Other books by Philip Hatfield, Ph.D.

*The Battle of Hurricane Bridge, March 28, 1863*
*With the Firmness of Veterans*

*The Other Feud*
*William Anderson "Devil Anse" Hatfield in the Civil War*

*The Rowan Rifle Guards*
*A History of Company K, 4th North Carolina State Troops, 1857-1865*

*North Carolina Draws the Sword*
*Capture of Coastal Forts, January-April 1861*

# SACRIFICE ALL

## *FOR THE*

# UNION

*The Civil War Experiences of*
*Captain John Valley Young and his Family*

*Company G*
*13th and*
*11th Regiments*
*West Virginia*
*Volunteer Infantry*
*1861-1865*

## PHILIP HATFIELD, Ph.D.

# Sacrifice All for the Union

*The Civil War Experiences of
Captain John Valley Young
and his Family*

*Company G, 13th and 11th Regiments
West Virginia Volunteer Infantry*

*1861-1865*

Philip Hatfield, Ph.D.

35th Star Publishing
Charleston, West Virginia
www.35thstar.com

ISBN-13: 978-1-7350739-1-0
ISBN-10: 1-7350739-1-1


35th Star Publishing
Charleston, West Virginia
www.35thstar.com

On the cover:
Image of Captain John Valley Young, courtesy of the West Virginia State Archives, Charleston, West Virginia.

Cover design by:
Angela Underwood, angie@pubbla.com

*This book is dedicated to the men and women of West Virginia
who sacrificed all for the Union.*

*They are eternal reminders of why
Mountaineers are always free.*

*Montani Semper Liberi*

# Contents

# Maps, Photos, Illustrations

# Acknowledgments

There are many people who deserve thanks for contributing to this project, and it would consume several pages if all were listed. Those who helped know that I am forever grateful for their input. Joe Geiger and his excellent staff at the West Virginia State Archives were extremely helpful accessing original source materials and photographs. Catherine Rakowski at the West Virginia University Library Regional History Collection patiently answered many requests for copies of source materials. Sarah Pendleton at Carlisle U.S. Army History Education Center was prompt and efficient answering requests for photographs. Amanda Larch provided much input editing. Mike and Sylvia Adams shared a wealth of family information on Captain John Young. Suzanne W. Silek at the Warrenton Rifles Museum kindly provided assistance accessing photographs of Pegram's Battery flag, and the Virginia United Daughters of the Confederacy shared information on Pegram's Battery. Terry Lowry, a long-time friend and influence, gave valuable feedback and guidance on this project. Bryce Suderow provided a great deal of insight and valuable assistance locating sources related to Petersburg. Historian and former Petersburg National Park Ranger Edward Alexander kindly shared much of his expertise and maps assisting with the Petersburg and Appomattox Campaigns.

I also recognize my life-long friend and publisher, Steve Cunningham of 35th Star Publishing, for his tireless ability to locate unpublished letters and other original sources. As I have stated before, Steve ever reminds me that West Virginia Civil War history is largely a story untold and deserves much deeper study. Scott Minske provided valuable assistance with the second and third battles of Winchester. David Jones contributed valuable feedback on the Petersburg Campaign. Howard McManus graciously allowed use of his maps of the battle of Cloyd's Mountain. Further, George

Skoch did excellent work on maps of Petersburg, and Neil Richardson of the St. Albans Historical Society shared photographs from the John S. Cunningham Collection. Special thanks also to Suzanne Spezik for sharing her photograph of Brigadier General Joseph Thoburn. Richard A. Wolfe of Bridgeport, West Virginia, provided photographs of Colonel Daniel E. Frost and Colonel William R. Brown. The Colonel Jacob M. Campbell Camp #14, Sons of Union Veterans of the Civil War, provided a war-time photograph of Colonel Jacob M. Campbell. John Koski, Ph.D., of the National Civil War Museum in Richmond, Virginia, shared his expertise on the captured battle flags from April 2, 1865.

Most of all, I am grateful for my wonderful parents, Calvin and Freda Hatfield. They are gone now but will always live in my heart. They are the reason I developed a passion for Civil War History.

# Introduction

An Ohio soldier once described the volunteer soldiers from West Virginia who served in the Civil War: "...the little mountain state, born amid the throes of war, rocked and shaken with the roar of cannon, and whose soil drank the blood of many of her own loyal sons, West Virginia, Child of the Storm. All honor to our little neighbor across the river, and may the words inscribed on her escutcheon always characterize the patriotism and valor of her people, *Montani Semper Liberi.*" These rugged, self-reliant mountaineer soldiers have a bloody and hard-fought story, but for the most part, remain an untold chapter in the vast Civil War literature. Serving in both the Eastern and Western theaters, they faced the same deprivations and hardships as their Confederate counterparts throughout the war, yet historians have written little of them. One of those men was Captain John Valley Young, a Union officer from Putnam County, West Virginia, who served in both the 13th West Virginia Volunteer Infantry and the 11th West Virginia Volunteer Infantry. Young raised a company of forty Union volunteers at the village of Coalsmouth in Kanawha County in April 1861 and served until the war's end. Both he and his family suffered many hardships during his term of service, and this is their story told primarily in their own words.[1]

Although there were only a few battles in western Virginia, Union troops serving in the region encountered hundreds of small skirmishes with both Confederate military and partisan, or "guerrilla," forces. These irregular troops were often known as "bushwhackers" and fought as aggressively as any regular Confederate forces. These small, but lethal bands were usually mounted on horseback and were typically citizens of the county or geographic area where they operated. As a result, they were often better versed in local culture and more familiar with roadways than the Union forces,

1

giving them an obvious advantage. This form of warfare was unpredictable and bloody, resulting in a general sense of instability in the region throughout the war, even when the Kanawha Valley was under Union control. In many ways, the war in western Virginia was more malevolent and personal than in larger theaters of war. Numerous accounts exist of men fighting on opposing sides that knew each other before the war and, in some instances, were even family members. Often, their families paid a dear price while soldiers were off in the field and unable to protect them. This added dimension when former friends, co-workers, business associates and even family become enemies was truly a fratricide and required an uncommon depth of courage and commitment on the part of both the soldiers and their families as hostilities increased.

John Valley Young was born in Kanawha County, Virginia (now West Virginia), on June 5, 1813. He grew up in Putnam County, and attended a small public school there as a youth. In 1850, his parents, Jacob Reed Young and Nancy Stevenson Young, lived near Pocatalico, a small village near the intersection point of Putnam and Kanawha Counties along the Kanawha River. The eldest of ten siblings, Young had five brothers: James (b. 1810), Alexander Samuel (b. 1816), Lewis N. (b. 1821), Jacob Jr. (b. 1827), and Samuel Early (b. August 26, 1828); and four sisters: Margaret, Melinda, and Sallie (birth dates unknown, possibly before 1825); and Nancy who was likely born in 1829. His paternal grandfather, John Young, was born in 1760, in either Germany or Virginia, and served in the Continental Army during the American Revolution from 1775 to 1778. Afterward, he received a 160-acre land bounty in Kanawha County for his service in 1783. He married Keziah (Kesiah) Lewis Tacket, the daughter of Lewis Tackett on May 20, 1783. Her father was one of the first settlers in the Kanawha Valley, and was also John Valley Young's maternal-great-grandfather. Tackett was a well-known scout, and established Fort Tackett in 1788, located about one-half mile south of the mouth of the Coal River, near modern St. Albans, West Virginia. The fort protected local families and served as a trading outpost on the Kanawha River.[2]

John Young's eldest son, Jacob Reed Young, was born at Fort Tackett on August 26, 1790. One day later, the Shawnee Indians attacked and burned the fort to the ground. His mother, Keziah Tackett Young, took the child and escaped by canoe the night before, paddling all the way to Fort Clendenin near Charleston. Jacob Reed Young later built a house along the James River and Kanawha Turnpike (present day U.S. Route 60) just west of Coal Mountain, near Sam's Fork and Snag Creek in the early 1800s. His father-in-law, Lewis Tackett, deeded them 100 acres for their home. By 1830, Jacob and Nancy lost one child who died in the interim decade, but also had four more children. The Young family included two sons and two daughters, with the youngest two children being twins. Descriptive information is limited, as census data preceding 1850 did not include the names of women or children, only recording their age range and gender. They continued to reside in Kanawha County. John was then eighteen years old and residing with his parents.[3]

John resided there until he married Paulina M. Franklin (b. October 25, 1820, in Wilson County, Virginia) at Charleston on January 18, 1840. He was then twenty-eight years old, and Paulina was aged eighteen years. They moved to a small farm in Kanawha County near his father's property. Jacob, his father, then had one employee living in his home, who is described in the 1840 census as a "free colored" woman, around twenty-four years old, assisting Nancy with the eight children remaining at home. There was no evidence indicating Jacob Young ever owned slaves. John and Paulina relocated to Putnam County sometime before 1850, when they were identified with a Teays Valley post office located in District Twenty-Nine, near the eastern slope of Coal Mountain, not far from Coalsmouth (modern St. Albans, West Virginia). Young's real estate was then valued at $800.00, and he was employed as a collier, which is someone who processes or digs coal for a living.[4]

*John Valley Young*
*West Virginia State Archives*

Young was then aged thirty-six-years and Paulina had given birth to four children during the interim decade. Their two daughters included Sarah Francis (b. February 4, 1842), whom Young affectionately nicknamed "Sallie" after his sister, and Emily Ann (b. February 14, 1844). They also had Benjamin Lewis (b. May 27, 1847) and Jacob Reed (b. January 14, 1849). Both of Young's daughters were then attending public school. Young was quite close to his wife and children. He regularly corresponded with them during his service. Several of his wartime letters also reveal an interesting tendency to disclose more details of the war to his daughter Sarah than to Paulina. By 1850, Young's parents had also relocated to postal district forty-six in Putnam County, some twenty miles away. Jacob Young's real estate was valued at $1,500.00, and his occupation was as a farmer. Twenty-three-year-old Jacob Jr. was residing with his parents and was employed as a "cooper", meaning he was a maker of barrels or other round containers. In 1856, John Young purchased 125 acres of land in Putnam County for an unknown amount. He later paid $4.30 in personal property taxes at Coal Township, Putnam County on the land, which was valued at $250.00.

Both of John's younger twin siblings were still residing with their parents in 1860, twenty-one-year-old brother Samuel, who later volunteered to serve in John Young's company during the Civil War, and his youngest sister Nancy Ann. Jacob Young passed away at age sixty-three years, and John and Paulina, aged forty-six and thirty-eight respectively, continued to reside in Putnam County when the 1860 census was taken, along with their four children. Sarah was then aged eighteen years, and Emily was aged sixteen years, with Benjamin aged fourteen years, and Jacob aged twelve years. There was no evidence that John Young ever owned slaves.[5]

John Young's military records describe him as five feet, seven and a half inches tall, with a dark complexion, gray eyes, and black hair. He listed his occupation as a farmer at the time of his enlistment on November 15, 1861. Working as a farmer agreed with Young, as his family physician, Dr. R. B. Thompson, described him as having "...every appearance of a Robust, Rugged man" before the Civil War. Another doctor, R.H. Lee, examined Young in May 1862 when he mustered into U.S. service and described Young as a "rugged, sound man."[6]

Another interesting aspect of Young's personality was that he was also a devout Methodist-Episcopalian and felt a strong calling into the ministry. He obtained his license to perform marriages in 1859. John frequently discussed his faith with his wife and daughter in their letters. Like many soldiers, Young believed that God favored the Union, but also admitted some doubt on the matter, particularly after experiencing the horrors of battle. His writings also reflect a deep devotion to liberty and preservation of the Union, and a strong disdain toward the practice of slavery. However, he also clearly voiced his disgust with the government for allowing it in the first place. Young had no difficulty pointing out that it did little, if anything, to prevent the practice until the matter became the dominant campaign issue when Abraham Lincoln was elected.

Aged forty-eight years when the war began, John Young had never attended college, and had no military experience. Despite this, Young's wartime correspondence reflects a strong sense of understanding his role as an officer, as well as a surprising grasp of military tactics of the era. Young was as dedicated as any of his professional officer cohorts, and when his rapidly deteriorating health manifested in 1864-1865, he was tested to the limits as his brigade served in more than one hundred skirmishes and full engagements in the Shenandoah Valley and Petersburg. In 1865, War Department documents identified Young as the only company officer from West Virginia to serve in over eleven major engagements. One of the first loyal mountaineers to step forward in service to the Union, he was still present when the Confederate Army of Northern Virginia surrendered at Appomattox on April 9, 1865.

Young rarely told his wife about his hardships, although oddly, he occasionally disclosed details of combat and other campaign experiences with his daughters, Sarah and Emily Young. Sarah kept a diary documenting her thoughts and reactions to war time events, and she also found a young male suitor with whom she often corresponded. Fortunately for them, he also had the favor of her father. Her beau was Edgar B. Blundon, an officer in Company F, 8th West Virginia Volunteer Infantry (later re-designated as the 7th West Virginia Cavalry). He and Sarah enjoyed an intense courtship largely through their letters, until they married on September 29, 1863. He was also a Methodist minister prior to the war, and his letters to Sarah and her mother offer an in-depth look into his faith, political views, as well as his courtship with Sarah. Her diary and Blundon's letters bring a rich context to the musings of Captain Young throughout the war and detail the often painful hardships that Young's family endured. Ultimately, John Young was hated by many of his former friends and neighbors for serving in the Union army, and his intense devotion to duty exacted a strict price not only on his family, but also on his health. He died from tuberculosis, contracted during his military service, at his home in 1867. This was a sad irony after surviving some of the worst battles of the Civil War. Truly, John Young proved his own admonishment, to "Sacrifice all for the Union."[7]

Introduction References

1. Joseph F. Sutton. *History of the 2d West Virginia Cavalry.* (Huntington, WV: Blue Acorn Press, reprinted 2001), 50. See also "Narrow Escapes: Some Exciting War Experiences No. 3." *Ironton Register,* December 2, 1896. Interview with General Enoch.

2. 1820 United States Census, Record Group 19, Microfilm Roll 33; 1840 US Census, RG 29, M704; 1850 US Census, RG 29, M432, National Archives, Washington DC; B. Ross. *West Virginians in the Revolution.* (Baltimore, MD: Johnston Genealogical Publishing, 1977), 121-123; Kanawha County, West Virginia, Clerk's Office, Record of Marriages, FJL Microfilm 521, 719; St. Albans Historical Society, Fort Tackett files.

3. Ibid; Joseph Griffith. *History of Company G, 11th West Virginia Volunteer Infantry, from Coalsmouth to Richmond 1861-1865.* (Roswell, GA: Self-published monograph, 1995), 220; 1830 & 1840 US Census, Database with images. *Family Search.* http://FamilySearch.org: 24 March 2020. Citing NARA microfilm publication M19. Washington, D.C.: National Archives and Records Administration, n.d.

4. John V. Young Letters and Young Family Record of Births, Deaths & Marriages and Summary of Proof, Marriage Certificate, January 18, 1840. Roy Bird Cook Collection, Call No. A&M 0895, Series 1, Correspondence, Box 1, Folder 1, West Virginia Regional History Collection, West Virginia University Library, Morgantown WV; 1840 & 1850 U.S. Census; Drake, Paul. *What did they mean by that?* (Bowie, MD: Heritage Books, 1998, Rev. Ed.), 47.

5. 1850 US Census; J.V. Young Family Record of Births, Deaths & Marriages; Drake, 51; 1856 Receipt to John V. Young for 125 acres bought from George Hicks in Putnam County in J.V. Young Letters.

6. 1850 & 1860 US Census; 1860 US Census Slave Schedules; M432-954, Rolls 119A, National Archives; J.V. Young, Deposition testimony for Pension Claim, Application No. 175.823, February 4, 1871, Dr. S.B. Thompson, Acting Assistant Regimental Surgeon, 13th West Virginia Volunteers, 1862-1865, filed by C. Mollohan, Attorney, Gallipolis, Ohio, with the U.S. Department of the Interior Veteran's Pensions Claims Office. Union Soldier Pension Files, MT288, Roll 542, US National Archives; Compiled Service Records, Union Regiments, 11th West Virginia Infantry, Record Group 94, M508, Roll 195, National Archives.

7. J.V. Young Pension File, February 3, 1871; Captain John V. Young discharge

certificate, May 15, 1861. On January 1, 1859 John V. Young testified in front of a board of examiners from the Methodist Episcopal Church at Winfield, Va., and was granted license to preach the gospel. In May 1859 he was granted a license to perform marriages in Putnam County through the Methodist Episcopal Church; the license is signed by Deputy Clerk J.L. Middleton, with deposit of $13.77 bond.

# 1

# Yankees in Virginia
# 1861

When the Civil War came to western Virginia in 1861, the Kanawha Valley was important to both the Union and Confederacy mainly due to the presence of salt works and waterways. The salt works were crucial to manufacturing gunpowder and meat preservation, and the rivers made travel in and out of the area much easier than crossing mountains. It was the Confederacy's most logical route to access the Ohio River, and allowed access from southwestern counties into the Shenandoah Valley of Virginia. Nonetheless, the rough, mountainous terrain represented not only large physical barriers between North and South as a border state, but also in many ways reflected a psychological barrier. A strong sense of geocentricity, or an "us versus them' mentality, existed among inhabitants of western Virginia when thinking of those outside of their immediate area. This cultural identity was deeply rooted in earlier political events leading many residents to favor forming a new state separate from Virginia. When John Brown's militia raided the Federal Arsenal at Harpers Ferry in 1859 with intention of inciting a slave rebellion, sectionalist ideologies rapidly polarized in western Virginia. As a result, when two competing political movements sought to establish a foothold in the region, residents were quite divided on the issues of secession, slavery and states' rights. Thus, it is important to briefly review both the social and political context in which John Young and his family lived prior to 1861, in order to better understand their wartime experiences.[1]

As with any civil war, there was a long history of smoldering political, legal and economic factors at work between opposing sides in western Virginia. Decades of frank political and economic domination of western counties by wealthy eastern planters in the General Assembly left many westerners feeling unfairly treated. For example, there were 1.6 million slaves living in Virginia in 1860, with 491,000 of them in the eastern counties working in large, wealthy plantations. In contrast, the forty-eight counties comprising western Virginia had a population of 376,667, covering one quarter of the state's geographic area. There were 18,731 slaves held by 3,605 whites, mostly farmers, in the western counties, of whom 2,572 (71%) owned five slaves or less. This translates to approximately one slave owner per one hundred white residents. The latter accounted for but one third of the total slaveholding population in Virginia.[2]

To get a sense of the larger picture in western Virginia, the second largest slave population in the region was in Kanawha County with 13.7%, most of whom worked in the salt mines. For perspective, in neighboring Putnam County where John Young and his family resided, there were 580 slaves (9.2%), and 13 freed blacks residing there. Also, Berkeley County had 13.5% slave population; Greenbrier County had 12.7% slaves; Hardy County had 11.2%; and Monroe County was 10.5%. Therefore, in theory, most westerners should have had little, if any, allegiance to the Old Dominion, and yet the western counties provided between eighteen and twenty-two thousand men to the Confederate armies. It is not surprising, then, that Lincoln obtained only 1,921 votes in western Virginia during the 1860 election, albeit mainly in the northern counties. It is additionally noted the western counties also contained most of the state's oil and natural gas resources, and the affluent land and business owners tended to view slavery as a source of competition, especially when attempting to negotiate in the state assembly. Additional data for slave population of six counties near Putnam County are shown in Figure 1-1.[3]

The historic tendency of Virginians to define themselves as either eastern or western primarily had its origins in the state constitution. Adopted in 1776, it granted voting rights only to white males owning at least twenty-five acres of improved land or fifty acres of unimproved land. This blatantly favored wealthy planters inhabiting the fertile lands of eastern Virginia with hundreds of prosperous acres. As a result, the western farmers and business owners were historically underrepresented in the General Assembly. As they voiced discontent with the discrepancies early in the Nineteenth Century, several attempts were made to modify the state constitution in favor of western counties from 1825-1849, but each resolution was soundly defeated in the powerful planter dominated legislature. In this context, the discussion of creating a new state from western Virginia emerged, and was ongoing for decades prior to the Civil War. To help appease growing sectionalist tensions, the General Assembly passed new laws in 1850 enabling white males over age twenty-one years to vote who owned any land valued at $25 or higher, and also approved making the office of governor and judges subject to election by the people, but it made little difference to western residents who had suffered painfully obvious economic discrepancies at the hands of wealthy eastern planters for over a century.[4]

Figure 1-1

1860 U.S. Census Slave Tables

| County | White | Slave | % Slave |
|--------|-------|-------|---------|
| Kanawha | 13,787 | 2,184 | 13.7 |
| Putnam | 5,708 | 580 | 9.2 |
| Mason | 8,762 | 386 | 4.2 |
| Cabell | 7,691 | 305 | 3.8 |
| Wayne | 6,604 | 143 | 3.8 |
| Logan | 4,470 | 148 | 3.0 |

Source: 1860 United States Census, Slave Schedules.

U.S. National Archives, Washington, D.C.

The *Wheeling Intelligencer* newspaper editorialized an accurate summary. "The slave population of western Virginia is only nominal, while her white population is some one hundred twenty-five or thirty thousand in excess of eastern Virginia. The consequence is that we suffer all the evils without any benefits of the system..." Another editorial published in the Grafton based *Western Virginian* news organ succinctly elaborates the sentiment: "We the people of northwestern Virginia... have no objection to slavery existing where it is wanted... but will never consent to become the menials of a slave oligarchy... The conflict in Virginia, between the East and West, virtually swallows up the national conflict between North and South, and we are for the West." In this sense, the division in Virginia was literally a civil war within a civil war, although the moral problem of slavery was not a key issue among residents of western Virginia. Rather, the economic inequity it created decidedly became "...a war of free labor of rough, self-reliant mountain men and slave labor in the east. It clearly was not fought there to free slaves by Union men; rather it was against unfair taxation by wealthy slave holders of the east who dominated the assembly."[5]

Eventually, the conflict proved irreconcilable, and when South Carolina seceded in December 1860, Alabama, Georgia, Florida, Louisiana, Mississippi and Texas soon followed. On February 4, 1861, delegates from each of the seven states held a convention in Montgomery, Alabama, and formed the Confederate States of America. Amidst the growing strife, John Young's nineteen-year-old daughter Sarah saw the great conflict looming ahead was imminent and mused in her diary that day, "My birthday. And Oh! What may transpire before my next. Our Country seems to be in danger of Civil War and it makes me shudder to think of it. May our blessed Union be preserved in spite of all traitors."[6]

When Abraham Lincoln was inaugurated as the sixteenth President of the United States on March 4, 1861, sectionalist tensions piqued in western Virginia. Solomon Minsker, a resident of Charleston, indicated "Most people do not like Lincoln's inaugural address. But I hope all be settled without coming to arms, although the south is preparing for it." Yet, most of the elected western representatives opposed secession and their constituencies often had mixed sentiments. As a result, law and order were in danger of breaking down completely. Citizens were becoming increasingly agitated and fearful, not knowing from day to day what would become of them and their families. On April 4, when the Virginia Secession Convention met in Richmond, Putnam County had one representative present, James Hoge of Winfield. Hoge was a popular attorney who owned six slaves, although he also strongly opposed secession. The convention voted against secession eighty-nine to forty-five, which appeared to temporarily appease conflicted emotions in many western counties, but it did not last long as Southern militia attacked the Union-held Fort Sumter in Charleston, South Carolina, on April 12.[7]

Immediately, President Lincoln called for 75,000 volunteers on April 15 to "put down the rebellion," and there was no turning back. The Virginia Secession Convention reconvened on April 17 and voted in favor of secession, with all delegates from the forty-eight western counties voting against it, many of whom were also slave owners. Those representatives protested by walking out of the assembly, including James Hoge of Putnam County. Soon afterward, Arkansas, Tennessee and North Carolina also seceded in May 1861, each having earlier voted against it. The four slaveholding states of Delaware, Kentucky, Maryland and Missouri opted not to leave the Union.

No one in the Kanawha Valley knew when it was going to happen, but all realized that a civil war was upon them. Union-minded delegates from the western counties quickly seized the chance to organize the Restored Government of Virginia and held their first convention at Wheeling on May 13. A second Wheeling Convention was held on June 11, and on June 20, representatives unanimously elected Francis Harrison Pierpont as the new governor. The result was a rather confusing and dangerous situation in the western counties. Citizens were now caught between two competing governments. For those undecided as to which side they were on, choices had to be made quickly.[8]

Francis Pierpont was aged forty-seven-years when he became governor. He grew up on his father's plantation in Monongahela County, Virginia, and his family held slaves. Raised as a staunch fundamentalist, he strongly identified with the Republicans, but discouraged blind allegiance to politicians, most of whom he considered corrupt. Pierpont believed that the Federal government did not have power to coerce a state but was conversely unwilling to concede that a state had any inherent right to secession. Although he opposed the notion of slavery, Pierpont did not align with the abolitionists either. He saw their behavior as extreme and found their "rule or ruin policy" to be a danger to the Federal Union. Being an industrialist, Pierpont favored free labor over slave labor, and he had long resented the heavy tax burden placed on horses, cattle and other livestock of small farmers, as well as discrepant land appraisal values given to non-slave holders in Virginia.[9]

## Militia Crisis of 1861: Union Citizens Unprotected

Virginia's secession also left Union-leaning citizens in a quandary, as nearly all of the extant militia companies in the Kanawha Valley were divided, with many of those men enlisting in regular Confederate service. There were only a few Union-minded state militia units in the area to protect them, but the new state Adjutant General, Henry J. Samuels, acknowledged that the general state of militia in western Virginia was in disarray in early 1861, blaming it on years of neglect during the antebellum era. In short, it was little more than a paper tiger in the early months of the war. The primary law governing state militia was the Federal Militia Act of 1792, which required compulsory military service of all able-bodied men ages eighteen to forty-five years. This law required men to enroll in a company within their district. The aggregate of companies formed in this manner were known as Line Militia, although they were not uniformed, and drilled only once annually, if at all. In many

*Captain Isaac Rucker*
*Commanded a company of*
*Independent Scouts in*
*the 181st Regiment Virginia Militia.*
*He also served as a Captain in the*
*7th West Virginia Cavalry.*
*Courtesy of Steve Cunningham*

counties, men simply failed to report for muster without legal consequences. The few militia companies that met for annual muster usually had no more than a drunken brawl with a picnic. One militia officer recalled a typical muster day: "On muster days... the boys after drill would usually indulge in a little horse trading, or swapping, talk of, and appoint log-rolling, rail-maulings, house-raisings, apple-cuttings, corn-huskings, and many other kinds of frolics..."[10]

In April 1861, the 181st Regiment Virginia Militia in Putnam County was ostensibly commanded by attorney and state assemblyman, James Hoge of Winfield. Although he was commissioned as the colonel, he had no experience drilling or serving in the field. There were seven companies with expressed Union sentiment assigned to the 181st Regiment including Captain James Bailey's Hurricane Creek Home Guard, Captain William Hudson's Company from Buffalo, Captain John M. Ball's Scouts, Captain John A. Ford's Company and Captain Isaac Rucker's Company of Independent Scouts. Although technically part of the 181st Regiment, none of these companies served together in the field until 1864. In 1861, most Union men in the area refused to report for musters, because they feared being drafted and sent away from their families and homes, which were in constant danger of raids and harassment from Confederates and guerillas.[11]

Although the exact date is unknown, John Young recruited a company of forty Union men in the Coalsmouth area during April 1861. They elected him as their captain, although the rank was not formally recognized by the state or U.S. War department until over a year later. Young's company was assigned to the 181st Regiment Virginia Militia, but they never served with the other companies. They generally operated autonomously during the first year of the war in the Coalsmouth area, providing regular patrols, until the Confederates took possession of the Kanawha Valley. Then, Union outfits went into hiding to avoid arrest and harassment.[12]

The village of Coalsmouth was particularly affected by the rabid sectional division occurring in the Kanawha Valley. Located at modern Saint Albans, West Virginia, the quiet village sat along the eastern bank near where the Coal River fed into the Kanawha River. With approximately 1,500 inhabitants in the village and immediate area, including a large slave population, Coalsmouth was a small but thriving community and strongly aligned with the Confederacy. The James River and Kanawha Turnpike, (also referred to as the James River Turnpike) connected the western Virginia counties along the Ohio River to Richmond, Virginia. The turnpike ran through Coalsmouth with a large covered bridge connecting the village to the western bank. In 1847, a series of eight dams and locks were built on the Coal River for the purpose of moving coal and timber downriver to the Kanawha. The system ran some thirty-five miles from the village of Peytona to Coalsmouth. The Chief of Construction who built the dams and locks was William S. Rosecrans from Ohio, who later became a Union general officer in charge of the Federal forces in western Virginia. Prior to the war, John Young was employed as a coal tinder for a brief period.[13]

There were a few Union supporters in the village, including John Overshiner, owner of Overshiner Wagon Works, and a close friend of John Young. On April 11, 1857, an advertisement in the *Kanawha Valley Star* newspaper states that he wanted to inform his friends and the general public that he made a "neat good and substantial wagon" and that folks would "not be disappointed." Overshiner was forty-nine years old when he joined Young's company, serving with him until 1865. Another Union man, John S. Cunningham, owned a drug store located next to the post office on the south side of Main Street. The post office was operated by Cunningham's father-in-law, Samuel Benedict. Cunningham was born January 15, 1827, at North Orange, Essex County, New Jersey. He married Helen Benedict in 1857 while living in Pennsylvania, and shortly afterward, Cunningham and his father-in-law relocated their families to Coalsmouth. Cunningham worked as a surveyor for several railroad companies prior to the war and was also involved in the construction of the Chesapeake and Ohio Canal. Samuel Benedict was sixty-four years old when the war began and was one of the largest landowners in the Kanawha Valley. He was also a strong Union supported who favored organizing the new state of West Virginia. Cunningham was initially commissioned as a lieutenant colonel in the 80th Regiment Virginia Militia, but resigned to accept a commission as 2nd Lieutenant of John Young's company on May 23, 1862.[14]

Stephen P. Capehart was also a Unionist resident of Coalsmouth, and described the situation, "The local Democrats divided over their interpretation of the Constitution leading to Lincoln's election. Neighbor rose against neighbor, with both North and South aligned families in strife – former friends and peaceful neighbors. The times were awful - soldiers would shoot at citizens just for fun..." Such neighborhoods were commonly known as "Union Holes" by Secessionists, a pejorative term meant to describe small pockets of Union loyalists in their midst, much like one would describe the discovery of a hidden den of poisonous vipers.[15]

John Young's nineteen-year-old daughter Sarah, whom he nicknamed "Sallie," kept a diary of her wartime experiences. She also began corresponding with twenty-four-year-old Edgar B. Blundon in the first months of the war. Blundon was born on September 24, 1836, in Morgan County, Ohio, and was raised in a devout Methodist family. His father passed away when he was aged fourteen years, at which time he believed he was called to preach the gospel. He was ordained as a Methodist minister in 1865, and also worked as a machinist. Sarah was also raised in an intensely devout Methodist-Episcopal family, and they shared similar religious and political views. Blundon initially enlisted as a private in a three-months regiment, the 18th Ohio Volunteers, and served in western Virginia from April to August 1861. Afterward, he enlisted as a private in the 8th West Virginia Volunteer Infantry at Red House, in Putnam County, on September 15, 1861. Blundon was elected Captain of Company F, 8th West Virginia Infantry on February 15, 1862, and served in both Putnam and Kanawha counties during 1861. John Young was also ordained as a Methodist-Episcopal Minister in 1859 and approved of his daughter's friendship with Blundon. The young officer's military prowess and strong faith no doubt played a key role in winning Young's favor as a courtship soon developed.[16]

Although they had not met in person, Sarah and Edgar's acquaintance quickly developed into a blooming romance, as she confided to her diary, "Edgar asked me if I would correspond with a soldier and asked me if I thought our acquaintance sufficient. I told him I had known him by reputation for a long time. He said he had known me for a long time, and he felt acquainted before he even saw me." Despite their sentiments for each other, the war soon began.

On May 1, the Virginia State Assembly called out the Virginia Militia in anticipation of a Federal attack. On May 10, Colonel Robert E. Lee, a West Pointer and career soldier, who was also a Mexican War Veteran, was promoted to Major General and given command of the Virginia militia forces and volunteer units.

*Captain Edgar B. Blundon*
*8th [West] Virginia Infantry*
*(later 7th West Virginia Cavalry).*
*Courtesy of Steve Cunningham.*

Meanwhile, on May 13, Major General George B. McClellan, a West Point alumnus, was given command of the Federal Department of the Ohio which then included western Virginia.[17]

Shocked by the rapid secession of several southern states, Sarah again wrote on May 23, "Everything is confusion. Several states have seceded, and War! War! is all we talk about. The Rebel Soldiers are going into camp at Buffalo, Putnam County, Va. They say the Yankees shall not invade West Va. I am sorry to see such preparations, for I know we will all suffer if two armies are in Virginia." The situation at Coalsmouth was not improving, and on April 20, a garrison of Confederate cavalry arrived and encamped at St. Mark's Episcopalian Church. Private J.D. Sedinger of the Border Rangers, 8th Virginia Cavalry, wrote in his diary that his company had to cook their own meals for the first time there, and that many men cut large pieces of pipe to carry as weapons since they did not yet have muskets. He also boasted, "We drilled cavalry drill and thought we could whip the world." Sarah Young didn't quite agree, however, as she recalled, "The soldiers have moved from Buffalo to Coalsmouth. The horsemen pass us every day. They still think they can whip the Yankees." At that point, Confederate military forces had control of the Kanawha Valley, and Union citizens daily petitioned their new government to send help.[18]

Shortly after the Restored State Government of Virginia held its first election in May, Major General George B. McClellan issued a proclamation to the Union men of the region on May 26. "...You have now shown, under the most adverse circumstances, that the great mass of the people of Western Virginia are true and loyal to that beneficent Government under which we and our fathers have lived so long...The General Government cannot close its ears to the demand you have made for assistance. I have ordered troops across the river. They come as your friends and brothers - as enemies only to the armed rebels who are preying upon you. Your homes, your families and your property are safe under our protection. All your rights shall be religiously respected. Notwithstanding all that has been said by the traitors to induce you to believe that our advent among you will be signalized by interference with your slaves, understand one thing clearly - not only will we abstain from all such interference, but we will, on the contrary, with an iron hand, crush any attempt at insurrection on their part." A few days later, Colonel Charles Q. Tompkins, commanding the Confederate volunteer forces in the Kanawha Valley, also made a proclamation. He ordered broadsides to be posted around Kanawha County encouraging men to step forward and take up arms with the South, admonishing them not to heed the Union "sophistry."[19]

Sarah Young's hope that the two opposing armies would soon leave the Kanawha Valley was quickly shattered when Brigadier General Henry A. Wise took command of Confederate troops in the region on June 6. Just three days earlier, three thousand Union troops from Indiana and Ohio, along with the 1st and 2nd West Virginia Infantry regiments attacked and routed roughly eight hundred Confederates at the town of Philippi in Barbour County. Union newspapers mocked the Confederates for the loss, satirizing the affair as the "Philippi Races" (sung to the tune of the popular song *The Camp Town Races*). Most warfare in western Virginia was not as simple, however. The numerous heavily wooded and serpentine mountainous roads gave roving bands of Confederate guerrillas, known as "bushwhackers," ample opportunities for ambushing Federal soldiers, who dreaded marching through the mountainous roads in long, heavily encumbered columns. The rough, hilly terrain also made it easy for guerillas to raid the rural homes of Union citizens, and then quickly vanish into the hills.[20]

The psychological impact of the unpredictability in guerilla warfare was profound on both the Union troops and citizens in western Virginia. Such unconventional, covert tactics were a marked contrast to traditional Napoleonic military tactics of the era, which prescribed large infantry units supported by artillery and cavalry units, engaged in open fields, using linear tactics. General McClellan, on the other hand, despite being a West Pointer trained in traditional Napoleonic warfare, understood the guerrilla problem in western Virginia, and promised the most severe consequences allowed by military law. His later successor, Brigadier General William S. Rosecrans, was president of the Coal River Navigation Company before the war and quite familiar with the people and culture of the Kanawha Valley. Also, a West Pointer, Rosecrans discerned that many of the guerilla bands in the Kanawha Valley were attacking former neighbors, often avenging personal vendettas against Union citizens. He proclaimed an order stating that all citizens must endeavor to take "prompt and vigorous" measures to end such "private wars" and went a step further than McClellan by announcing that he would treat those who failed to take proper steps to suppress such violence as "accessories to the crime."[21]

## Citizen Patrols

As the situation became increasingly dangerous for Union citizens in the Kanawha Valley during periods of Confederate occupation, those opposing secession quickly learned to either refrain from speaking out or risk severe retaliation. A few Union leaning community leaders attempted to make speeches but were usually harassed and forced to leave. Most of the Union-minded citizens soon began to meet covertly in their homes, trying to organize and protect their families. Union men were being arrested and taken away from their homes at night by force, and were often "conscripted," i.e. drafted into Confederate service. One such Union supporter was asleep in his home one night when a Confederate patrol arrived and entered his home. The man sought to defend himself with a homemade sword, and as he swung it at the assailants, it lodged into the rafters in the ceiling, and he was taken away.[22]

General McClellan told the U.S. Secretary of War on June 10, "If we don't muster Virginians into service according to proclamation and arm them, we must quit the territory or prepare to hold it with Federal troops." He also wrote, "I cannot urge too strongly the importance of this matter, on which hinges, I think, the fate of Western Virginia...The anxiety in this regard to this condition arises, I think, not from any unwillingness to fight the battles of the Union on any battle-field, but from the natural solicitude of a simple people for their homes and families. We have it in our power to unite that people firmly to us forever." The Secretary of War agreed and directed McClellan to muster the Union troops from western Virginia into Federal service on June 12.[23]

On June 11, the Restored Government of Virginia met at Wheeling and passed an order calling out the militia into active state service, although the War Department directed that new regiments be mustered into Federal service but remain styled as state Volunteer Militia. Hence, when it came time to clothe, equip, arm and feed the regiments, no one seemed clear whether the volunteers were operating under state or Federal authority, including Governor Francis Pierpont. In response to numerous complaints from Union citizens in fear for their safety, the Wheeling Convention also passed House Bill Number Five, designated as "An Act to Prevent Offences against the Commonwealth, and to provide for the Organization of Patrols during the War, June 1861." This act enabled the immediate organization of citizen patrol groups across the state, which were armed para-military organizations with a captain, junior officers and privates, with arrest and detainment authority for anyone found opposing the new state or "inciting others to attempt the overthrow of said government." Many such groups failed to keep muster rolls due to fear of being identified by Confederate forces, but those with documentation who later enlisted in the Federal army were given time in service credit for pay by the Federal army.[24]

Governor Pierpont petitioned President Lincoln for help on June 21, pleading that Confederate military and guerilla forces, "...are now making war on the loyal people of the State. They are pressing citizens against their consent into their military organizations, and seizing and appropriating their property to aid in the rebellion. I have not at my command sufficient military force to suppress this rebellion and violence... I therefore earnestly request that you will furnish a military force... to protect the good people of this commonwealth from domestic violence." Lincoln promised to send "a large additional force," but Union citizens would not see relief any time soon. A few Union men, such as John Young, had shown initiative and organized their own patrols shortly after Virginia seceded. While details are sketchy, Young later recalled that he recruited and organized his company at Coalsmouth during spring

1861 and served on "scouting" patrols around the Coalsmouth area for "many months" afterward.[25]

Union citizens persistently complained to state authorities that they did not feel safe, particularly after the 8th West Virginia Infantry left the area in May 1861 with orders to join Major General John C. Fremont's forces at New Creek and went onto participate in the pursuit of General Thomas "Stonewall" Jackson in the Shenandoah Valley. The state adjutant general appointed a local physician, thirty-four-year-old Dr. Edward Naret of Buffalo, as adjutant of the 181st Regiment Virginia Militia for the purpose of organizing the various militia companies in his area into a full regiment for active service. French-born Naret was quite popular in the county and a successful physician but could only organize three companies to serve as citizen patrols in Putnam County, and only two in Mason County and two in Kanawha County, including John Young's company. Naret was unable to establish contact with several local militia companies, as many refused to be part of a formal military unit for fear of exposing their families to retaliation or being sent away from their homes. Although Citizen Patrols in Putnam and Kanawha County were better organized than the state militia companies in the early months of the war, many lacked arms or only had their own personal shotguns or outdated hunting rifles. At Coalsmouth, where John Young's company was based, each night prior to beginning their rounds, they held a formal guard mount. Most of the men carried only axes or shotguns and looked ridiculous going through the rigors of a formal guard mount drill while only pretending to have firearms.

Captain Naret pled his case for firearms to the state adjutant general in Wheeling. "We're being threatened by secessionists who are organizing in large numbers within a very short distance of this place... their purpose is to destroy all of the property of the Union people and to drive them off. The troops in the upper Kanawha Valley are unable to protect us; we shall depend on our own exertions, and we have no arms – our men would fight if placed in a position to do so... Sinister reports are spread about to frighten us away from our homes, and already a number of families from Hurricane and Coal have left rather than be exposed to the attacks of their enemies; among them are many brave men, who would fight if they had arms, but they are powerless and they go away. Much depends in the new state of things on the protection afforded to our valley – if the Secessionists are suffered to gain strength here; our future is uncertain." The process was overwhelming, and Naret eventually became so frustrated that he tendered his resignation.[26]

# Caught Unprepared: The Supply Quandary in Western Virginia

As the new state government in Wheeling was still struggling with how to protect Union citizens from constant harassment and Confederate raids, as well as slow recruiting for new regiments, Governor Pierpont found himself in a dilemma in June 1861. He was receiving daily letters and telegrams from field commanders begging for new weapons, uniforms and other supplies, but had none to send. This had an adverse effect not only on morale among the volunteers, but also on recruiting. Secretary of War Simon Cameron promised full support backed by the United States treasury, but also stipulated that this was contingent upon his filling the full quota of troops from the new state for each regiment.

*Governor Francis H. Pierpont,*
*Restored Government of Virginia.*
*Library of Virginia.*

This was no small matter. The Federal government would not take over the state supply depots until much later, and as a result, the early volunteers in western Virginia suffered immensely during the early months of the war. Pierpont informed President Lincoln on June 26 that he finally had three full regiments in the field, and again requested he direct the War Department to send proper supplies.

Frustrated, the governor noted that most of his regiments were still without tents or blankets, which were difficult to obtain, as well as knapsacks and other camp equipment. Many of the new troops lacked adequate shoes. One officer described the condition of his troops' feet as "appalling." The industrious governor soon acquired a minimal stockpile of 1855 U.S. rifled muskets manufactured at Harpers Ferry, along with a few hundred M1816 and 1820s percussion conversion weapons stored in arsenals at Martinsburg. In addition, there were five hundred Belgian rifles stored in Wheeling by December 1861. Eventually, however, Pierpont happily acquired ten thousand .69 caliber smoothbore 1842 U.S. Springfield muskets from Massachusetts in July 1862. A few fortunate volunteer companies acquired the highly coveted .577 caliber British made Enfield rifles from Federal quartermasters, and some were also privately purchased by officers or other benefactors.[27]

Cameron eventually ordered General McClellan to send supplies intended for his own troops, who were mostly from Ohio and Indiana, to the new western Virginia regiments. However, McClellan knew that giving up arms and equipment to the western Virginians was not going to be well received by his regiments for whom the supplies were originally intended, and blithely attempted to delay executing the order. Only with much pressure from Governor Pierpont and the War Department did McClellan begrudgingly comply in late July 1861, and ordered the U.S. Army Supply Depot in Cincinnati, Ohio, to begin supplying the western Virginia regiments. This would not actually begin in earnest until November 1861, unfortunately, and proved quite problematic initially because Ohio had fallen severely delinquent in maintaining proper state weapons and supplies during the antebellum era. Another problem was the Cincinnati Depot relied on contractors, with no quality control or inspections. The substandard clothing and equipment often wore out quickly, if it fit at all. Hence, any notion of a finely uniformed, well-armed and supplied "Billy Yank" serving in western Virginia early in the Civil War is a myth. For the most part, the Union volunteers fared no better than their Confederate counterparts in terms of clothing, arms and other supplies.[28]

On July 11, General McClellan's subordinate, Brigadier General William S. Rosecrans, defeated Confederates under Brigadier General Robert S. Garnett at Rich Mountain in Randolph County. Garnett was killed three days later while retreating during a skirmish at Corrick's Ford. Meanwhile, at Governor Pierpont's behest, the War Department finally agreed to direct General McClellan to deploy even more Federal regiments from Ohio into western Virginia in early July. They hoped to dislodge 3,500 Confederates stationed at Charleston under Brigadier General Henry A. Wise, a former governor of Virginia, who had control of the Kanawha Valley where tensions were rapidly escalating.[29]

## Federals Move on the Kanawha Valley

General McClellan ordered Brigadier General Jacob Dolson Cox, who commanded Union troops in the Kanawha Valley, to move the 12th Ohio Volunteer Infantry and two companies from the 21st Ohio Volunteer Infantry toward Coalsmouth from Camp Dennison, Ohio, on July 9, with plans to remove the Confederates from the valley. Jacob Dolson Cox was born on October 27, 1828, in Montreal, Canada, to American parents. Cox was previously an attorney who served in the Ohio state senate in 1859-1861 and was also a recognized microbiologist. Despite having no prior military experience, his political ties led to an appointment as Brigadier General of Volunteers, and when the war began Cox immediately began studying military tactics, strategy and military history. It paid off, as unlike many of his contemporaries who were also political appointees, Cox proved to be an efficient commander.[30]

On July 13, Sarah Young was relieved to see the Federal troops move into the Kanawha Valley: "Oh, What a time! The Federal troops are coming up Kanawha. The secessionists are running with their guns to bushwhack them. They are mad because my father doesn't raise arms against our Government. No, we are too glad to see our protectors come. General [Jacob] Cox has landed at Winfield and will move on in a few days." She noted a small skirmish occurred near their home the next day, when Federal scouts appeared and encountered some Confederate pickets from nearby Camp Tompkins. The scouts also encountered artillery located near the mouth of Scary Creek, about two miles from Young's home near Coal Mountain. They fired one shot

*Brigadier General Jacob Dolson Cox*
*Library of Congress*

at the Federals, who quickly dispersed, "but hurt no one." Sarah's earlier fear of what could happen with two opposing armies in the valley proved correct, however, as the first significant battle in the Kanawha Valley was about to occur just over one mile from her home. On July 15, Cox's troops were marching toward Scary Creek in Putnam County, where the Confederates were posted along the southern creek bank. Many Coalsmouth residents panicked and immediately evacuated the area. One of Sarah Young's southern contemporaries, a young woman named Victoria Teays Hansford, lived in Coalsmouth and wrote in her diary on July 16, "I left home the day before the battle of Scary... We started in the afternoon for Paint Creek... The road was full of refugees going up the valley and from all directions [Confederate] soldiers and armed civilians were going down the valley towards the advancing [Union] foe. Weeping women and sad unhappy children were all along the road... I found many others in the same fix as I was..."[31]

The Confederates were posted along the southern bank of Scary Creek, with the right extended to where the creek feeds into the Kanawha River. Lieutenant Colonel George S. Patton, grandfather of the famed World War II General George S. Patton, posted the artillery on the heights behind their lines, approximately two hundred yards above the infantry. Fighting began early the next morning as Federals marched in from the north and encountered Rebel pickets around 9:00 a.m. and by 11:00 a.m. had pushed them back across the bridge spanning Scary Creek. Sarah Young encountered some Confederate soldiers foraging for food at her home that morning. "Two Rebel soldiers came today, begging for something to eat... They had been gone but one hour before the Federals attacked the Rebels at the mouth of Scary. Oh, how our hearts ached while the sound of the booming cannons reached our ears! We could distinctly hear the report of small arms..." The battle began in earnest shortly afterward and continued to ebb and flow throughout the hot July afternoon. During the fight, a company of Federals managed to cross the creek and flank the Confederates' left. Severe hand to hand fighting occurred for several minutes there, and the battle appeared to be turning against the Confederates by mid-afternoon. However, after three more hours of heavy fighting, the Federals withdrew and the battle ended around 6:00 p.m.[32]

Sarah Young said she "felt afraid the Federals would be whipped", but when news came of the battle results, she was elated. Sarah heard a rumor that "three Rebels were killed and eight Federals captured... may they soon escape to join their regiments." General Cox, on the other hand, stated his losses were fourteen killed, thirty wounded, and several missing, while Confederate commander General Henry A. Wise reported his losses as between one to five killed and six wounded. Sarah also mentioned that she heard several Federal officers were captured. That incident occurred around dusk, when a small group of Federal officers, all green volunteers, foolishly decided to walk on the battlefield area to view the aftermath of the fight at about sunset. They encountered what they thought were Union pickets, but it turned out that they were Confederates, who quickly took them prisoner. When General McClellan learned of it, he was furious with the bumbling, inexperienced officers. "A wounded colonel of ours taken prisoner, and a possibility of having lost two colonels and a lieutenant-colonel, who amused themselves by a reconnaissance beyond the pickets... In Heaven's name give me some general officers who understand their profession. I give orders and find some who cannot execute them unless I stand by them. Unless I command every picket and lead every column I cannot be sure of success... Had my orders been executed from beginning, our success would have been brief and final." Although General Wise achieved a tactical victory at Scary Creek, he ordered a general withdrawal of Confederate forces from the Kanawha Valley on July 20.[33]

Sarah Young was happy to see the Confederates leave. "General Wise has left the Kanawha Valley. Several of the Rebel soldiers have deserted and come home. They say they don't want to fight against the Stars and Stripes. I hope Wise may never see

Kanawha again. The Federals have possession of Charleston. They are received by the Union men with great joy." Edgar Blundon was so excited that he wrote a poem about Wise's defeat, and sent it to Sarah. Entitled "Wise's Retreat" the poem was sung to the tune of "Auld Lang Syne." Blundon wrote,

"Should old acquaintance be forgot, And never brought to mind,
To think old Wise had run away, And left one hog behind.
He stole away the last old goose, He ate the cow,
He did not spare the horse, But left one poor old sow
He used up all the oats and corn, He fed up all the hay;
And when the eleventh came in sight, Old Wise he ran away.
He ran so fast he could not stop, For valley and for hill,
He had no time to call around, To pay his washing bill.
And when old Gabriel blow his horn, And the devil claim his own,
May he throw wide his arms, To welcome old Wise home.
And when he takes old Wise below, With Jenkins and his host,
May he, with fear and trembling, No longer swear and boast.
When Floyd comes home to meet him, Which he is sure to do,
May the devil and his angels, Put both the traitors through.
But good devil, be you careful, And give them all they need,
Or, by the great Old Moses, They'll get mad and secede.
Watch Floyd in every movement, Be sure to guard him well,
For if you don't be careful, He'll steal Wise out of h-ll."[34]

General McClellan was ordered to report to Washington, D.C., on July 22, and left Brigadier General William S. Rosecrans in command of Union forces in western Virginia. Known for his fiery temper and tendency to argue with superiors, Rosecrans also shared a similarly low opinion of the new western Virginia volunteers as General Jacob Cox. Realizing how undisciplined and green the new West Virginia volunteers were, he complained, "Every day's experience with volunteer troops convinces me of the absolute necessity of having some officers of military education among them... regiments are mustered into the services and sent upon active duty without a single officer who knows thoroughly company drill, much less the organization or drill of a regiment. I am convinced that the detail of a second lieutenant from the Military Academy to act as major even would in six weeks increase the military power of a regiment at least one-third." General McClellan was placed in command of the Army of the Potomac on July 27. The army was demoralized following their recent defeat at the Battle of Bull Run (Manassas) on July 21, just three days after the battle at Scary Creek, and McClellan's presence rejuvenated the troops.[35]

Sarah Young wrote on September 3 that, "Several Union men from Nicholas, Kanawha and Clay counties are here. The Rebels were going to press them into service or take them to Richmond. They made their escape, and will stay until they think all the Rebels have left." On September 10, General Rosecrans sent more than 6,000 Union troops to Carnifex Ferry and attacked a force of about 2,000 Confederates at Camp Gauley under Brigadier General John B. Floyd, a former U.S. Secretary of War and governor of Virginia. Rosecrans ultimately failed to dislodge the entrenched Confederates, who despite the tactical victory, prudently chose to withdraw and escaped toward Meadow Bluff in Greenbrier County. Union troops then regained control over the Kanawha Valley as well as much of the territory in western Virginia. John Young had recently become ill, as Sarah noted on September 6, "Pa is quite sick with pneumonia," but he continued with his company.

As Union troops established a stronger foothold on the Kanawha Valley and Gauley region, Sarah Young was elated. On September 23, she reflected: "Good news! Capt. [John] Vance, 4th Va. Vol. Infty. has arrested all of the leading Rebels in the Valley. They are very angry. He has taken them to Charleston. I hope the worst ones will be sent off. Pa is almost well."[36]

John Young remained ill for several weeks but continued regular patrols around the Kanawha Valley. He arrested several Confederate guerillas and southern sympathizers, although this led to retaliation against his family. According to Sarah Young, October 5 was "All confusion. A party of Guerillas, commanded by the notorious Herndon. Two came for Pa, but he had gone to Winfield. Ma sent Ben to meet him and tell him not to come home." They did not give up, though, as Sarah stated on October 6: "The Rebels went to Winfield. Eleven came by and searched the house for Pa, but he had gone to Charleston. They robbed Mr. Cox's store of some clothing and took Mr. Cash prisoner, but released him. A Government boat was coming up. They fired on it, but the boat turned around and went back. Then they took Mr. Frederick prisoner and went back to Hurricane Bridge." Sarah also indicated a regiment of Zouaves arrived on October 8, along with part of the 4th West Virginia regiment, intending to "drive the Rebel Herndon off." By the time the Federals arrived at Hurricane Bridge, however, the Confederates had left the area.[37]

By mid-October 1861, Young's reputation as a strong Unionist was growing. A prominent citizen from Kanawha County, Greenbury Slack, Sr., wrote to the War Department about him advocating for his commission, "...there is a Capt John V. Young in Putnam County who at considerable expense of time and means raised a company in his neighborhood near Winfield of some 40 more or less who have been advantageously employed for some time in scouting and capturing dangerous persons who wishes to organize (with the company he has got) a company of cavalry for the purpose of contradicting raids that are from time to time in that section by the rebels from the Southern army who dash into unprotected neighborhoods and plunder and murder the inhabitants and dash off again and defy pursuit in consequence of our lack of that necessary arm of defence (cavalry). Mr. Young is a man of unflinching courage and would doubtless render good service if commissioned..." Young was elected as the captain by forty-two of the men of his company on November 10, 1861, although the U.S. War Department would not recognize his rank for several months because extant army regulations required eighty men for a captaincy. Instead, he received a commission as a 1st Lieutenant in the 3rd Regiment Mounted Volunteers on November 15, although his company never served as cavalry or mounted infantry. Sarah Young was quite pleased with her father's commission. "Pa received his commission to make up a volunteer company. Oh, I hope if he fills his company they may never be captured by the Rebels. May they come out in glowing colors, without the loss of one." On the same day John Young was elected captain, seven hundred Confederate cavalrymen attacked the newly forming 9th West Virginia Volunteer Infantry at the village of Guyandotte in Cabell County, resulting in ten Union soldiers killed, ten wounded, and over one hundred captured.[38]

At the end of 1861, the Restored Government of Virginia was still plagued with fiscal and jurisdictional problems related to paying and supplying the state regiments. This had a profound impact on the morale of John Young and his company, who, despite having served consistently since the war began, still had not received any pay, and were without uniforms or adequate firearms. Young's company formally mustered into three years United States service on December 1, 1861, although they were essentially still operating as an independent Citizen Patrol outfit. Adding to the confusion, on December 15, they were mustered into the 3rd West Virginia Cavalry, but Young later said he never served with that regiment. The original company was comprised of 1st Lieutenant John Young, age forty-nine, 2nd Lieutenant Robert Brooks, age forty-eight, and forty-five enlisted men at the end of 1861. The average age of enlisted men in the company at that time was 30.5 years, arguably much older than most volunteer units in the region, which typically ranged 18-25 years. Their occupations were reported as laborers, farmers, tanners, and a wagon maker. Roughly 68% of Young's men came from the Coalsmouth vicinity, and 22% of them resided at Winfield. The remaining 10% came from Cabell, Mason and Wood Counties, and one man was from Meigs County, Ohio.

On Christmas Day in 1861, Sarah Young expressed her disappointment that earlier fears had proven true. She wrote: "Christmas! And our beloved country still engaged in a deadly war. I flattered myself with the hope that the war would have ended before today, but vain hope."[39]

## Chapter One References

1. J. Duane Squires. Lincoln and West Virginia Statehood. *West Virginia History,* Vol. 24(4), (July 1963). Online article: www.wvarchives.gov; Granville Parker. *The Formation of the State of West Virginia.* (Wellsburg, WV: Glass & Son Publishers, 1875), 1-2.

2. 1860 United States Census; Wilma A. Dunaway. *Slavery in the American Mountain South.* (Cambridge MA: Cambridge University Press, 2003), 26-29; Jack Hutchinson. *Divided Loyalties: The Border States of the Upper South.* (Loganville, Georgia: Signature Printing, 2005), 110-111.

3. 1860 US Census, Slave Schedules. Jack L. Dickinson. *Tattered Uniforms and Bright Bayonets: West Virginia's Confederate Soldiers.* (Huntington, WV: Marshall University Foundation, 1995), 1-10; See also: Linger, James Carter. "Confederate Military Units of West Virginia." State Archives, 1989; also Jack L. Dickinson. "Confederate Soldiers in West Virginia." e-WV: The West Virginia Encyclopedia. 13 June 2011. Web. 10 March 2020. Estimates of the number of men serving in Confederate military organizations in western Virginia tend to vary among various researchers; many Confederate units did not keep, or lost records, and some men simply refused to put their names on muster rolls for fear of retaliation to their families. Also, a large number of men served in guerilla or partisan units, most of which did not keep records. Hence, caution is advised when considering statistics related to the number of men serving in Confederate regiments in western Virginia.

4. P. Wallenstein. *Cradle of America: Four Centuries of Virginia History.* (University Press of Kansas, 2007), 169-173.

5. John A. Williams. *West Virginia: A History.* (Morgantown: WVU Press, 2001), 35-43; 46; *Wheeling Daily Intelligencer,* Vol. 35, December 25, 1860 and April 24, 1861, Vol. 9; Chronicling America Series: https://chroniclingamerica.loc.gov/lccn. Library of Congress; D.W. Mellott and M.A. Snell *The Seventh West Virginia Infantry: An Embattled Union Regiment from the Civil War's Most Divided State.* (Lawrence, KS: Univ. of Kansas Press, 2019), 8; 35-43; 46.

6. Diary of Sarah Francis Young 1861-1862. Typescript. West Virginia Regional History Collection, Roy Bird Cook Collection, Call No. AM 1651, WVU Library. Morgantown, WV.

7. Solomon Minsker Family Letters, Civil War Manuscripts, PL 2004-109, WV Archives; 1860 US Census Slave Schedules; William J. Hoge House, National Register, West Virginia Landmarks, January 21, 2007. ID No. 86536037. National

Archives.

8. Squires, 19, 63; Parker, 1-2.

9. Charles H. Ambler. *Francis H. Pierpont: Union War Governor and Father of West Virginia.* (Chapel Hill, North Carolina: University of North Carolina Press, 1937), 3-11; 16-23; 29-32; 34-50; 62-73.

10. West Virginia Adjutant General Papers, AR 373, Union Militia 1861 to 1865, Box 21, Folders 1-5; 9 & 10, 181st Regiment Virginia Militia, Letters of H.J. Samuels, February-June 1862, WV Archives; Records of the Colonial Militia through World War I. Ca. 1936, MS80-22, 50; 53, WV Archives; *Kanawha Valley Star*, Buffalo, Va., May 21, 1860, Misc. Reels M-16, 54; 57; 126, WV Archives; Frazier Family Records, MS90-96; 1859, WV Archives; Hoge House; Joseph, Geiger, Jr. *The Civil War in Cabell County 1861-1865.* (Charleston, WV: Pictorial House Publishing, 1991), 43-48; Terry Lowry. *22nd Virginia Infantry.* (Lynchburg: H.E. Howard, 1986), 3; WV AG Papers, MS76-13; Kanawha Riflemen, 1859-1861. WV Archives; John Morgan. *The Last Dollar.* (St. Albans Historical Society, St. Albans, West Virginia, 2012, Original printing 1909), 2; Michael Egan. *The Flying Gray-Haired Yank or the Adventures of a Volunteer.* (Leesburg, VA: D.L. Phillips (Ed.), Gauley Press, 1992), 19-38; CSR Union Regiments from West Virginia, M507-508, National Archives; James C. James C. Confederate Military Units of West Virginia. Revised Ed. (Tulsa, Oklahoma: Self-published, 1990, 2-23; 59-82.

11. Ibid; Lew A. Wallace, Jr. *A Guide to Virginia Military Organizations 1861-1865.* (Lynchburg, VA: H.E. Howard, 1986), 234-235.

12. WV AG Papers, AR 382, Union Militia Muster Rolls, Box 2/2, WV Archives; WV AG Papers, Union Regiments, 13th West Virginia Infantry Files, AR 382, Folder 7, West Virginia Archives.

13. Griffith, 12-13; US 1860 Census.

14. Ibid, 13-15. Note that while John Overshiner is shown as a private on the Company G muster roll from December 1, 1864, Captain Young often referred to him as Sergeant Overshiner in his personal diary and letters; WV AG Report December 31, 1864; *Kanawha Valley Star*, April 11, 1857, Kanawha Court House Edition, M57-April 1857-April 1859 Misc., WV Archives; WV AG Papers AR 373, Box 2/2; Box 10, Union Militia, Kanawha County, Folder 10-A. Muster Roll of September 14, 1862; WV Adjutant General Order Book No. 1, Commissions; Griffith, 16-17; WV AG Report December 31, 1864; WV AG Papers, AR 382, 11th West Virginia Infantry; Misc. folder, Letter by J.V. Young, July 8, 1864;

Atkinson, G.W. and A.F. Gibbens. *Prominent Men of West Virginia.* (Wheeling, WV: W.L. Callin, 1890), 419-421; CSR, RG 94, M507, Roll 205, National Archives. No other men from Company B, 80th Regiment Virginia Militia, appear on later muster rolls for Captain Young's Company G. John S. Cunningham resigned from the 13th West Virginia on December 21, 1864 due to his family being robbed three times by Confederate guerillas, and also due to his elderly father-in-law Samuel Benedict's failing health; Benedict's son passed away in 1862. After the war, Cunningham served as the First Superintendent of Free Schools for Kanawha County, and later served as a member of the Republican State Central Committee; he was also President Judge of the Kanawha County Court. Cunningham's brother-in-law was Park Benedict was also pro-Union. He operated the drug store until appointed post master in 1860. Benedict's youngest son Samuel was later identified by John Young as a private in his company in 1864, although is not found in Company G muster rolls.

15. "Stephen P. Capehart of Coalsmouth." *West Virginia History*, Vol. 5(1), (1905), 22-31; Lowry, 152; David Turk. *The Union Hole: Unionist Activity and Local Conflict in Western Virginia.* (Bowie, MD: Heritage Books, 1994), xxi, 9, 14, 21.

16. WV AG Papers, AR 373, Union Militia, Box 21, Folders 1-5, 9 & 10. Official Roster of the State of Ohio in the War of the Rebellion 1861-1866, Vol. 1. (Akron, OH: Published by the State of Ohio. Akron OH: The Werner Company, 1893), 379-380; Sarah Young Diary, undated entry March 1861, 1; CSR, RG 94, M508, Roll 69, National Archives.

17. Sarah Young Diary, February 4, 1861; Official Records of the War of the Rebellion, Series 1, Vol. 2, 51.

18. James D. Sedinger. "Wartime Reminiscences of a Border Ranger: Company E, 8th Virginia Cavalry, April 20, 1861." Typescript. West Virginia Archives Manuscript Collection, MS78-1, Series 1, West Virginia Archives; see also West Virginia History, Vol. 51, 1992, 55-78; Sarah Young Diary, May 23, 1861; undated June 1861.

19. OR, Series 1, Vol. 2, Part 1, 48-49; 51; Lowry, 202. Colonel Christopher Q. Tompkins was a West Point alumni (Class of 1836) and previously served in the U.S. Artillery, and was a veteran of the Seminole War. Tompkins was also a successful iron manufacturer and mining agent prior to the war.

20. Mark Mayo Boatner, III. *The Civil War Dictionary.* (New York: McKay, 1959; revised 1988), 123-124; Sarah Young Diary, June 3, 1861; Daniel E. Sutherland. *A*

*Savage Conflict: The Decisive Role of Guerillas in the American Civil War.* (Chapel Hill, NC: UNC Press, 2009), 65-67 OR, Series 1, Vol. 2, 195-196; Curry, R. O. & G. Ham. "The Bushwhacker's War: Insurgency and Counter-Insurgency in West Virginia." *Civil War History,* Vol. 10(4), (December 1964), 416-433; Daniel E. Sutherland. *A Savage Conflict: The Decisive Role of Guerillas in the American Civil War.* (Chapel Hill: University of North Carolina Press, 2009), 61-67; 319-325.

21. OR, Series 1, Vol. 2, Part 1, 674; 679.

22. Turk, 28-29, 30-32.

23. Ibid.; OR, Series 1, Vol. 2, Part 3, 673.

24. Militia Called into Service: June 11, 1861. An Ordinance of the Convention Assembled at Wheeling, June 11, 1861. Cited in Records of Colonial Militia through World War 1. Ca. 1936. MS80-22, West Virginia State Archives, 46; WV AG Papers, Union Regiments 1861-1865, AR 383; Box 36; Broadsides and Oversized Items, No. 3. House Bill No. 5 Broadside, June 1861, WV Archives.

25. Griffith, 225; J.V. Young Pension Files: Paulina Young, Widow of Captain John V. Young, testimony for Pension Claim, February 1, 1871: filed by C. Mollohan, Attorney at Law, Gallipolis, Ohio, with the U.S. Department of the Interior Veteran's Pensions Claims Office. Union Soldier Pension Files, MT288 Roll 542, US National Archives; Young's Pension File contains a letter from C. Mollohan, Attorney, of July 22, 1867 stating that he was already in active service for several months on date of his commission, November 15, 1861; Records of Colonial Militia through WW 1, 5-11; 47.

26. WV AG Papers, AR 373, Union Militia, 1861-1865, Box 21, Folder 1, and Box 2; 181st Regiment Virginia Militia. Letter from Captain Naret to H. J. Samuels, February 17 & 28, 1862; Letter from S. H. Grose to H. J. Samuels August 19, 1862; Captain Naret Resignation June 12, 1862; Naret Letters September 2 & 4, & 26, 1861, WV Archives.

27. OR, Series 1, Vol. 12, Part 1, 730-731; Vol. 2, 730-731; Francis H. Pierpont Restored Government Executive Papers, 1861-1865. Accession 36928, State government records collection, The Library of Virginia, Richmond, Virginia. November 21, 1861; *Cincinnati Daily Commercial,* Vol. 22(185), June 6 1861, sn84037036. Newspaper Reading Room, Library of Congress; Charles Leib. *Nine Months in the Quartermaster's Department; or, The Chances at Making a Million.* (Cincinnati, OH: Moore, Wilstach, Keys & Co., 1862), 7-9. Pierpont Telegraphs, October 3 & December 30, 1861, WV Archives; West Virginia Civil War Collection,

Pierpont-Samuels Data Base-Memory Project; No. 1010, Box No. 6, Pierpont letters: August 22, 1862; November 15, 1861; WV AG Papers, AR 382, 9th West Virginia Infantry, Box 16, Kellian V. Whaley letters November 1861; WV AG Papers, AR 373, Box 2/2, Letter from Lieutenant Colonel J.C. Wheeler, November 1861; Letter from Colonel J.A.J. Lightburn, January 16, 1862, WV Archives; Francis H. Pierpont Telegrams in the Civil War, 92. Gr. 281. West Virginia Regional History Collection, August 3, 1861, WVU Library.

28. OR, Series 1, Vol. 2, 705-706; 737; 766; Matthew Oyos. "Mobilization of Ohio Militia in the Civil War." *Journal of Ohio History*, Vol. 98 (Summer-Autumn 1989), 147–174; Ohio Adjutant General's Letters. 1861, Series 147, File 1A:15, June 2, 1861. Ohio State Archives, Columbus, Ohio; Leib, 13-27; Richard A. Warren. "3rd to 5th and 7th to 13th Regiments, Ohio Volunteer Infantry, 1861." *Military Collector and Historian*, Vol. 57 (Fall 2005), 151; Bell I. Wiley. *The Life of Billy Yank: The Common Solider of the Union*. (Baton Rouge, LA: Louisiana State Univ. Press, 1971), 229–231; *Cincinnati Daily Gazette*. June 10 & 15, 1861; SN 84028718. *Jeffersonian Weekly Democrat*. Vol.4(27), June 28, 1861. Chronicling America Series: https://chroniclingamerica.loc.gov/lccn/sn82015737/1861-06-28/ed-1/seq-1/, Library of Congress; Lester L. Kemper. The Salem Light Guard: Company G, 36th Regiment, Ohio Volunteer Infantry 1861-1865. (Chicago, IL: Adams Press, 1973), 36; 44.

29. OR, Series 1, Vol. 2, 202-214; 259-272.

30. Jacob D. Cox. *Military Reminisces of the Civil War*, Vol. 1, April 1861-November 1863. (Great Britain: Hard Press Books, 2016), 119-122; Jacob D. Cox. *Military Reminiscences of the Civil War*, Vol. 5. October 1900. (Cincinnati, OH: Cochran Publishing. Reprinted by Kessinger Publishing, Whitefish, MT, 2008), 26; 34; 58; Eugene D. Schmiel. *Citizen-General: Jacob Dolson Cox and the Civil War Era*. (Athens, Ohio: Ohio University Press, 2014), 225-248; CSR, RG 94, M508, Roll 206, National Archives. General Jacob D. Cox later served as the twenty-eighth governor of Ohio and U.S. Secretary of Interior.

31. Sarah Young Diary, July 13 & 14, 1861; Diary of Victoria Teays Hansford, Boyd Stutler Collection, MS78-1, Series 1, No. 8, July 1861, WV Archives; William D. Wintz. *Civil War Memoirs of two Rebel sisters*. (Pictorial Histories Publishing, Charleston WV, 1989), 25-26.

32. Lowry, 141-145; 146; Richard Andre, Stan Cohen,& William Wintz. *Bullets and Steel: The Fight for the Great Kanawha Valley 1861-1865*. (Charleston, WV:

Pictorial Histories Publishing, 1995), 64-69; OR, Series 1, Vol. 2, 1010-1012; Sarah Young Diary, July 24, 1861.

33. Ibid.

34. Sarah Young Diary, July 24, 1861; J.V. Young Letters, Undated, likely July-August 1861.

35. OR, Series 3, Vol. 5, 118-119; WV AG Papers, AR 382, Union Militia, Box 5, Letter from General Rosecrans to Governor Pierpont, January 8, 1862, WV Archives; J.C. Olsen. *The American Civil War: A Hands-on History.* (Indianapolis, IN: Farrar, Straus and Giroux, LLC, Publishers, 2006), 167-175. The Union rout at Bull Run was afterward mockingly known as the "Great Skedaddle" because hundreds of spectators came from nearby Washington, D.C. to watch the battle, and were overran by Confederates and forced to run when the Union lines broke.

36. OR, Series 3, Vol. 5, 128-132; 136-139; 144-165; 616. Pierpont Telegrams, August 14, 1861; Sarah Young Diary, September 3 & 6, 1861.

37. Sarah Young Diary, October 5, 6, and 8, 1861.

38. WV AG Papers, AR373, Box 21, Putnam County, Union Militia, Folder 8, Letter from G. Slack Sr. to H. J. Samuels on November 10, 1861; see also Letters, account books, 1865-1868. Ms80-122, WV Archives; WV AG Papers, AR 382, Box 2, N-Z, 1866-1870, WV Archives; CSR, RG 94, M508, Roll 195, National Archives; WV AG Papers, AR 903, West Virginia Volunteers & Militia Orders & Appointments Book No. 1, January 26, 1861 to June 9, 1863, WV Archives; Pierpont-Samuels Record No. 1020, Box 6, Letter November 12, 1861; Naret Letters, November 11, 1861; Sarah Young Diary, November 15, 1861; OR Series I, Vol. 5, 411-412; Joseph Geiger, Jr. "The Tragic Fate of Guyandotte." *West Virginia History*, Vol. 54, 1995, 28-41; Pierpont Telegraphs, November 14; 24 & 25, 1861. Note that "Greely Slack" is a misspelling of Greenbury Slack. Greenbury Slack, Sr. (1807-1863) served as a justice of the peace and member of the 1861 and 1863 Constitutional Conventions from Kanawha County. He served in the West Virginia Senate 1863-1868. His son, Greenbury Slack, Jr. was an officer in the 13th West Virginia Infantry.

39. WV AG Files, AR 383, 11th West Virginia Infantry, Boxes 1 & 2, Folders 7; 41; 42; & 43; Muster and Descriptive Rolls and Morning Reports; Letter from C. Mollohan, Attorney, to Pierpont, January 10, 1864, on behalf of Lt. Robert Brooks; Sarah Young Diary, December 25, 1861.

# 2

# A Divided State
# 1862

The winter of 1861-1862 was bitter cold with heavy snows covering the ground. Solomon Minsker, a resident of Charleston, noted: "We have had one of the most disagreeable winters I ever experienced." At that time, there was only one Federal regiment in Charleston, the 12th Ohio Volunteers. Unable to spend much time at their homes due to the risk of capture by Confederate guerillas, John Young and his company continued patrolling the Kanawha Valley despite inclement weather. There also remained a great deal of confusion regarding who had jurisdiction over Young's company. On January 11, state Adjutant General Henry J. Samuels petitioned the U.S. Secretary of War, Simon Cameron, requesting that Young's company muster into Federal service in the 11th West Virginia Volunteer Infantry as "mounted infantry." Samuels reasoned that since West Virginia then had six infantry regiments in the field, Young's outfit should be attached to a regiment under a close chain of command. This caused "...embarrassment because of the uncertainty existing in regard to whose jurisdiction parts of companies are..." according to the state adjutant general.[1]

Sarah Young's beau, Lieutenant Edgar B. Blundon, wrote to her from Winfield on January 8, discussing how a civilian attempted to play both sides of the conflict to avoid arrest, a "turncoat." Blundon reflected a general distrust toward locals, "...I am informed that the Rebels are coming into town and observing the Federal Flag displayed from the window I arrested him and took him forty or fifty miles on the road to Richmond. Perhaps he can appreciate the blessedness of making long marches, as he told me he had to march all the way. I hope he may be compelled to take a sufficient number of trips of the same kind to change his traitorous heart that he may learn to appreciate a good and beneficent government..." He also mentioned that his regiment would likely be leaving the area soon. "I cannot say how deeply I regret the necessity that calls us away; if indeed, it is a necessity. We all have doubts with regard to it..."

On January 11, U.S. Secretary of War Simon Cameron resigned, and was replaced by Edwin M. Stanton, who was sworn in on January 20. Known as more of a shrewd politician than an administrator, Stanton had a reputation for corrupt dealings. He was also one of Lincoln's strongest critics, but Lincoln felt obliged to add him to his cabinet for his assistance in the 1860 election. Despite the tension, Stanton proved to be an affective administrator and quickly organized the massive logistical resources in support of the Union army and navy into a more reliable and efficient machine.[2]

*St. Mark's Episcopal Church*
*site of wartime Camp Defiance, circa 1900*
*Licensed by Alamy.com*

John Young's company went into camp on the grounds of St. Mark's Episcopal Church in Coalsmouth in early February 1862. He wrote to his wife, Paulina, on February 3, "I understand you have been robbed again. Well, poor devils, it is the only way they have to get their rights. Courage my dear wife, they may take our horses, and all we have but one thing they can't take – that is, principle and the love of country. I know that it is hard to bear, but the time is coming when we and our children will be rewarded. Stand firm to the good old Cause. I have just come from Charleston, and found while there that there will be a change of Commanders in the Department of [West] Virginia. The authorities feel determined that we shall have protection. But if we cannot have better protection than we have had, the country is ruined. But I assure you there will be a change for the better. I don't know how you will get up to see me now. Well, we must bear it the best we can. Sacrifice All for the Union."[3]

Sarah Young celebrated her twentieth birthday on February 4, while the Kanawha Valley remained under martial law. Federal authorities were convinced the majority of residents in the area were Confederate sympathizers, and there were numerous confrontations between citizens and Union troops. "My birthday! I sincerely hope ere my next we will be enjoying the blessings of Peace. Oh how I tremble when I think of so many orphans, widows and broken hearted lovers made by this unholy war. Oh God in thy infinite mercy restore peace to our once happy land. Endow our leaders with wisdom and teach them to lead our soldiers on to Victory." On February 11, John Young received two new recruits into the company, Fretwell Hensley of nearby Brown's Creek, and his older brother Shelton Hensley. Shortly afterward, Coalsmouth residents John S. Cunningham, who had recently resigned from his post as lieutenant colonel in the 80th Regiment Virginia Militia, and John Overshiner, who owned a wagon shop there, also enlisted in Young's company.[4]

Although her father was only a short distance away from their home at Coalsmouth, Sarah Young was anxious on February 11, "Pa has gone into camp at Coalsmouth...He has only a few men yet. Oh, what shall we do without him? But we would much rather he was there, or on the battle field, fighting bravely for his country, than to be a coward and run to the Federal troops for protection unless he was not able to fight. And we know if he remains at home the Rebels will take him to Richmond as Prisoner." Soon, Edgar Blundon paid Sarah a visit on March 9 and informed her that he recently saw John Young in his camp at St. Mark's Church, and that he had "a noble company." Young's company did not stay at Coalsmouth long, as they moved out on patrol again on March 11. Also, on that date, the U.S. War Department re-designated the Department of West Virginia as the Mountain Department, under command of Brigadier General Robert H. Milroy.

Brigadier General Jacob D. Cox had approximately 12,071 troops scattered across the Kanawha Valley and Gauley River area. The 11th Ohio Infantry and the newly forming 13th West Virginia Infantry were at Point Pleasant; eight companies of the 8th West Virginia Infantry were scattered around the valley, with the 12th Ohio Infantry and one company of Ohio Cavalry at Charleston. Also, at Camp Piatt, some twelve miles above Charleston, was the 44th Ohio Infantry and one company of the 1st [West] Virginia Cavalry. To the west at Guyandotte, Cox had eleven companies of the

2d West Virginia Cavalry with six companies of the 9th [West] Virginia Infantry, and at Barboursville was the 34th Ohio Infantry, while at Ceredo was the 4th [West] Virginia. On March 28, Major General John C. Fremont was given command of the Mountain Department, and rumors began about an upcoming spring campaign. Sarah Young was concerned after reading Blundon's letter of that date indicating the 8th West Virginia had just received orders to join General Fremont in northern Virginia and would likely march toward Richmond.[5]

Union citizens in western Virginia struggled with who to trust. Confederate supporters were being arrested, only to take the Oath of Allegiance and return home to continue their anti-Union activities. A contingent of leading local Union men met at the county courthouse in Winfield on March 24, with the objective of discussing the problem of "turncoats," those southerners who pretended to be Union when Federal troops were in the area. One man was identified as an "arch traitor," and said to be "the most loud mouthed and the meanest of all of the infamous pack of Secessionists who have disgraced the Kanawha Valley." Another case discussed was a prisoner taken from Colonel Albert G. Jenkins' Confederate cavalry regiment who had earlier returned to the area "...dressed in female attire...distributing letters to the friends of Jenkins men – as he passed through the neighborhood as a strange lady..." Attendees included Dudley S. Montague, Mason County Clerk of Court, who was later suspected of being a Southern sympathizer when he accused John Young of stealing his horse. Also present was John Bowyer, a close friend of John Young who later helped him obtain a captaincy.[6]

On April 15, Sarah Young received news that the 8th West Virginia was leaving Buffalo for Richmond, and she became depressed as the realities of war sunk in, "A letter from Edgar today. He says their Regiment marches today – destination Dixie. Oh, God, save them! Spare them the cruelties of the vile Rebels. We know if they move toward Richmond we shall never see all of them again. The Company in that regiment that we presented the flag to seems to think so much of it, and the Captain assured us that it shall never be disgraced so long as they have the strength to sustain it. I feel very melancholy today. My father is scouting in a very dangerous country; and one of our Virginia regiments leaving makes me feel sad." Sarah's despair was justified, as the 8th West Virginia served in the 1862 Shenandoah Valley Campaign against Major General Thomas "Stonewall" Jackson, and Edgar Blundon saw action at Harrisonburg and Cross Keys. The 8th West Virginia later also fought at the second battle of Bull Run in August 1862.

Meanwhile, Young and his company went about their usual patrols, still based out of their camp at Coalsmouth. Guerilla attacks were also increasing in Putnam County, especially along Hurricane Creek. One irate Union citizen informed General Cox he would take matters into his own hands, "Guerilla warfare appears to be the determination of the Rebels...I am at liberty to act guerilla to guerillas and their aiders of rebellion..." On April 29, Young was ordered to detain two local Secessionist men at Winfield who were arrested for "bushwhacking" and "horse thievery" near Garrett's Mill along Mud Creek in Cabell County on the previous day. Young's acquaintance John Bowyer was a prominent figure in Putnam County, and knew both men taken prisoner. He wrote Young a letter on one's behalf requesting his release, but to no avail, as Young had little trust in Bowyer and refused to let either man go.[7]

On May 6, Governor Francis Pierpont acted on the War Department's recommendation to commission Young as a 1st Lieutenant in Company G, 11th West Virginia Infantry. On May 20, the War Department formally re-designated Company G as an infantry company. They were initially designated to be cavalry. The new regimental assignment took a while for the authorities in Young's area to recognize. General Cox afterward often referred to them as "Young's West Virginia Company." This led to yet more aggravation when Young filed to receive back pay from his service in1861, which was declined because he had not formally mustered into U.S. service until May 6, 1862. The matter was not fully resolved until nearly two years after the war ended. At least one of Young's problems was settled on May 10, however, when General Jacob Cox promised to send Company G a shipment of the much coveted .577 caliber British made Enfield rifles, then considered by most soldiers to be the finest long arm available. Heretofore, Young and his men were armed with axes, squirrel guns and shotguns. General Cox also telegraphed Governor Pierpont in May, indicating he wanted to establish a new outpost at Hurricane Bridge in Putnam County and others at Coalsmouth, Charleston and Chapmanville, with orders to the officers to be "extremely vigilant," promising to "spare no pains to protect" the Union citizens in the area.[8]

## Betrayed by a Friend

Because Young and his men wanted to remain with the 13th West Virginia, they were frustrated by their new orders assigning Company G to the 11th West Virginia Infantry, Young wrote to military and state leaders attempting to have his company reassigned. He also requested to be commissioned as a captain, arguing that since his men had duly elected him, he deserved both the rank and equivalent pay. The War Department did not agree, due to army regulations requiring eighty-three men for a captaincy. When he received Young's letter, Governor Pierpont sent for him to come to Wheeling in person to discuss the matter and pick up the new Enfield rifles recently given him by General Cox, because military regulations required a commissioned officer's signature to transport them. Young declined, stating he was too uneasy leaving his company with a persistent threat of guerilla activity in the area. He sent instead 2nd Lieutenant Robert Brooks, a long-time friend and resident of Coalsmouth. As it turned out, Young learned Brooks was not really his friend, but had devised a plan to usurp his authority.

Robert Brooks began military service as a private in Company E, 153rd Regiment Virginia Militia in 1861. Young petitioned the governor to have him commissioned as his second lieutenant, which he came to regret as Brooks became a painful thorn in his side. When he met with Pierpont in Wheeling, Brooks asserted that morale was poor in the company under Young's command, and that the enlisted men looked to him for leadership, and that he should be given command. Pierpont did not believe him and was frustrated that Young had not come in person to see him. He refused to let Brooks have the new Enfield rifles since he was not commissioned. Brooks insisted that he could sign for them since he was elected as a 2nd Lieutenant, but Pierpont refused. Brooks returned to the company empty handed, but arrogantly assumed he had convinced the governor that he should command the company. He proceeded to mount a slanderous campaign against Young among the men and sent a series of letters to Governor Pierpont requesting a commission as captain. He also wrote to the state adjutant general complaining that Young was incompetent.

Despite Brooks, Pierpont commissioned Young as 1st lieutenant of Company G on May 20, and directed that Young, not Brooks, was to be the company commander. Also, in a surprise move, Governor Pierpont ordered Young and his men on a "temporary" assignment with the 13th West Virginia Volunteer Infantry, which was struggling to fill their ranks at Point Pleasant in nearby Mason County. Neither Young nor Brooks was pleased with the governor's decision. The feisty lieutenant again wrote to Pierpont contending that the "true" reason Young did not want to be assigned to the 13th West Virginia was that he did not want to lose his company's autonomy and be forced to deal with rigid, military discipline within a formal chain of command. Brooks next petitioned the U.S. Secretary of War, Edwin Stanton, on May 24 accusing Young of incompetence, and again arguing that the men wanted him, not Young, in command and that morale was suffering under him.[9]

Frustrated, Brooks made another trip to Wheeling to once more attempt to persuade Pierpont that it was he who should be in command of the company. Unaware that Brooks had written Secretary of War Edwin Stanton, who refused to honor the request, the governor this time gave in to Brooks' agitation and gave him a commission as 2nd Lieutenant and placed him in "temporary command" of the company. This infuriated the enlisted men in Company G, most of whom were also long-time friends of Young. Ignoring Brooks' schemes, Young continued to lead the company on patrols. Brooks was apparently unaware that the ultimate decision rested not with the War Department, but with Governor Pierpont. Shortly after he left Wheeling, the Secretary of War informed the Governor that it was Young, not Brooks, who should be in command of Company G.[10]

Young wrote to Pierpont on May 24 requesting then to have the matter settled in his favor once and for all, but by the time the letter arrived, the governor had left Wheeling on business for Washington, D.C. The state Assistant Adjutant General, George Bowyer, responded to Young on the governor's behalf. He was the son of John Bowyer of Winfield, a close friend of Young's.

Bowyer wrote, "Lieut. Brooks is assuming entirely too much authority – I know all about the matter, I understand exactly how Brooks got his commission...when Brooks was up here the first time the Governor went up to Gen [John] Fremont's Head Quarters and Gen Fremont said the Government would not accept any more cavalry and that your company would have to be mustered into the service of the United States as infantry...Brooks said he would not take responsibility for having the company mustered in as infantry without first getting their consent...when Brooks came back the second time the Governor said that he would have to commission him (Brooks) in order to sign the receipt and in that way you could get your arms [the Enfield rifles]– But the Governor told me himself that you ought to have come...just as soon as he returns I will have the matter set right, because I do know it was not the intention of the Gov to deprive you of the command of your brave men after you done so much to raise the company..."

Meanwhile, Brooks, who was obviously too self-absorbed to realize that he could not effectively lead a group of men who resented him, gloated over his temporary victory. He sought to stir up even more negative sentiment against Young within the company, but with no substantive effect, as the non-commissioned officers were furious with him. In response, they collectively wrote to Governor Pierpont vouching for not only Young's leadership but also clarifying he had formed the company and demanded to have Young reinstated. Pierpont promptly restored Young as the rightful commander of Company G on June 5, which was also his forty-ninth birthday. Needless to say, Young was quite pleased with his gift.[11]

Edgar Blundon wrote to Sarah Young on August 5, indicating that the conflict between Lieutenant Robert Brooks and Captain Young was now well-known among other Union regiments in the Kanawha Valley, and that camp rumors held Brooks was going to resign soon. Blundon wrote, "I am glad to know that Mr. Brooks has become disgusted with the military life and of course, will return to the real pleasures of private life. What a great advantage it would have been to the service had this pious purpose presented itself to his mind long since. Surely, Captain Young feels greatly relieved. The fact that Mr. Brooks was trying to supersede your Pa in commanding was made known to me even before we left the Valley; and I, deeming it my duty, appraised him of it, although I did it indirectly, fearing that I might possibly create difficulty and prevent them from filling up... It is so strange that men will repay kindness by using their effort and influence to destroy the very hand that has conferred the favor. But thus it is with selfish humanity. However, in most instances they destroy themselves. I do hope that the men of your Pa's command saw clearly the motive of Brooks, that there may be no dissatisfaction hereafter."12

## Coalsmouth Under Martial Law

When news reached the area of Confederate victories in the Shenandoah Valley during Major General Thomas J. "Stonewall" Jackson's infamous campaign during April and May, as well as the Seven Days battles around Richmond in June, oddly, Sarah Young doesn't mention either campaign in her diary, although Edgar Blundon was in Jackson's Valley Campaign. The spring of 1862 found tensions running high at Coalsmouth in particular, as Southern citizens buckled under martial law. During his tenure as garrison commander at Coalsmouth, Captain Young encountered daily conflicts with Southern supporters. One resident, Jacob Douglas, was arrested on April 28, 1862, by an officer in the 11th Ohio Volunteer Infantry. Young charged him with taking up arms against the government, on grounds that Douglas had participated in the battle of Scary Creek in July 1861, and he was imprisoned at Camp Chase, Ohio. Douglas was well liked by both Southern supporters and many Unionists, however, as several citizens and even Union soldiers later petitioned Governor Francis Pierpont on his behalf begging for his release, asserting that he was an otherwise peaceful citizen. Among the soldiers was Joseph Griffith of Company G. Douglas was released on December 18, 1862. It should be noted, however, according to the formal charges signed by Captain Young, Douglas had said that if he took the Oath of Allegiance, "he would not consider it binding."

Sarah Young's Southern contemporary, Victoria Teays Hansford, found it particularly harrowing when she received a visit from some Federal soldiers one chilly

April evening. Although speculative, it was quite likely men from Lieutenant John Young's company, as they were the only Federal unit occupying Coalsmouth at that time. Victoria penned, "I was left entirely alone. It was a cold overcast day, and I was sitting by the fire reading some old Dixie letters I had spread out before me. I also had a small silk flag draped over the back of the chair they were on... About then I heard the gate slam and looking out I saw four Yankee soldiers armed to the teeth headed for the door. The orderly sergeant in front wore a sword, a red sash, pistols etc., etc. etc. behind him were three men with muskets and I only had time to thrust my letters into the fire."

Victoria continued, "The flag which I so highly prized went into my bosom, all this within a matter of seconds. With my heart pounding and thumping so loud I could hear it, I put on a calm face and met them at the door. They did not knock as they were a low down squad that had been sent out by the Home Guard to search for contraband articles. The sergeant said he had been told I had a Rebel Flag which they had come for...I looked him straight in the eye and said, 'If you can find one here you can have it.' I also told him he was perfectly welcome to search the house. Finding me so willing for them to search left him standing abashed. I then told him it was not necessary to have brought many men with muskets, swords and pistols when there was only one woman in the house to contend with. He finally sat down and I became more polite and entertaining. I told him that I did have some flags he was welcome to. 'Where are they?' he said, 'There,' I said pointing to a framed picture on the wall of all the presidents. There were four small stars and stripes in each corner but he was so ignorant he had a hard time telling them from 'Stars and Bars.' He finally said if that was all I had I was welcome to keep it. So I bowed them out very dignified, while my little treasure still lay close to my heart. This taught me a lesson to be always alert and never get caught napping...If those four men had been turned loose to search the house I would have lost valuable articles and perhaps been arrested. Our town was under martial law, and we were entirely under their power. We learned to be very discrete but also learned to be cunning."[13]

Although the Kanawha Valley was under Federal control, Confederate guerilla parties continued to conduct frequent nocturnal raids against Union families. Many such raids were led by Peter M. Carpenter, a.k.a. Peter Slick, who was a resident of Coalsmouth. Known as Captain Slick, he was thirty years old and had mainly worked as a laborer prior to the war. His company operated in both the Kanawha Valley and Big Sandy River region, and frequently encountered John Young and his men in small skirmishes. Young and his men also frequent dealt with Colonel Vincent A. "Claw Hammer" Witcher's 34th Battalion Virginia Cavalry, who were still lurking about, routinely attacking Union outposts and harassing Union supporters. Many citizens on both sides assisted troops in their efforts to oust the opposing side from their home, acting as spies and insurgents. Victoria Teays Hansford indicated the Union soldiers also often questioned the local slaves, to gain information of the Confederates' activities: "The Yankees were always interrogating the Negroes. Most of them were true and steadfast, but a few would let out little things that could get us in trouble. However, our colored people never in any way caused the Yanks to bother us, as long as they were with us."[14]

## Attached to the 13th West Virginia Infantry

Early in the morning of August 6, Company G was ordered to an outpost at Mud Bridge (later named the town of Milton in 1870), in Cabell County, located along the James River and Kanawha Turnpike. Young wrote Paulina shortly after arriving there,

*Union Baptist Church, Milton, West Virginia*
*Mud Bridge and the Union fort were nearby*
*Photo by Steve Cunningham*

"Dear Paulina: I am here at Mud Bridge, busily engaged in fixing our tents. The boys are making their bunks...We will be very busy for two or three weeks, building our fortifications. My Company are not all here yet. I only have 60 men here, the rest are at Coal [Coalsmouth] and will be down tomorrow. I have new tents and they look very pretty, and besides all of this I am proud of my men. They are the finest looking men that can be gotten up. Lt. [Robert] Brooks has sent up his resignation. I hope it will be accepted...I like this place very much. It is a pretty place. We are now camped around the Union Church (Baptist) but there is no Union in this neighborhood, nor never was in a Baptist Church. I feel very uneasy about home."

Young continued, "I can't hear from home like I could at Coal. But I don't expect to have the trouble with the Secessionists here that I had at Coal. We will get our letters from Winfield after this. I will try and arrange it so as to send the Post Boy by our house that you may send your letters down by him...Major [John T.] Hall's remains passed by here on way to the Point. I think Colonel [James R.] Hall will be down tomorrow. If he does Colonel Brown will take command here until he returns. He is here now. There are several Gray backs come in since we have been here. Colonel Hall sends them to Charleston as fast as they come in. They will do to swap for Union men who are in the Southern dens. I wish the war was over so I would be able to return home in peace, but I don't want peace made until it is made honorably and the Rebellion put down and the Union established as it was."[15]

Young refers to Major John T. Hall of the 4th West Virginia Infantry, the brother of Major James R. Hall of the 13th West Virginia. John Hall was killed in action on a recent expedition to Logan County (in an area now part of modern McDowell County) on August 6. Sadly, he had tendered his resignation from service in July in order to return home to care for his father but was not yet aware that Governor Pierpont had accepted it when he was killed.

On August 10, Young's company was officially detached from their earlier assignment to the 11th West Virginia and ordered to rendezvous with Lieutenant Colonel William R. Brown and his newly forming 13th West Virginia Volunteer Infantry regiment at Point Pleasant. Brown had five companies partially filled and was rigidly drilling them daily on the old Mason County fairgrounds. As if the enlisted men and junior officers in company G were not already sufficiently aggravated with the conflict between Young and Brooks, when they met Lieutenant Colonel Brown, who was a stern, rigid disciplinarian, they became inconsolable. Unaccustomed to working in a strict military chain of command, Young became so frustrated that he petitioned, albeit unsuccessfully, General Jacob Cox asking him to intervene and remove his company from Brown's command.[16]

Unknown to Young, several citizens familiar with his company as well as some of his enlisted men wrote to the state Adjutant General, Henry Samuels complaining that Lieutenant Colonel Brown was a "dictator" and accused officers of the 13th West Virginia Infantry, many of whom were from Ohio, of treating them unfairly with excessive discipline because they were thought "inferior" due to being from western Virginia. Brown was a Pennsylvania native, born October 11, 1823. During his youth, he tended to drift through the western territories from Iowa to Kansas, and eventually settled in Pomeroy, Ohio, where he became foreman of a brass foundry and machine shop. As the Civil War broke out, he recruited forty men from his foundry and went to Point Pleasant, Virginia, where they enlisted in the 4th West Virginia Volunteer Infantry, and Brown was quickly elected their captain and assigned to Company E. He proved to be

*Colonel William R. Brown*
*13th West Virginia Infantry*
*Courtesy of Richard A. Wolfe*

a strict, but efficient officer; Brown was soon promoted to colonel on September 16.[17]

Once Company G arrived at Point Pleasant, Colonel Joseph A.J. Lightburn, the post commander, was still unaware of Governor Pierpont's recent decision reinstating John Young commander of his company. The irascible Lieutenant Robert Brooks still claimed to be in charge and was pressing the issue with Colonel Lightburn. Puzzled, the colonel had earlier written to the Adjutant General, "Who am I to regard as having command of the company of the 11th Va. Regt known as Young's company? Young or Brooks? It is necessary that someone should command and but one officer can be allowed." Governor Pierpont informed Lightburn of his decision on August 27. The next day, Young received a commission as captain, and his forty newly recruited volunteers raised the Company G census to eighty-seven men. He then petitioned Pierpont to have Sergeant Clark Elkins commissioned as a 2nd Lieutenant, describing him as a "solid and reliable soldier."[18]

When Lieutenant Colonel Daniel Frost, commanding the 11th West Virginia

Infantry, learned a few weeks later that Governor Pierpont had reassigned Young's company to the 13th West Virginia Infantry, he responded with a barrage of letters to the War Department protesting the transfer. Frost even threatened to resign unless Company G remained in his regiment. This was ironic, considering that Young's men had never served with the 11th West Virginia in the field, but as extant army regulations directed that the regimental budget was determined by the number of men on their rolls, it is not surprising Frost was disturbed. Captain Young, who had still not been paid for his time in service, wrote to his wife boasting that he cared little about which regiment he would serve in, as long as he was serving in the Union army.

Meanwhile, two of John Young's relatives, Noah Young and Alexander S. Young, had each requested Governor Pierpont commission them as lieutenants, after organizing a militia company at Winfield comprised of about sixty men. Two of Young's enlisted men, George W. Leadmon and Van Morris, were sent on recruiting duty at Winfield and Coalsmouth. The Putnam County militia was still unorganized and the state Assistant Adjutant General George Bowyer wrote to Adjutant General Henry Samuels on August 15 that he wanted to see more troops placed at Coalsmouth as well as troops placed at Hurricane Bridge. He warned, "If something is not done immediately, we will have warm work in Putnam..."[19]

Due to increased guerilla activity in the area, Captain Young soon received orders to join Companies A, B and D of the 13th West Virginia at Winfield under Lieutenant Colonel James R. Hall. While there, more trouble arose when some Confederate leaning citizens accused Young and his men of stealing their horses. Young denied it, but there is evidence he had in fact taken at least one horse from a local resident earlier in the year. A letter written to Young's brigade commander on his behalf indicated the horse was taken prior to any affiliation with the 13th West Virginia Infantry, however, and also intimated that "Capt. Young has been placed in very peculiar circumstances ever since his entry into the service, his command has most always been right in the midst of inveterate enemies. He has lost by these enemies I believe all of his horses and was in the service some nine months. If I mistake not, has received as yet nothing for his services. He is a brave man, a good Captain, and uncompromisingly for the Union, and hates Secessionists intensely - has showed them little clemency. The consequence is they are trying to hunt him down. I make these remarks simply because I feel for the man, and do not want his character destroyed through the influence of those who hate him only because he tries to do them justice."[20]

## General Cox Leaves the Kanawha Valley

Elsewhere, events in the Eastern Theater of war were about to bring more dramatic changes to the Kanawha Valley. On August 8, Brigadier General Jacob D. Cox was ordered to take the Kanawha Division, with approximately 5,000 troops, and join Major General John Pope in northern Virginia. Cox turned over command of the district to Colonel Joseph A. J. Lightburn when they met at Gauley Bridge on August 17. On August 27-30, Cox's 1st Brigade participated in the Second Battle of Bull Run (a.k.a. Manassas). Captain Edgar Blundon, Sarah Young's sweetheart, had been on active campaign in the Shenandoah Valley since February, and was also engaged in heavy fighting at Second Manassas. He wrote to Sarah Young on September 5, "You desire me to give you a description of the late battle fought along our lines during the past three, and to us, long weeks. I would gladly comply with your wishes were it in my power, but I conclude that the horror which I have observed during the 15 days fighting cannot be described...The war may be protracted indefinitely but the finale must result in the perpetuation of the principles made sacred by the blood of our fathers." Later in September, Blundon's regiment, the 8th West Virginia Infantry, returned to the Kanawha Valley, much to the delight of the soldiers. While stationed at Coalsmouth, Edgar Blundon began pursuing a more serious relationship with Sarah and she responded favorably. Her father John Young granted his permission for them to marry shortly afterward, and a wedding date was tentatively set for February 18, 1863.[21]

After a brief tenure in Washington, D.C., General Cox's Kanawha Division fought at the battles of South Mountain on September 14 and the battle of Antietam (Sharpsburg) on September 17. At South Mountain, Major General Jesse Reno, who commanded the 9th Corps, was mortally wounded and General Cox was given temporary command of the corps. He resisted this idea, pleading with General McClellan that he was too inexperienced at such level of command, but was placed under direct supervision of Major General Ambrose Burnside. Late in the day at Antietam, Cox advanced the 9th Corps on Lee's right and nearly overwhelming the Confederates, until General A.P. Hill's 3rd Corps arrived to reinforce them, forcing Cox to withdraw. Antietam was afterward known as America's Bloodiest Day, with more than 23,000 men killed, wounded or missing in action. President Abraham Lincoln was so impressed with Cox's aggressive style that he recommended him to Congress for promotion to Major General.[22]

The impact of losing more than half of the Union force in the Kanawha Valley left it glaringly vulnerable to Confederate attack. Colonel Albert G. Jenkins' 8th Virginia Cavalry and five companies of the 14th Virginia Cavalry planned to take advantage of the situation. Brigadier General William W. Loring ordered Jenkins to create a diversion as a force of 6,000 Confederates advanced on the Kanawha Valley from Pearisburg, Virginia. Loring, a native of Wilmington, North Carolina, was known as a hard-edged fighter. He lost his left arm in the Mexican War, and yet continued to lead troops in combat. Jenkins had a promotion to Brigadier General pending at Richmond and had only recently resigned his former seat in the Confederate Congress. He soon arrived at Buffalo in Putnam County on September 6. He immediately occupied the vacant home of Dr. Edward Naret, the former Adjutant of the 181st Virginia Militia Regiment. There, he not only enjoyed an afternoon tea taken from Naret's pantry, but he also took a horse and sixteen tons of hay for his troopers. Naret, who was already aggravated from the militia debacle, was furious when he learned of Jenkin's plundering of his house. He was later overheard gloating when he learned one of Jenkin's men drowned crossing the Kanawha River.[23]

When Governor Pierpont learned that Jenkins was back in the Kanawha Valley, he telegraphed Colonel Joseph A.J. Lightburn at Point Pleasant admonishing him to send a large force out to find the Confederates. Lightburn knew that Loring was heading toward Charleston, however, and that doing so would require dividing his 5,000-man force, leaving the region even more dangerously exposed. As a result, he wisely declined Pierpont's request. On the other hand, Lightburn knew he couldn't ignore Jenkins either, and ordered six companies of the 2nd West Virginia Cavalry under Colonel John C. Paxton, along with three companies of the 4th West Virginia Volunteer Infantry to find Jenkins. Colonel Paxton's detachment arrived at Coalsmouth at approximately 11:00 a.m. on Sunday, September 7, and received word that Jenkins was spotted near Hurricane Bridge, with plans to attack Winfield and Coalsmouth that night.[24]

## Skirmish on Coal Mountain

When Colonel Paxton heard that Jenkins was spotted near Hurricane Bridge, some twelve miles away, he sent Captain Young's Company G, and Company K, 2nd West Virginia Cavalry, to reconnoiter. At about 9:00 p.m. that night, Young's Company G and Company K of the 2nd West Virginia Cavalry moved along the James River Turnpike toward Coal Mountain and soon encountered Jenkins' pickets. Colonel Jenkins was said to be familiar with Captain Young and had sent word to him that he would "eat supper in Coalsmouth or in Hell" that night according to Sarah Young's diary. Around 11:00 p.m., Company G and the cavalry drove Jenkin's pickets in, and an intense skirmish ensued on Coal Mountain resulting in two minor casualties in Company G and two Confederates killed. One Union soldier reported they were "fighting like the devil" but were heavily outnumbered and had to fall back toward Coalsmouth after waiting for nearly three hours on expected reinforcements that never arrived.

Sarah Young wrote that night, "Great excitement! We have heard that the Rebels are marching toward Buffalo, and that they have taken Roane C.H. [Court House] with Colonel Rathbone...of the 11th Va. Volunteers...The Union men have all run to the woods. The steamboats have stopped running. Pa was at Coalsmouth with only his company, but he has been reinforced by Cavalry and Infantry. Oh, may they be successful in holding the post and driving the detestable traitors off!" The incident at Roane Court House Sarah mentioned occurred earlier on September 2, when the inexperienced Colonel John Rathbone of the 11th West Virginia Infantry surrendered his command, along with elements of the 9th West Virginia Infantry, to Confederates without even putting up a fight. The affair ultimately resulted in his dismissal from service.[25]

Sarah Young was sad when she heard more details from her father the next day, "...Pa went to meet him [Jenkins] with horsemen and footmen. They had a skirmish on Coal Mountain last night. The Rebels retreated. We heard that two of Pa's men were wounded, but don't know how true it is. They are pursuing them yet. Oh, when will we enjoy the blessings of sweet peace? When will we be clear of annoying Guerillas...Ah, I fear not until many brave and gallant soldiers fall on the battlefield. Our dead soldiers who have offered their lives on the altar of victory; crown their efforts with success; aid them in every trial, and oh, be their hope in distress. May our leaders and Generals call upon Thee for divine wisdom; and, as the immortal Washington did in the old Revolution, humble themselves before Thee, and ask Thee for Thy assistance. God, give them all they require." Company G and the other units in Colonel Paxton's cavalry detachment also participated in minor skirmishes at Barboursville and Guyandotte on September 8 and returned to Camp Coalsmouth that night. Young's wife, Paulina, visited him in camp that evening and returned home the next morning, informing Sarah that her father and the men were "...in fine spirits."[26]

On September 9, Sarah learned still more of the recent skirmish on Coal Mountain, confirming: "Two of them were wounded – James Davis and James Paule. [Paul] They are not dangerous. They were all very brave, and deserve to be praised. The 2nd Va. Cavalry are pursuing the Rebels yet. We heard that the beautiful flag which we presented to Co. F, 8th Va. Vol. is the only one in the regiment. Oh, may the gallant officers and brave soldiers of that company rally around it, and vow that traitors shall never trail it in the dust so long as they have strength to sustain it! May the gallant Captain [referring to Edgar Blundon, her suitor] be endowed with divine wisdom, that he may lead his noble company under that flag to certain victory. May he survive the Revolution, and be honored in after years for his services and bravery during the Rebellion." She noted also her father had sent six men from Company G to their home on September 10 to see if the "...Rebels had disturbed us last night."

Sarah wrote, "He was uneasy about us. Oh, I wish the detestable Rebels would stay away from West Virginia! They have come in and caused the Federals to burn up some of the most influential rebel's property..." She also quipped that the Federals had not even given one Secessionist "...time to get his hat out of his house" before burning it. Young and Company G were ordered out on patrol in search of Jenkins on September 10, passing into Cabell County where they engaged in two small skirmishes along Charley's Creek, with no casualties before returning to Coalsmouth. Company G was involved in another skirmish near Hurricane Bridge in Putnam County on September 11 or 12. Details are sketchy, other than Company G was ordered to pursue Jenkins as he fled from Guyandotte. They caught up with him near Hurricane Bridge and had a brief skirmish, but Young did not give more details.[27]

## Confederates at the Door

As rumors of a general Confederate advance flowed across the Kanawha Valley, Sarah Young became anxious and was constantly on the lookout for Confederate raiders and found comfort in recording events in her diary. She and her family received a visit from not only her father and some of his soldiers on September 12, but also a party of Confederates led by Captain James Nounnan, who were looking for him. Nounnan and his company joined the 16th Virginia Cavalry under Colonel Milton Ferguson as Company K in August 1862, and a month later were then on Young's doorstep. The experience of having the enemy in his own home had a profound effect on Young, who, by his daughter's description, appeared somewhat haggard after the affair, "Oh, little Journal, I have things to write that make my heart ache! Yesterday evening we heard of some Rebel soldiers in the neighborhood. Ma sent Ben [Benjamin Young, her fourteen-year-old brother] to Coalsmouth immediately to tell Pa, if he had not heard it; but others informed him and after dark Pa and three of his men pressed some "secesh" horses and borrowed one of Mr. Mynes, who is hiding from the Rebels, to come down in this neighborhood."

Sarah continued, "They had been there but a short time before the men became sleepy, and Pa told them he would watch if they wished to sleep a little while. They all laid on the floor and I thought Pa looked tired. Emilie and myself told him we would watch if he wanted to rest. He laid down and in the course of an hour we heard horses coming. We wakened Pa directly, and he and the men ran out through the back door, passed around the corner of the house, but seeing too many Rebels to attack they slipped down the hill back of the house into a ravine thickly set with alders. Two of the men ran on. One concealed himself along the fence to get a shot at them. Pa hid in a large bunch of alders. When the rogues stopped they found the horses tied, and asked us, very authoritatively, what those horses were doing here. Ma told them, as they answered her when she spoke to them, that it was an unfair question, and she would not tell them. I never in my life experienced such a time."

She further penned, "They stayed around the house about two hours, scouting through the yard and listening; no doubt expecting Pa to come after their horses. I never felt so much like abusing men in my life. One rough, ill-bred fellow would not tell me his name. I suppose he was ashamed of it. Burns, one of the set, told Ma his name was Dotson from Guyandotte. All the time they were here they would not move the horses. They were fastened in the back yard, and I reckon they thought Pa would come after them. While Pa was in the alder bush, a large, over-grown horse-thief came sneaking around him, and would stand listening within about ten steps of Pa. Pa said he fixed to shoot him, but he heard some more talking, and he thought he had better not. They came to the house and we talked with them some. Indeed, my heart ached so I could scarcely talk. Old Dotson said he thought he could get married somewhere on this road. I told him Rebel beaux could not shine with the Union girl, but Yankees went like hot cakes. He said, 'I think I could make a Secesh out of you.' I gave him to understand quite different. He said something about 'homespun Yankees.' I told him they were home-spun Rebels. He said, 'I would like to stay about a week and quarrel with you.' After a while, the notorious horse thief, and blood-thirsty Rebel, Jim Nounnan, came along and called for a candle to search the house.

Emilie carried the candle and helped to search, laughing all the time at them. I told Nounnan I would not tell him who came here, and if I knew where they were I would not tell him. He said it was immaterial to him that he only asked for information here. I think he was mad, but I did not care. Dotson told us we would have to go to the North with our sweethearts or submit to Jeff Davis. I hope he may never live to see the time. Well, I suppose they got tired of searching and waiting. They bade us goodnight, wishing us good luck. Em [Emily] told them when gentlemen called on us we wanted them to come at a fashionable hour and not scare us half to death in the night. I told them I was not glad to see them, and did not wish them good luck at all. And I don't. After they had left the house, one of the soldiers fired at them. It scared them so that they went double quick down the road."

Lastly, Sarah recalled, "The soldier declares that he wounded one of them. Pa then came close to the house. I declare he looked so strange it frightened me to look at him. He had left his hat in the house. Ma took it to him and he said he would hide and wait for the boys but he started back to Camp. Ben was at Coalsmouth when he came, and said Pa had to crawl through the Rebel pickets. I suppose they were posted along to catch him. He went most of the way through the woods, and waded Coal river. After a while two of the others came in. They were very uneasy about the other one but before noon he came in. He was the one who fired at the Rebel." Sarah again observed on September 13, "The same evening the Rebels were here, the Federal Cavalry came through Hurricane Bridge and captured six of their men. Good. They had no business here...Some of the Cavalry went to Winfield but made no discoveries."[28]

## Battle of Charleston – Lightburn's Retreat

The town of Charleston was home to approximately 1,500 citizens. When Colonel Joseph A.J. Lightburn confirmed that Major General William W. Loring's force of 5,000 Confederates was marching toward Charleston, he placed all Union forces on alert in the region, with Captain Young's company posted at Coalsmouth. Loring had orders to create a diversion from General Robert E. Lee's upcoming Maryland Campaign, and capture the salt mines near Charleston. The Confederates marched from Giles County, Virginia, arriving at Fayetteville on September 11 where Loring found two Federal regiments waiting. After a small, but intense battle, Loring forced them to withdraw toward Charleston. With Loring in fast pursuit, Lightburn ordered a general retreat of all Federal outposts from Fayetteville to Charleston, burning the Union powder magazines and other military stores left behind along the way. The retreating Federal troops reached Charleston near 2:00 a.m. on September 13 and took up positions on the western bank of the Elk River and on the east end of town along the Kanawha River.

As the Confederates approached Charleston early on the morning of September 13, the advance guard made contact with Federal troops there, and the battle began in earnest. Citizens were advised to evacuate, and many became trapped under heavy artillery and small arms fire from both sides of the river. The downtown and west end areas were severely damaged by artillery and several buildings were burned also. After several hours of heavy fighting, the Federals withdrew toward the Elk River and crossed a large suspension bridge to the western bank where Lightburn had posted two regiments to cover them. Confederate artillery quickly zeroed in on their position, and bombarded them until about 5:00 p.m., while the Federal artillery provided heavy counter-battery fire. Once all of the Federals had crossed, they cut the bridge's cables on the west bank, and let it fall into the river to prevent Confederates from pursuing them further. Realizing the town was lost, Colonel Lightburn ordered a general withdrawal toward Point Pleasant, and thousands of dollars in government stores were burned to prevent capture. As Lightburn's troops made their way along the Ohio River toward Point Pleasant by way of Ravenswood with Confederates rapidly pursing, one soldier described it as "a continual skirmish for fifty miles" under rapid, forced-march conditions.[29]

Confederate supporter Victoria Teays Hansford was twelve miles away at her home in Coalsmouth when the battle began and heard the cannonading and rattle of muskets as terrified Union supporters evacuated the village. She recalled in her diary, "Such sight about me I never saw nor ever expect to see again. The river as far as the eye could reach up and down was covered with boats of all kinds, large flat boats, jerry boats, jolly boats, skiffs and canoes...When I say the river was covered with boats I mean just what I say, and a person could have almost crossed the river by jumping from one boat to another...I will never forget a woman and a man were on two short pieces of gunnywayles lashed together. A tub sat at one end of it containing their property. The woman sat in a rocking chair at the other end, while the man stood in the middle and paddled them on as best he could. The woman was wet to her waist from the water washing over the planks; the man seemed to be wet all over from pushing and pulling. I felt so sorry for them and said, 'Poor fools, the Rebels won't hurt you.' But on they went. This was the famous Lightburn's retreat... all this time the cannonading went on and it was music to us."[30]

Sarah Young was unaware that her father and his company had joined Colonel Lightburn's troops just in time to avoid capture on their retreat, but was quite unhappy about the Confederates return, "Oh such bad news. We heard the Rebels were coming into the Valley with such a superior force the Federals could not drive them back and that the Union families are moving down the river fast. I sincerely hope they will be reinforced before the Rebels get to Charleston. I went to Coalsmouth today to see Pa, but his company had left there. They reached the river Saturday night. His pickets were opposite Coals Mouth. Emilie and I crept and talked with them. I am so afraid the Rebels will get possession of Kanawha Valley. God forbid that they should hold it. We heard today that the Rebels had possession of Charleston and Pa has moved down the river somewhere. Oh Lord, in Thy kind mercy, be with him and his Company. Save them from the savage rebels."[31]

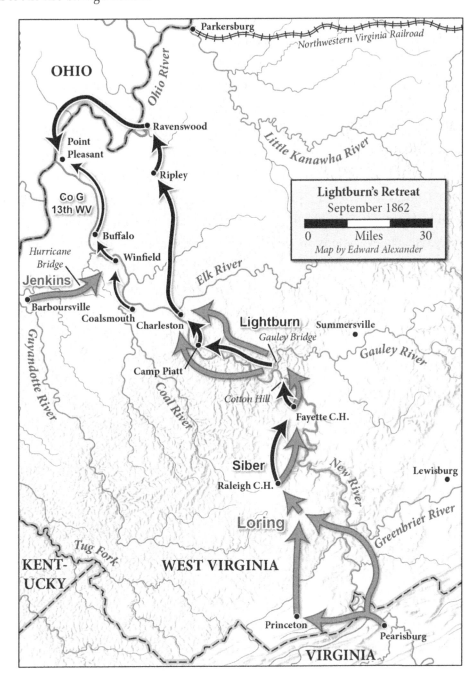

Lightburn arrived at Point Pleasant on September 17 and the exhausted soldiers went into camp. John Young was unable to contact his family for several days, but later wrote to his daughters, describing Company G's retreat, "We got here without any difficulty by twenty-four hours march, the Rebels at our heels...These military men here think I made a most glorious retreat from Coals Mouth. They think very few men would have conducted the retreat better, and I got great praise for it. Some had said Captain Young would never get out; others that Captain Young would report at Point Pleasant. When Colonel Lightburn came to Point Pleasant he inquired at once if Captain Young had gotten out." Young also praised them for their courage after the Federal troops evacuated the area, "...It is now nearly midnight and I am cold, and have the headache. I have had the earache very bad but am better...the prospect of hearing from home keeps me from sleep. You can't conceive how badly I want to hear from home. I am tented out in the field and just have a little stove in my tent, and it makes it very comfortable; and if I knew you all had plenty I would be very well satisfied, but until I hear from you there is no pleasure for me. I read your letters to Colonel Brown and he said he wanted to see you for he knew you were the right stripe. I was proud of your letters. Nearly everybody in Point Pleasant read them and praised you for your valor. Some said, "they are heroes," others said. "they had the ring of their Pa."[32]

Once they had control of Charleston, the Confederates quickly seized control of the *Kanawha Valley Star*, a popular local newspaper. Also, another newspaper soon emerged, *The Guerilla*. This organ had clear intentions of persuading Union men to side with the Confederacy. The first issue appeared on September 29, describing the plight of Union citizens under Confederate martial law, "During the past few days the Kanawha and Ohio rivers have been full of flatboats...laden with the families of Unionists, who find themselves compelled to flee...fearing the rebel General will carry into execution his recently made threat to hang every citizen "Yankee" he found in the Kanawha Valley... they are obliged to leave behind them what they depended on to subsistence during the coming winter...most of them have to seek a charitable home among strangers...It is a pitiful sight to see families adrift... to find a home they knew not where - and all because their father or husband would not renounce his allegiance to the Government of his Fathers. The rebels in Western Virginia have declared themselves unsatisfied with anything less than armed resistance to the Federal power on the part of citizens whom they meet in their raids. It will not do to say you have not taken sides with either way, or that your sympathies only are with one side or the other. They demand active participation in their cause, and "confiscation" robbery and outrage are the punishments for Federalism."[33]

On September 17, the same day that the battle of Antietam was fought near Sharpsburg, Maryland, a group of Confederates, including one man whom Sarah Young was familiar with came to her house. Sarah chronicled the events, "The Rebels came again today. They thought they would scare us. Old Bob Thompson came riding up and asked Ma how many minutes she wanted to get things out of the house. He found out we did not care, and then he said he was not going to burn. We heard that Pa and his Company crossed the Ohio river, and that a very large force of Federal troops are at Point Pleasant. Oh God, aid them in re-taking this Valley!"[34]

When Company G reached Point Pleasant, they assumed regular garrison duties with the 13th West Virginia Infantry. Young had a change of heart toward Colonel William R. Brown after realizing the benefits of a stronger military discipline, "We drill twice a day, have Battalion drill once a day; dress parade once. We have eight companies in the 13th Regiment - all full. Three companies from Kanawha. They are fine looking men and I believe will fight. At least they want to come up the Kanawha Valley very much. Most of their families are up there." Young approached Colonel Lightburn requesting that his company receive a permanent assignment with the 13th West Virginia Infantry. Lightburn agreed, and telegraphed Governor Pierpont on September 19: "Capt Young's Company is here, he desires to go into the 13th. If it can be so arranged, I think it will be best." After the Confederates returned to the Kanawha Valley, guerilla outfits began seeking recourse in earnest against Union citizens in several areas, and Loring's men pressed dozens of horses and forced eligible males into Confederate service.[35]

Sarah Young became increasingly distressed with her father and Edgar Blundon away from the area. On September 22, she observed: "Oh dear little journal, how I wish I could write something today that would cause my heart to beat with joy! Ah, nothing but trouble, trouble. The Rebels are pressing every man into service, from eighteen to thirty-five, and taking every horse from the Union men. Several of our neighbors have gone to Ohio to escape them. They say they intend staying in West Virginia. I hope they will be driven from here before winter; if not, what will become of suffering families for Rebels don't care who they cause to suffer. We can't hear one word from Pa. We don't know where he is. Oh God, give him health, and may he soon return." Sarah noted on September 25 that, "The Rebels are swarming around. Some of them are doubtful about staying in the Kanawha Valley others seem to be very positive about it." Sarah also mentioned that another skirmish occurred between Confederate cavalrymen under Albert G. Jenkins, who recently became a brigadier general, and Union cavalry in the vicinity of the Young family home, only adding to her anxieties.[36]

Soon after capturing Charleston, Confederate General William Loring established his headquarters in the small village of Coalsmouth at the home of Unionist Samuel Benedict, whose son-in-law, John S. Cunningham, was in John Young's company. Benedict had helped organize the Restored Government of Virginia and helped write the new state constitution. Loring found it humorous that he used Benedict's home as headquarters as a result. Benedict, however, was furious but helpless to stop Loring. Southern leaning residents quickly informed Loring of Captain Young's activities around Coalsmouth prior to Lightburn's retreat, and the Confederates tormented local families of Union soldiers in Company G as well as other outfits. Sarah Young desperately missed her father, and heard only bits and pieces of information, "Oh, how lonely we feel. We can't hear one word from Pa – only what the secessionists please to tell us." The hardships under an enemy occupying army were felt throughout the Kanawha Valley, with shortages of food, clothing and often medical supplies. Union citizens were often afraid to leave their homes, and others had evacuated the area completely, leaving many isolated and feeling very alone.[37]

Sarah elaborated further, "Sometimes they say that they have captured him. How long will we have to live with Rebels? It makes me feel indignant to see them riding by on horses that they have stolen from Union men. And to think of our own friends in the Federal army. Oh, God, give them victory. May they soon return to us. We are living here almost destitute of everything. Common calico one dollar per yard. But that is a mere nothing compared to being deprived of freedom of speech and the blessed privilege of enjoying the society of our friends. But oh, dear friends, though you are driven from us by a lawless band, you are fresh in our memory. Absence cannot erase you from our thoughts. Although absent, and perhaps it may be for some time, we will still retain one sacred corner of our hearts for you. Our prayers will often waft your names to Him who upholds the right and crushes the falsehood. Believe us, dear friends, and stand bravely under the Flag of the Free. God save you!"[38]

Union citizens had virtually no protection now, although there were still a few militia companies posted at Buffalo. They continued to pressure Confederate troops with regular patrols and had a few small skirmishes, but Citizen Patrols ceased operations while the Kanawha Valley was under Confederate control. Sarah Young's family was marked due to their father's Union service, as she penned on September 29, "Three mean looking rebels came today and searched our house for guns. They did not find any but seemed to think we had some hidden somewhere. We heard that the Rebels and Federals had a skirmish yesterday near Buffalo. The Rebels reinforced, and the Federals were compelled to retreat. I sincerely hope that our dear soldiers will soon be here. Ah! gladly would I meet them. Gladly would I say, 'Welcome dear soldiers! We have missed you and have longed for your return.'"[39]

Sarah also scribbled a small prayer for her sweetheart, Edgar Blundon and her father, "May the blessings of our kind and benevolent Father be on you. May no ball discharged from a Rebel gun have the desired effect; and may they fly before you realize the fact that they can't stay in our Valley." Not all Confederates behaved aggressively toward Young's family, however, as one paid a visit on October 4, whom Sarah noted was the "politest and most gentlemanly Rebel I have seen since they came to our Valley." Two Confederates from guerilla James Nounnan's outfit also came by her house later that evening in search of one of Young's horses, but somehow Sarah and her mother had managed to hide it in the bushes nearby. Sarah again encountered two other gentlemanly Confederates, who came by requesting dinner on October 6; she noted, "Some of them are very kind to us, and treat us as gentlemen should, but some are perfect nobodies; they have not one gentlemanly principle about them." Brigadier General Quincy Adams Gilmore was ordered to replace Colonel Joseph A.J. Lightburn and take command of the Kanawha District on October 2. The next day, General Loring issued a proclamation to the citizens of the Kanawha Valley area, warning them, "We do not intend to punish those who remain at home as quiet citizens, in obedience to the laws of the land, and to all such clemency and amnesty are declared; but those who persist in adhering to the cause of the public enemy, and the pretended State Government he has erected at Wheeling, will be dealt with as their obstinate treachery deserves."[40]

John Young finally found time to write to Paulina, whom he often called "Marsh" (derived from her middle name Marsha) on October 6, "I am here with my company and all well and in good health, but want to come home. I got here without any difficulty by twenty-four hours marching, the Rebels at our heels. I want to hear from home very bad indeed. I have 86 men here now and are willing to start up now any hour. We hear many doleful tales about the Rebels and what they are doing in the Kanawha Valley. We expect to come up soon...I have a horse in Gallipolis for you as soon as the way is open. General [Quincy Adam] Gilmore is here. General [Robert H.] Milroy will be here tomorrow. Dear "Marsh," you must stand it as well as you can until there is a way open for you to get out of that filthy place...I would say to my noble daughters that they must be as quiet as possible. I want them to write to me all that they have seen and heard since I left. I want it for publication. Write it carefully. Tell me the condition of things generally. I would like to know how many there are and where located. I have sent a horse to the Ohio for you when you come. Tell me how much the Rebels have taken from you since I left, and how they have talked to you. Dear Paulina, if you think you can get out with your things safely, come; but I don't think they will let you come. But if they take your provisions, leave everything but the children and make your way to the Ohio. Use your own judgment in the affair, but keep a sharp look."[41]

Young's family received the letter on October 9 and Sarah was elated, as she exclaimed: "How glad we feel! We have received a letter from Pa. His company is well and anxious to come home...he would not tell us how many troops are at Point Pleasant, but said we would soon know. O, God, let them come safely. Last night the Rebels were passing like bees. I know something great was to pay. Some went down the road walking, and back riding. We could see them hunting for our horse. They kept us awake all night." The flow of Confederates moving along the roads that night that kept Sarah, her mother and sister awake was in fact the beginning of the Confederates' retreat out of the Kanawha Valley. Confederate General William W. Loring had learned Union forces had massed some 10,000 soldiers at Point Pleasant, with more on the way, and were planning to regain the Kanawha Valley. Loring wrote to Confederate Secretary of War George W. Randolph on October 8, informing him of the Federal build-up, but was only given a thin promise to send more artillery and infantry "when able." Loring prudently decided to plan his withdrawal from Charleston the next day.[42]

On October 10, Sarah Young confirmed that Confederates were leaving: "Good! Good! The Rebels are preparing to make a grand retreat. I suppose they will take enough out to keep them this winter. They have taken out, or rather, stolen, every horse from the Union men that they could find; and besides all the kindness they have received from the Rebel friends, they have stolen from some of the most prominent ones. They stole one poor Union man's horse while one of his children was dying. He is left in a bad condition. He only had one horse and a large family. One of his sons is in Pa's company. I can't mention all the meanness they have done. Indeed I almost blush to see Virginians do so; but what can we expect of persons who openly rebel against our Government. Their Generals say that taking horses is positively against orders; and when a man goes to the Commanders for his horse, they tell him if he can find the horse and the man who took it he can have it. And perhaps, if he finds the horse, which is a seldom occurrence, they say 'If you had some prominent Secessionists from your neighborhood to prove it to be yours, you could have it.' This is the way the Generals have their orders obeyed. They tell their men to do just as they please, and great doings they have; still they say the Yankees are the worst things in the world. God forbid we should be troubled with Rebels again." The terminally ill man Sarah mentioned was the brother of 2nd Lieutenant John Cunningham, the son-in-law of Samuel Benedict of Coalsmouth, who served in Company G with her father.[43]

## One Cannot Serve Two Masters

The conflict between Colonel William Brown, commanding the 13th West Virginia Infantry and Colonel Daniel Frost of the 11th West Virginia Infantry over the question of who had rights to Young's company intensified to almost ridiculous proportions, although the morale in Company G had improved since arriving at Point Pleasant. Frost telegraphed Governor Pierpont on October 11, complaining that "Young had not reported per orders…" although he was also aware Company G was still attached to the 13th West Virginia. Frost argued that Young, despite only having a temporary detachment to the 13th West Virginia, had recruited forty-seven new troops for his company since August 1862, and they were all mustered into the 13th West Virginia at Colonel Brown's insistence instead of his own, thinking the original War Department order assigning Company G to his regiment took precedence. Colonel Brown adamantly disagreed; reasoning that Young was only able to recruit so many new men in the first place because of his affiliation with the 13th West Virginia. Young made several attempts to resolve the matter through his chain of commands in both the 11th and 13th West Virginia regiments, and he also requested that Colonel Brown send his company to Winfield again so they would be closer to their homes. The matter eventually wound up on the desk of recently promoted Major General Jacob D. Cox, who had not yet returned to the Kanawha Valley following his success in the Maryland Campaign.[44]

Cox often expressed marked reservations about the volunteer troops from West Virginia, knowing that they came from an area dominated by loyalty to the Confederacy. He also harbored significant doubts about the military aptitude of what he deemed rough cut, simple "mountain people," quipping that many such men assured him "they had never before seen the American flag", and their families had never been further than "a few miles away from home." While he carefully reviewed the matter, Cox was unable to resolve the issue. He deferred to Governor Pierpont, who recently received another telegram from Young's antagonist, 2nd Lieutenant Robert Brooks on October 14 alleging the "true" reason Young wanted to be posted at Winfield was to avoid strict discipline posited by Colonel Brown. Pierpont again fell victim to Brooks' manipulation and told Colonel Frost he wanted Company G in his regiment because they apparently lacked discipline. However, this was also the same regiment that surrendered to Jenkins' Confederates at Spencer on September 2 without even so much as firing a shot. Many of those same men eloped into the hills due to a lack of discipline.

Cox eventually wrote to the U.S. Secretary of War asking for jurisdictional guidance on the matter. He was not pleased with Colonel Frost's demand, "I hand you a communication from Lieutenant-Colonel Frost, Eleventh [West] Virginia Volunteers, in reference to the position of Captain Young's company. The company is acting with the Thirteenth, into which part of its men has been mustered, but Captain Young, the other officers and the rest of the men were originally mustered into the Eleventh. Will you be kind enough to give me such information as to the course taken in that matter as may enable me to determine what should be now done in the premises? The tone of Lieutenant-Colonel Frost's letter is unmilitary and improper in its reference to yourself and Adjutant-General Samuels, and he will be reprimanded for it."[45]

Shortly afterward, Secretary of War Edwin Stanton intervened and decided that Captain John Young and his men were to remain with the 13th West Virginia, at least for the time being. General Cox was then also contemplating putting troops at Hurricane Bridge in Putnam County, but a lack of wagon transportation to the area due to poor weather, had deterred him from doing so until that time. He also mentioned that he was pondering establishing a permanent outpost at Hurricane Bridge, insisting no precaution be omitted "...to give the people of that region full protection." Cox's general mistrust of western Virginia regiments had also affected the quality and type of firearms they received, as on October 13, Governor Pierpont received another telegraph from a disgruntled officer in the 13th West Virginia, "The Thirteenth Regt is only furnished with old condemned guns, it is a regiment of superior men and if possible, ought to have good guns immediately."[46]

As rumors flooded the Kanawha Valley area that Union forces would return any day, Sarah Young was reeling from the constant flow of misinformation and was not sure what to believe. She maintained hope the Union army would soon return, writing on October 14, "Glorious news, if it be true! – The Federals are at Buffalo, and the Rebels have skedaddled across Gauley. May they never come to Kanawha in arms again. By the blessings of God our men will soon be home. We hear from Pa often now. He is very anxious to come home. Oh, what joy when we will be free from Rebels!" On October 21, Sarah confided: "How I wish I could write something that would be pleasing to me. How lonely and melancholy we feel. All our friends gone! I feel like desponding when I think of our situation, but there are others who are suffering for the necessities of life. I am thankful that we have plenty yet, but where are our protectors? We hear various rumors about the Army. Sometimes we hear that the Federals are marching up the river, and today we heard there were two thousand infantry and two hundred fifty horsemen at Mud Bridge; after that, we heard there were Rebels at Coalsmouth. This evening, about sundown, twenty-five or thirty Rebels, horsemen, passed here. When they passed our stable they saw the horse which Mr. Sims was kind enough to lend us."[47]

Sarah continued, "One of them rode back and asked whose horse that was. I suppose he thought it very strange that a Union family should have a horse. They went back during the night. I haven't heard what their business was down the road." Paulina Young celebrated her forty-second birthday on October 25, and Sarah's mood was improving some also, as she indicated: "Ma's birthday. O, dear little journal, I have good news this time, without doubt! Our beloved soldiers are at Winfield, Captain Blundon is there. He sent word he would come out as soon as possible. We are so glad to know General Cox is commanding here again, and that the 8th Va. Vols. have come back to West Virginia. Yesterday five of the Rebellion thieves rode down the road as though no Yankees were this side of Ohio River; but I guess they went back double quick. Forty Union Cavalry were in the neighborhood. I hope we will never see them scouting here again. Such a pitiful set. We received a letter from Pa and Mr. Elkins yesterday. Their Regiment is at Point Pleasant. They have been attached to the 13th Va. Vol. Infty. Oh Lord, may our troops be victorious! In Thy Kind mercy, remember them in their trouble. Give them health and wisdom to fight for the glorious, old star-gemmed banner."[48]

Sarah's speculation proved correct; Major General Robert Milroy assumed temporary command of the Kanawha Valley in mid-October, as General Cox had not yet returned from the Maryland Campaign. The Union force soon grew to approximately 20,000 troops stationed at Point Pleasant, as the Cumberland Division, under Major General George Washington Morgan, gradually arrived from eastern Kentucky during the next few days. They had recently experienced hard service during the Cumberland Gap Campaign and were exhausted and ragged, marching slowly not having received fresh supplies or uniforms in months. Morgan then had three brigades in his division, comprised of troops from eastern Tennessee, Kentucky, Ohio, Indiana and Illinois. The majority of Tennesseans and Kentuckians had something in common with the western Virginians; they hailed from areas with large Secessionist populations and were used to dealing with the problems faced by Union citizens in the Kanawha Valley. Loring began his retreat from Charleston in a gradual and orderly manner on October 9 but chose to digress from the plan ordered by General Robert E. Lee. He was replaced by Brigadier General John Echols on October 16, who promptly halted the withdrawal, and moved back toward Charleston, arriving there on October 22, and immediately posted broadsides threatening to arrest any citizen suspected of disloyalty to the Confederacy.[49]

## Lightburn's Advance on the Kanawha Valley

Three days earlier, Major General Cox ordered Colonel Lightburn to begin his advance to re-take the Kanawha Valley, and move his division toward Buffalo. He arrived the next day in unseasonably warm, windy weather, accompanied by a detachment of men from Captain Young's Company G. Colonel Lightburn found the

Confederates waiting with three pieces of artillery posted in line of battle near Red House on October 23, and after a sharp skirmish, the Southerners retreated down the Kanawha River toward Charleston. There were no casualties in the detachment from Company G. Echols knew his days in Charleston were numbered after learning of the large Union force heading his way and ordered a general withdrawal once again on the cold, snowy evening of October 25. It took a few days to organize this retreat, however. General Cox had left Point Pleasant and traveled down to Pocatalico to join Colonel Lightburn, arriving there on October 27. He immediately sent out scouting parties to Scary Creek in Putnam County, and also to Tyler Mountain (located near modern Cross Lanes). General Echols began his eastward retreat early in the morning of October 28.[50]

John Young was still at Point Pleasant on October 28 and wrote to his wife that he was "...doing nothing but cooking and eating, and I am really tired of staying here. I want to hear from home so much. I have been wishing and listening for some news from home but I can't hear any...I also sent you my horse (Alex) and some flour, coffee and soda; and wrote you to come down as soon as you could. I don't know what to do until I see you. I wish you would come as soon as you can...I will be up as soon as I get my money. It is no use for me to come without it, but if you can come down I can get you such things as you need without the money. I can get groceries from the Quartermaster Department at government prices. Lieut. Col. Hall started this morning with 200 men toward Teays Valley. 40 of my men are with him...I just now hear, while I am writing, that our men are fighting at the mouth of Coal, and if this is true you will soon be delivered from the rebels. There are now about 25,000 troops in the Kanawha Valley. Gen. Milroy is on his way to Gauley with fifteen or twenty thousand, and you may guess what will become of Jeff [Davis] and his vandals."

Young also expressed, "...I am afraid you and my children are suffering for the necessities of life. I hear so much about what the rebels have done up there. I don't know how you can get along without a horse, but I told Col. Lightburn if any women who lived in the Valley could, you would. Oh, Paulina, I want to see you and the children so bad. I dream of you at night and think of you by day. I think of the happy hours and years we have enjoyed at home at our hard labor. The happy hours! When will they return? But our consolation – those who have disturbed our peaceful home will be disturbed in return, and that right speedily. I love to think of "home, sweet home" indeed to me; and those four ties that bind is more closely together. Col. Frost has ordered me and my command to Parkersburg, but Gen. Crook says he has use for Capt. Young's company in the Kanawha Valley."[51]

Young continued on October 29, "It makes me indignant but I intend to retaliate fourfold on their heads...Paulina, do come as soon as you can. I repeat it. I don't know what to do until I see you and get your advice. I am in a great deal of trouble about my family and cant hear from home at all, and don't expect to hear correctly until I see you. My troubles since I came down here have reduced me considerably, but I try to bear it as well as I can under the circumstances. But I assure you it is hard to do when I know my dear family is insulted and abused by thieves and traitors and have their living taken from them when I know they have worked hard for it. Well, I must quit writing and go on dress parade. The drum is now beating, the Captains are shouting 'fall in, fall in.' I must go. Colonel Brown has his uniform on all ready, so goodbye at present. I will say more sometime shortly. Dress parade is over now and I will finish my letter...Yours in love until death..."[52]

On the afternoon of October 29, Colonel Lightburn's main force came within two miles of Charleston, while the 37th and 89th Ohio regiments reached the mouth of the Coal River near Coalsmouth. At about 2:00 a.m, they reached Charleston and found the Confederates had left without a fight. The Kanawha Valley was once again in Union hands. During the next few days, Union troops filled the valley and soon recaptured the numerous salt works in the region. One elderly gentleman in Charleston was so elated he yelled out to the passing troops, "God Bless you, God bless you, everyone!" and sang the Star Spangled Banner aloud to them as they marched by, on October 30. Another excited citizen yelled out to them, "By the Blessing of our Heavenly Father our soldiers occupy Charleston again!"[53]

On October 30th, 1862, Major General Jacob D. Cox ordered a large expedition of Union troops in Guyandotte and Barboursville to reopen communication with Charleston, now that the Confederates had withdrawn from the area. The 84th Indiana Volunteer Infantry Regiment was stationed at Guyandotte and was ordered toward Hurricane Bridge "scouting for Rebels who may be lingering in Putnam County." Once at Hurricane, Pvt. Samuel Huddleston found the effects of war had ravaged the once beautiful area, noting it "...bore the marks of war. The bare chimney – monuments standing over the ashes of once peaceful and happy homes – and the absence of all able-bodied men told the sad story of a town which was one of the first to reap the bitter fruits of war. And this was only a sample of towns among the Western Virginia hills." Sarah Young diarized a day later, "With a light heart I can write today. So much has taken place within the last few days. By the blessing of our Heavenly Father our soldiers occupy Charleston again. To Him we owe all our victories. To Him we should bow in meek submission, and ask for a continuance of His mercies. I hope our Chief Command of West Virginia, Major General Cox, may be endowed with divine wisdom. May he humble himself before our Father, and he will surely uphold the truth. I am so glad the

8th [West Virginia] Regiment has come back. Ma started to Point Pleasant yesterday to see Pa. His Regiment is there yet."[54]

Corporal Fretwell Hensley of Company G wrote to his wife on October 31 from Point Pleasant that he had still not been paid. He had earlier told her: "I have not received any money yet, but we expect to be paid off before long and it is the opinion of the soldiers that when we get our money we will come home and not before. I am getting very impatient to see you and the children once more but we must suffer sorrows and disappointments now and hope they may better prepare us for each other's society when we are permitted to return to our home in peace, and oh how I long to see that happy time when soldiers may return to the loved ones at home and enjoy the pleasures of the affectionate embraces of a faithful wife and loving children, and I hope that time is not very distant...If you are in need of anything, sell anything you can and get it..." Hensley also mentioned rumors were going around their camp that they would be coming back to Charleston or Coalsmouth soon for the winter, which he and the other men much anticipated.[55]

The 8th West Virginia then had companies stationed at Guyandotte and in the area known as Brownstown. (modern Marmet) Edgar Blundon wrote to Sarah Young on November 2, "I have been very anxious to receive intelligence from you direct but, of course could not as the Rebels always bring terror instead of peace with them. But they are gone now. Communication has again been opened between the Loyalists and the world, and we anticipate an early restoration of the privileges enjoyed by us formerly. We are glad in our hearts that we have been permitted to proclaim deliverance to the captive Union families of this valley and vicinity...For two months past I have been perfectly indignant, and ready to adopt the most severe and strenuous measure to crush the Rebellion and restore peace; and while I have watched earnestly the policy of some of our officials I have become so angry that I have been compelled to doubt the possibility of the existence of Religion in such a heart. Nevertheless, I have tried to pray that the chastisement which the Almighty sees proper to bring upon us might cease. Oh, that I could by one strong effort exterminate the Rebellion with oppression of every form. But what can the influence of a few avail when those to whom we look for guidance seem to have become estranged to the desires, the wants and necessities of the country..."[56]

Coalsmouth resident and Southern supporter Victoria Teays Hansford was once more unhappy to see the Confederates retreat from the Kanawha Valley. She observed on October 31, "After the Rebels had gone into the vastness of the mountains; the blue coats (Union soldiers) soon returned and took possession of the valley again. They came back with scowls on their faces. They were incensed at the good treatment we had given our dear Confederate boys. Those who had been kind to them were now called to account for it. At least they were made to feel so by bad treatment and harassment. The Union officers were a great deal more strict and, of course, we were all under martial law. The Union soldiers encroached on us in many ways. If it was known that any Rebel had more than he needed to keep body and soul together they came boldly and took it with guns in hand. They took our corn, the best of our meal, 18 large hams, middling's, all our coal, chickens, turkeys, pigs and everything else they could get hold of. We dared not open our mouths to the commanding officers or our men could be arrested and sent off to prison and the ladies would be insulted... Now of course, there were exceptions as once in a while we could find a gentleman among them."[57]

Sarah Young reflected on November 3, "How like the declining years of mortals is Fall. The leaves are falling fast, and sound on the roof like rain. The trees are beginning to look bare, and the flowers have faded like the cheeks of young maidens when old age comes. The grass has withered, and snow-flakes turn it like the advance of age turns the lovely locks of Youth. Ah, soon will stern winter come, and snow and ice will cover the ground. When it is like the weary Pilgrim, when beauty and strength are gone – will close with the lovely things of summer; will be gone forever. Heard from Pa today, Pa's men were all paid yesterday." Initially, there was a great deal of ambiguity as to who was responsible for paying the West Virginia troops (i.e. the War Department or the fledgling state government). The issue was unresolved for several months, because at that time the volunteers were viewed as "state troops" although West Virginia was not yet admitted into the union. However once mustered into Federal service, it became the War Department's responsibility. Regardless of who paid them, Captain Young and his enlisted men were overjoyed to receive monetary reimbursement for their service.[58]

Union patrols once again continuously operated throughout the Kanawha Valley, as rumors circulated that the government would soon begin conscription (i.e. a military draft). Private David Burrows, Company F, 13th West Virginia, was stationed at Point Pleasant on November 9; he wrote to his wife at home in Gallia County, after his company returned from a scouting mission to Hurricane Bridge, a distance of more than forty miles, "We was out to Hurricane and it was a hard trip. There is a very hard talk down here of conscription, and I would like to know what people think about it here." Sarah Young and her sister Emily, and a friend were present at Coalsmouth on a visit when "to our great joy the 8th Regiment Vols. came in" on November 9. Ecstatic, she wrote "I love all the Federal soldiers, especially the Virginia boys, but I have a particular feeling for the 8th. I have one dear friend in that regiment. Edgar has been down several times since his Regiment returned. Our friendship has grown to devoted love. Is there one in the world half so noble? I have promised to become his wife soon. Now, our Father, I ask Thee to make me in every way worthy of him. May no act of mine cause him to regret his choice." Sarah's sister Emily Ann was born February 14, 1844, in Kanawha County, Virginia. She was then aged eighteen years, and she was often mentioned in Sarah's, her father's, and Edgar Blundon's writings. She apparently bore the same devout faith as they and also had a similarly dry and sarcastic wit that her sister possessed and was capable of comprehension beyond her age as well. Emily also regularly discussed complex military and political matters disclosed by her father in his letters to her.[59]

## Horse Thieves and Soldier Shenanigans

On November 10, General Cox ordered Companies A, B, D and G of the 13th West Virginia to establish camp at Winfield along the southern bank of the Kanawha River, under command of Lieutenant Colonel J. R. Hall. Companies C, E and F were then located at Point Pleasant. The regiment would remain so disposed as such until January 28, 1863. However, there were numerous Southern sympathizers who were most displeased to learn that some three hundred Union soldiers were now encamped in their midst. As Cox busily contemplated solutions for protecting the Union citizens in the Kanawha Valley, he also needed to keep crucial supply lines open from Charleston into Putnam and Cabell Counties, but was frequently distracted by irate civilians. Angry Southern residents rendered near daily accusations against his troops alleging they stole horses and other farm animals or were harassing their families. In most instances, it was proven false, but several also turned out to be true.[60]

One soldier in the 13th West Virginia was a young boy known as an excellent hunter but was also said to be quite lazy. He was popular for his tendency to sneak away from camp into the woods, returning with wild game to supplement his comrade's meager diet. One day he trekked some eleven miles into the woods and bagged several birds for dinner. Unwilling to walk back, and knowing he had to be present for evening parade or face harsh consequences, the industrious lad devised a ruse hoping to scare civilians into giving him a ride back to the army camp at Winfield. He went to a farm house and told the family he was a Confederate, and that a large rebel force was nearby, thinking they would take him prisoner and return him to camp. Instead, the family quietly eloped, and took their neighbors along too. As his scheme failed, the youth had to walk back to camp anyway. He made it just in time to participate in evening drill. However, the group of terrified citizens arrived, and informed Lieutenant Colonel James Hall of what had transpired. In the process, they identified the perpetrator, who was mortified when they recognized him. After a rather unpleasant interview with Lieutenant Colonel Hall, the guilty soldier confessed and was punished by being forced to carry a large load of bricks on his back during dress parade for the next ten days. As these often lasted two to three hours, he wasn't long showing remorse. According to soldiers who witnessed the affair, his comrades made no effort to restrain their laughter and insults as he loped along with his burden every evening at parade time.[61]

General Jacob D. Cox was not as amused with the soldier's antics when he learned of it, particularly when he received a letter from one of his subordinate officers stating that another irate citizen, who was also the local tax collector, complained that one of the locals requested he waive their taxes on a horse stolen by Captain John Young. The citizen griped that Young had "pressed the animal" into Federal service without paying for it. Cox ordered Young to return the horse, but refused to press any charges when it was determined "this pony was taken previous to his connection with the 13th Regt..." Young defended himself by showing how he had no less than two horses stolen from his own farm by local Confederate guerillas, and that the government failed to provide him with a replacement mount, to which he was entitled as a captain. General Crook thought formal charges ought to have been brought against Captain Young when he learned of the issue, but the matter was eventually dropped. Young developed a strong resentment toward Crook during the process.[62]

Dudley Montague was the Revenue Collector in Putnam County frequently complained to General Cox accusing Union troops of stealing horses and abusing loyal citizens. Cox was annoyed and did not believe the accusations. He responded: "Mr. Montague's wholesale assertion that Union men in the valley have 'no more favors shown them than the meanest dogs' deprives the rest of his communication of reliability, as, if he knows anything of the matter, he knows he is making a misstatement, and it is quite probable that he is trying to cover up his neglect of duty in his department by such abuse of military officers. Any specific complaints will meet with prompt investigation. The troops stationed at Winfield are part of the 13th Virginia Volunteers, and I desire that you will require Mr. Montague to report at once whether he complains of them or of the general officers in command in the valley, giving full and specific details of the ground of his complaint, informing him that he will be expected to make good the charges, or be held responsible for a malicious effort to make trouble between civil and military authorities in West Virginia."[63]

## Edgar Blundon's Proposal to Sarah Young

On November 27, the 13th West Virginia Regiment was given a day of Thanksgiving, for prayer and fasting. John Young and Company G was still at Point Pleasant, and remained there until later in December, when they were ordered to Winfield. Company G then had eighty-four men and received a few new recruits while at Winfield. Sarah Young's intuition about her relationship with Edgar Blundon proved correct; their affection had grown into love, and he soon proposed marriage. Sarah agreed, yet he still felt the need to clarify some things between them, "Will you waive formalities and give the following your consideration? I do not introduce my thoughts with any foreboding so far as committing a wrong is concerned, although providence might dictate otherwise. If in this I do err, I do it with sincere assurance that I have carefully weighed the subject and cannot see that anyone will be injured should I fail to accomplish that which I so much desire."[64]

Blundon further inquired, "Our acquaintance and correspondence has to me been very pleasant, although circumstances have been unfavorable. I hope it may have been to you. I now very earnestly desire, if consistent with your wishes, or can be made so, to sustain a nearer and much dearer relation to you than has heretofore existed between us. Will you permit the change? It is not necessary for me now to recapitulate the circumstances which have compelled me to make the important request. I hope I may have an opportunity to do it at the proper time. Neither will I try to adduce arguments, make solemn affirmations, write pretty or affectionate sentences to convince you of my sincerity, because I deem the importance of inquiry sufficient. Hoping to receive a favorable reply." Sarah again agreed to his request for increased intimacy, and he went to see her on the evening of December 10. Edgar noted that now having received her affirmation, "I can better explain my satisfaction verbally than write it."[65]

Neither Sarah nor Edgar had yet mentioned this new development to her father, however. Blundon wrote to him on December 16, requesting his consent to marry her: "Captain, I have the honor to submit the following for your consideration. About one year since, as you know, I formed the acquaintance of your daughter Sarah. You are also informed thoroughly of the manner in which it has been continued, which of course, renders an explanation unnecessary. I now very respectfully request your consent that I may, at a period not far distant, make her my wife. Do not think that I have an incorrect appreciation of the responsibility I assume by taking this favor, because I Thus boldly request it; on the contrary let me assure you that I have deeply and carefully reflected upon the subject and cannot see that it is improper or wrong. You are doubtless very anxious for her future prosperity and happiness, and doubts may arise in your mind as the propriety of consenting to blend her destiny with those of a soldier in the field, but let me again assure you, which is all I can do now, that no act of mine, as a soldier or citizen, shall reflect discredit upon her or cause you to regret that you gave her interests into my hands." Young gave his consent, and Edgar and Sarah were elated. They began discussing wedding dates, which unfortunately could not occur until long after the New Year.[66]

As 1826 drew to a close, President Abraham Lincoln was preparing to release the Emancipation Proclamation. He was also struggling with complex legal issues related to admitting West Virginia into the Union as a new state. Fully aware that consent from the Virginia legislature would normally be a constitutional necessity, Lincoln decided that since those serving in the Virginia assembly under the Confederacy were "engaged in open rebellion" against the government, that the Restored Government of Virginia was not required to concern itself with consent of the mother state under such circumstances. Lincoln was working in his office late on the evening of December 31, deeply reflecting on the matter. He wrote, "We can scarcely dispense with the aid of West Virginia in this struggle; much less can we afford to have her against us, in Congress and in the field. Her brave and good men regard her admission into the Union as a matter of life and death. They have been true to the Union under very severe trials."

Lincoln continued, "We have so acted as to justify their hopes; and we cannot fully retain their confidence, and co-operation, if we seem to break faith with them. In fact, they could not do so much for us, if they would. Again, the admission of the new State turns that much slave soil to free; and thus, is a certain, and irrevocable encroachment upon the cause of the rebellion, the division of a State is dreaded as a precedent. But a measure made expedient by a war, is no precedent for times of peace. It is said the admission of West Virginia is secession and tolerated only because it is our secession. Well, if we can call it by that name, there is still difference enough between secession against the Constitution, and secession in favor of the Constitution. I believe the admission of West Virginia into the Union is expedient."[67]

Chapter Two References

1. Minsker Letters, December 1, 1861 and March 12, 1862; OR, Series 3, Vol. 1, 788-789.

2. Blundon & Matthews Family Papers, Edgar Blundon Civil War Diary and letters, typescript, 1861-1920, West Virginia Civil War Manuscripts Collection, Ms 89-94, Folders 1 & 2, WV Archives David H. Donald. *Lincoln.* ( New York: Simon & Schuster Publishers, 1996), 266-267; Noah Brooks. *The Nation's Leader.* ( New York: Putnam & Sons, 1888), 425-429.

3. J.V. Young Letters, February 3, 1862.

4. Sarah Young Diary, February 4, 1862; WV AG Papers, 11th West Virginia Volunteer Infantry Muster Rolls, Company G, October 1862. WV Archives.

5. Sarah Young Diary, February 11, 1862; March 9, 11, & 28, 1862; Griffith, 44-45; OR Series 1, Vol. 12, Part 3, 8-12.

6. WV AG Papers, Union Militia, 80th Regiment Virginia Militia; AR 373, Misc. File, Letter from A.I. Waterson, May 2, 1862; *Gallipolis Journal,* April 3, 1862, Vol. 37(21), Chronicling America Series, Library of Congress: https://chroniclingamerica.loc.gov/lccn/sn85038121/1862-06-26/ed-1/seq-3/. *Weekly Register* March 27, 1862, Vol. 1(4), Chronicling America Series. Library of Congress: https://chroniclingamerica.loc.gov/lccn/sn84026817/1862-03-27/ed-1.

7. Sarah Young Diary, April 15, 1862; Cunningham, Steve. Major Edgar B. Blundon, 7th West Virginia Cavalry, Civil War Service. Unpublished Manuscript. (1992). Author's collection.

8. WV AG Papers, 11th West Virginia Infantry, AR 382, Box 7, Letter by J.V. Young, April 18, 1962, WV Archives; OR, Series 1, Vol. 12, Part 3, 120; 164; Roy Bird Cook Collection, Box 1, Folder 2, Call No. A&M 0895, Series 1, Correspondence. Letter to J.V. Young from John Bowyers, April 1862, WV Archives; CSR, 11th West Virginia Infantry, RG 94, M508, Roll 188, National Archives; OR, Series 1, Vol. 12, Part 3,165; 308-309; Pierpont Telegraphs, May 11, 1862.

9. OR Series 1, Vol. 12, Part 3, 308-309. Pierpont Telegraphs, May 11 & 20, 1862; Pierpont-Samuels, Nos. 153 & 515, Box 1 & 7; Letters by Robert Brooks, May 15 and 20 & 24, 1862.

10. Ibid.; Letter by George Bowyer, May 24, 1862. Roy Bird Cook Collection, Box 1, Folder 2, Call No. A&M 0895, Series 1, Correspondence; Letter from Non-Commissioned officers to Governor Francis Pierpont, May 24, 1862; Letter from J.V. Young to Pierpont May 20, 1862. WV Archives.

11. J.V. Young Letter to U.S. War Department May 24, 1862; William D. Wintz. *History of Putnam County*, Vol. 1. (Charleston, WV: Pictorial Histories Publishing, 1988), 54-59; "House of Delegates: Sketches Personal, Political and Biographical. George C. Bowyer, of Putnam." *Wheeling Intelligencer* newspaper, July 21, 1863; WV AG Papers, WV Adjutant General Order Book No. 1, Commissions. WV State Archives; Sarah Young Diary, June 5, 1862. John Bowyer of Winfield was often referred to as Captain Bowyer from his service in the War of 1812. His son George C. Bowyer received a commission in 1861 as Colonel in the 181st Regiment Virginia Militia, replacing Colonel James Hoge of Winfield. He was often taunted by Confederate guerillas to call up his regiment and fight, but he is said to have "put them off by one device or another" and never commanded the regiment in actual field service. He served in the Virginia Assembly in May 1861 as a pro-slavery Union candidate, and later as Assistant Adjutant General. His political connections eventually led to an appointment as a Brigadier General of Militia in his district in 1863 and is often remembered as "General Bowyer" although he had no combat experience.

12. Blundon letters, August 5, 1862.

13. Hansford Diary, 3-4. CSR, Documents Relating to Civilians who came into contact with the Army during the Civil War, including deserters, thieves, and spies. RG 109, M345, Roll 76, National Archives. Jacob Douglas' brother, John Douglas, served in the 4th West Virginia Infantry. Although Douglas obviously had convincing testimony against him when charged with taking up arms against the government at the July 1861 battle of Scary Creek, service records from the Confederate units engaged there do not contain his name, including the 22nd Virginia Infantry, 36th Virginia Infantry and Kanawha Artillery. Note also that many of the cavalry units present were originally organized as companies which later became part of the 8th and 16th Virginia Cavalry; those company records similarly failed to show Douglas as a member in July 1861.

14. Ibid.; 1860 US Census, Coalsmouth, Virginia; Hansford Diary, May 1862; Griffith, 47-48.

15. WV AG Papers, AR 654, Folder 10-11, Part 1, Field History of the 13th West Virginia Volunteer Infantry. WV Archives; J.V. Young Letters, Undated, early August 1862 from Mud Bridge. WVU Library.

16. Ibid.; CSR, RG 94, M508, Roll 114, National Archives; WV AG Papers, AR 382 Box 18, 11th West Virginia Infantry, Company G Muster Roll, April 30 to

December 31, 1862, WV Archives; J.V. Young to Brigadier General Jacob D. Cox, June 17, 1862.

17. Ibid.; WV AG Papers, AR 382, Boxes 7, 12, & 23, Samuel Benedict, August 28, 1862; P. Ellis to H.J. Samuels August 5, 1862; J.S. Cunningham to H.J. Samuels, August 16 & 28, 1862; Letter by H.J. Samuels, August 28, 1862; Pierpont-Samuels, Box 6, Letter by W. H. Tomlinson September 1, 1862; Company G Non-Commissioned Officers and other enlisted men to H.J. Samuels, September 1, 1862; Civil War Recollections of George Rucker, Co. E, 13th West Virginia Infantry, Letter of September 19, 1862, Rucker Family Papers, MS-94.45, WV Archives; CSR, RG 94, M580, Roll 117, National Archives; *South Kansas Tribune* newspaper, Friday March 27, 1891; *The Star and Kansan*, March 25 1891. William R. Brown was later brevetted as a Brigadier General on March 15, 1865. After the war he relocated to Kansas City, Missouri, where he later served as a county commissioner and probate judge, and a member of his county board of education. At age sixty-five years, he died at home of pneumonia on March 24, 1891.

18. WVAG Papers, AR 382, Boxes No. 7 & 12, J.A.J. Lightburn to F. Pierpont, August 10, 1862; J.V. Young to F. Pierpont, August 27, 1862, WV Archives.

19. WV AG Papers, Union Regiments 11th West Virginia Infantry, AR 383, Box 18, WV Archives; WV AG Papers, Union Militia, AR 373, Putnam County, Box 2, G. Bowyer to F. Pierpont, August 11 & 15, 1862; WV Archives; J.V. Young Letters, August 12, 1862, WVU Library.

20. WV AG Papers, AR 383, 11th West Virginia Infantry, Boxes 1 & 2, Co. G Muster-In Roll, WV Archives; CSR, RG 94, M594, Roll 196, Letter by R. P. Kennedy to J.R. Hall, December 22, 1862, National Archives; 13th West Virginia Field History, Part 1.

21. OR, Series 1, Vol. 12, Part 3, 551; 582; 619; WV AG Papers, Union Regiments, 4th West Virginia Infantry, AR 382, Box 12, J.A.J. Lightburn letters September 1862 (Hereafter Lightburn Letters); Blundon Letters, September 5, 1862.

22. OR, Series 1, Vol. 12, Part 3, 407; 534; 540; 543; 567; 570; 577; 619; 629; 698-699; 712; 722; 726; also Part 1, 738; 742; 754; Part 2, 405-411; OR, Series 1, Vol. 19, Part 1, 419; 424-426; 427-431; 458-474; Cox, *Military Reminisces of the Civil War.* Vol. 1, 77-79; 80-81; 96-98; 114-115; 118-122. General Jacob Cox's promotion to Major General expired in March 1863 due to Congressional reports indicating there were too many general officers of that rank. Cox was later re-commissioned as Major General in 1864.

23. James I. Robertson, Jr. (Ed.). *Soldier of Southwestern Virginia: The Civil War Letters of Captain John Preston Sheffy.* (Baton Rouge, LA: Louisiana State Press, 2004), 77-84; Journal of the Congress of the Confederate States of America, 1861-1865, Vol. 5. 1905. Washington DC: Government Printing Office, 340-341. Library of Congress, Washington DC; Terry Lowry. *The Battle of Charleston and the 1862 Kanawha Valley Campaign.* (Charleston WV: 35th Star Publishing, 2016), 77-78.

24. Lightburn Letters, September 1862; Lowry, Battle of Charleston, 84-86; Sarah Young Diary, September 7, 1862; OR, Series 1, Vol. 12, Part 2, 756-764; *Weekly Register,* September 18, 1862, & January 22, 1863; Jack L Dickinson. *16th Virginia Cavalry.* (Lynchburg, Virginia: H.E. Howard, 1989), 9-10; 109; OR, Series 1, Vol. 19, Part 1, 1058-1060; Griffith, 49-52; Joseph J. Sutton. *History of the 2nd Regiment, West Virginia Cavalry Volunteers.* (Huntington, West Virginia: Blue Acorn Press, Reprinted 1992; Original publication 1892), 59-61.

25. Ibid.; 13; OR, Series 1, Vol. 12, Part 1, 759-764; 13th West Virginia Field History, Part 1.

26. Sarah Young Diary, September 7& 8 , 1862.

27. Ibid., September 9 & 10, 1862; WV AG Papers, Union Regiments 1861-1865, AR 383, Box 18, 11th West Virginia Infantry, Co. G Muster-In Roll, October 1, 1862. WV Archives. Privates James Davis and James Paul enlisted in Company G May 23, 1862 at Coalsmouth. Davis was wounded at the battle of Winchester in 1864; OR Series 1, Vol. 19, Part 1, 1058-1060; Dickinson, 9-10; 109; Griffith, 49-53.

28. Sarah Young Diary, September 12 & 13, 1862.

29. Roy Bird Cook. "The Civil War Comes to Charleston." *West Virginia History,* Vol. 23(2), (January 1962), 153-167; Letter from unidentified Union soldier from Ohio written on September 18, 1862 from Gallipolis, Ohio. *Cincinnati Daily Commercial,* Vol. 46(244) October 5, 1862; OR, Series 1, Vol. 19, Part I, 1057-1090; Cook, 153-167.

30. Hansford Diary, 6-7.

31. Sarah Young Diary, September 14 & 15, 1862, 15; Cook, 153-167.

32. J.V. Young Letters, October 6 & 29, 1862.

33. *The Guerilla, Vol. 1(2), September 28, 1862, Charleston WV, SN: 85059834. Newspaper reading room, Library of Congress.*

34. Sarah Young Diary, September 22 & 25, 1862, 16.

35. J.V. Young Letters, October 29, 1862, WVU Library; Pierpont Telegraphs,

J.A.J. Lightburn to F. Pierpont, September 19, 1862, WVU Library; OR, Series 1, Vol. 19, Part 1, 1057-1090; 13th West Virginia Field History, Part 1.

36. Sarah Young Diary, September 22, 1862, 16.

37. Ibid., September 22, 1862.

38. Ibid.

39. Lowry, Battle of Charleston, 292-293; *The Guerilla*, October 3, 1862; OR, Series 1, Vol. 19, Part 1, 1057-1090; Sarah Young Diary, September 29, 1862.

40. Ibid., October 4 & 6, 1862; Lowry, Battle of Charleston, 292-293; Telegraphic Dispatches to the Governor of Ohio, Series 145, Ohio Historical Society, Columbus, Ohio.

41. J.V. Young Letters, October 6, 1862; Lowry, Battle of Charleston, 301-302.

42. Ibid., October 9, 1862.

43. Sarah Young Diary, October 10, 1862; Atkinson & Gibbens, 419-421.

44. Pierpont Telegraphs, October 11 & 13, 1862; OR, Series 1, Vol. 19, 857; OR, Series 1 Vol. 12, Part 3, 308-309; Cox, Vol. 5, 26; 34; 58; Pierpont Executive Papers, Box 9, Folder 1, October 11 & 14, 1862.

45. Ibid.

46. Ibid.

47. Young Diary, October 14 & 21, 1862.

48. Ibid., October 25, 1862.

49. Lowry, Battle of Charleston, 315-329; 335-355.

50. Ibid.; J.V. Young Letters, October 28, 1862; 13th West Virginia Field History, Part 1.

51. Ibid., October 28, 1862.

52. Ibid., October 29, 1862.

53. Lowry, Battle of Charleston, 315-329, 335-355; *Pomeroy Weekly Telegraph* newspaper, November 21, 1862, Library of Congress.

54. Jacob T. Foster Papers, ca. 1847-1929. [1st Wisconsin Light Artillery] October 29, 1862, Wisconsin State Historical Society; Lowry, 303-315; Huddleston, Samuel B. Papers 1843-1917. Rare Books and Manuscripts Collection, Folder S694. "A Civil War History of the 84th Indiana Regiment as Recorded by Samuel Huddleston." Transcribed by Sharon Ogzewalla, 2007. Indiana State Library, Indianapolis, IN; Sarah Young Diary, October 31, 1862.

55. Letters of Corporal Fretwell Hensley, Company G, 13th West Virginia Infantry, October 21 & 31, 1862, cited in Griffith, 62-63; 64, originals in private

collection.

56. OR, Series 1, Vol. 19, Part 2, 522-523; Blundon Letters, November 2, 1862.

57. Hansford Diary, 10-11; Sarah Young Diary, November 3, 1862.

58. Sarah Young Diary, November 9, 1862.

59. Herbert L. Roush, Sr. *If Thou Wilt Remember: A Historical Narrative.* The story of David M. Burrows, Company F, 13th West Virginia Volunteer Infantry. Call No. 973.781 R863, WV Archives. (Lowell, Michigan: Modern Printing, 1995), 26. David Burrows lived in Meigs County, Ohio. He enlisted in Co. F, 13th West Virginia on September 9, 1862 at Point Pleasant in Mason County, Virginia.

60. 13th West Virginia Field History, Part 1; OR, Series 1, Vol. 19, 857; 1905.

61. Davis Washington. *Camp-fire Chats of the Civil War: Being the incidents, adventure and way-side exploit of the bivouac and battle-field, as related by the Veteran soldiers themselves.* (Detroit, MI: W.H. Boothroyd and Co.,1887), 204-209.

62. CSR, RG 94, M594, Roll 196, Letter from Captain R.P. Kennedy, December 22, 1862, National Archives; WV AG Files, AR 383, 11th West Virginia Infantry, Boxes 1 & 2, Folder 42, Co. G Muster In Rolls, WV Archives.

63. Ibid.; OR, Series 1, Vol. 19, 857; 1905; OR Series 1, Vol. 21, Part 1, 880-881; 997.

64. 13th West Virginia Field History, Part 1; WV AG, AR 383, 11thWest Virginia Infantry, Boxes 1&2, Folders 7 Morning Reports, Folder 42, Muster-In Rolls, Folder 43, Muster-Out Rolls, Folder 44, Descriptive Rolls. WV Archives; Sarah Young Diary, November 12, 1862; Blundon Letters, December 6 & 10, 1862.

65. Ibid., December 6 & 10, 1862.

66. Ibid., December 16, 1862.

67. Abraham Lincoln Papers, MSS30189, General Correspondence, Reel 42: Lincoln, Abraham. Opinion on the Admission of West Virginia, December 31, 1862, Library of Congress.

# 3

# First Blood
# 1863

President Lincoln proceeded to issue the Emancipation Proclamation on January 1, declaring all persons held as slaves in the Southern states will be "thenceforward, and forever free." Following the Battle of Antietam in September 1862, President Lincoln published his first edition of the Emancipation Proclamation. He afterward revised the document, although it did not affect slavery in the Northern or border states and exempted those areas in the South already under Union control. Lincoln faced another problem however, when anti-slavery Congressmen were inflamed because he was planning to admit West Virginia into the Union as a slave state. They argued it was a *Pandora's Box* to divide Virginia into two slave states, and that it was inherently contradictory to the Emancipation Proclamation to do so. However, while Governor Francis Pierpont was opposed to slavery, he favored a gradual emancipation, arguing that sudden freedom would result in chaos for both the farmers and business owners as well as the former slaves. In the end, Lincoln ultimately soon also approved the statehood bill, therefore making the admission of West Virginia into the Union as a slave state inevitable despite the Emancipation Proclamation.[1]

Company G remained at Winfield until January 28 when ordered to Coalsmouth. John Young wrote to Paulina earlier on January 24, "I have just returned from Charleston and heard that you were sick, which gives me much uneasiness...I want to come home so bad that I am almost sick. I stayed at Uncle John [John D.] Young's and had quite a time with Harriet about her John. The postmaster has gone to Charleston and I think we will get our pay next week. I will come home in a day or two if I can. My

79

men are nearly all sick. Tell Emma the big Corporal sticks out bravely. While I was in Charleston five of my men deserted. Two Racers are gone." William, George and John S. Racer enlisted at Coalsmouth on May 31, 1862, and August 13 and 30, 1862, respectively. All three were "cut off" by Rebels (i.e. captured) and missing since early December 1862.[2]

Young again wrote to Paulina on January 25, "I am very sorry that you are no better. I sent the doctor out this morning but Ben says that he had not come when he left. The Colonel gave me leave to come tomorrow and I think I will be there very early. The 8th Regiment, Ohio, is here and we expect more Regiments in a few days. There is a great move among the troops in the valley but what is the cause I don't know. I fear that we will be ordered away. I would dislike to go very much but if the government needs me I am willing to go. God knows that I am willing to make any and every sacrifice for our country and our holy religion. And I hope that we will be amply paid for all our sacrifices that we have made for the sake of our country. The time is coming when we and our children will be applauded for our loyalty to the Union. In regard to General Crook's orders to me to return those horses, making me enemies, it has made me many friends. The loyal people of West Virginia are after him with a sharp stick. His order to me was sent to Washington and he is now ordered away from this Valley...My friends at the Point wrote to General Crook that Captain Young did right in taking those horses and if that was the course he allowed to pursue he had better leave the Valley and let someone else take the command that would not protect rebels. I tell you he is in a hot place and if he gets out he may be thankful. I will come tomorrow and tell you all about it."[3]

A day later, Young was back at Winfield and penned a note to Paulina, who was still sick, "The doctor will be out tonight to stay with you all night. I will send John out this morning and if you are worse will you write to me and I will come with the doctor. The paymaster has gone to Ceredo to pay the 5th Regiment, Va. Volunteers, and will return this week to pay us, and I think in all probability he will be here between now and Saturday. Nothing new here. The troops are all gone, General Crook's with them. Don't say anything about General Crook being ordered away to anybody, for they might court martial me for it. Sarah, write to me by John how your Ma is, and tell me what she wants...Lieut. Cunningham has not yet returned; I think he must have quite a time of it." 1st Lieutenant John S. Cunningham, the 13th West Virginia Adjutant, wrote to Governor Pierpont on January 25 on behalf of Lieutenant Robert Brooks, who had yet to be paid. Cunningham petitioned that Brooks had not been paid for his service since enlisting as a private in Captain John Young's Company in December 1861 due to "some informality in his muster" and contended that Brooks, despite his persistent and rather mutinous conduct attempting to take over Company G, was "a brave man and efficient officer, who has a general knowledge of West Virginia, particularly this part of the state, and has performed some difficult scouting whilst in service."[4]

Young was likely unaware of Cunningham's letter, as he did not mention it on January 29 writing again to his wife, "I hear by the doctor that you are much better; all but your mouth and he says that is not dangerous, but I will send some medicine for your mouth this morning. The Pay Master has not come yet, but as soon as he does come I will come out home. But if you get worse send one word and I will come. Charles A. Ellis died last night and Noah J. Hamrick is very low. I don't think he will live. I have quite a time here with my sick men; but if you were well I could stand it much better. I received a letter from Captain Blundon. They are at Clarksburg and expect to stay there until Spring. Poor fellow! He grumbles considerably, about being sent away. He thinks it would have done just as well to let the 8th stayed here and killed the Rebels in the Kanawha Valley. But he wants me to do it." Private Charles Ellis had only recently enlisted in Company G on November 29, 1862, at Winfield, but had been in the field hospital there since December. Upon his demise, Captain Young had his personal effects sent to his father. Private Noah Hamrick enlisted on July 26, 1862, at Coalsmouth. He survived until February 10, 1862, when he succumbed to Typhoid.[5]

## Murder of Calvary Gibson

Despite the harsh winter, Confederate guerrilla activities continued in the region; local newspapers reported many incidents of Union citizens encountering their antagonists, usually with violent results. Young was worried about his wife and family; he wrote on February 5, "I sent Sergent [Clark] Elkins out this morning to see how you are. I have been very uneasy about you through the night. I have dreamed many things about you. I was gratified to hear from Mr. Elkins you were better. Myself and company are improving in health. General Scammon sent me word yesterday that he would send a company of Cavalry here in a few days, therefore I don't think there will be any danger here. Write to me how you are getting along, and if you want anything. I can't come out until the Cavalry comes, then I think I can get leave to come home."

Young's fears were not ungrounded, as the *Gallipolis Journal* newspaper reported on February 26 a recent incident on Hurricane Creek in Putnam County involving the family of Calvary Gibson, a known Unionist. He was killed by a band of Confederate guerrillas in his home led by the notorious Lieutenant William Keaton late on Sunday night, February 8 when the guerrillas surrounded his home, fired into the house, then broke open a window, and swarmed into the house.

His wife, Lucretia Gibson, recognized several of the assailants as former neighbors, including one who she and her husband had helped raise. The newspaper reported that "Gibson cried out, 'for God's sake don't murder me,' but the man crushed his skull with the butt of a gun, and seven shots were fired into his body, blowing out every vestige of life, and mutilating the remains in a terrible and sickening manner. As Gibson's young daughter ran into the room screaming to her mother, 'they've killed Pa, they've shot Pa,' and got in the way of a large lieutenant, he threw the child into the fire. The wife and mother sprang to the child exclaiming, 'Don't burn up my child after killing my husband' and the officer responded, 'Shut up, you damned union bitch, or I'll kill you too.' They reportedly shot him seven times and bayoneted him several

*Lucretia Leadmon Gibson*
*Wife of Calvary Gibson*
*Courtesy of Bob Gibson*

times...to make the crime more hideous, they with the butts of their guns broke his skull in until the hammer of the lock was buried in his brains up to the barrel, all this was being done while he was begging for his life, and to make the crime of a deeper dye, caught the wife of the murdered man, and choked her until she was insensible..."[6]

Since Company G was "temporarily attached" to the 13th West Virginia Infantry in August 1862, 2nd Lieutenant Brooks found opportunity to renew his quest to remove Captain Young from command. His new argument was that since they were reassigned, there should have been a new election of officers, giving him a fair chance to become the captain. Although he again wrote to Governor Pierpont and the War Department, his sham thus far had no evidence of making negative impact with the officers in the 13th West Virginia.

*Elizabeth Gibson Billups*
*Daughter of Calvary Gibson*
*Courtesy of Bob Gibson*

To the contrary, they too discerned Brook's agenda and supported Young. As usual, Brooks failed to learn from experience, and continued to agitate discord within the regiment against Young. This time, however, it backfired on him. The officers went to Colonel Brown following his most recent tirade, and with his support, collectively petitioned West Virginia Adjutant General Henry J. Samuels on February 15. Their supplication states: "We the undersigned Commissioned Officers of the 13th Regiment V.V. [Virginia Volunteers] feeling a deep and intense interest in the cause of our country & the good of this Regiment and for other reasons herein after mentioned do earnestly and insist the Co. under command of Capt J.V. Young be permanently attached to this Regiment. First, Captain Young who alone raised the company and has commanded it since its organization is exceedingly anxious to be connected with said Regiment and further more aperts in most positive terms that if the company is taken away and attached to any other Regiment it will become completely demoralized."

The officers also noted, "They were enlisted in the first place for cavalry but were forced at the point of the bayonet and now that the Regiment will probably be mounted they claim, that it is but just and right that they be permitted to remain with the Regiment. This company was raised in this region of [the] country and know it thoroughly from the great Kanawha to the Kentucky line & from the Ohio to Tazewell County [Virginia] and would therefore be at invaluable service as scouts and spies. This company has been doing a great deal of hard service all through this country and are willing still to labor and toil on for the good of the country and if the Regiment is to remain in this region there is no one company here perhaps that would be so effective for the above and other considerations not named, we urge the necessity of complying with our requests..."

Unknown to Young at the time, the officers and non-commissioned officers of the 11th West Virginia had also written to Governor Francis Pierpont earlier on December 17, 1862, asking him to bring Young's Company G into their regiment because the commander, Colonel Daniel Frost, had threatened to resign unless Company G was permanently assigned to that regiment. The soldiers asserted how they had "become attached to him" during their time of service under him because of his "uniform kindness and constant energies for ours, and the Regiment's prosperity..." Soon afterward, (the exact date is unknown) Colonel William Brown was tired of Brook's persistent agitation against Captain Young and transferred him into Company K at Barboursville. It would not be the end of Brooks' campaign for power, however, as he began recruiting and immediately began efforts to have himself made captain.[7]

Edgar Blundon was promoted to captain of Company F, 8th West Virginia Infantry on February 15, 1862. He wrote to Sarah Young the next day indicating Robert

Brooks, aware of his potential influence in his case against John Young, attempted to manipulate him into supporting his cause, "I am sorry that Mr. Brooks should again become so mean, as to resort to his previous plan of gaining promotion. He reminds me of one of Aesop's Fables, where the man found the serpent in mid-winter. It was in a torpid state, and he thought, very cold. His kindness of heart induced him to take it in to his home where it shared with him the pleasant influences of a cheerful fire. The snake soon became warm, having been brought to life by the farmer's fire. As soon as it came to life, it bit its kind donor for his goodness to it. Brooks is most assuredly worse than the serpent. I received a letter from him last week containing a very kind and courteous request to give him all the facts connected with the capture of a horse which he says was taken by my order and given to your Ma. I have not answered, neither will I."

Blundon continued, "He knows very well that I never captured a dimes worth of property and made disposition of it in any other way than that prescribed by law. I regard him as a poor, aspiring villain, who would, for the purpose of obtaining information, sacrifice every sense of personal honor or respect. I regret that Pa had anything to do with him in the onset. The dunce ought to know that every effort he makes to oppose right he will betray himself. He cannot injure an honest man, who has been known in our locality as long as your Pa. I expect he will have me summoned, should he conclude to prosecute the case further. I wish he would. Perhaps I might get a wife through his efforts to do injustice to the best friend he ever had. Don't laugh at my folly. That would be the best motive, or rather principle one in my coming...Please tell the Captain that if he does not write soon, I will. I would like to plead his case before Brook's Court of Inquiry...I think it strange that I have not received a letter from your Pa...I hope he has not been superseded by the inimitable Brooks. I heard through one of my Lieutenants that your Pa was to be court martialed. He said he did not know what for. I do not know where he obtained the information. I have my conjectures..."

Military records do not show if John Young ever faced court martial. Blundon was likely correct in speculating that Lieutenant Brooks had initiated the rumor. Blundon and Sarah were to be married on February 18; however, he was unable to obtain leave from his regiment at Buckhannon. He wrote again on that date, "Today we were to have been married. I have used every means in my power to fulfill my engagement, and be there at the time, but could not get away honorably. I may come soon, if Providence will favor me." The couple agreed to delay their marriage until September 1863.[8]

On February 18, Company G received their first pay since entering service. Young wrote home to Paulina that day indicating he had only received part of it, however, "I have just returned from Point Pleasant and hear on my return that you are all on the mend, for which I am thankful to God for his great mercy. I will be at home as soon as possible. I have settled with the paymaster only from the 23rd of May, 1862, which amounted to $900.18; the balance I will get from the State...I have just returned from Point Pleasant and hear on my return that you are all on the mend, for which I am thankful to God for his great mercy." As Union citizens in the area continued to complain of harassment from Confederates, an unidentified member of the 13th West Virginia Infantry editorialized in the *Wheeling Intelligencer* newspaper on February 11 that the solution would be to create mounted infantry or cavalry regiments: "The rebels are still pursuing their old game of arresting and carrying off peaceful, unoffending Union citizens of West Virginia, and in the humble opinion of Union men in this part of the country it is high time that some protection was extended to them..."[9]

The unidentified soldier continued, using the case of Putnam County Sheriff Benjamin P. Morris, who was recently captured by guerillas, to bolster his case for having several infantry regiments transposed into cavalry outfits, noting that when Morris was captured, "The guerrillas could not be overtaken by infantry soldiers...The rebels have also captured and carried off, within a short time past, fourteen horses from the lower end of this county, and I am safe in asserting that they will continue to carry off men, horses, and whatever else suits their pleasure so long as we have nothing but infantry to meet them with. Perhaps the authorities at Wheeling are not aware that the success of the new State is seriously endangered by the very considerable force of rebels now ranging the country between the Kanawha and Sandy rivers. This force will undoubtedly, unless vigorous and effectual measures are taken to prevent it, play an important part in the general election soon to be held...What is likely to be the result? The prospect certainly is anything but cheering... Indeed those who have the best opportunities of knowing and judging, say it will defeat the new State altogether. All of these men have been raised in that portion of the new State referred to; they thoroughly know the people, and every road and by-path within the boundary...the defeat of the new State in the counties below the Little Kanawha is morally certain, unless the Government can be induced to mount and equip four or five of our Virginia regiments - say the 8th, 9th, 11th and 13th..."[10]

Young next wrote to his wife from Coalsmouth on February 21, after receiving a visit from one of his neighbors who assured him that Paulina and the children's health was improving, "You don't know how glad I am to hear that you and the children are getting well... I expected to come home yesterday but the excitement in the country prevented me from coming. [Brigadier General John] Floyd is bearing down on Guyan River with twelve hundred Cavalry and you see that it behooves us to be on the alert. [2nd Lieutenant Robert] Brooks has gone to Point Pleasant and Lieut. [John S.]

Cunningham is out with a Scout, therefore you see that I can't leave my post. But, dear Paulina, you can't tell how bad I want to come home and see you all...I have my money here and if you think you can keep it I will bring it home. I have paid out already $250 dollars, and owe more yet, but I think I can leave you four hundred for your own use. I can't get eggs or butter here without paying two prices. The soldiers buy all that comes in. I have no letters from the 8th Va. yet. If you want hay and corn you had better buy it down in the Valley..."[11]

Company G was ordered to the post at Barboursville in early March, where Young was temporarily placed in command until Colonel William Brown arrived. Young wrote to his daughter Emily on March 9, "I have written to your Ma but have no answer. I received a letter from Ben [Young] and said that you wrote that his Ma was sick. I am very uneasy about her. I can't hear from home at all. I do think that if your Ma was well she would write to me. Colonel [William] Brown has just arrived and I have turned over the command to him again, which relieves me very much. I wish you would hurry that old woman up and make her write. Tell her that I don't want her to let her business crowd out all affection for me. I know that she has much to do and to think about in her lonely condition, but she must remember I, too, have many troubles and perplexities that she is a stranger to, but yet I never forget home and you can tell her how anxious I am to hear from your Ma. For one whole week I have had many forebodings about your Ma, and why it is that I can't tell, but I suppose it is because Ben said she was sick. Ben says his school will be out in three weeks, and he is very anxious that his bills be paid when it is out, that he may come home at once. I think, if I don't see your Ma before that time, that she had better go up and pay all but his board...Ben says fifteen dollars will pay all but his board and have enough over to bring him home. I don't want him to stay a day over time. He is anxious to get home...You can't imagine how I love to hear from home. I want to see Sallie so much." It is unknown where Young's son Benjamin was attending boarding school, although it was unlikely at the Buffalo Academy in Putnam County, as it had ceased operating by this point in the war.[12]

As he continued the letter to Emily of March 9, Young was responding to an ongoing discussion with Emily regarding his own motivation for service, as well as mentioning the latest histrionics from 2nd Lieutenant Robert Brooks, recently transferred to Company K , as he wrote, "General [George Crook] Crooks has put [2nd Lieutenant Robert] Brooks and his company under command of Company K. Lieut. [1st Lieutenant Joseph E.] McCoy was here last night and says Brooks is very mad and says that he will report General Crooks to the Governor and if he don't do something for him he will disband his company. This is what he ought to do and do it quick, for he is a disgrace to any people and a perfect tyrant. I suppose he is done making raids on helpless women and children. I hate treason as much as Brooks but when Secessionists submit to the laws they should have protection and shall have as long as I have a sword or a gun. I want Virginia restored with the citizens in it, not a waste territory with people and property destroyed. No, Emma, I have not been fighting to destroy but to restore Virginia to her wanton greatness; and if tyrants are permitted to make raids on helpless families and destroy them and their property we have missed our aim. May the Lord restore Virginia and bring back her poor, deluded children."[13]

Captain Edgar Blundon poked fun at Emily Young in his letter to Sarah on March 10, teasing her that he knew she was corresponding with a certain overweight Corporal in his regiment. He advised: "Tell her I...hope she will succeed in catching that Corporal. He is large enough for a Major General. Tell her that I don't think he will do any good in the Cavalry service as there is nothing except an elephant that would be sufficiently large to transport him over the hills of the Mud River country; and such an animal would be too slow for active service. However, he might apply to Barnum and obtain old Hannibal, for instance, and at the conclusion of the war he could make an independent fortune exhibiting his War Horse."

Due to the frequent attacks on Union citizens, John Young was contemplating relocating his family from their home near Coal Mountain to Winfield, where there was a Union army post and a strong Unionist population. Blundon also confided his anxiety to Sarah because he heard rumors from other soldiers that she and her mother had been seriously ill, with her father camped nearby but unable to come to their respite.[14]

Edgar encouraged Sarah to accept relocating to Winfield in his next letter of March 18, "...that you might enjoy the society so necessary for comfort. I often fear that the sudden appearance of some of those vile characters who have so long threatened the life and property of Union families in Putnam. I heard of the murder of some of the citizens near you a few days since and have been very much alarmed for your safety. Persons who would be guilty of such a diabolical outrage would resort to any act, no matter how vile, could they but get what they term revenge, but which is simply violence and plunder. I am heartily glad you are protected but military movements are so uncertain that we cannot rely upon any disposition of troops, and especially when they are liable to be moved at every demonstration of the enemy...It does seem that you have suffered sufficiently to atone for the patriotic efforts made for the Country's honor and cause...The result is anticipated and will soon prove a reality...Heretofore, Virginia has been cursed with a few monied aristocrats who have sought with all ardor of their hearts the oppression of the humble and poorer class. They saw the madness of their efforts to crush the remaining elements of manhood which had been so long struggling with the great enemy of the free institutions of the country; and while they saw the gradual progress of the principles inculcated in our declaration of rights as a nation, they resort to the last remedy, viz: Secession, and have so far succeeded in carrying the popular sentiment of the country that anarchy and despotism may at once be established by one vast united effort."[15]

## Murder of Calvary Gibson Avenged

While at Barboursville, Company G had a small skirmish with some guerillas in the area where the Guyandotte and Mud Rivers meet. In response, Captain Young ordered two of the guerillas' homes burnt to the ground, one belonging to Lieutenant William Keaton who murdered Unionist Cavalry Gibson on Hurricane Creek on February 5. On March 18, Captain John C. Witcher of the 3rd West Virginia Cavalry took six troopers and rode through "drenching rain"to Poore's Hill in Cabell County, searching for Keaton. The affair was reported in the *Ironton Register* newspaper by an unidentified soldier of the 5th West Virginia Infantry on March 26, whose company had been on a two-day scouting mission along the Guyandotte River, "We encamped that night without supper in a barn and in our wet clothes. Next morning we resumed our march and brought up in the Keaton settlement, a distance of 40 miles from camp. Here is the place that a few days ago a company of the 13th Virginia was fired upon from the bushes in retaliation for which a house or two soon disappeared. Here we found that a horseman had lately passed; we followed the trail up a by-path and a short turn in the way...upon a log house, at which were hitched four cavalry horses."

The writer further described the incident, "A charge was ordered, four men came hastily out, armed and equipped; after a slight resistance and the exchange of a half a dozen shots, they were captured. They seemed well rationed as among the haversacks were found two cooked chickens, two or three suspicious looking black bottles, &c., &c., all of which were duly confiscated...This proved to be a very important capture, as among the squad was the leader of the gang, a Lieutenant [William] Keaton, a desperado, that has been annoying the citizens of this part of Virginia for twelve months past, and has eluded vigilance, heretofore of the military authorities. This same Keaton was engaged in the murder of Mr. Gibson, a citizen of Virginia, who lived on the waters [Hurricane Creek] of Hurricane..." Keaton and the other prisoners were sent Atheneum Prison in Wheeling the next morning.[16]

## The Battle at Hurricane Bridge

On March 28, 1863, the small, quiet village of Hurricane Bridge was host to a small battle when Confederate cavalry under Brigadier General Albert G. Jenkins attacked a Union garrison there. Jenkins' command was part of a series of raids planned throughout western Virginia that spring and intended to capture the Union supply depot at Point Pleasant. General Jacob D. Cox, who commanded Union forces in the Kanawha Valley, had for months debated placing a Union outpost at Hurricane Bridge to protect loyal citizens in the area, as well as to maintain critical supply lines traversing the Kanawha Valley from Gauley Bridge to the Ohio River. On February 28, 1863, Cox ordered a detachment of four companies from the 13th West Virginia to establish an outpost at Hurricane Bridge, comprised of Companies A, B, D and H, under command of Captain James W. Johnson. Companies C, E and F remained at Point Pleasant and Company G remained at Coalsmouth. Captain Young and Company G was not

*Captain James W. Johnson*
*13th West Virginia Infantry*
*Battle of Hurricane Bridge*
*West Virginia State Archives*

present during the battle on March 28, as several researchers have suggested. Rather, they were at Coalsmouth, roughly ten miles away. Once they arrived at Hurricane Bridge, Companies A, B, D and H busied themselves establishing a large earthen fort on the western heights near where the James River Turnpike and Midland Trail intersected, but it was unfinished on the day Jenkins attacked.[17]

Jenkins was conducting a series of raids through the Kanawha Valley for supplies and horses and was also supposed to obtain a herd of beef-cattle from Confederate sympathizers in Ohio. His troopers were dismounted and had marched more than two hundred miles across the rough, snow covered mountains, with most of the men barefoot prior to arriving at Hamlin (modern Lincoln County) late on the evening of March 27. They arrived near Hurricane Bridge early the next

*General Albert Gallatin Jenkins*
*Confederate commander at the*
*Battle of Hurricane Bridge*
*Library of Congress*

morning, March 28, and attacked the Union garrison, who were entrenched behind the unfinished earthen fort. Jenkins' troopers had trained as infantry during the winter. With sharpshooters posted on the eastern and southern heights, they fought for five hours, before the Confederates withdrew. Federal casualties were four killed, six wounded, and the Confederates lost at least two men killed, and as many as thirteen wounded, although sources conflict on the actual number of casualties.[18]

Prior to leaving, some of the Confederates familiar with Union residents of Hurricane Bridge burned several houses and the log building used by the Baptist and Methodist churches. Jenkins then headed for Point Pleasant, where he attacked the remaining Union garrison (Company E, 13th West Virginia) and some home guards on March 30, sustaining more than seventy casualties. Following the battles at Hurricane Bridge and Point Pleasant, Companies E and F were sent to Mud Bridge in Cabell County, where they quickly dug earthworks around the Union Baptist Church. The remaining companies A, B, D, and H spent the next month at Hurricane Bridge improving and strengthening their earthen fort, and Company G remained at Coalsmouth.[19]

Young wrote to Edgar Blundon on April 5, "I will try and give you some of the news of the valley. Well, first of all, my family is well, except Emma, who is not much better. Old Jenkins has made his raid in the valley and has gotten out again, but he never called on me. But went around me and attacked the Hurricane Bridge, got whipped there, then marched to the Point, where Captain [John] Carter and his brave lads flogged him again. Then, he turned his course up the river, crossed at Ten mile, and struck a bee line for Mud, but Captain Rucker, with his Home Guards, pitched into him and bushwhacked him to Mud River. The thief came in with eight hundred but I don't think he got out with three hundred. He stole about one hundred head of horses and a great deal of other property and it all might have been saved. Jenkins might have been caught, but escaped. Colonel Brown wanted to go but was unable. So, as it is, he is out and gone. The whole country full of squads of robbers. Three companies maintained their ground against six hundred."

Young further reported, "The firing commenced at 6 a.m. and lasted until half past eleven. (I mean at the Hurricane Bridge). The whole country is in a state of excitement. Lieutenant [Robert] Brooks has just returned from a two days scout in the Mud country, and says Jenkins is camped two miles above Barboursville on Guyan river, and is reinforced by Clarkson. They say that he has about eight hundred men, and when they rest he intends another attack on the 13th at this place and the Hurricane Bridge. I wish we were mounted and had a commander who cared for Virginia, or would let us go after them. But while we have commanders who won't let us drive the Rebels out of our country we might just as well quit, throw down our arms and make friends with the South. I have my company and Company I here, in all about one hundred men, but if old Jenk does come I think he will have a good time of it. I have written three letters to you but have no answer yet. Write soon. Give my respects to Col. [John] Oley and tell him I want him in the valley, mounted. We want the 8th Va. here. Must have it. Captain, I am almost disheartened. But I know we are in a good cause. Your friend, J.V. Young"[20]

Edgar Blundon also wrote to Sarah on April 5: "I am really glad that in the Providence of our Heavenly Father no fatal results have attended the sickness of your family, and deeply regret that Emily's illness is so intensely severe. It seems hard that one possessing a brilliant mind and possessed of so good and generous a nature as she should suffer so much." Blundon had also shared the news he recently received from her father, Captain Young: "I received a letter from your Pa some days since. He seems to be very much discouraged. I do think he has had the severest experience of any loyal man in the Valley, and that too because he has had true moral courage and sufficient patriotism to sacrifice the comforts of home, and even the good wishes and influences of those who were warm friends before the war, to save the hope of our country and the world. Because he has dared to enlist the sympathy and influence of some of his fellow citizens in the same great and noble cause, he seems to be the great center at which the fiery darts of our enemies are hurled. And in addition to this, some low, cunning aspirants are at work to destroy his labor the past two years. I wish that Brother Gregg and myself could have a minute's conversation with some of his enemies there at Coal's Mouth and vicinity. I think we would remind them of some important facts that they could not soon forget. They cannot do him injury with any who know him, but they can resort to the lowest and most contemptible means in order to succeed in prejudicing the mind of some influential men who do not know him. He is troubled about Emily's health, which of course makes the burden heavier."[21]

John Young wrote to his wife on the same evening, April 5: "My dear 'Marsh,' I am so sorry that you are not able to come up. I am very uneasy about your eye. If it doesn't get better you had better go to Charleston where you can get medical aid; and if you want to go I think Mr. Freeman will go with you. I thought indeed I would get a chance to come home but Col. [James R.] Hall is going to the Point tomorrow and will be gone one week, and Gen. Scammon has turned over the command to me until he returns, which will keep me here one week longer. But, my dear wife, you don't know how bad I want to come home. Really, I am almost homesick when I think of the happy hours that we have spent at home with our lovely children, and then think what we have to suffer by this wicked Rebellion. It makes the blood run warm in my veins. Indeed, sometimes I think that it would be doing God's service to kill the last rebel in the government. Indeed, 'Marsh,' I am tired of the command of a Post. You don't know the trouble that it causes me. The she-devils are running to Headquarters reporting me every week - But thanks to General Scammon - he is not General Crook. Sam Wilson's negroes ran away last night - the last one, big and little, and two of Sam Rust's. Will let them go - it is their Southern rights. Mr. Lewis tells me this morning that the Secesh are cutting up on the lower side of Coal about their negroes, and say Captain Young won't give them any protection at all. Well, suppose I don't. I didn't leave my happy home to protect 'rebels' property - won't do it. There are three companies here now, and it will give me something to do this week. But if you get any worse please send me word. There is no medicine up here..."[22]

In April 1863, Confederate Major General John Imboden was preparing for a raid on the Baltimore & Ohio railroad in northwestern Virginia. General Albert G. Jenkins was still in the Kanawha Valley region with Union troops rabidly searching for him. Captain David Love, 2nd West Virginia Cavalry, was on a three-day expedition from Camp Piatt through Logan and Cabell Counties when he encountered Jenkins at Mud River on April 6, "About 3 o'clock I struck the Mud River road and traveled up it 1 mile to where the trail again left the road, and crossed the river and ascended a very steep and rough hill, covered by a thick woods. When the advance was about halfway down the hill, on the opposite side, it came upon the enemy in a very deep ravine, into which it was almost impossible to force the horses. After a sharp skirmish, we drove them from their position, when a very exciting and dangerous chase ensued, the enemy scattering in every direction. During the engagement the enemy lost 1 man killed and 15 prisoners, 15 horses, and 50 stand of arms, which we destroyed. After resting an hour, I started for Hurricane Bridge, arriving there at 8 o'clock, and remained there during the night."[23]

Sarah Young received another letter from Edgar Blundon on April 16, discussing the recent battle at Hurricane Bridge. Blundon intimated that one of the Union soldiers killed there, Henry Sands of Company D, had a brother in the 8th West Virginia, Thomas Sands of Company A, and that everyone who knew the deceased were "indignant toward the Rebels" now, no longer wishing them anything but the harshest punishment. He also hinted in a not-so-subtle fashion that Sallie ought to send him a photo of herself, griping that he deserved it as much as any other family member, and that "It is the prevailing practice in Love..." A few days later on April 20, Blundon expressed concern that some of his mail may have been opened by the courier – who was also a friend of Lieutenant Robert Brooks. Blundon noted also he had written five letters to her father that oddly went unanswered, speculating that "...it is not improbable that they have been intercepted by the same curious, inquiring friend." Blundon opined: "I am afraid that your Pa will venture too far and be captured. He should have a strong guard to go with him at all times when away from camp. If there was no other danger than a simple capture, it would be somewhat different. They don't want to capture him or me, and if they did it would only be to find the nearest tree. He might with safety make a night visit occasionally, but there the utmost secrecy would be necessary...I am going to write a word of caution to him. I feel uneasy about him constantly because I know he is not safe."[24]

Blundon wrote on, "Nothing but fear has prevented them from destroying him before now. It is certainly pleasant to have him at home, and I know if anyone can realize the blessed influences of a good and peaceful home, and appreciate its benefits, it is a soldier. When I read your letter, I saw the home group; with the marked satisfaction indicated by each countenance. But there is an uneasiness manifested by all save the old Veteran, which is not unusual in places of like character in Ohio or other States where the awful consequences of war are not seen except in miniature." Obviously, Captain Young and his men in Company G were not making many friends among the Confederate troops of the region, particularly in Jenkins' outfit, which was comprised of at least eighty-one men from the Hurricane Bridge vicinity, and more from the Putnam, Cabell, Wayne and Kanawha County areas, whose families were doubtless terrified of the Union troops.[25]

After months of debate on the question of constitutionality, on April 20, Abraham Lincoln signed a proclamation admitting West Virginia into the Union as the thirty-fifth state, but it would not take effect for sixty days. Despite his six-member cabinet being equally divided, Lincoln steadfastly maintained his position that the act was made expedient by a war, particularly since Virginia had seceded and was no longer entitled to the protections afforded by the United States Constitution. With enactment of the bill, the last step to statehood was for the people of West Virginia to ratify a revised state constitution allowing the gradual emancipation of slaves within its territory. After the citizens of the new state overwhelmingly voted in favor of the document in March 1863, Lincoln issued his proclamation: "Whereas by the act of Congress approved the 31st day of December last the State of West Virginia was declared to be one of the United States of America..."[26]

On April 20, Wood County resident and attorney Arthur Ingram Boreman was elected as the first governor of West Virginia, to be sworn into office on June 20 when West Virginia obtained statehood with Wheeling as its capital. A former member of the Virginia House of Representatives, from 1855 to 1861, and anti-abolitionist, he was decidedly a Union supporter who fervently tried to stop Virginia from seceding in 1861. He served as President of the Second Wheeling Convention in 1861 and played a key role in establishing the Restored Government of Virginia. Francis H. Pierpont continued to serve as Governor of the Restored Government of Virginia, although only for counties under Federal control until 1865. While still recognizing Richmond as the official capital, his de facto seat of government moved to Alexandria until the war's end, and then moved to Richmond where he served until 1868. Pierpont's nephew, Francis P. Pierpont, an officer in the 12th West Virginia Infantry, was appointed as the new state Adjutant General of West Virginia by Governor Boreman.[27]

*Arthur I. Boreman*
*First Governor of West Virginia*
*Library of Congress*

As of April 20, the 13th West Virginia Infantry was then posted in the following manner: Companies E and H were at Point Pleasant, while Companies B and G, along with a detachment of new recruits, were still at Coalsmouth, and Companies A, C, D and F remained at Hurricane Bridge in Putnam County. Following the battle at Hurricane Bridge, Colonel William Brown had 2nd Lieutenant John S. Cunningham of Company G appointed as the regimental Adjutant, to replace 1st Lieutenant Emory Bridgeman, the former Adjutant who was killed in action there on March 28. Cunningham was from Coalsmouth and often wrote home to his wife. He penned a letter to her on April 24, stating: "I send you this note to inform you that I am well. I wish you would send me any late papers that you may have as I find it quite lonesome here and no news. Save all your newspapers and send them to me. If you have any news write to me. Tell Father that as soon as my commission comes I will have to get me a horse. I was under the impression that the Government furnished one already..."[28]

During the next two weeks, Company B of the 13th West Virginia Infantry was sent to assist Company G at Coalsmouth. On April 30, Lieutenant Colonel James R. Hall ordered Companies B and G to Mud Bridge, Cabell County. The road connecting the two Union army posts was known as the James River & Kanawha Turnpike, a well-known and important travel link for the region in the 1800's. Known locally as both the James River Turnpike and the James River Road, the route was originally surveyed by Lord Fairfax of Colonial Virginia in 1748, and in 1769 George Washington's survey party also measured the road. It was intended to establish a trail from Jamestown, Virginia, to the Ohio River in hopes of facilitating trade from eastern settlers with Native Americans residing in the Ohio River Valley. The James River Road terminated at the area known as Virginia Point in what is now Kenova, West Virginia, where the Ohio and Big Sandy Rivers meet. After the Revolutionary War, Congress made the James River Turnpike into a toll road. On April 30, General Jacob D. Cox ordered Colonel William Brown to move Companies B and G of the 13th West Virginia from Coalsmouth to Mud Bridge and establish an encampment there. Also, a detachment of infantry from the 5th West Virginia stationed at nearby Ceredo was sent to Mud Bridge on that date, under command of Captain R.B. McCall. This was the second time Company G had garrisoned Mud Bridge. Once they arrived, John Young was the senior captain and took command of the garrison per orders of Lieutenant Colonel James R. Hall. He immediately directed his men to begin erecting a large earthen fortification near the Union Baptist Church, close to the James River Turnpike.[29]

Young wrote to Paulina from Mud Bridge shortly after arriving there: "I am tolerably well at present, except the rheumatism in my arms, which is no better. But I hope that you are improving in health at home. We are fortifying here and that strongly; and I think if Jenkins or any other Rebel leader comes he will find something to do. I understand that there is a considerable Rebel force in North Western Virginia, and what has become of our men I cant tell. But I heard this morning by the doctor of the 4th Va. that the 8th is at Parkersburg, but how true I can't tell. I shall move tomorrow to the fort, and fix myself to stay some time here, and when I get fixed and you get well I shall look for you down. 'Marsh' I shall prepare my tent for you. I am cooking for myself and I think you could enjoy camp very much. Chickens and turkeys are plentiful and don't cost anything but an effort to get them. Paulina, I do wish you could come down but I dont want you to come until you get well. Write and let me know how Emma has gotten...Let me know how the Rebs are doing up there..."

Young continued, "Keep me posted about your neighborhood. There is considerable excitement now at Headquarters but the cause is kept from us, for good reasons I suppose. But as I learn the facts I will let you know. I don't expect to get leave to come home until the excitement is over. I am very anxious to hear from home and I think I want to come home worse than I ever have since I have been in the service. But I look forward to when I can return home to the arms of my little family, an honor to them and my country. Surely I could not stay at home in peace and see my country struggling with traitors, and not raise my arm as well as my voice in the defense of the liberty of our depressed people; and of our holy religion May God strengthen the arms of the

Union and hasten the time when the Rebellion shall be put down and peace be restored."[30]

During May 1-3, just barely one month prior to West Virginia becoming a state, General Robert E. Lee and the Army of Northern Virginia achieved what most historians recognize as his most brilliant tactical victory at the Battle of Chancellorsville. On May 2, in western Virginia, Confederate Major General John Imboden moved his forces toward Summersville, and destroyed Union store houses and barracks at Bulltown, Sutton and Big Birch Mountain along the way. Meanwhile, Colonel William Brown received orders to form the entire regiment at Camp White in Charleston and proceed to Fayetteville. The Union garrison at that post was commanded by Colonel Carr White, a Mexican War veteran who was expecting an attack any day. For unknown reasons, Captain Young did not receive his orders to rendezvous at Camp White until over one week later. Companies B and G left immediately on May 9, once he had the instructions in hand. On May 10, Private David Burrows of Company F, 13th West Virginia Infantry, wrote in his diary that his company had marched "all night" to reach Coalsmouth, after several days of "improper food, long night duty, lack of sleep, and frequent skirmishes" in the Kanawha Valley going toward Charleston. Colonel White warned Colonel Brown to take extra caution and guard against "surprise" en route, as there were frequent ambushes by bushwhackers and recent attacks by Confederate cavalry. Brown also recalled being warned that "...the place was probably infested...and that I would most likely have to cut my way through them in order to relieve the garrison." This bode for a tense and uncertain march to Fayetteville, where Company G would see their first open engagement of the war. On May 12, General John Imboden's Confederates forced Union troops under Brigadier General E.P. Scammon to leave Fayetteville and occupied it the next day.[31]

## Battle of Fayetteville

By May 11, the entire 13th West Virginia regiment had arrived at Camp White, and remained there until May 17, when Brown received orders to report to Fayetteville without delay. The 13th West Virginia had to leave their supply wagons on the north bank of the Kanawha River when crossing the waist-deep water at Kanawha Falls at approximately 8:00 p.m. Earlier that morning, a group of fifty troopers from the 2nd West Virginia Cavalry were posted about eight miles from Fayetteville at the intersection of the Raleigh Road and Paint Creek, when they saw a large force of

Confederates approaching, consisting of Brigadier General John McCausland's 36th Virginia Infantry, six companies of the 60th Virginia Infantry, four guns of Bryan's Battery, and a company of cavalry. McCausland immediately opened fire on the Union cavalry, and after a brief skirmish, the Confederates withdrew.

Meanwhile, the 13th West Virginia Infantry shuffled along to Fayetteville in four long columns, arriving there just after midnight on May 18. There, Colonel White placed the regiment in line of battle next to the 12th Ohio Infantry; two companies of the 2nd West Virginia Cavalry and two sections of McMullin's Battery of six 3-inch rifled cannons. The 13th West Virginia were ordered to "sleep on arms" that night, resting on the ground with their weapons close at hand.[32]

Captain Young wrote to his wife that night, "I am here yet and well all but the rheumatism in my arms. Company G is all right, ready for a fight, and I think when the time comes you will hear from, and hear too, that Co. G. has done her duty. What we are going to do, or where we are going I can't tell. But one thing I can tell - we intend to make our mark wherever we go, as long as there is a traitor left in Virginia. The boys like this place very well and I believe would rather stay here than at Coal. But I want to see home. I want to be in your arms. You may think this is childish for a soldier fighting for his country and the liberty of his children, but I can't help it. When I think of the happiness I have enjoyed with my dear wife and children, and remember who it is that deprived me of those blessings, I grow indignant and feel like exterminating the last rebel that has given aid or comfort to the rebellion. The drum is beating for guard mounting. The sound is heard far up and down the river. The 5th Va. is above us and the 23rd Ohio is below us. Witcher's Cavalry is on our right and a heavy battery on the hill at the ferry branch, with one company, 1st Va. Cavalry, besides other troops in the neighborhood. Therefore you may see that we are not afraid of Jenkins or any other horse thief. The Rebels drove the 91st Ohio from Summersville night before last, and captured their trains, and it is rumored that they have with their army from 3,000 to 8,000 head of cattle, and 500 head of horses, all stolen from North West Virginia. What the country will come to I can't tell, while we have such commanders."

Young anxiously wrote further, "But we must be patient and trust in the friend of the oppressed. I wish you would come up and stay with me a few days for I don't know how soon we may be ordered away from here, and where the General only knows, for I don't. I have some things to send home and can't send them well at present. You can ride up or come up on a steamboat. They all know where the Thirteenth is camped. You can stay at Albert Tulley's who lives here. Write soon and let me know how you are getting along, and how Emma is getting. 'Marsh,' come if you can. I can't get leave to come to see you, and I want to see you and the children so bad. May God protect our loved children; and If I fall in the defense of my country and the liberty of my dear children, I shall fall with my face toward the enemy. I never intend to bring disgrace on my family by cowardice. My company is in better condition this morning than it has been for some time. We report 70 for duty this morning. We think Col. Brown and Col. Hall almost the best men in the world. They have the entire confidence of the officers and men of the Regiment, and I have no doubt but the officers and men would fight for them as long as one was left to raise an arm; or a voice to cheer them in their efforts to re-establish our Government. We hear many rumors about the 8th Va. The last report was that Co. C. and Co. F. had three fights with the Rebels, got whipped once and whipped them twice; but how true we don't know...I want to hear from you soon..." Brigadier General Rutherford B. Hayes commanded the brigade to which the 13th West Virginia was assigned, and generally lacked confidence in most of the West Virginia regiments; however, he agreed with Captain Young's assessment of the 13th West Virginia commanders, noting they were "...capital officers and they promise well in all respects."[33]

Early on May 19, McCausland attacked Federal outposts near Blake's farm in force; he had brought up more infantry overnight, causing the Federal detachment to retreat over the mountains. McCausland continued his advance, pushing the Federal pickets back along the way. Around noon, they reached the Federal earthworks at Fayetteville, and the 12th Ohio Infantry took position in the two front redans. McCausland's artillery opened on the Federals from a hill located one half mile away near Raleigh Road, and the 13th West Virginia lay under heavy cannonading until about 1:30 p.m. Firing continued until it became more desultory along the lines at dark, with minimal effect. On May 20, firing resumed at 3:30 a.m., rapidly at first, but it had slackened by noon and had stopped by 2:00 p.m., with one Federal killed and four wounded.

John Young's first experience in an open engagement occurred May 20, around daybreak, when Confederate artillery opened a "vigorous fire" upon Federal troops and "closely shelled the battalion of this Regiment under Lt. Col. [James R.] Hall, which was stationed on the slope of the hill South of the town..." The artillery barrage was rapid for a while, but diminished about noon, and by two o'clock had ceased altogether, when McCausland retreated. Company G suffered no casualties in the attack. By late afternoon, Colonel White saw that the Confederates were retreating, although he waited until well after dark to begin his pursuit. Colonel White then ordered the 13th West Virginia to "...be ready at 10 O.C. PM with three days rations to march..."

The Federal brigade left Fayetteville consisting of two thousand men from the 12th Ohio Infantry and 13th West Virginia, including Young's Company G, and a part of McMullin's Battery. They marched toward Raleigh Court House (modern Beckley), more than twenty-five miles, chasing the Confederates all night, until they arrived within ten miles of the courthouse, occasionally skirmishing with McCausland's rear guard without casualties. Just before sunset, the 13th West Virginia halted roughly one mile from the Raleigh Court House. Two cannons were brought up, and the 13th West Virginia was placed on the left of the brigade in support of the 91st Ohio Infantry on a small hillside. Captain Young and Company G slept on arms again that night. At approximately 8:00 a.m. the next morning, Union artillery quickly shelled the town, and Colonel Brown ordered Companies B, F and G to deploy as skirmishers and reconnoiter the area. Upon entry, they found the village void of Confederates, having evacuated the night previous "when the first shell was thrown." Brown reported there were no casualties in his regiment on this expedition, and late that evening the 13th West Virginia marched back toward their camp at Fayetteville, arriving there on May 23.[34]

Young wrote more of the battle at Fayetteville and pursuit to Raleigh Court House to Paulina from Fayetteville on May 24: "Dear wife and children: I am well at present and Co. G. is all right. We left Charleston last Sunday and have been marching ever since, night and day. We ran the Rebels to Raleigh Court House, shelled them out, and returned here last night tired and sore feet, without the loss of a man, but one got his finger shot off. I had the biggest company in the Regiment and was sent out to take the town, which we did with Company A. But when we get there the Rebels had left and we were all broke down and could not follow them any further. I tell you Colonel McCauslen [McCausland] did good running this time. On Wednesday we lay under his cannons all day, the shells bursting over our heads, but nobody hurt. Co. G. made a great deal of sport about their bad shooting. I can't write much this time. I have no place to write but on my knee. We are camped out in the field without tents or anything else. We left our wagons and tents and knapsacks at Gauley. Where will go next I cant tell, but I am willing to go any place if I can help put down this infernal rebellion, that I may return home. Home! home! home! I love it. I think of my sweet wife and children by day and by night, and my prayer is that the Lord may preserve us until peace is made and the Government is established. Write often, send your letters "to follow regiment." Dear Paulina, I must stop. The mail goes out at twelve, and I have no time. I am officer of the day and will be busy, so goodbye for this time."[35]

Although the battle at Fayetteville was relatively small, it was a significant event in military history as it witnessed a tactical precedent for modern warfare. This was due to Artillery Sergeant Milton W. Humphreys of Bryan's Battery, who made the first recorded attempt to shell enemy troops by use of "indirect cannon fire." Humphreys effectively discerned the location of Federal infantry by use of men he had posted as forward observers, who relayed the location of enemy forces, with information on the effectiveness of fire, back to the battery. This process enabled the gunners to fire over the intervening forest into the Federal fort with an unprecedented efficiency. When Bryan's Battery opened fire, however, the Federals answered "so vigorously and accurately with several guns that we were compelled to move to a place nearby where we could not be seen for the timber in front of us, and the smoke behind us rising from the woods which were on fire." On May 25, the 13th West Virginia returned to Camp White, and Companies A, C, D, F and H were sent to Hurricane Bridge; also, Companies B, F, and G were sent back to Mud Bridge.[36]

*Camp of the 12th Ohio Volunteer Infantry at Fayetteville, 1863*
*A) Fort Scammon, B) Battery McMillin,*
*C) Camp of the 12th OVI, D) Fayetteville Courthouse*
*Sketch by Charles Riedel, Co. H, 12th Ohio OVI*
*West Virginia and Regional History Collection, West Virginia University Library*

After a brief respite, the 13th West Virginia returned to Coalsmouth on the evening of May 28. On June 1, Companies G, B and E, were ordered back to Mud Bridge, where they remained until June 29. Young wrote to Edward Blundon shortly after their arrival at Mud Bridge: "Dear Friend: I received your official letter but as there has been so much rumor about the raid in North West Va. and your retreat, I don't know where to direct my letters; but I shall write anyhow and if you don't get it, it won't be contraband. My family is tolerably well, except Emma who is no better, and I am afraid she never will be any better than she is now. I am now at Mud Bridge. Company C 13th, and two companies of the 5th Va. and Company H 13th will be here in a few days. We are fortifying here. We are making our works very strong, and expect to give the Rebs a welcome reception if they do come. I was very glad to be relieved of my command at Coal. No one knows the trouble I had with those Rebel women running to Charleston almost every day reporting me or my men. But, sir, the Secessionists at Coal will long remember Young and his men. Captain, when I think of my quiet home and the condition of my family at the present, and their helplessness, I don't feel like showing favors to the enemies of our country."

Young continued, "If you get this letter write soon and let me know where you are and what you are doing, and if you are mounted yet. We hear no more about horses here, but, oh that we were mounted. Then, we could settle with those mounted robbers who invade our homes and country...General [E.P.] Scammon is making a line of forts from Charleston to Guyandotte on the turnpike. But, O how I wish the 8th was here. But we have a work to do and we must be willing to do it anywhere, so we know that we are in the defense of our country. I hope the time will come when you and I will be rewarded for all our labors. I have no news of importance to write you but if anything turns up I will inform you. Tell Capt. [James] Cassady that Sallie [his daughter Sarah] says she is not a 'Butternut,' but she hopes to have the pleasure of helping the Captain crack butternuts when the war is over. I send enclosed a letter from Sallie. I broke the seal, thought it mine, but did not read it. My company is in good health and spirits, wishing for Jenkins and his ragamuffins to come. Lieut. [Robert] Brooks has sent up his resignation. I hope it will be accepted, he has caused me much trouble. Lieut. Cunningham is promoted to the Adjutancy of the 13th. You see I am left without a Lieutenant. Give my respects to Capt. Cassady."[37]

## Lieutenant Robert Brooks Resigns

Young's former friend and recent antagonist, 2nd Lieutenant Robert Brooks, realized that he would not be given command of Company K and tendered his resignation on April 25, 1863. However, he was not officially relieved from duty until May 23, 1863, when his name was dropped from the regimental rolls. He then returned home to Coalsmouth, and soon rejoined the 80th Regiment Virginia Militia. Brooks finally obtained the commission as a captain in July 1863 he had so long coveted. Brooks served as the regimental Adjutant until commissioned as lieutenant colonel in August 1863. Muster rolls from the 80th Regiment show he was commissioned as captain in the Kanawha Scouts company on April 30, 1864, for a one-year term of service, although thirty-two of his forty-four men resigned by mid-1864. While Young was happy to be rid of Robert Brooks, it did not stop the seemingly endless flow of accusations against himself as well as other Union troops in the Kanawha Valley by Southern citizens.

Edgar Blundon wrote to Sarah Young on June 7, noting that his regiment, the 8th West Virginia Infantry, expected to soon be transferred into the cavalry, and were learning cavalry tactics using new drill manuals they received. Edgar also mentioned that Southern supporters and Confederate soldiers alike in the area were furious about West Virginia soon becoming a state and described how many prominent citizens had attempted to hinder election of a new governor. Blundon was especially proud to learn that Captain Young and Company G had been assigned the "post of honor" by leading the skirmish line into Raleigh Court House on the morning of May 21, "I have almost prayed for an opportunity in which your Pa would, by the same determined spirit of resistance towards the Rebellion, accomplish such an achievement that would forever stop the mouths of John Young haters. If he could have just one privilege of doing some act where General Scammon could see his acts for himself, I don't think those cunning aspirants who have been looking for the courage commanding would ever assay him again..."[38]

Captain Young again wrote home on June 11 from Mud Bridge, "Dear wife and children: As I have been in bed a part of two days with pain in my back and side, but tonight am able to sit up and write, I thought it would not be wrong to tell you. But you know those pains in my back are common. When I returned to camp I found all right side up. Colonel [James R.] Hall is fortifying here just as though he was going to remain here during the war. But I think it very uncertain how long we will stay here. However, I shall keep myself in readiness to gather up when I am ordered. Well, I will commence this again this morning. All the troops are out on inspection and general review, but I have not gotten able to attend...There are not more than a dozen sick men left in camp, and Colonel Hall left me in charge of the Fort, and gave me orders that if I was attacked to fight until the last man was dead; while he would not be out of sight. Your barrel of flour is at Mr. Walls. I couldn't get it hauled out but I think you can get it."

Young continued, "Tell Emma that I rested better satisfied since I was at home than I have for four months on account of her health, for I know she is much improved. Tell Ben and Jacob they must be good boys and obey their Ma. Tell them the Lord hates disobedient children, and if they disobey their Ma now the Lord will hate them and they will never do any good while they live. The Lord will not prosper bad children but he does love good and obedient children and will cause everybody to love them. Tell them every morning when they first waken to pray the Lord to give them grace to do their duty as good boys and that they may be good and kind to their Ma and sisters; and, Ma, you must let them come down when they can and see their Pa. Charles Allen and James Paul left yesterday morning without leave, and have not yet returned. I reckon they will come back... My books, orders, men and everything else had been inspected this morning by a general inspecting office [Inspector General] of General [Robert] Schenck's staff, Colonel Jones, but they are all right..."

Private James Paul enlisted at Coalsmouth on July 27, 1862; he returned to camp a few days later, and Captain Young did not charge him with desertion or being Absent without Leave. On the other hand, Private Charles Allen, who enlisted at Coalsmouth on February 28, 1862, did not return on his own volition. He was caught near his home by the Provost Guard and arrested as a deserter. Allen was then confined at the military jail in Charleston until October 1863.

On June 15, Young scribbled a brief note to his family, again from Mud Bridge, "Dear Wife and Children: I am tolerably well today and will start in a few minutes on a scout to Mud and Guyan River, and as I am in a hurry to go I can't write much. I have written a letter to you...which I think you will get today..."[39]

## West Virginia Becomes the 35th State

On June 20, 1863, the new state of West Virginia was formally admitted into the United States, but for Union troops in the Kanawha Valley, it had little immediate effect. John Young wrote to his old friend, John Bowyer, who was now Sheriff of Putnam County on June 26: "...as you up there appear to be much excited and have not time to write and let a body know what you are scared about, I will try and give you a hint of our troubles down here. Well, in the first place, the Rebs are stealing all of our horses, and if the Governor of Virginia don't do something for us on this side of the Kanawha River we might just as well hang up the fiddle, and I assure you that nothing but mounted men will do any good here. Now, Sir, I have been scouting this country hard for two years, and you must know that I understand the country and the people by this time. If you think the people are willing to submit to the new Government of Virginia over here you are mistaken although they claim protection from us."

Young further related, "Last week it was reported here that there were Rebs upon Mud, [Mud River] and Col. [James R.]Hall ordered me to take thirty men and look after Jeff's [Confederate President Jefferson Davis] horse thieves. Well, I proceeded up Mud to the mouth of Middle Fork, then up the Middle Fork...Here I captured two rebel soldiers...the squad of horse thieves about a mile above this place. An attempt was made to rescue the prisoners. A squad as large as our own fired on us. Three of the party shot at me, which came very near hitting me, the rest fired on the company, but as Providence would have it, none were hurt. On last Monday I was sent out again after other horse thieves that had been stealing the neighbor's horses out of the plow. This time I found their Camp where they had kept their stolen horses for more than twelve months. Not one man or woman would tell me one word about those thieves, but denied that they had ever been there, when the fact is that they fed and harbored them all the time, and those men and women say they claim protection from the northern government."[40]

Young continued, "I struck the trail of the stolen horses, 8 in number, which had started for Dixie the day before I got there, but I back trailed them to their camp near one Peter Burns, whose wife stated that they had been there and boarded at their house and cut grass in their meadow for their horses. (This I forced out of her by telling her I would burn - - ) I saw where they cut the grass, where they had carried it to the horses, but for all this Peter Burns denies that he knows anything about them or who they were. I have two Burns in the Guard House here but I think Col. Hall will release them. I have taken several horses from these kind of men, but they are given back again. But when the Rebels get a Union man's horse he is gone forever from him - Therefore the loyal citizens here are losing confidence in our Government."

Exhausted, Young came to a close, "They say, and truly too, that the Secesh is protected while they are unprotected just because they did not rebel against their Government and for this they are leaving this part of Virginia - and they think it is very hard, indeed, that they have to leave their homes and the graves of their fathers and everything that is near and dear to them just because they are loyal and the Secessionists are permitted to remain at home and enjoy their property and be protected too by their sons who flew to their country's call to put down this infernal rebellion. I must stop. It is now nearly twelve. Write soon. My family is well - neighbors well. This detachment is generally well." After their tenure at Mud Bridge, Companies A, G and H, along with a new squad of green recruits relocated to Coalsmouth, where they continued to carry out numerous patrols and expeditions in the Kanawha Valley. Most of the regiment was ordered back to Camp White on June 29, except Companies A and H, who remained at Coalsmouth.[41]

Following the state's formal admission into the Union, several changes occurred in Federal regiments from West Virginia. Volunteer regiments were then officially deemed "West Virginia" troops and underwent more reorganization on June 30. The geographical area comprising the new state became known as the Department of West

Virginia and was assigned to the 8th Army Corps, under command of Major General Robert C. Schenck. He placed the 13th West Virginia Infantry in the 1st Brigade of his 1st Division, under Brigadier General E.P. Scammon, along with the 23rd Ohio Infantry, 5th and 9th West Virginia Infantry; also Company I, 1st West Virginia Cavalry and Company L, 2nd West Virginia Cavalry, and Company G, 3rd West Virginia Cavalry, in addition to Captain S.J. Simmonds' Kentucky artillery, with six cannons.[42]

## Return to Gauley Bridge

The 13th West Virginia remained scattered throughout the Kanawha Valley region until July 2, when Company B moved to Point Pleasant, and on July 6, Company F went to Loop Creek near Gauley Bridge. On July 8, the balance of the regiment went into camp on Cotton Mountain (sometimes referred to as Cotton Hill) until Company F arrived there July 10, and then the regiment returned to Fayetteville. They were ordered to Camp White near Gauley Bridge again on July 8, and after marching all night to the south side of Cotton Mountain reached the "old camp of the 89th Ohio" where they stayed until again ordered to Fayetteville on July 12. Young reflected increased optimism toward the Union war effort, as newspapers trickled into camp showing the fall of Vicksburg, Mississippi, on July 4 and the Battle of Gettysburg July 1-3.

Young wrote to Paulina on July 6: "I will try to write a letter to let you know that I am well. But there is some sickness in my company at this place. There is no excitement up here. We are all watching with breathless emotion the struggle of our army in the East and West with the Rebels for freedom and the Union - the whole Union. I hope they will be successful and triumphant over the rebellion and send the whole thing to Hell where it belongs. I hear from Colonel Brown that there are some Rebs down on Mud, and in the valley. I expect Company G will have to be sent back again, and the devil help them if I am sent back. You may say to the Rebs in your neighborhood that Colonel Brown says if the Rebels take one dollar's worth from you, he will send my Company G down there and turn them loose in the valley on the Secesh, and make them tired of bringing horse thieves into the neighborhood."

Irate, Young promised Paulina, "Tell them this, and tell them that they shall make all the Union losses good. Their protection won't do them any good if they dont stop their friends from stealing. It is believed here that they are the cause of it. Mr. [Alexander] Handley need not boast his protection for all the written protection that he could carry would not save him if my family is again interrupted; and you may send him word of the fact, for all the officers up here believe that he and Jim Gray and J. Seasholes are the head and front of all the mischief done in the valley. There is strong talk up here of sending many of the Putnam Secesh to Dixie, both male and female. I think it would be a good thing. You had better take care of your horses, and, if you think proper, you may send me one and I think you can take care of the other. We are two miles above Charleston on the old Four Farm. There is tolerable good pastures here. The 9th [West] Va. has gone to Fayetteville. We expect to stay here some time. You might come up and see me often. I know if you were up here and at home I would find many excuses to come. I know the girls can keep house and I know also that they would be glad for you to come often. But I know also that you have many things to do at home and will not think hard. Write soon."[43]

On July 10, Young wrote to his daughter Emily, indicating that Company G was at Cotton Hill between Fayetteville and Gauley Bridge, guarding the wagon trains, where he expected to stay for some time. He penned: "...I am well this morning and most of the boys who are here are well, but there are many of the boys sick, some at the hospital and others on the way here. This is a lonesome place, nothing to eat except what we brought out here with us. My Lieutenant and I have taken board with a farmer but he has not meat but plenty of milk and butter. They are good cooks, just from Buckingham County, old Virginia. On the 7th of this month the Rebs attacked our trains on Cotton Hill and took all the teamsters prisoners, and the best of the horses, and made their escape. There are several companies, or bands, of horse thieves and bushwhackers in this county, and they are very troublesome to our transportation. I am willing to deed all this country to Jeff Davis if he will stop his 'Gray Backs' from stealing, and if he doesn't stop them I reckon we will have to do it, or stop them from breathing, but we will have to catch them first."

Young also expressed, "I feel very uneasy about home. I have written three letters and have only received one from Sallie on the 4th Inst. I am afraid the Rebs will get your horses and if they do I dont know how you will make out to live. But we must be willing to sacrifice everything for our Government and our holy religion. I mean the religion of our fathers - in other words, old Methodism. You can't imagine how much I think of home and my loved ones there; and what great pleasure it would give me to be at home. But I know I must bear it with the patience of a good soldier until this rebellion is put down and our Flag is honored and not only by the world but by the Rebels too."

Young wrote further, "I don't intend, by the help of God, to leave any reproach upon my family. If I fall on the battlefield, or at the hands of those infernal thieves that invest our country, I shall try to fall as a brave man - as one who thinks he is right and is battling with treason and traitors. I don't think it will be long before rebellion is put down. Lee's army is whipped to death; Rosecrans has driven Bragg out of Tennessee; Grant has taken Vicksburg, and you can see that rebellion is much crippled. I really think Jeff Davis can feel the rope around his neck. Colonel McCausland (Rebel), I understand, is at Raleigh with considerable force, but we dont know how many. But if he wants to know how many there are of us, all he has to do is to come and see. We dont want Raleigh; and if he wants the Kanawha Valley he will have to come and get it. But I assure you, Emma, he will have a sweet time of it when he does come. There are three regiments at Fayetteville - the 12th, 11th and 9th Va. The 13th is at the foot of Cotton Hill, the 34th at Camp Piatt, the 23rd at Charleston; one battery of 12 guns at Fayetteville; another of as many more at Charleston. You can see by this that there will be some fighting down before they get the valley. I forgot the 2nd Va. Cavalry and party of the 1st, and also the 5th Va. at Mud Bridge, and Barboursville, which would round up some eight or ten thousand troops in the Valley, enough to hold it from the Rebels."[44]

Young told Paulina on July 10: "I was in hopes that I would of had the pleasure of seeing you again before we left the valley but I was disappointed. The order came and we had to obey. But we are here at the foot of this miserable hill, six miles from the River, and six miles from Fayetteville, for the purpose of guarding the transportation to Fayetteville. Well, if we can do any good here I am willing to remain here. I am well this morning except the rheumatic pains in my arms. If there is no excitement here about the 20th of this month I expect to be at Charleston for the purpose of being mustered into the service, and I would like it very much if you could meet me there...it wont hurt you to take a little ride about and see your old friends at Charleston. I will be sure to be there if nothing serious happens. Don't fail to come. Write as soon as you get this whether you can come or not. Tell me all the news in the Valley, and what the Secessionists are doing. I shall send my trunk home the first opportunity with the most of my clothes. I have got a writing desk made to hold my papers, and will not need my trunk."[45]

## Expedition to Piney - Battle of Buffington Island

Brigadier General E.P. Scammon ordered Colonel Rutherford B. Hayes to move his brigade from Fayetteville toward Raleigh Court House again in pursuit of an old nemesis, the Confederate force under Major General William Loring, on July 12. Hayes took the 13th West Virginia along and moved out early that morning. Upon arriving near Piney River, Hayes found the Confederates had abandoned their fortifications and left behind several supply stores, which were captured. Colonel William R. Brown indicated the brigade camped overnight, marched back toward Raleigh Court House on July 14 and arrived there at midnight. A day later, Colonel Hayes received orders to proceed with the 23rd Ohio Infantry and 13th West Virginia Infantry toward Gallipolis, Ohio, to assist in the pursuit of Confederate Cavalry

*General and future President*
*Rutherford B. Hayes*
*West Virginia State Archives*

General John Hunt Morgan, who had recently been on an extended raid across Indiana; Kentucky, and Ohio. He was then traversing through the eastern part of the Buckeye state, attempting to escape capture.[46]

Hayes also wanted the 9th West Virginia Infantry to join the expedition, but General E.P. Scammon ordered them to remain at Fayetteville to provide security for the garrison. Hayes arrived at Gallipolis via steamer on the morning of July 18 and proceeded to Pomeroy. En route, they encountered Morgan's Confederate cavalry attempting to cross the Ohio River about two miles south of Pomeroy. Morgan ordered his men into a line of battle to receive the advancing Federal infantry. General Scammon ordered Hayes to take Companies A, B and H of the 13th West Virginia and one company from the 23d Ohio Infantry and deploy them as skirmishers to their front for probing Morgan's strength. As they engaged, John Young's Company G awaited further orders with the rest of the brigade. As the skirmishers exchanged shots at each other, a brief but furious fight quickly developed, resulting in one 23rd Ohio corporal wounded, while Morgan lost five killed and sixteen wounded. The Confederates quickly mounted their horses and moved northward up the Ohio.[47]

The 23rd Ohio and 13th West Virginia next boarded a steamer and cruised upriver to Buffington Island, where they disembarked and were formed in line of battle along the West Virginia banks of the Ohio River. On the morning of Sunday, July 19, Morgan again attempted to cross the river at the village of Portland near Buffington Island but was discovered, and the Union forces attacked. After several hours of fighting, Morgan was defeated; Private David Burrows of Company F recalled the 13th West Virginia poured a "murderous fire" into the Confederates just before they surrendered over 800 men to Union troops. Afterward, the 13th West Virginia pursued Morgan's cavalry on their retreat, chasing the "flying rebels" northward to Big Hocking River in Ohio. That night, the 13th West Virginia was again deployed along the West Virginia shore to prevent any Rebels from crossing, while the 23rd Ohio was sent to scour the wood lines along the shore seeking any stragglers who may have managed to cross.[48]

Private David Burrows of Company F noted one hundred twenty Confederates drowned trying to cross the river that night. Overall, Hayes' Brigade captured two hundred eight of Morgan's troopers on that expedition and were credited with assisting in the capture of General John Hunt Morgan and preventing his crossing of the Ohio River into Virginia. As Colonel Hayes was traveling back to Camp White aboard the steamer *Victress*, he wrote a letter to his uncle on July 22. He described the recent battle as, "...The Rebs couldn't fight soldiers at all. We lost one man. We had a most glorious time."[49]

John Young wrote about the expedition after returning to Point Pleasant on July 23, where the regiment remained until August 13. He advised Paulina to remain vigilant now that Morgan's raiders were disbanded, as stragglers were combing the western Virginia area in search of new horses and other booty: "After a long and wearisome march on land and water, we have all returned to this place safe and sound. We were in some skirmishing with Morgan and were in sight of the battle fought at Buffings [*sic* - Buffington] Island but were not engaged in it. We were drawn up in line on the Virginia side to prevent his closing, which we did, all but Morgan and about eighty of his men made their escape in Virginia. We captured nearly one hundred prisoners, one inspecting General, some captains and several Lieutenants. About three thousand of his men and horses are now in our hands with all his artillery, small arms, wagons, buggies etc. Old Morgan is gone up sure. There are a good many of my men sick and unable for duty. Henry Allen and Gabe [Gabriel Bryant] Brian is in the hospital and I think will die."[50]

Young exclaimed, "Poor fellows! They have gone through many hardships for the sake of the Union. But they must now die away from their once peaceful homes while their Rebel neighbors are enjoying some protection. We think this a great hardship in

Virginia, but it is so. Company G are all here but Harvey Burns and the last I saw of Harvey he was one mile above Buffington's Island and had captured a 'Gray Back' and had him a prisoner, but the wind was blowing so hard that I could not land for him and his 'Gray Back.' I cant tell how long we will remain here, or where we will go from here, but one thing I do know that Company G is willing to go any place to put down this infernal rebellion. You must do the best you can and watch your horses. Morgan's men are scattered all over the country and must have horses..."[51]

At approximately 3:20 p.m. on July 24, Young again wrote to Paulina: "As I have had one day's rest here I will now try to write. We are all well except Mink Brian (Private Gabriel Bryant's nickname was Mink) and Henry Allen who are very sick, and dont think they will live until tomorrow morning. They have the fever. We had a long and tiresome march both by land and water, but the good of it is that we have destroyed Morgan's whole force. We have captured about three thousand of his men, and all the ammunition of war fell in our hands (Old Morgan is done). We fought them at Pomeroy, then again at Buffington's Island - here we whipped and scattered the whole force. It is said that Morgan and staff have gotten over into Virginia with 80 men. I saw the men on the Virginia side but whether General Morgan was with them or not I can't tell; but one thing I do know they are bringing his men in here every day. Two have just come. The 13th Regiment did not lose a man, notwithstanding we made a charge on the Gray backs back of Pomeroy with a yell that made them fly in every direction. We charged down a steep hill right on them."

He continued: "If you ever saw devils double-quick, you may imagine their speed. I cant write and tell you all but I hope to see you soon, and then I will tell you the whole affair. But would just say to you, take care of your horses for the woods are full of Morgan's men. They have all left their horses and are trying to make them way to Tennessee or Kentucky, and if they can steal horses they will do it. I want to come home very bad indeed. I have not heard one word from home since I received your letter at Raleigh. I wrote you a few lines on the steamboat with a pencil and left it at Winfield. I think the Regiment will be ordered to Coal [Coalsmouth] or Winfield as soon as we get together again. Two companies were left up the river to guard the prisoners. If you have any business down here you had better come down while I am here and I can assist you...There is quite an excitement now in this place. They have discovered a squad of Rebs eight miles above here. Company F and Company C are just now starting after them. I hope they will get them. Nothing more at present." Private Gabriel H. "Mink" Bryant enlisted on May 24, 1862 at Coalsmouth; he died that evening, aged twenty-years. Private Henry Allen, one of Young's first recruits in 1861 at Coalsmouth, died three days later, on July 27, in the army hospital at Point Pleasant.[52]

Emily Young and a friend were pleased to finally visit her father at Point Pleasant on July 28. He had been quite ill for a few days. That evening, Young also managed to pen a few lines to Paulina, "I was very glad to see Emma. Wish she could stay longer. I can't tell where we will go from here. I was very glad to hear from home and to hear that you are getting along so well. I hope that as soon as Morgan's men are gathered up, the country will be pretty well cleared of horse thieves. And the best of all is that we have old Morgan himself. I wonder now if he is willing to carry out his favorite plan - take no prisoners! Many poor, Union men, and families, have suffered at the hands of his demons - not demons but devils in human shape, for I hardly think that 4000 such men could be scraped up in the balance of the world. However, the backbone of their rebellion is broken, and they will soon get their Southern rights, and I don't care how soon. I think in all probability I will get leave to come home in a few days, if we are not ordered from here soon. I don't think there is any force of rebels in West Virginia. None but a few scattering horse thieves, and they finally will be gobbled up. Do the best you can. Endure hardship as a good soldier, and you will finally be rewarded. As Emma and Mrs. Cash want to go to bed, I must stop. They both have seen the elephant this time and are willing to return home in peace."[53]

Emily Young's friend, Mrs. Cash, was the wife of nineteen-year-old Private Ferdinand Cash of Company G. He enlisted at Coalsmouth on August 23, 1862, and was a farmer prior to the war. Young's expression that they had "seen the elephant" was a common term during the Civil War, meaning that a soldier had their first combat experience; however, it not clear what Young meant by his daughter and her friend Mrs. Cash "seeing the elephant" as there is no evidence of any raids or other fighting at Coalsmouth on that date, but it is likely he was using the phrase in jest. On the evening of August 4, Colonel Brown ordered the entire regiment to Coalsmouth, which was then renamed "Camp Defiance." Once at Coalsmouth, Company G reestablished their former camp site near St. Mark's Episcopal Church.

Young wrote Paulina on August 6: "Dear Wife: Through the blessing of God I am here, and in tolerable health; and expected to come home this evening but Colonel Brown wants me to go to Charleston tomorrow on business. But as soon as I return I will come home. You spoke of wanting bacon and flour. I would just say that in a few days we will have everything you want here, and you can send a wagon here and get it. I saw Sallie [Sarah Young] yesterday. She is well. The whole Regiment is here, and camped where the Rebels camped two years ago. It is such a nice place, cool and shady. I hope we will remain here some time. William Racer reported himself to camp this evening. The whole Regiment is in fine health and spirits. Nothing more until I come." Thirty-nine-year-old Private William Racer was Absent without Leave (AWOL) from

June 21, 1863. He was previously captured by Confederate cavalry in Cabell County during 1861, along with his two brothers. There is no record Captain Young made him face a Court Martial, however.[54]

The 13th West Virginia regiment remained at Coalsmouth, and on August 11, Young was still feeling poorly. His two sons, Benjamin and Jacob, were in his camp visiting when he wrote to Emily, "I shall look for you and Miss Mary tomorrow and I think I can go with you to Coal on a 'spludge,' but if I don't it makes no difference, you and Miss Mary can spludge [refers to swimming] alone. I think it more than likely that I will be down next Sunday, as I am gaining Health and strength so fast. I feel quite as well today as I have since I entered the service, only not quite so strong. Ben and Jacob are here. I will send you my trunk and my old 'duds.' I want your Ma to mend one pair of pants and send them back soon. The Cavalry pants you will keep. I haven't but one pair and don't want to spoil them. Tell Miss Mary to come up and I will introduce her to all the Union boys (up here); and I do think she can enjoy herself some better than she can among them infernal Rebels in Putnam. I would like to see Miss Mary do well, and I intend to do all for her that I can. If it kills the Rebs I can't help it and shan't try."[55]

As Company G was still technically on "detached service" with the 13th West Virginia Infantry by orders of the War Department, this created a problem because army regulations required company officers to have a minimum of eighty-four men in order to receive captain's pay. Also, one had to be permanently assigned to a regiment to draw pay through its rolls. Again, the ambiguity over who had jurisdiction over West Virginia troops became an issue when the regiment met army paymasters near the Elk River on August 12. They refused to pay Young as a captain when their records showed he was mustered into the 11th West Virginia as a 1st Lieutenant. His assignment to the 13th West Virginia was perceived as an informal agreement; the paymaster argued even though Young had recruited forty-seven new men into his company for an aggregate of eighty-seven men, those forty-seven were mustered into the 13th West Virginia and therefore did not legally belong to his company in the 11th West Virginia. Young argued he was commissioned as a captain in August 1862 and had functionally acted in the role of captain since May 6, 1862, and had the necessary number of troops to justify his rank, and ought to be paid as such. The paymaster recommended that Company G transfer into the 13th West Virginia since forty-seven men already served with that regiment.[56]

Young contacted Francis P. Pierpont, the West Virginia Adjutant General on August 15, "I would respectfully request permission to make the following statements with regard to my company which has and is now doing duty in the 13th Reg't Va. V.I., and has been since October 1862. In the first place I was mustered in as 1st Lieut November 15, 1861 the company then numbering 44 men. On the 6th of May following I was promoted to Captain and mustered with my men into the 11th Reg't Va. V.I. In October 1863 [1862] I was ordered to report to the 13th Reg't Vol. Inft. With some 40 or 50 more recruits - these were then mustered into the 13th by R.R. Crawford under instructions from Adjt. General Samuels with the understanding that the company should be consolidated and permanently attached to the 13th but the thing has remained in this state ever since which you will perceive at once produces a very unpleasant and dissatisfactory state of things and I am exceedingly anxious to have the thing permanently settled one way of the other."

Young further wrote: "If I am to go into the 11th which I would very much regret indeed I want to know it or if the company is to be consolidated and remain where it is which would be much more satisfactory...that there are not more than 25 or 30 men of those that were mustered into the 11th remaining and they are exceeding unwilling to leave the 13th or to be separated from the balance of the company. I think that the good of the company and service both demand that the company be consolidated at once and remain where it is. I hope that if the power is in your hands to do anything in the matter that you will do it at once. I may further state that I have frequently refused to be mustered into the 11th knowing that it would result injuriously to the cause to divide the company and this would necessarily follow. If you can do anything for me in this matter you will confer a great favor and I would respectfully urge that be done immediately."

What Young did not say overtly was the reason there would only be twenty-five to thirty men remaining was because Colonel Brown was already aware of the conflict with the 11th West Virginia, and he shrewdly reassigned those men to other companies in the regiment to prevent them from being reassigned also. Despite Young's frustration, his case would not be fully resolved until 1864. His back pay due from 1861-1863 was a different matter, which was not settled until nearly twenty years after his death.[57]

Governor Arthur Boreman received frequent complaints from residents of Mason and Putnam Counties about Confederate guerillas raiding farms and stealing horses, bacon, flour, etc., like those made earlier in the war. Many citizens also indicated that the local home guards, a company of roughly fifty men under Captain Isaac M. Rucker, had been "of little benefit in repelling the enemy." In response, Boreman issued a proclamation on August 20, identifying by name over one hundred men from Putnam County, who in 1861 had "deserted their homes and are actively engaged in aiding the so called Confederate States of America, and the rebel State Governments at

Richmond, in their attempt to objurgate the good people of this State, but in consequence of the war evidence of their rebellious and criminal acts cannot be obtained; Now therefore, I, Arthur I. Boreman, Governor of the state of West Virginia, do issue this my proclamation declaring the said...enemies of this State, unless they shall within sixty days from the date of this proclamation take and file in the Clerk's office of the Circuit Court for the said county of Putnam an oath to support the Constitution of the United States and the Constitution of the State of West Virginia, and thereafter demean themselves as good citizens." One citizen also pointed out that many of the home guards had moved their families across the river into Ohio and were hiding out there with them to avoid military service.[58]

On August 22, Colonel Brown wrote to Governor Boreman recommending Sergeant Clark Elkins of Company G for commission as 1st Lieutenant, contending that he had been doing the duties of a 1st Lieutenant since before June 1. He also mentioned Company G had mustered into the 13th West Virginia, with only enough men to justify the rank of a 1st Lieutenant, much to Young's chagrin. Young penned a letter to Paulina that evening noting he was in better health, "I regret that I was not in Camp when you came up, but was in the line of my duty. I was out three days but never saw the track of a Rebel but I understand that there is quite a force on the Middle Fork of Mud, stealing horses and plundering houses. But I did not have time to go after them. My business was to make the Secessionists fork over their tax and they did fork, and when they didn't we forked their horses. Oh, wonderful! Six of Garret's Negroes followed us in, but nobody followed them - yet. I learned that that notorious Harvey Bowyer is in the neighborhood again. He was on the head of Chimer last Sunday night, and of course he is lurking about until he can steal some more horses. I think there are several in and about Teays Valley, and the first thing the citizens know they will be minus their horses. Sallie is at Winfield and will be home soon and then I think you might come up and stay two or three days with me. All is well."[59]

## Edgar Blundon and Sarah Young Married

On the morning of August 26, Edgar Blundon was with the 8th West Virginia, which was recently transformed into Mounted Infantry, under Brigadier General William W. Averell at the battle of White Sulphur Springs, (Rocky Gap) near the West Virginia-Virginia border. The fighting lasted all day, and into the next morning. Blundon was wounded and hospitalized for three weeks. Afterward, he received fifteen days convalescence. Blundon arrived in Putnam County on September 22. During this hiatus, he and Sarah Young were finally married on September 29 at the Methodist-Episcopal Church in Winfield, Putnam County. Sadly, there are no letters or diary entries available at the time of this publication from Edgar, Sallie or John Young to provide more details on their marriage.[60]

As of August 31, the 13th West Virginia remained in Colonel Rutherford B. Hayes' 1st Brigade, as part of Brigadier General E.P. Scammon's 1st Division, in the Department of West Virginia. Also, in Hayes' Brigade were the 23rd Ohio Infantry, 5th West Virginia Infantry, two companies of the 1st West Virginia Cavalry, and a Kentucky artillery battery. Several 13th West Virginia soldiers stationed at Mud Bridge, Guyandotte and Barboursville became severely ill during September-October 1863. Young and several other officers drafted a letter to Governor Boreman on October 12, requesting that Dr. Charles Dally, the 5th West Virginia Assistant Surgeon, be transferred into their regiment as surgeon, as he had been effectively treating many of the sick men stationed in Cabell County. Company G remained at Coalsmouth, where on September 3 Young wrote to Paulina, expressing how he regretted missing her when she came to see him recently, but was grateful he was nearer home than before. Again, he expressed concern over horse thieves roaming the Teays Valley area and revealed another of his ancillary roles as a Union officer in a predominantly Southern area, that of enforcing tax collections.[61]

On September 3, Colonel Brown received orders to relocate the regiment to Barboursville, "without delay and camp at that place." They left Coalsmouth immediately, marched along the James River Turnpike, passing through Hurricane Bridge that afternoon, and continued onto Mud Bridge and into the village of Barboursville that evening. Once at Barboursville, it became clear their purpose was not only to maintain patrols throughout Cabell and Wayne Counties, but also to recruit enough men from Cabell County to fill the entire regiment. Young was apprehensive about this, however, knowing the new recruits would likely be assigned to other companies than his own. He again petitioned Adjutant General Francis P. Pierpont regarding his assignment in the 11th West Virginia Infantry. Pierpont then contacted Major General Benjamin F. Kelley, commanding the Department of West Virginia, "There is a difficulty between the 11th & 13th Infantry regiments in regard to a company of recruits by Lt. John V. Young...In October 1862 he was ordered to report to the Cmd'g officer of the 13th with some 40 or 50 more new recruits, which were mustered into the 13th Reg...with the understanding as he says that the Company should be consolidated and permanently attached to the 13th with which regiment they have been doing duty all the time ever since and they are very anxious to be attached to that regiment... There should be something done for this Company, as it is they cannot be paid..." General Kelley responded "...the cause referred to within this has recently been submitted to the Secretary of War for opinion and decision." For time being, Young would continue to wait on a resolution.[62]

On September 9, Joseph A.J. Lightburn, who was recently commissioned as a Brigadier General, ordered Lieutenant Colonel James R. Hall to bring his command from Winfield and Coalsmouth to Point Pleasant immediately, while Company G was directed to remain at Barboursville. Young wrote on September 10: "Dear Wife and Children: I am well this morning and have just returned from a scout in Wayne Co. I was on the Beach Fork of Twelve Pole but did not find any Rebs. This is a good farming country and the people have once lived well here but Secessionist, that foul fiend, has destroyed the country. There are very few Union families, either in Cabell or Wayne; and they say they haven't any neighbors. But all the Secessionists down there are trying to be Union. In all my Scout I did not find one man or woman but who claimed to be Union. But they refuse to associate with the loyal citizens, which shows what they are. I want no better mark. But the time is coming when they will be glad to have the privilege of associating with Union families. The poor, contemptible devils have the impudence now to claim protection from us. But as far as Company G is concerned they wont get it. I tell them they cant get protection from me while my own dear family is unprotected. I will tell you how one old rich fellow on Beach Fork got protection from us yesterday."

Young continued, "We got there about three o'clock and the first thing the boys did was get in his milk house, then his good things generally. Next they found an old fiddle; ordered supper, then took possession of the parlor and went to dancing and had a regular Ball. Danced until supper, making the Reb and his negroes wait on them. This old devil claimed protection just because he had been at Camp Chase. When we left the boys thanked the old traitor saying that they would call on him again. We had a good time on our scout. Everything is plenty in this country...we will winter here, and I think it will be a very good place. I am boarding at Mr. Blankenship's tavern - $2.50 per week. A very good place. The boys are all well and in fine spirits, none in the hospital but McDowell and the boys scared him in. Company G is in better condition at this time than it has been since last Fall. It is next to Company B in numbers, and in fact is called the best company in the Regiment."

He further opined, "I think it likely that some of us will be up at Court, and probably with a large Scout. I dont know whether they will let me come or not, but I want to come. You must do the best you can until I get my money, but I think you had better sow some wheat for fear something may turn up that we are not looking for. You can't lose by it. If I dont come up, you must come down before the roads get bad. I have a good place for you to stay down here. Tell the children to be patient. I think the time is fast coming when all things will be right. Thank God, the backbone of this infernal Rebellion is broken, and Southern chivalry is trying to creep back into the Union. To hear a Rebel say that he is Union makes me indignant, but it is true that they are denouncing their principles, but they cant help looking mean while they are doing it. Write as soon as you get this, and let me know how everything is going in the valley."[63]

Colonel William Brown again wrote to Adjutant General Francis P. Pierpont on the matter of Young's rank and pay on September 15, "There are 47 men of Co. G mustered into the 13th Regt. and 38 men mustered into the 11th Regt who are doing duty in the same Co., which makes the whole No. 75 men. Not having sufficient men in the 11th Regt I cannot get Clark Elkins mustered into service on the commission issued to him in the 11th Regt June 6/63. He has been performing the duties of 1st Lt. ever since the date of his commission of 2d Lt. in the 11th Regt. There being a different No. of men in this Regt. to enable him to be mustered in as 1st Lt. in the 13th Regt. Va. V.I. to fill a vacancy to rank as such from June 6th, 1863. This will enable the Co. to have a Lieut which I deem absolutely necessary." Colonel Brown soon received a response from the War Department stating that Company G ultimately belonged to the 11th West Virginia, and not the 13th West Virginia.[64]

Young wrote to Paulina on October 13 letting her know he was still well, and he mentions the 1864 Congressional election. Kellian V.R. Whaley, a former colonel commanding of the 9th West Virginia Infantry, ran for the 3rd Congressional District seat. He also mentions an interesting plot twist in the conflict over who had jurisdiction over Company G, "...Colonel Frost [Daniel Frost, commander of the 11th West Virginia Infantry] was here yesterday and made a rousing speech. The Colonel is all right and will be elected for Congress...The boys are voting today and Mr. Whaley [Kellian V. Whaley] has gotten 4 votes. I dont think he will get ten votes in the Regiment...What are they doing in Putnam? Who are the candidates? I will send Van [Morris] up to see what you are all doing, and to see if any butternuts are running for Putnam for office. Write by him everything you know about the candidates, and who they are...I expect I shall go to Wheeling next week and I would like if you could go with me. It would be a pleasant trip for you..."[65]

Edgar Blundon wrote to his new mother-in-law, Paulina Young, on October 31 from camp near Beverly, West Virginia, reassuring her of Captain Young's safety, and a religious revival in camp, "The news from the army is meager...You will hear many rumors as to our success or defeat but you must not be anxious about that Captain in the 13th, as I learn he and his Regiment will join us at some point on the route...Our regiment is now in the midst of a great and grand religious excitement. Many of our men have not only joined the church but have been most powerfully converted. We have had service every evening since the 18th of this month. The Sacred Fire has been transferred...and it seems to be the subject of conversation in every camp in the Brigade. Surely Israel's God is making His stately stepping's visible among the soldiers of the 1st Separate Brigade."[66]

## Young Family Relocates to Winfield

At Coalsmouth, Union families were still unsettled as to their safety, even with the large Union force occupying the Kanawha Valley. Samuel Benedict, who was 1st Lieutenant John S. Cunningham's father-in-law, made numerous complaints to Union military leaders that citizens were quite disturbed with the risk of further Confederate raids. Benedict wrote to Adjutant General Francis P. Pierpont on November 3 requesting fifteen "short Enfield Rifles with leather accoutrements, and 100 rounds of ammunition," for use by the citizen patrols. They expressed concern they were in "imminent danger" from Confederate raids. Their fears were not ungrounded. Also, during this time, John Young was making arrangements to have his family relocated to Winfield due to constant harassment from guerillas. He purchased ten acres from the estate of Ann M. Milam, of Charleston, in November 1863. The property was Lot 2, located on modern Ferry Street along the bank of the Kanawha River.[67]

Captain Edgar Blundon's regiment, the 8th West Virginia Mounted Infantry, took part in the last major battle of the Civil War in West Virginia at Droop Mountain near Hillsboro, in Pocahontas County. Union General William W. Averell earlier launched a series of raids in August 1863, hoping to disrupt the Virginia and Tennessee Railroad in southwestern Virginia. During this time, Averell hatched a scheme to trap Confederate troops around Lewisburg but failed. He managed, however, to attack some 1,700 Confederates under General John Echols and General William Lowther "Mudwall" Jackson at Droop Mountain on November 6. Jackson's nickname stemmed from his being a cousin of Major General Thomas J. "Stonewall" Jackson. The battle opened early in the day, with nearly six hours of artillery fire and musketry. It climaxed in vicious hand-to-hand combat when Averell's infantry finally forced their way through the Confederate left wing, turning the action into a Union rout. Although he played an active role, Edgar Blundon said little of the fighting in subsequent letters to Sarah Young as he had one previously in the 1862 Shenandoah Valley Campaign. The Confederates lost about 275 men, and the Federal losses were reported as 119 killed and wounded.[68]

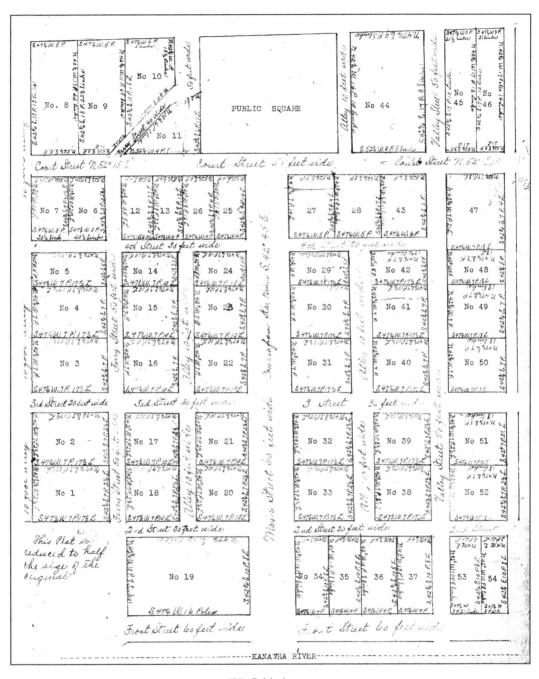

*Winfield plot map*
*John Valley Young's family moved to Lot No. 2 along Ferry Street*
*Putnam County Clerk of Court Records, Winfield, West Virginia*

John Young's two-month repose at Barboursville soon ended, as Colonel William Brown advised him in early November that the War Department had officially decided Company G actually belonged to the 11th West Virginia and was now "to be considered and treated as such." Brown recognized this meant Young's imminent departure and prepared for the eventual transition. Measures were immediately taken to form a new company to "replace that of Young's." Interestingly, Brown mentions nothing of having mustered forty-seven men, whom Young recruited in 1862, into his own regiment, which caused Young a great deal of trouble with the army paymasters. On November 12, Company G was then ordered to take post at Hurricane Bridge.

General E.P. Scammon, who commanded the Union troops in the Kanawha Valley, was anticipating further Confederate cavalry raids and needed to maintain a presence at that outpost. With transfer into the 11th West Virginia imminent, Young wrote to his new commander, Colonel Daniel Frost, from Hurricane Bridge on November 16, advising that he now commanded the garrison there, and recommended promoting Sergeant Clark Elkins to 1st Lieutenant and 1st Sergeant George McDaniel to 2nd Lieutenant, stating they were both good men and "faithful soldiers since the formation of my company." Sergeant McDaniel was earlier promoted to First Sergeant in June 1863, following former First Sergeant Clark Elkins' promotion to 2nd Lieutenant.[69]

While at Hurricane Bridge, Company G maintained daily patrols, and Young was able to catch up on his correspondence with Paulina. On November 18, he received a letter from Colonel William Brown that a former political prisoner was being released and would pass through Hurricane Bridge on his way home under guard. Young also found that his old nemesis Robert Brooks was then a captain in the 80th Regiment Virginia Militia, and was patrolling in Putnam County. Brooks came to Hurricane Bridge during Young's tenure there, although their interaction was amicable. Young also received correspondence that a company of the 2nd West Virginia Cavalry was going to be scouting in his vicinity soon. He wrote to Paulina on November 20, "I would have sent some men up today but for the rain and warm weather. But if it turns cold this evening I will send up in the morning. I have sent Lieut. [Clark] Elkins to Coal this morning to inquire about our horse. He will return in the morning. And then I will send you the mare. Then I want you to go to Winfield and try to buy that property...I have no doubt but we could get better bargains at Coalsmouth but I dont want to lose my citizenship in Putnam County. I have an idea that the time is not far distant when "Old Young's family" will raise to one of the first families in Putnam, but this must take time and perseverance, and in all probability the sacrifice of all that we have."[70]

He continued: "But triumph is certain. The scriptures say we shall place our feet on the necks of our enemies, and I believe it will hold good in this infernal Rebellion. It is really humiliating for the poor devil to have to come to Young for a pass to go to their neighbors. Mrs. Conner says, if Young's Company stays at the Hurricane Bridge she wont stay at home. I say, let her go to Dixie if she wants to. I am getting very anxious about Ed. I have heard nothing from the 8th [West Virginia] yet. General Averell says that he lost 100 officers and men. [Captain Robert] Brooks caught thirteen of them and some horses, I don't know how many, and yesterday the 23rd caught four more who had been back and stolen more horses on Browns creek. I hope among the captured we will find Van [Morris]. We are looking for the Paymaster every hour. As soon as you come to Winfield you must come down and let me know what you have done..."[71]

As of November 22, Young only had the original forty-four men in Company G at Hurricane Bridge. He requested thirteen new recruits, but thus far only ten had arrived; the "fresh fish" had an average age of eighteen years. On November 23, Young once more wrote to Paulina, indicating he had a new horse to send her, noting one of theirs had recently been stolen by Confederates. It is not clear how Young acquired the mare, but it is noted he was often accused of horse thievery by locals at Coalsmouth and surrounding areas earlier in the war. He wrote: "I intended to come up today but I can't come. But I will send you the mare...You had better not keep her long at home at a time. When you come back from Winfield, come down and let me know what you have done. We are looking for the Pay Master every day, therefore I will have to stay close to the camp until he comes...I will send the boys up this evening to kill your hogs, and you had better kill that calf and salt it. It will always be a pest. I received a letter the other day referred by the Provost Marshal at Charleston...written by D.S. [Dudley S.] Montague, begging for the release of Patrick Meddings, and stated in his letter that I arrested him for some old family difficulty. He prayed for humanity's sake, his country's sake, and for his God's sake, to release Mr. Meddings and let him come home to his family." Dudley Montague had also earlier accused Young of horse theft when Company G was posted at Winfield in 1862.[72]

On December 3, Young sent Paulina another letter: "I think you had better come down again and see Van [Morris] and make some disposition for his board. I think you had better get your business drawn up in a smaller compass, that is, you had better visit me...more frequently and see how we are prospering. The old fellow looks mean since he has been caught in company with Rebel horse thieves. You will have to visit him very frequently while he is down here or he will forget you. The old chap is very much jaded. I would like to know what you have done, and I don't know how I can know it unless you come down and tell me yourself. That would be the most agreeable message to me. I will send to Winfield tomorrow by messenger and he will come by and you could ride down with him without difficulty. Tell Emma not to think that I am childish because I draw on your visits so often, for I am very lonesome here and the distance is not great and the sacrifices don't amount to much. We are getting along very well down here. No Rebs in the country. All whipped out of their breeches..." Young's confident prognostication for a peaceful stay proved quite inaccurate, however, as the outpost would soon face another attack from the Confederates.[73]

## Second Attack at Hurricane Bridge

Young had a lot on his mind; he received a dispatch from Union headquarters in Charleston on December 10, ordering him to send a lieutenant and twenty-six men to Coalsmouth, leaving him with fifteen men at Hurricane Bridge. This was due to recent complaints by Samuel Benedict and other prominent Union citizens at Coalsmouth, who told state officials they felt unsafe with no Union troops there, even though they now had new firearms provided by the state. While the outpost at Hurricane Bridge was recently improved with heavier earthworks, affording riflemen more protection than was available during the March 28 battle there, it was still a remote and dangerous assignment. Incensed, Young wrote to Colonel Brown on December 11, "...to my surprise on their receipt, to think that I have been placed here on this rebel thoroughfare with my Company, where we are in danger day & night and then by other representation to have the company divided so as to be sure that some of us may be captured or killed. (It makes me indignant) You know that I never have flinched from duty since I have been in the service but this trys my patience and I think the request is beyond precedent. I suppose that you have not learned that Provost Marshall has arrested a great number of rebel women and men in Putnam, this week, and taken them to Charleston and they are now in the Guard House, and the rebels here says they will have revenge in a few days. I understand today, that they are threatening that they will have Union women taken as hostages and that in a few days. I learned yesterday that notorious horse thief Wake Dudding is in, I had Sergt [1st Sergeant William G.] McDaniel and 12 men after him last night, and but for this order would have at him tonight."[74]

It is no surprise that Young did not immediately comply with orders to further divide his company, and it proved to be a wise decision; the outpost at Hurricane Bridge was soon attacked. On the bitter cold afternoon of Sunday, December 13, 1863, Young was alerted by his pickets that a large force of enemy cavalry was rapidly approaching the post. The Confederates were later identified as some 300-500 men from the 16th Virginia Cavalry, which belonged to Brigadier General Albert Gallatin Jenkins' cavalry brigade. This was the same regiment that attacked the outpost with the 8th Virginia Cavalry on March 28. Colonel Milton J. Ferguson, commanding the 16th Virginia Cavalry, sent Young a note demanding surrender, stating he had Young surrounded. Recalling the majority of the 13th West Virginia were then stationed at nearby Barboursville some thirty miles west, and knowing he was significantly outgunned, the contentious Young decided to fight anyway rather than surrender the post.

Probably due to both their fighting tenacity and a great deal of protection afforded by the improved earthworks, Young's small company resisted the Confederate attack for nearly six hours, until just after dark, when Young realized he had to make a decision whether or not to evacuate his post. It is not known who retired first, but the only official report on the matter indicates Union officers believed Young's account that: "The enemy left, probably about the same time in great haste...It is doubtful whether they discovered that our force had left." There were no casualties, and the Confederates withdrew toward Barboursville. Company G traversed the James River Turnpike as far as Milton searching for the Confederates but found nothing.

A few days later, Young received orders to join the Union garrison located at Barboursville, commanded by Lieutenant Colonel James R. Hall of the 13th West Virginia. Hall organized a search party of about two hundred infantrymen, including Young's company, and scouted throughout Cabell and Wayne counties looking for Jenkins' Confederates; only this time, they found them. Hall reported: "We passed through the country between this and Wayne-Court House, and found that they were camping in the neighborhood of Wayne-Court House. I found it impossible to force them to fight, as they were well mounted and appeared to be only disposed to

*Private David Burrows*
*Co. F, 13th West Virginia Infantry*
*West Virginia State Archives*

interrupt us by harassing our advance and rear guards...I would have remained out longer but for the want of rations and the sudden change in and inclemency of the weather, which rendered it impossible for the men to march." Thus, the year 1863 ended with no casualties in Company G from combat, although two died from illness. Several men in the 13th West Virginia became severely ill with fever in the damp, cold weather of December 1863, but this did not stop military activities in the region.[75]

Private David Burrows, Company F, 13th West Virginia, was one of the sick, although he managed to recover in time to receive a furlough home to visit with his family during the Christmas holiday. He wrote a poem in his tent during the time he was ill, and shared the missive with his family:

"When I am dead my dearest, sing no more songs for me
Plant there no roses at my heard, nor shady Cypress tree
Because the green grass above me, with showers and dew drops wet
And if thou wilt remember, and if thou wilt forget;
I shall see not the shadows, I shall not feel the rain
I shall not hear the nightingale singing, as if in pain"[76]

Chapter Three References

1. First Edition of Abraham Lincoln's Final Emancipation Proclamation. Alfred Whital Stern Collection of Lincolniana, Library of Congress; D. Shaffer. "Lincoln and the Vast Question of West Virginia." *West Virginia History*, Vol. 32(2), (January 1971), 86-100; B.F. Wade Papers, 1800-1878, Letter from A.W. Campbell, June 26, 1862. Manuscripts Division, Control No. MM 78044263. Library of Congress; R. Morris. "The *Wheeling Daily Intelligencer* and the Civil War." (Unpublished doctoral dissertation. West Virginia University, 1964), 36-55; Diary of Orville H. Browning. Historical Collections, Part I, 1933. (Illinois State Archive, Springfield, Illinois), 550-551; 596-599; Robert Todd Lincoln Family Papers, 1864-1938. Control No. MM 97084148, Letter from Francis H. Pierpont, December 30, 31, 1862. Library of Congress; R. O. A. Curry. *A House Divided.* (Pittsburgh, PA: Univ. of Pittsburgh Press, 1964), 100-115; Salmon P. Chase Letters, General Correspondence 1810-1989: Letter from E. W. Crittenden July 21, 1861, MSS 15610, Reel 14, Library of Congress; Seth A. Nichols. "Let us Bury and Forget: Civil War Memory and Identity in Cabell County, West Virginia 1865-1915." (Undergraduate Thesis, Marshall University; May 2016), 1-30; OR Series 1, Vol. 21, Part 1, 964.

2. J.V. Young Letters, January 24, 1863; CSR, RG 94, M507, Roll 208, National Archives; WV AG Papers, AR 382, 13th West Virginia, Box 2/2, Folder 72, December 17, 1862 Co. G Muster Roll, WV Archives; Griffith, 69; Blundon Letters, January 8, 1863.

3. J.V. Young Letters, January 25, 1863.

4. Ibid., January 26,1862. CSR, RG 94, M504, Roll 186, National Archives.

5. WV AG Papers, AR 382, 13th West Virginia Infantry, Field & Staff Letters, Folder 1, Letter from J.S. Cunningham, January 25, 1863, WV Archives; J.V. Young Letters, January 29, 1863, WVU Library; CSR RG 94, M508, Roll 188, National Archives.

6. *Gallipolis Journal,* Vol. 28(14), Feb. 26, 1863; J.V. Young Letters, February 5, 1863.

7. WV AG Papers, AR 382, 13th West Virginia Infantry, Misc. Folder. WV Archives; Pierpont Letters, December 17, 1862; J.V. Young Letters, March 9, 1862.

8. CSR, RG 94, M508, Roll 69, National Archives; Blundon Letters, February 16 & 18, 1863; Union Army Court Martial Case Files 1809-1894, RG 153, M1105, Records of the Judge Advocate General, Proceedings of General Court Martial; Dept of West Virginia, 13th West Virginia Infantry, 1862-1865, National Archives.

9. J.V. Young Letters, February 18, 1863; *Wheeling Intelligencer* newspaper, February 11, 1863.

10. Ibid.

11. J.V. Young Letters, February 21, 1863.

12. J.V. Young Letters, March 9, 1863; William Wintz. "Buffalo Academy." e-WV: The West Virginia Encyclopedia. January 10, 2011.

13. Ibid., March 9, 1863.

14. Blundon Letters, March 10, 1863.

15. Ibid., March 18, 1863.

16. *Ironton Register*, March 26, 1863: http://www.wvculture.org/history/sesquicentennial/18630208.html. Note that the 8th and 16th Virginia Cavalry regiments were also in the area at the time Company G skirmished with Lt. Keaton's guerillas on February 5. Some writers have speculated Keaton was part of one of those units, but his name does not appear in either regiment service records: See CSR, RG 94, M324, Rolls 83& 147, National Archives.

17. OR, Series 1, Vol. 25, 2; Series 1, Vol. 51, Part 1, 176; 13th West Virginia Field History, Part 1, Appendices A & B; Griffith, 5-12; 70; Dickinson, *16th Virginia Cavalry*, 17-18; O.R. Miller. "The Skirmish at Hurricane Creek Bridge." June 24, 1993. *Hurricane Breeze*, Hurricane, West Virginia, 1. Copy in Authors Collection; Jack L. Dickinson. *8th Virginia Cavalry.* (Lynchburg, VA: H.E. Howard, 1989), 28; 37-38; J.D. Sedinger Diary, March 28, 1863; Philip Hatfield. *The Battle at Hurricane Bridge.* (Charleston WV: 35th Star Publishing, 2019), 133-175.

18. Ibid.

19. OR, Series 1, Vol. 25, 75-77; Hatfield, 177-200.

20. J.V. Young Letters, April 5, 1863, WVU Library.

21. Blundon Letters, April 5, 1863.

22. J.V. Young Letters, April 5, 1863.

23. OR Series 1, Vol. 25, Part 1, 90-105; 79-80.

24. Blundon Letters, April 16, 1863.

25. Ibid., April 25, 1863.

26. R.P. Basier, (Ed.). "The Collected Works of Abraham Lincoln." Vol. 5. (New Brunswick, NJ Rutgers Univ. Press, 1953), 35-38; 166; Vol. 2, 255-256; Vol. 6, 26-28; 181; Crawford, Bruce. *West Virginia: A Guide to the Mountain State.* (New York: Works Progress Administration, 1941), 8; Squires, 27; Otis K. Rice. *West Virginia:*

*The State and its People.* (Parsons, West Virginia: McClain Printing, 1972), 202-203.

27. Rice, O.K. *West Virginia: The State and its People.* 1972. Parsons, West Virginia: McClain Printing, 202-203.

28. Field History of the 13th West Virginia, Part 1; Dorothy Locke. (Ed.). "Letters of John S. Cunningham, 2d Lt. 13th WV Infantry 1863-1864." *The Coalsmouth Journal,* (St. Albans Historical Society, St. Albans, WV, Fall 1986), 7.

29. 13th West Virginia Field History, S. Heck. Part 1: "The James River Turnpike." (May 2008). Online: http://www.militonwv.org; J.V. Young Letters, April 1863 from Mud Bridge.

30. Ibid., J.V. Young Letters.

31. OR, Series 1, Vol. 25, Part 1, 174-256; 308-316; 631-674; 906-926; 977-1051; 1110-1111; 13th West Virginia Field History, Part 2, Appendix B, 10; Roush, 3; M.W. Humphreys. *Military Operations, 1861-1863, Fayette County.* (Fayetteville, WV: Self-published monograph, 1926), 21-22; William H. Robarts. *Mexican War Veterans: A Complete Roster 1846-1848.* (Washington, DC: Brentano's, A.S. Witherbee & Co. Prop., 1887). Original copy found at Harvard University Library, Boston, MA), 66.

32. Ibid.

33. J.V. Young Letters, May 19, 1863; C.R. Williams. *Diary and Letters of Rutherford B. Hayes: Nineteenth President of the United States.* Vol. 2. (Columbus OH: F.J. Heer Printing, 1922), 409.

34. 13th West Virginia Field History, Appendix B, 10; OR, Ser. 1, Vol. 25, Part 1,1110-1111; J.V. Young Letters, May 24, 1863.

35. Ibid., May 24, 1863.

36. Humphreys, 23; OR, Ser. 1, Vol. 25, Part 1, 1111; Moore, 622; 13th West Virginia Field History, Appendix B, 10.

37. J.V. Young Letter, June 1863 from Mud Bridge.

38. Ibid.; CSR, RG 94, M508, Roll 186, National Archives; WV AG Papers, AR382, Union Militia Oversized Muster Rolls, 1861-65, Drawers 80-87. WV Archives; Blundon Letters, June 7, 1863.

39. J.V. Young Letters, June 11 & 15, 1863 from Mud Bridge; CSR, RG 94, M508, Rolls 194 & 192, National Archives.

40. J.V. Young Letters, June 26, 1863.

41. Ibid.; June 26, 1863; 13th West Virginia Field History, Part 2, 2-3; 9-10.

42. OR, Series 1, Vol. 27, Parts 1 & 3, 2; 449.

43. J.V. Young Letters, July 6, 1863, WVU Library.

44. Ibid., July 10, 1863.

45. Ibid.

46. 13th West Virginia Field History, Part 2; OR, Series 1, Vol. 51, Part 1, 207; Hayes Diary, Vol. 2, 420-422; Roush, 15.

47. Ibid.

48. Ibid.

49. Ibid., Hayes Diary, July 22, 1863, 422.

50. J.V. Young Letters, July 23, 1863, WVU Library.

51. Ibid.

52. Ibid., July 24, 1863; CSR, RG 94, M508, Roll 185 & 186, National Archives.

53. J.V. Young Letters, July 28, 1863.

54. CSR, RG 94, M508, Roll 186 & 193, National Archives; 13th West Virginia Field History, Part 2; J.V. Young Letters, August 6, 1863.

55. J.V. Young Letters, August 11, 1863.

56. Revised Pay Regulations for the Pay Department of the United States Army of 1861. (Washington, DC: U.S. Government Printing Office, 1863), 9-11; 18-21;341-387; WV AG Papers, AR 382, 13th WV, Box 1 of 1. Co. G Muster Roll. WV Archives; CSR, 13th West Virginia, RG 94, M594, Roll 196: Letter from Thomas Vincent August 22, 1863, National Archives.

57. CSR, 11th West Virginia, RG 94, M506, Roll 195: WV AG Papers, 13th West Virginia, AR 382, Folder 10, Letter by J. V. Young, August 12, 1863, WV Archives; 13th West Virginia Field History, Part 2; Young Pension File, Paulina Franklin Young's Widow Application: Letter from U.S. Adjutant General, W.G.H. Carter, September 27, 1910.

58. The *Wheeling Intelligencer* newspaper, August 20, 1863.

59. WV AG Papers, AR 382, 13th West Virginia, Folder 10, WV Archives; J.V. Young Letters, August 22, 1863.

60. OR, Series 1, Vol. 29, Part 1, 32-59; 47; 1016; OR, Series 1, Vol. 29, Part 2, 138-139; 616; CSR, RG 94, M508, Roll 69, National Archives; Young Letters and Family Marriage Records, September 3, 1863.

61. OR, Series 1, Vol. 29, Part 2, 138-141.

62. 13th West Virginia Field History, Part 2; CSR, RG 94, M508, Roll 195, National Archives; WV AG Papers, AR 382, 13th West Virginia, Field & Staff

Letters, Folder 10; J.V. Young to WV AG F. Pierpont, September 2, 1863; Pierpont to General B.F. Kelley, September 3, 1863; General B.F. Kelley to Pierpont, September 3, 1863. WV Archives.

63. 13th West Virginia Field History, Part 2; J.V. Young Letters, September 10, 1863, WVU Library.

64. WV AG Papers, AR 382, 13th West Virginia, Field & Staff Letters, Folder 1, Colonel William Brown to WV AG F. Pierpont, September 15, 1863. WV Archives.

65. J.V. Young Letters, October 13, 1863, WVU Library. Kellian Whaley ran unopposed for the 3rd Congressional District in November 1863 and served until 1865.

66. Blundon Letters, October 31, 1863.

67. WV AG Papers, 11th West Virginia, AR 373, Box 21, Folder 7, Letter from Samuel Benedict, November 3, 1863, WV Archives; Putnam County Clerk of Court Records Room, Putnam County Court House, West Virginia, Deed Book No. 4, 423; 485.

68. OR, Series 1, Vol. 29, Part 1, 498-550; Blundon Letters, November 1863.

69. WV AG Papers, 11th West Virginia Infantry, AR 382, Box 1, Folder 41, WV Archives; WV AG Report, December 31, 1864, Co. G Muster Roll; 13th West Virginia Field History, Part 2; WV AG Papers, 11th West Virginia Infantry, AR 383, Box 1, Folder 7, Letter from J.V Young to Colonel D. Frost, November 16, 1863. WV Archives; CSR, RG 94, M508, Rolls 188 & 191, National Archives.

70. J.V. Young Letters, November 18 & 20, 1863.

71. Ibid.

72. Civil War Muster Rolls, RG 94, 13th West Virginia Volunteer Infantry, Loose Letter files, Company G Muster Roll, November 1863, National Archives, Washington DC; J.V. Young Letters, November 20, 1863, WVU Library; WV AG Papers, 11th West Virginia Infantry, AR 383, Boxes 1 & 2, Folder 7, WV Archives.

73. J.V. Young Letters, December 3, 1863.

74. 13th West Virginia Field History, Part 1; WV AG Papers, 11th West Virginia, AR 373, Box 21, Folders 7, 42, 43 & 44. Letter from Samuel Benedict, December 6, 1863 and Letter from J.V. Young to Colonel William Brown, December 11, 1863, WV Archives.

75. OR, Series 1, Vol. 29, Part 1, 977; 51. OR, Series 1, Vol. 51, Part 1, 1139; 13th West Virginia Field History, Part 2; WV AG Papers, 11th West Virginia Infantry, AR 383, Boxes 1 & 2, Folders 7, 42, 43 and 44, WV Archives.

76. Roush, 19.

# 4

# Valley of Death
# 1864

Winter encampments in both Union and Confederate armies were cold and dull. On January 12, Major General B.F. Kelley, commanding the Department of West Virginia reported: "...All quiet in the western portion of my department. The snow in the mountains and excessive cold weather preclude any operations on my part or the enemy's. The Kanawha River is frozen over..." After weeks of only sedentary activity in his winter camp, Private William Cobb, Company E, 13th West Virginia, wrote, "I am as fat as a hog..." Many Confederates were granted furloughs home during the winter, and hundreds returned to the Kanawha Valley and also the border counties. Union authorities were aware of this, and in spite of the frozen weather, General Kelley ordered his troops to maintain frequent patrols advising, "There are great numbers of rebels home on furlough in all the border counties, and many of them can be captured if scouts are vigilant."

There were also organizational changes among West Virginia regiments in January 1864. General E. P. Scammon's command transferred to the 3rd Division, along with the 23rd Ohio Volunteer Infantry, 5th and 13th West Virginia regiments, and Companies A and G, 1st West Virginia Cavalry. On February 11, Colonel Brown ordered Company G to Barboursville and directed them to prepare for transition into the 11th West Virginia Infantry. Soon, Brown received orders from General Scammon to instruct Captain Young and his company to join the 11th West Virginia at Parkersburg, then commanded by Lieutenant Colonel Van H. Bukey.[1]

Since the war began, Confederates tried disrupt the Union government in Putnam County, and during the winter of 1864 increased the number of raids into the area

131

hoping to shut it down. Ferguson arrived at Winfield on February 2 with several companies of guerillas, having learned from locals that General E.P. Scammon was aboard the steamer B.C. Levi, which was moored at nearby Red House Shoals. Just before daylight, Confederates under "the famed horse thief" Peter Carpenter and nine of his men, along with Major James Nounnan and a company of cavalry, attacked the guard of roughly forty Federal soldiers and boarded the ship, capturing Scammon, along with the guards, a cannon and several staff officers, as well as destroyed the armory and robbed them of several valuables. The Confederates then burned the steamer.

Captain Isaac Rucker's company of Union home guards on Hurricane Creek in Putnam County received word of the attack from one of their scouts who ran six miles to bring the news. Rucker took twenty-two of his men and "double-quicked" over twelve miles toward Hurricane Bridge, where he caught up with Carpenter and his raiders, then "raised the yell, gave chase, ran them two miles, and being entirely exhausted, came to a halt. Afterward, Rucker's men returned to camp, picking up what their "flying enemies had thrown away in the race." They gathered up arms, tobacco and dry goods, to the amount of about $1,000, and about sixty rebel letters directed to residents of Mason and Putnam counties, and arrived safe in camp about 7 p.m., "without a scratch, or the shedding of blood." General Scammon, who was known among local Southern sympathizers and Confederate troops for his fair treatment of them, was quickly paroled and sent to Washington, D.C., for a prisoner exchange. Meanwhile, Captain John Young was preparing to transfer into the 11th West Virginia Infantry. A review of that regiment's history is needed to better understand the new circumstances Young and his men faced.[2]

## Brief History of the 11th West Virginia Volunteer Infantry

John C. Rathbone principally organized the 11th Regiment [West] Virginia Volunteer Infantry on October 29, 1861. He recruited men from Wood, Wirt, Roane, Braxton and Calhoun Counties of Virginia. The regiment was initially meant to guard railroads and protect Union citizens from guerilla forces. Rathbone owned many oil fields in the mineral-rich districts of Burning Springs and Wood County, West Virginia, and obtained his commission through political connections. Unfortunately, his ingenuity for industry did not transfer to military skill, as he made a series of humiliating tactical blunders, including surrendering his command of several hundred Union troops at Roane County Court House on September 2, 1862, without even putting up a fight. Eventually, military authorities demanded his resignation in February 1863; however, Lieutenant Colonel Daniel Frost was given command of the regiment and promoted to Colonel shortly after Rathbone was removed in October 1862.

Frost was a strong advocate for West Virginia statehood. A former newspaper entrepreneur, he owned the *Virginia Chronicle* at Ravenswood, in Jackson County, West Virginia. When the war erupted in 1861, Frost suspended publication. The franchise's contents and records were mysteriously burned "by accident" in 1862. In May 1863, the regiment was assigned to the new 8th Army Corps in the Middle Department. On June 30, 1863, when West Virginia achieved statehood, Colonel Frost was reassigned to take command of another brigade, and Lieutenant Colonel Van H. Bukey took command of the regiment. As of January 31, 1864, the 11th West Virginia was spread out with companies posted at various locations in the Parkersburg, Grafton and Clarksburg areas. The regiment remained in the Department of West Virginia, under General B.F. Kelley, as part of the 8th Army Corps, 2nd Division, 3rd Brigade; on February 11, 1864, Brigadier General George Crook was placed in command of the 8th Corps 3rd Division, and General B.F. Kelley

*Brigadier General George Crook*
*National Archives*

was replaced by Major General Franz Sigel on March 10. Sigel had formerly commanded the 11th Corps, and he was considered generally inept by career army officers, who viewed him as little more than a political appointee. Despite this, Sigel immediately began planning a large campaign into the Shenandoah Valley in the spring, of which the 11th West Virginia would participate. Overall, other than guarding the railroad, and an occasional small skirmish with bushwhackers or Confederate cavalry, the 11th West Virginia saw little action during those years and was viewed by military leaders as green and inexperienced.[3]

## Company G Transfer to the 11th West Virginia Infantry

Young marched his men twenty-eight miles from Barboursville to Coalsmouth on March 20, and then he gave his men a three-day furlough to go home and visit their families. He gave them strict orders to report back to Coalsmouth on March 23. Company G boarded the steamer Victor and traveled to Winfield on March 24 and then continued to Gallipolis, Ohio, the next morning. They arrived at Parkersburg on March 26 and camped there until April. Effective March 29, the Department of West Virginia was expanded to include areas extending from the Potomac River in the east, to the Ohio River and beyond the Kanawha River in the west, southwestern territories, and the Northwestern Railroad from Grafton to Wheeling. Governor Boreman insisted that Sigel protect Union citizens in those areas, which were of vital importance for maintaining both supply lines and communication. Sigel placed the majority of troops in that region of West Virginia at various points located from Monocacy to Fredericktown, Maryland, and from Harpers Ferry to Parkersburg and Wheeling. The 8th Army Corps became known as the Army of West Virginia, with some 15,680 men and officers in the infantry, 5,441 men and officers in the cavalry and 2,276 men and officers serving in the artillery from West Virginia at that time. Sigel also had 1,800 cannons available in the field. By March 29, the 11th West Virginia was assigned to the 3rd Brigade, 2nd Division, and scattered along the railroad from Sleepy Creek, near Hancock, to Parkersburg, with advanced posts at Philippi, Buckhannon, Bulltown, Glenville, and Wirt-Courthouse.

Similar to Major General Jacob D. Cox, who earlier expressed reservations about the coarse mountaineer troops, General Sigel shared similar reservations, "Brave as the soldiers may be individually, and with the exception of a few well-drilled and well-disciplined regiments, they have become loose and degenerate by inactivity and garrison life. They may be made soldiers, but at this moment they are very far from understanding their duties." Sigel ordered also that his "Troops should be required to travel as light as possible and to live off the country where it can be done." The 11th West Virginia was soon ordered to concentrate at Clarksburg, where they rendezvoused and quickly marched to Beverly, West Virginia, on April 4. Young noted in his diary that night it had "rained today and mud almost to our knees." The bad weather continued, rain mixed with snow, as they passed over the old battleground at Rich Mountain the next afternoon heading toward Lost Creek in Lewis County, covering eighteen miles.

After a brief stay, they returned to Clarksburg, and Young's Company G, along with

Companies B, C, D, I and K, were then ordered to join the command of Brigadier General George Crook, Commanding 1st Brigade, 3rd Division, Department of West Virginia, under Major General E.P. Scammon. Young's company was delayed about two weeks while obtaining the needed provisions and rations from army quartermasters. On April 25, they and the other five companies marched to Camp Piatt. Meanwhile, Companies A, E, F and H remained at Beverly. Colonel Daniel Frost was given command of another brigade on April 22, 1864, again placing Colonel Van H. Bukey in command of the regiment. He was ordered to take six of his companies to Webster County, then rendezvous with Brigadier General J.C. Sullivan at Cumberland. He arrived there the next morning, with "...not quite two thousand effective men in five regiments under him."[4]

Young's son-in-law, Edgar Blundon, was given a veteran's furlough from his regiment March 10 through April 25 and was home visiting his wife and in-laws. Also, during the previous two months, Young finalized the transaction on his new home on Ferry Street at Winfield and had Paulina and his children moved to that location, which was immediately adjacent to the Kanawha River. Also, on April 25, Young received orders that he was being detached to the scouting service in the Kanawha Valley by order of General Crook and remained so until September 1864, much to the delight of his wife and family. At Clarksburg, Young quickly found he shared Sigel's dislike of the green West Virginians in his regiment. He wrote to Paulina on April 14, "...you dont know how glad I was to hear from you. Since I left home we have been the rounds. We have marched fourteen days in the mud and snow and rain, and every other kind of weather that a soldier could wish; and we are right back where we started from on the 31st of March."

Young further wrote, "Where next I don't know, but I would not be surprised if we did not remain here some time. My reason for this is that the 11th is the greenest Regiment I ever saw. They don't know how to drill a company drill, nor can they form a line of battle. They have no discipline, no rules; every man for himself. To give you an idea of Colonel Frost's military control over his men, I will give you a sketch of our march from Beverly to Clarksburg. Col. Frost told me to be ready to march at 8 o'clock on the 10th. Six companies of the 11th were to march to Clarksburg. Well, I was ready at 8 but you cannot imagine my surprise when I found that five companies were gone. Col. Frost and staff was gone also. I marched my company the first day alone. The next day we found the men and officers scattered along the road in squads, killing fowls, sheep, pigs, and committing all kinds of depredations on the citizens that could be thought of."

He continued, "I kept my men together until we arrived at this place, and when we got here there was only one man missing Samuel Saunders was left at Beverly with the measles; and now we are here and the men are shooting all over the country, and go where they please and do as they please. They are nothing more or less than a set of Home Guards; and therefore it can't be expected that they will be led into battle without drill or organization. I would rather suppose that the 11th Virginia will be left behind to guard the country when the main forces advance (or destroy it). The smallpox is raging in this place and Co. G. is badly scared and keeps very close. I tried to get Col. Frost to let me take my men to the woods to camp, but he has refused up to this time. I am again out of money. When I arrived here last night I had twenty-five cents left, and we will not be paid until May. I wish you would send me twenty dollars as soon as you get this. I can't do without money here... I am glad that J.W. West refuses to take the saddle. It shows that he is guilty. I suppose that Sallie will stay with you this summer. I hope she will. As for Company G's coming back to the Kanawha Valley, that is played out. I don't care. We can serve our country the balance of our time here as well as there. Yes, my dear wife, if I am thankful for anything it is that you are comfortably situated on the River, [at Winfield] in a house that you can call your own. I must close. May the richest blessing of Heaven rest upon you and my dear children."

On April 23, Young again wrote to Paulina: "After many long marches and with tired legs, we are again on the Kanawha, but our destination I don't know. Perhaps Dublin Depot. My company is aboard with the 14th Va. Regiment. The 11th will be in tomorrow. We are ordered to report to Charleston. I wish if you have time you would come up. I don't expect to get leave to come home...We left Clarksburg day before yesterday. The mountains covered with snow, and very cold. The 11th, 14th and 15th Regiments [West] Virginia Vol. Infty are on their way; also the First and Third Cavalry. If you can't come to Charleston write as soon as possible. We don't expect to be there but a short time. Nothing more..." The saddle was not the first one stolen from him during the war; earlier in 1863, he lost another, taken by an officer of the 22nd Virginia Infantry, and he eventually managed to receive reimbursement by the government in 1864. On April 29, Young discovered that Colonel William Brown had reported two Company G members, Privates Adam White and Benedict Burgess, had enlisted after Company G was ordered into the 11th West Virginia from Wood County, although both had enlisted in 1862. Both Burgess and White were born in Switzerland; White migrated to Wood County, Virginia, in the 1850s, and Benedict lived at Coalsmouth. The problem arose when the army paymaster inquired as to their county of origin and enlistment dates, finding that each had lost their record of muster.[5]

## Crook's Raid on Dublin

Young did not have time to write much during the next few weeks as Crook's Division participated in the Dublin expedition, with plans to destroy the railroad and supply depot. Companies B, C, D, G, I and K of the 11th West Virginia marched from Beverly and joined a new brigade under Colonel Horatio G. Sickel on April 24, when they arrived at Camp Piatt. Sickel's Brigade was comprised of the 3rd and 4th Pennsylvania Reserves and the 11th and 15th West Virginia Infantry regiments. After remaining at Camp Piatt for six rainy, cold and muddy days, the brigade broke camp and "...proceeded up the Kanawha River toward the Great Falls, making two marches to Montgomery's Ferry, bivouacking for the night at Paint Creek, reached the ferry at 3 p.m. May 1." That evening, Young was ordered to form his company and receive new firearms; they turned in their old Enfield rifles and received another new shipment of the same weapons. Sergeant Major Michael Ayers of the 11th West Virginia found the seventeen-mile march intolerable, noting the prospect of sleeping on the water-drenched earth "not the most pleasant contemplation..." They made the most of it,

*Colonel Horatio G. Sickel*
*from History of the 198th Pennsylvania Infantry*

though, as there was a large field enclosed with a high, wooden fence near their camp. The same officer recalled, "About five minutes after our arrival, the whole of this fence disappeared in one loud crash. Almost the entire command assisted in its demolition. Soon there were many pleasant fires, and over their cheerful blaze coffee pots, tin cups, and frying pans were doing good service."

Their warm repose did not last long, as a sudden and unusual "snow squall" occurred that evening, making the men "very uncomfortable." There were also heavy rains the next morning, "rendering the road very slippery." Despite the foul weather, Crook's army resumed their march across Cotton Mountain toward Fayetteville on May 2. Colonel Horatio Sickel wrote, "A heavy rainstorm prevailed during the afternoon, making the roads very muddy, and rendering the march most fatiguing... Nothing of interest took place on the march." May 3 and 4 were consumed marching to Raleigh Court House, halting only thirty minutes for dinner that day. They next moved toward Mercer County with the 11th West Virginia Infantry posted as rear guard, while the brigade marched more than twenty-two miles through the county. Numerous obstacles, such as fallen trees, were found along the rough roads, making it more difficult to move the lengthy columns through the mountains. Late on May 5, the brigade came to Camp Creek, and the exhausted troops camped for the night.[6]

## Skirmish at Princeton

On May 6 the weather improved, and the roads also became more passable as Sickel's Brigade advanced on the road toward Princeton. There was frequent skirmishing throughout the day between the advance guard and Confederate pickets, who were eventually driven back upon their works near the Mercer County courthouse. In a short but sharp engagement with Brigadier General John McCausland's cavalry, Colonel Carr White's 2nd Brigade routed the Confederates. Sickel's 3rd Brigade took no part in the skirmish. During the next two days the brigade marched to Shannon's Bridge, on the northwestern slope of Walker's (Cloyd's) Mountain, covering forty-five miles. Colonel Sickel recalled that "nothing worthy of note occurred during this march, except the occasional firing of straggling bands that we paid no attention to." Young described the countryside there as "the most dreary country I ever saw. The roads blocked in every way imaginable." Company G was ordered out on picket duty all night on May 6, and Young commanded companies. The next morning, they were exhausted, but had to continue their march.

General Crook placed the 3rd Brigade in the advance, with Company G deployed forward as skirmishers. Passing through Rocky Gap in Bland County in pursuit of General John McCausland's force, they encountered "considerable skirmishing" throughout the day with the Confederate advance guard, "without casualty on our side..." Sergeant Major Michael Ayers recalled the 11th West Virginia camped on the farm belonging to a "Rebel Quartermaster," and they captured several thousand dollars in Confederate money; Ayers mentioned all his livestock, including sheep, calves, hogs, chickens, turkeys and even geese, were all taken, so that "not a live animal was left" on his farm.

On May 8, the 3rd Brigade again found itself posted as train and rear guard. General Crook placed the brigade in the following order: "Fifteenth Regiment Virginia in advance of the train, Third and Fourth Pennsylvania Reserves distributed along the train, the Eleventh Virginia, with one section of...battery, brought up the rear." Colonel Daniel Frost, 11th West Virginia, indicated they had "some skirmishing" on the march, with "bushwhackers concealed in the surrounding hills..." Frost also noted the 3rd Pennsylvania killed the commander of a notorious gang of bushwhackers frequenting Walker's and Brush Mountains. Sergeant Major Ayers noted the march across Brush Mountain was "very tedious." Crook's Division was then located near Walker's Creek in Pulaski County, roughly sixteen miles from his objective at Dublin Depot.[7]

## Battle of Cloyd's Mountain

Overshadowed by the major campaigns at the Battle of the Wilderness and at Spotsylvania Court House occurring in early May 1864, the action at Cloyd's Mountain has generally received little more than a nod by historians. However, this small, but brutal engagement evidenced some of the most vicious hand-to-hand fighting of the war. It was highly significant for the 11th West Virginia, being their first combat experience as a regiment; although Captain Young and Company G had seen smaller battles, they had yet to experience such violence as well. Early on May 9, Crook's Division left Walker's Creek and marched to Cloyd's Mountain, where they found the Confederates under Brigadier General Albert G. Jenkins strongly posted on the mountain summit, roughly four miles from the railroad. Sickel's 3rd Brigade was to attack their front and quickly deploy to the left of the road, through dense, heavy underbrush and rough, rocky broken ground.

As they approached, Sergeant Major Michael Ayers was becoming intensely anxious; upon hearing "the sharp report of muskets" every few minutes from skirmishers as they approached the Confederates, he was acutely aware that the sound "told too plainly that we were nearing the battlefield where some of us would fall to rise no more." At about 9:00 a.m. Jenkins' batteries opened on Crook's Army of West Virginia from their breastworks at the foot of the mountain. Colonel Sickel hastily formed the brigade in line of battle in the woods and ordered to advance upon the enemy's left center. Sickel's men emerged from the woods under severe fire of musketry, grape, shell and canister and charged across the meadow in front of the enemy's works, firing several volleys upon them before falling back. Colonel Frost recalled the early phase of the battle: "Our regiment was the first in the left defenses of the enemy...Brig. Gen. George Crook ordered his three brigades into a column, which he immediately set in motion."

Sergeant Major Ayers continued, "The column was ordered as follows: Colonel Carr White's Second Brigade was in the advance, followed by Col. Horatio G. Sickel's Third Brigade second in line, and the First Brigade acted as rear guard. Upon reaching the base of Cloyd's Mountain, the Third Pennsylvania Reserves and Eleventh Virginia Volunteers were temporarily detached from the brigade and directed to cross the mountain left of the Dublin Road, supporting Colonel White's brigade, which had advanced in that direction. The Fifteenth Virginia and Fourth Pennsylvania Reserves advanced steadily up the mountain on the Dublin Road until near the summit, when the advance was met by a shower of musketry from the enemy, who had two companies of infantry posted on an imminence commanding the road." Sickel stated further, "I immediately dispatched Captain Egan, of the Fifteenth Regiment Virginia, with his company to the right, up a small gorge, to gain their rear, while myself and the Fifteenth Virginia climbed a steep bluff to our right, and gained the road on the left of their position."

The Confederates immediately perceived Crook's attempted flanking movement, and according to a Federal officer in the 12th Ohio Volunteer Infantry, "beat a hasty retreat down the south slope of the mountain and gained their works, situated behind a deep stream passing through the clearing at the base of the mountain." Sharp skirmishing ensued as Crook's Division reformed a line of battle along the edge of an open clearing. They found a large meadow and paused for several minutes as Crook assessed the Confederate lines. While they waited, an occasional artillery shell exploded near the 11th West Virginia but did no damage. Soon they again advanced up the mountain; Sickel described, "We were here met by a fearful fire of shell and spherical case-shot from the enemy's batteries." The column was immediately halted and placed under cover of woods; meanwhile, the Third Pennsylvania Reserves and Eleventh Virginia Regiment accompanied Colonel Carr White's command slowly moving up the north slope of the mountain, while Sickel waiting on them to catch up.

At 11:00 AM, Sickel placed his brigade in a new order of battle, and at noon, Crook ordered a general advance. The skirmishing rapidly emerged into a general engagement. Colonel Carr White's 2nd Brigade advanced first, and when they were fully engaged, Crook ordered the remaining two brigades to charge across the open meadow, which they did with a shout. Moving upward toward the heavily fortified Confederate works, the division was now under "the most galling artillery and musketry fire I ever witnessed" according to one soldier. While taking cover, Young wrote in his diary while awaiting orders during the battle, "Several shells have exploded over our heads. Eleven o'clock – the shells are flying and cannon roaring." This was a habit Young would practice throughout the war; it was likely a means of distracting himself from the realities of possible death or wounding. Michael Ayers recalled that as they moved closer to the Confederate positions, the artillery fire intensified, with shells bursting closer with each step, producing "a queer sensation among many of our men who had never been under fire before." The artillery became incessant and so heavy that Colonel Sickel had to halt the brigade and order them to lay down a few minutes, to prevent them from decimation by artillery shells that the gunners were "flinging at us with a vengeance."[8]

*Federal soldiers prepare to cross Back Creek and attack*
*the Confederate line at the Battle of Cloyd's Mountain.*
*Sketch of the battlefield by a Union soldier.*
*Cloyd Family Papers, Virginia Museum of History*

The heights ahead of Colonel Horatio Sickles 3rd brigade were as equally steep as those previously scaled, described as at an "angle of sixty degrees" in most places. Crook again ordered the division to move forward, climbing the heights under a galling fire the entire time and over natural obstacles impeding their advance. Colonel Sickel noted, "On arriving at the foot of the slope upon which the enemy were posted we encountered a sunken muddy stream waist deep. The men plunged in and crossed to the opposite side, where they were under shelter from the enemy's bullets." As they again climbed from the safety of the small ravine, Sickel's Brigade was met with a series of murderous volleys, and general firing began all along the lines. General Crook later described the sound of the Confederate artillery pounding them as "a graveyard whistle." Crook indicated the deadly Confederate artillery seemed to be "everywhere we made our appearance" as they tried to ascend the heavily wooded slope. During this phase of the advance, a part of the 3rd Brigade, including the 11th West Virginia, was thrown into confusion by a galling fire of musketry and artillery coming in large part from the 45th Battalion Virginia Infantry, who was posted in their front.[9]

After falling back behind a small ridgeline which afforded a slight shelter, Colonel Sickel rallied his men, who "came up in good style." As the 3rd Brigade again advanced, the 2nd Brigade was moving concordantly on their left, until one of their regiments, the 91st Ohio Volunteer Infantry, managed to get inside of a series of works located to the right of the 45th Virginia Battalion's position, and poured a deadly enfilade fire [firing from the flank or side] into them. Captain John Young later recalled both he and Lieutenant William G. McDaniel, along with several men of Company G were "knocked down by the concussion of a shell in our midst...but not badly hurt...all recovered. I walked through an open field while 8 cannon were playing on me, about four hundred yards distant, throwing shell, canister grape railroad iron, and every other infernal missile that could kill. I had no idea of getting through but I passed through the storm unhurt, although men fell on every side." Young also indicated "Sergeant [John R.] J.R. Holstein carried the flag right up to the Rebel fortifications and kept it floating in the air while the shells and bullets were flying round him by hundreds. I say this to his praise...The field was strewn with wounded and dead as far as I could see. Poor fellows, they have their rights."

Crook's Division mounted a fierce final charge to enter the Confederate works. Sergeant Major Michael Ayers described, "most gallantly did the Colonel lead his regiment forward, [Daniel Frost, 11th West Virginia] at double-quick, and with a shout that made the enemy tremble, for it was the deep, shrill yell of the true Virginians..." Vicious hand-to-hand fighting now occurred for several minutes, resulting in a rout. The Confederates, most of whom lacked bayonets, fought hard, but panic quickly spread, and they abandoned their defenses at a full run. General Crook recalled: "...the general line moved steadily on until near the enemy's formidable breast-works on the crest of the ridge, a species of *cheval de frise* made of rails inverted, when the men rushed forward with a yell, the enemy remaining behind their works, until battered away by our men. Heaps of their dead were lying behind their works, mostly shot in the head." Once inside of the Confederate earthworks, Ayers found four dead horses "in one mangled pile" killed by artillery shells.

Captain Young later reminisced, "When I look back upon the battles of the 9th and 10th [Cloyd's Mountain] and what we passed through without losing a man, seems to me like a dream. When the 11th was ordered out in the open field I was much exhausted from long marches and skirmishing, and when we came into the field we had to double quick four or five hundred yards through the hottest of the enemy's fire...The boys ran on for the shafts of death were flying like hail. When I recovered I walked through the fire which had grown more furious. I passed through unhurt, fell again exhausted right

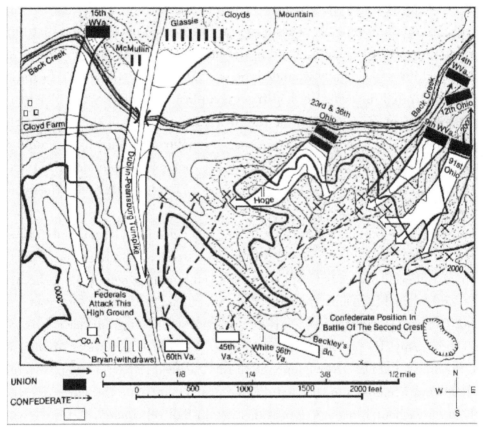

*Final phase of the Battle at Cloyd's Mountain*
*Courtesy of Howard McManus. Used with Permission.*

between the two batteries, and they fired over me for twenty minutes. When the cannon ceased and the shout went up, the Rebels fly, I started up and staggered over the battlefield to look for my boys, for I thought one-half were killed. And while I was hunting among the dead and dying for my boys they thought I was killed and they were hunting among the dead for me. Oh, you cannot imagine my joy when I saw...others running among the dead looking for me. We left the battlefield with all its misery, and pursued the flying Rebels to Dublin. There I found all my brave boys but one, James Davis I left for dead on the field. As I ran through the field I found him lying senseless, and as I ran I caught him by the shoulders and dragged him out of the range of the Rebel cannon and ran on. He recovered and joined the company three days later. But tongue nor pen can describe my feelings and my joy and gratitude when I found all my men safe; and now I feel grateful to God for his mercy to us in our great danger." Private James Davis was one of the two men wounded in an earlier action near Coal Mountain in September 1862. He was only slightly wounded and returned to the company after the battle.[10]

General George Crook reported losing 107 killed, 508 wounded and 28 men missing at Cloyd's Mountain. Confederate casualties are estimated between 800 to 1000. The 11th West Virginia lost one killed and nine wounded. Confederate Brigadier General Albert G. Jenkins was mortally wounded; he was taken to a Federal field hospital, and surgeons amputated his arm. He died from complications on May 21. The 9th West Virginia Infantry under Colonel Isaac H. Duval lost one third of their men, including the entire color guard who were killed in succession during the hand-to-hand fighting inside of the Confederate earthworks. General Crook's army pursued the retreating Confederates until after dark; a detachment was also left behind to bury the dead from both sides on the field.[11]

Elsewhere in the region, Major General Franz Sigel suffered a sound defeat at New Market on May 15. At President Lincoln's insistence, overall Union commander Lieutenant General Ulysses S. Grant then removed him from command of the Army of the Shenandoah and the Department of West Virginia. On May 21, Sigel was replaced by Major General David Hunter, a strong advocate of enlisting former slaves to fight in the Union army. He previously served in the Western Army under Major General John C. Fremont and was given command of the Western Department on November 2, 1861, following Fremont's unsuccessful attempt to emancipate the slaves of rebellious slave holders without Lincoln's approval. Lincoln had reprimanded Hunter when he zealously attempted to form a regiment of black soldiers to garrison the South Carolina area without his blessing. Hunter immediately set about the task of organizing his available forces and planning his move into the Shenandoah Valley. Robert E. Lee anticipated the coming danger, and deployed Lieutenant General Jubal A. Early's corps to the Shenandoah Valley to confront Hunter.

## Skirmish at New River Bridge

On May 10, General Crook marched his division toward New River Bridge before dawn, and after a hard march, found Brigadier General John McCausland's

Confederates posted at the bridge at 11:00 a.m. McCausland replaced General Albert G. Jenkins after he was mortally wounded at Cloyd's Mountain. Crook deployed his men to the opposite bank, across from where McCausland had constructed earthworks once again. Company B of the 11th West Virginia and Company B of the 15th West Virginia were posted as the advance guard. They immediately engaged McCausland's skirmishers, quickly driving the Confederate pickets into their lines. Michael Ayers recalled "a grand artillery duel" occurred for about two hours, and Colonel Sickel indicated the affair did not take long to escalate into a "...fierce artillery engagement" while Union infantry also attacked, soon "...driving the enemy at every point." One company of the 11th West Virginia and seven from the 15th West Virginia were posted along the river, supporting a section of the artillery located west of the railroad. As the Confederate battery began to shell Union troops from their front, Sergeant Major Michael Ayers observed their rounds went overhead and "mostly to our rear."

As the fighting pitched, the Confederates began to leave their earthworks and left behind two cannons. As two companies from the 11th and 15th West Virginia came upon the bridge, a lieutenant from the 11th West Virginia took a match from his vest pocket and gave it to the captain, who set the bridge on fire. They also burned the buildings surrounding the bridge. Colonel Horatio Sickel reported the capture of two large siege guns, a new caisson, a large amount of ammunition and commissary stores, all of which were destroyed for want of transportation. Casualties in this engagement consisted of twelve wounded, three killed in the 11th West Virginia and three wounded from the 15th West Virginia. That afternoon, the brigade crossed the New River and camped for the night. Before dawn on May 11, Crook resumed his march toward Blacksburg in Montgomery County, posting the 3rd Brigade again as train and rear guard. Captain John Young indicated while on the way, his company marched past a dead Confederate officer laying face down in the middle of the road, and no one stopped to move the body; they simply walked by it without saying a word. The effects of combat and campaign life was transforming them into hardened veterans. Reaching there about noon, Crook's Division encamped amidst a drenching rain that had prevailed all the morning. Colonel Daniel Frost recalled "At this point our rations were completely exhausted."

After an uneasy and soggy night, the division awoke to pouring rain again on May 12. They resumed their march toward Newport, Virginia, with the 3rd Brigade placed behind the 1st Brigade. As the long column of muddy blue uniforms made its way along the sloppy roads, heavy skirmishing occurred throughout the morning, in downpours that continued throughout the day. While crossing Walker's Mountain, Crook encountered a small force of Confederates who had taken position at a spot overlooking the road running along the base of the mountain, near the village of Newport. Crook directed Colonel Horatio Sickel's 3rd Brigade to pass through a deep ravine on their left and flank the Confederates. Colonel Sickel recalled, "As we approached their lines, my skirmishers fired one volley on them, when they broke to the rear, retreating on the New River Narrows road. Their knapsacks, blankets, camp and garrison equipage, with a considerable amount of commissary stores, fell into our hands, all of which were destroyed by our troops." Michael Ayers of the 11th West Virginia stated his regiment lost one man killed and fifteen wounded in the latter engagement, although Crook reported there were no casualties in this skirmish. The Army of West Virginia slept on arms without shelter that night in a heavy rainstorm.[12]

On May 13, Crook's Division again resumed their march toward Union, West Virginia, and crossed Peter's Mountain. The 11th West Virginia was deployed in advance; soon they encountered a company of Confederate infantry guarding a lone twelve-pound brass Howitzer cannon, posted along the northern slope. Company B was deployed forward as skirmishers, and as they advanced, they also discovered a supply train with eleven wagons and some ambulances, guarded by a small escort squad. They attacked the Confederates, who quickly retreated, abandoning both the supply wagons and the cannon. A large amount of supplies and ammunition was captured, along with rations. Lieutenant Colonel Thomas Morris of the 15th West Virginia analogized their plunder with a biblical reference, "...like the Israelites of old, they found food strewn through the wilderness, furnished not from heaven, but from the rebel's commissary department, which enabled them to move cheerfully on their way." After encamping a few moments in the land of bacon and bread, the Army of West Virginia reached Union on the evening of May 15, after marching twenty-three miles, and camped along Salt Sulphur Springs Road that night.[13]

Other than marching in very stormy, wet weather, the rest of May was relatively uneventful. In this period Crook's army obtained little rest, typically marching all day on wet, muddy roads. Sergeant Major Ayers also complained that "grub was getting scarce and there was nothing to be obtained but corn and mutton." Crook's army found much difficulty trying to cross the Greenbrier River at Alderson's Ferry. Swollen from recent storms, it took two days to reach the other bank. Moving west twelve miles, Crook passed through Meadow Bluff and continued along the Blue Sulphur Springs road. The 3rd Brigade posted again as train and rear guard, and things were relatively quiet, but both men and animals pulling the supply wagons were exhausted for want of proper food and were greatly annoyed with the excessively muddy condition of the roads. Captain John Young noted in his diary on May 19, "The boys grumbling...Nothing to eat for four days. Marched 11 miles."

During much of Crook's spring campaign in southwestern Virginia, the Army of West Virginia found itself "hungry, faint and weary" from lack of, or inadequate, rations, and many of the soldiers were often found barefooted. They had marched more than 240 miles in the previous twenty days. According to Colonel Horatio Sickel, they had thus far "...whipped the enemy at all points" and captured "immense amounts of commissary, quartermaster, and ordnance stores, together with depots, store-houses, and barracks, about seventeen miles of railroad, several bridges, trestle works, &c." As a result of this campaign, the Federal army seized the following items: "Firearms 630, Ammo -60,000, Artificers Tools, (chests), 4, wagons, 14, harness, 12, uniform coats, 70, uniform trousers, 32, blankets, various kinds, 320, knapsacks, 1,200, Gun carriage, 1, Caissons, 2."[14]

## Retreat to Meadow Bluff

Crook's beleaguered army next moved, albeit very slowly, across the mountains toward Meadow Bluff in Greenbrier County, West Virginia, with its lead elements arriving there approximately May 20. The men were given a brief respite, ostensibly to rest and resupply with ammunition, clothing, rations, etc. John Young found some paper, and continued correspondence with his wife, bringing her up to date on the recent expedition, "Through the manifold goodness of God we are all alive yet, although we have passed through many dangers. We arrived here last night, Co. G all safe but tired and hungry. Haven't had anything to eat for ten days except what they gathered on the road, and that was not much for the whole command. It is twenty days since we left Camp Piatt...On the 9th we came up with Jenkin's force fortified on Floyd's [Cloyd's] Mountain, Pulaski Co. We attacked him in his fortification and, after five hours and one-half hard fighting...Great Gen. [Albert G.] Jenkins is among the wounded. Our men fought like tigers. The 11th Va. had 11 men wounded, one killed. Company G, one man wounded – James Davis..." At the time he wrote to Paulina, Young was not aware that Jenkins was mortally wounded at Cloyd's Mountain. He continued, "...Our boys lost everything they had in the fight on the 9th inst., and a great many are barefooted, and some nearly naked, but they don't grumble...I have marched the whole round while most all the officers broke down and were put in the ambulance and wagons; but I don't think I could have gone much farther. We are lying here waiting for rations and when they come we will be all right...I see they are putting up a telegraph line from Gauley to this place, and I understand it will be completed to

Lewisburg at once..."

Writing further, Young prompted Paulina, "I would like to hear from the Kanawha Valley very much indeed. I want to know what the Rebs have done, or are doing since we left. I think you will have a raid there soon. Morgan is at Withville [Wytheville] with a large force. He met us at Floyd's [Cloyd's] Mountain but we whipped him so quickly that he made back in double quick time and we saw no more of him...I assure you that there is not much on our route to subsist the Rebel army. Men who were rich a few days ago are now poor – have got their rights in full. Not one pound of bacon or bushel of corn was left on our whole march. How the people are to live I can't imagine. But the citizens bushwhacked us all the way from Bland Co. to Greenbrier Co., and many of the poor, deluded creatures have got their everlasting rights. Gen. Crooks had every bushwhacker that we caught shot. I saw one old gray headed man laying on the road side, shot in the head for bushwhacking. Poor, old fellow! He could not get out of the way of the Yankees. We have lost a number of our men since we started, but not as many as we expected. Co. G has not lost any, although they are tired and worn out they are all here. Our boys think Genl. Crook is the man. He is a feeling man and loves his soldiers. It is said that when he came to Meadow Bluff and found no supplies for his men he wept like a child." Having served with General Crook under the duress of combat and exhausting marches, Young's tone toward him had clearly changed; he now saw him as more paternal rather than his former perception of him as a bit of a dictator.

Young further wrote, "My dear wife, I can't tell you but very little about our raid until I see you. I am writing on my knees, down in a dark hollow alone. The boys lying all over the field resting. Poor fellows! They are worn out, tired and hungry. Oh, what has this wicked Rebellion done? But I think it is nearly over. May the Lord hasten the time when the Rebellion shall be put down, peace restored, the tired and hungry soldiers be permitted to return home to their families in peace and honor...Tell my children to write to me often. I can't hear from Capt. [Edgar] Blundon. Nothing more for this time, I must stop writing and go hunt something to eat. I would give fifty cents today for one ear of corn to parch, but it isn't here... I have just made my supper on parch corn and rye coffee. F. L. [Ferdinand L.] Cash has just come in with a Rebel beef. The boys are cutting and roasting without bread. Rations will be here tonight."[15]

Not having written for several days, Young told Paulina on May 21: "...We arrived here on the 19th, hungry and tired. Had no rations for ten days, only what we snatched, and that was but little...Company G was in the 5 hours fight on Floyds [Cloyd's] Mountain, and, strange to tell, not one was killed. I was knocked down by a shell but not hurt badly. Five of Company G also fell but recovered...it is said that Jim ___ was left wounded on the field, but how true I can't say for I was hunting up my own boys and did not busy myself about the Rebels, although they called on me for water many times...But the best is we burned Dublin Depot, the resort of horse thieves."

On May 21, Major General Franz Sigel ordered General Hunter make a demonstration against Staunton as soon as possible. However, when Crook received the orders, he was apprehensive, noting his division was yet "scantily supplied with rations" and chose to wait there until such supplies could be brought from Gauley Bridge. Crook blamed the quartermasters, grumbling the delay was due to "the miserable transportation furnished by the quartermaster's department (many of the animals thus furnished being not two years old)...many of my men barefoot and scantily supplied with rations."[16]

Crook's army marched to Bunger's Mill in Greenbrier County on May 23. Young wrote to his daughter Emma that evening from camp, still numb from what he saw at Cloyd's Mountain, "My dear Emma: I have just wandered off from camp away out in the woods, in order to write a few lines home. I am well and hearty, but worn out on this raid. When I tell you that we marched two hundred and fifty miles in 19 days and whipped Jenkins at Floyd's [Cloyd's] Mountain, followed up and whipped their forces at New River bridge, besides skirmishing with the enemy some ten days, marching night and day, without rations, in the rain and mud, you can guess at the condition we are in. I have marched the whole round at the head of my company. Although Co. G was ordered to skirmish with the enemy over East River Mountain, and fought them for eight miles, killing and wounding quite a number; also in the heat of the battles on Cloyd Mountain and New River Bridge, not one was killed, and only one slightly wounded, while shells, canister, grape, railroad iron, telegraph wire, musket balls, and everything else that the enemy could throw to keep us back, and officers and men falling on every side, how myself and Co. G escaped is a wonder to me and always will be...but we left some three hundred of our brave officers and men on the field at Cloyd Mountain. Peace and honor to their dust. We left hundreds of the enemy on the field of battle, and all along the road. Tongue or pen cannot describe the scenes we have passed through since we left home...we have crippled the enemy in South West Va. badly. I think it will be some time before they can make another raid in the Kanawha Valley..."

Young further related: "You may guess what would be left when ten or twelve thousand hungry men and horses would pass through the country. I have seen the hungry soldier take the last bite from families on the road and leave the women crying – saying their children must starve while all the men are in the Rebel service...the country is gleaned. The hardships and battles that we have passed through are nothing new to men. Those brave men that have followed me faithfully for two years are now worn out. Some fifteen or twenty are sick with dysentery. Fresh beef and limestone water does not agree with them. I weep every day for my brave boys. I do all that I can for them. They look to me for everything they want. Next to my children I love my brave boys...Our column trains and all was nearly eight miles long, and when it was our lot to be in the rear we knew nothing of what was going on in front unless a cannon told us that Rebs were about. Every third day our Brigade was in rear of the trains, with two pieces of artillery. There are a great many Union families in Giles County, and were glad that the Yankees had come but they suffered with the rest. A hungry soldier knows no man. A great number of Union men came out with us, and almost an army of negroes."

Knowing his precocious younger daughter Emily would demand such detail, Young continued, "We are now camped on Sinking Creek, four miles from Lewisburg...Where we will go next we don't know, but I know that we can't move until the men are equipped, for many are barefoot, some have lost their hats; Company G stripped of the things for the fight – knapsacks and blankets, and lost everything they had only what they had on their backs. The 14th Va. lost all. The 9th Va. suffered more than any other Regt we had. Co. G, 9th Va. had only 15 men left...The field was strewed with dead Rebels and besides what were left on the field, they were hauling their dead off all the time the battle was going on. The Negroes say the cars at Dublin Depot were loaded with dead and wounded; therefore, this loss will not be ascertained. It is great. Just as we routed the Rebels out of their fortifications General John Morgan, with four hundred men, dashed in. He thought the Rebs had whipped, but he dashed out again in double quick. We captured some of the same men that we captured in Ohio. Came very near capturing the General himself...We also ran [into] General Echols and captured three cannon, ten wagons, four ambulances and all his supplies...We just pushed the Rebels before us wherever we went. I must stop writing for the want of space...Please send me eight or ten post stamps...The boys lost all their paper and ink at Cloyd's Mountain. None to be had here."[17]

On May 27, Young penned another note to Paulina when he was near Lewisburg, "It is with pleasure and gratitude to God that I can say I am well, notwithstanding our long march and fatigue and laying out in the rain on the cold ground. I have enjoyed my health as well as I ever did, and today could eat anything, but we can't get it to eat. This morning we had ½ pound issued to us, that is, to each man. The first bacon we have had for twelve days. But the citizen's sheep and hogs suffer, notwithstanding strict orders against it. My boys are improving fast and I think we will soon be able for another raid. We expect to start soon towards Jackson's River. This is rumor in camp. The 22nd [Virginia] Rebel Regiment has nearly all come in and taken the oath...We have heard nothing of the Pay Master yet. Your twenty dollars found me at Gauley and I have spent two dollars of it...if you get out of money you must borrow some from some friend until we are paid; and as soon as I get my pay I will send it home."

Young proceeded, "I feel so much better satisfied since you have gotten into your new home and out of that infernal neighborhood." Young also admonished his wife to tell his old antagonist Robert Brooks and Southern supporter Mr. [Dudley] Montague, who were both slandering him again, that he would "Take care" of each when he returned. Summarily, Young opined: "I think the Rebels are crippled badly in this country They say that they are whipped. However, there is a great deal of bushwhacking done here by the citizens, and our officers issuing rations to their wives and children. I reckon it is right. You may tell those Rebel women in the Valley that their beloved Confederacy has gone up the spout, and left them in disgrace, and their rights are gone. But O, what will be the winding up of all this rebellion? You know that Company G has a settlement to make with many Rebels who are now at home, and so it is with all other companies of the Virginians. Those men who have been engaged in driving them from their homes and taking their property must lookout whenever our boys return home. They won't then have leave to run to Headquarters to report."[18]

Young scribbled in his diary that it was pouring rain on May 28, and eighteen of his men in Company G were sick. With pickets firing all day, he also indicated more than half of his company were barefoot. Young wrote to his wife from camp on May 30, "I am well but much worn down, although we have rested here some ten days. But we are preparing today for an onward move. We will pull up stakes tomorrow for where I can't tell, but for Staunton, I suppose. The Q.M. [Quartermaster] is sending back everything but one wagon to the Regiment. When we will be permitted to return God only knows. But the signs of the times show that 'Rebeldom' wont last much longer. They are only fighting in desperation. They know they are whipped. There are quite a number of my boys who will be sent back from here to the Kanawha Valley – sick. I was up to the 7th Va. [7th West Virginia Cavalry] Camp yesterday and took dinner with Capt. [James] Cassady. Saw Col. Ohley [John Oley] and he told me that Capt. [Edgar] Blundon was still in the valley buying horses. I also saw Capt. [Isaac] Rucker. He said that he was in Winfield and you were well. The 7th boys are not mounted yet, and they grumble awfully. Co. F. wants Capt. Blundon to come very badly indeed. They think if their Capt. was with them they would fare better."

Young proceeded, "I have the headache today, I think from fasting. We have had no rations since day before yesterday. Our Brigade Q.M. is a mean man. He is 1st Lt. in the 3rd Pa. reserves, and is trying to make a fortune off the soldiers. He has been selling crackers to the privates at 6 cents per pound when he knew it was the soldiers own bread. Well, Col. Frost has made the Quartermaster shell out what he called private bread, and we got a cracker a piece and just ate our dinner, and now we feel considerably better. As I said before you will have to borrow some money for I can't tell when I will be paid and I want you to have what money you want. You can get it from Capt. [John] Bowyer or...[James] Hoge." Captain James Cassidy of the 7th West Virginia Cavalry was corresponding with Young's daughter, Emily, and would eventually become his son-in-law. Young refers to friends from Winfield in Putnam County, including the brother of one of his soldiers, Private Cy Cary, who served in Company A, 26th Battalion Virginia Infantry from Greenbrier County.

He further wrote, "I visited [George] Cary's wife yesterday in Lewisburg. George is in the Rebel army and she is a burning hot secessionist, but she is in a destitute condition and says she wants Cy Cary to send his father and mother some clothes for they are nearly naked and can't get any clothing out here. She says she wants the Yankees to leave here and go to their own country. When I told her that we were Virginians she seemed to be surprised that we would fight so hard against our own State. Poor, deluded creatures, I pity them in my heart. The negro appears to be their God. But Mrs. Cary frankly acknowledged that the rich are the cause of the war and all their troubles; and says the rich men around Lewisburg won't let a southern soldier's wife have one bushel of corn to save their lives without the money, and expressed a desire for the Yankees to take all they had, which I suppose will be done...She says James Cary says he is just as good a southerner now as ever but doesn't like bullets. Lewisburg looks like a dead carcass. Nobody there but women and some old men and they look scared. I long for a letter from home but can't get one...My Company has the praise of being the best skirmishers in the Division and Col. Sickel gave the honorable title of 'Hero of East River Mountain,' and also on the battlefield."

Young continued, "Col. Sickel leaves us today for home. His time is out and I am very sorry for he is a good man; and if he had stayed with us he would have given Co. G a chance to win laurels of honor for herself. He told me that Co. G was the best Co. in the Brigade and he could trust it farther, and it was better able to take care of itself. Co. G doesn't like the 11th nor never will be satisfied in the Reg't. They think they are imposed upon and think there are some pet companies in the Reg't which get all the favors, which causes me much trouble and much hard feeling with the staff officers. But whenever Co. G is imposed upon the Col. hears from me very soon, hard feelings or no hard feelings. I would just as soon they would impose upon my children as my brave men who have left their homes to fight for their country. My dear and much loved little wife, I must close my imperfect letter. Excuse bad writing for I am sitting alone under a bush, writing on my knee. Oh, how I would love to get home. But my country needs me. My duty to God and my country is here. May God bless you and my dear children – Amen...William Enicks is not very well but some better. He will go with us. Serg't Van B. Morris is well and has command of a picket post up Greenbrier River with 17 of our men. Eli McDowell is in good health; as fat as a pig. Lieut. Clark Elkins is Adjutant of the 11th Va."[19]

## Lynchburg Campaign

Crook's Army of West Virginia stepped off toward Staunton in Augusta County, Virginia, on June 1. As they left Lewisburg moving northward, the division encountered almost a "continual skirmish with enemy scouts and guerillas." From June 2-6, Crook's forces traversed through White Sulphur Springs, moving also through Hot Springs in Bath County, to Warm Springs Mountain and Bath Springs. They also passed through Panther Gap, where they found Confederates posted in force. There, Colonel Frost recalled executing "a flank movement" during slight skirmishing, causing the town to be evacuated, and afterward continued their march to Goshen Station near the Virginia and Tennessee railroad and encamped for the night. Crook also ordered his men to destroy the railroad from Millborough to Craigsville and Pond Gap, which was "done with alacrity."

After Crook's troops returned to the Shenandoah Valley, and camped within eight miles of Staunton at Middlebrook on June 7, the Army of West Virginia met up with the divisions of Major Generals Julius Stahel and Jeremiah C. Sullivan. At that time, Crook's army came under the overall command of Major General David Hunter, who replaced Colonel Horatio Sickel with Colonel Jacob M. Campbell of the 54th Pennsylvania Infantry as the 3rd Brigade commander. The constant marching through the mountainous terrain and ongoing attacks from the Confederates was taking a toll on Crook's men; Private David Burrows, of

*Major General David Hunter*
*National Archives*

Company F, 13th West Virginia (2nd Brigade), described his comrades with "tired and worn faces, their ragged clothes, wondering if they would ever see home again…"

Burrows observed they "seemed so young and haggard, with so little understanding of the war they fought." Crook's Division next marched through Pond Gap where they encountered both McCausland's and Jenkins' Confederate brigades in strong positions. In a brief skirmish, they attempted to impede Crook's march, but "to no avail." Crook next burned Calf Pasture Bridge and destroyed about four miles of railroad tracks of the Virginia and Tennessee Central Railroad. On June 9, Crook's army engaged General John McCausland's brigade of 1,500 men, some two miles from Staunton, driving the Confederates beyond the town. Colonel Frost reported that his "Eleventh Regiment was ordered to deploy to the right of the road, and throwing forward a line of skirmishers, marched on the right of the road, skirmishing the entire distance to Middlebrook, where we were relieved, and marched in column to Brownsburg, Rockbridge County." Crook's casualties were minimal in this affair, and they continued marching all night toward Lexington.[20]

## Battle of Lexington – Hunter Burns VMI

Crook's force arrived near Lexington at 5:00 a.m. on June 11, where they found the Confederates waiting on the outskirts. Nestled in the extreme upper portion of the Shenandoah Valley, Lexington had hosted the Virginia Military Institute since 1839. When the Confederate pickets saw the Federal column briskly approaching, they opened a heavy fire of musketry and artillery. The 2nd Brigade under Colonel Carr White was sent to ford the river about two miles above town, which crossed and pushed Confederates through town until they retreated west toward Buchanan. The 1st Brigade's advance guard entered Lexington "on the heels of the enemy" and was the first Union force to enter the town.

John Young found time to write to his daughter Emily: "It is with extreme gratitude to God that I can say I am well and have been able to march at the head of my company thus far. But few other officers have done this. We started from Lewisburg the first day of June, and march through Greenbrier, Allegheny, Rockbridge, and into Augusta County, 105 miles, driving Jackson, McCausland, Echols, and Horten before us towards Staunton, and when we got here General Hunter had whipped them and run them over the Blue Ridge. The truth is we have driven the whole Rebel force out of West Virginia. The citizens here say the South is whipped and the valley is willing to give up. But, O, mercy, how badly the women are scared about their yellow negroes, for fear the Yankees will take them off. They seem to be willing for the Yankees to stay here if they will let the negroes alone. I think the Yankees will stay, negroes or no negroes. We have had very little fighting since we left Lewisburg...But I understand this morning that General Hunter will start after the flying Rebels this evening with his whole force, some twenty thousand men, and I expect the next time you hear from me it will be from Richmond. The Rebs here say that if General Grant takes Richmond the Rebellion is gone up. He is sure to take it, and I think the time is not far distant when we can return home to our loved ones in peace."

Young further supposed: "I think we will go from here to Fredericksburg and from there to Richmond. The Rebel citizens have all run over the Blue Ridge, especially the men, but where next I don't know, for we will follow them up. I don't think there will be anything left for the Rebels to live on after we leave this valley. Just think of twenty or thirty thousand men and horses eating off a country like this, and too after the Rebels have gleaned the country before us. No Rebel force can subsist after we leave and besides this all the railroads are broken up that lead into this valley. I don't think you need fear another raid in Kanawha valley, unless it may be a small one from Wytheville for we have captured nearly all their supplies, broken up their communications and, I think, we will either capture them or drive them into the Gulf states. They cant turn back for the want of transportation. They must go ahead for their rights. I am truly glad that Captain [Edgar] Blundon was left in the valley...We have some men left at Meadow Bluff sick and Silas J. Davis left as nurse. Tell Captain Blundon that his company was mounted this morning on captured horses. I have not received a letter from home since I left. All others have. I cant tell why. Perhaps you have no paper. I will write every opportunity. Goodbye Emma, for this time – may God bless my dear family."[21]

General Hunter ordered the Virginia Military Institute burned on June 12, including the "professor's buildings." During a series of raids through West Virginia in 1863, Confederates burned the home of Governor Francis H. Pierpont. In retaliation, Hunter also ordered Virginia Governor John Letcher's home burned. Nearby Letcher's home was Confederate General Thomas J. "Stonewall" Jackson's former residence, but it was unharmed. Captain Young visited Jackson's grave that afternoon while VMI burned. Colonel David H. Strother, Hunter's Chief of Staff, rationalized this destruction, writing that VMI was "a most dangerous establishment where treason was systematically taught." 2nd Lieutenant John S. Cunningham was formerly in Young's company but stayed with the 13th West Virginia after Company G transferred to the 11th West Virginia. Cunningham wrote to his wife, "All the public buildings connected with the institution are being destroyed. Quite a large number of guns and small arms were captured...Tell Mrs. [John] Overshiner there are no casualties in Co. G, Capt. Young's Co. that I know of." Lieutenant John S. Cunningham was not the least bit bothered by the burning; he later disclosed to his wife that he had helped himself to a book and magnet from VMI as "mementoes of that place." Crook stayed in Lexington until June 14, when General Hunter ordered a renewed pursuit of the Confederates, traveling twenty-six miles that day to Buchanan, Virginia.[22]

*Ruins of Virginia Military Institute after Hunter's Raid, 1864*
*Public Domain*

## Battle of Lynchburg

Buchanan was occupied by a division of Union cavalry under Major General William W. Averell. When Crook arrived, the bridge spanning the James River was still burning, and Crook noted it would have "probably...been destroyed but for the efforts of our soldiers in subduing the flames." On June 15, Averell received word that a large body of Confederate infantry was nearby at Balcony Falls, gaining on Crook's left flank and rear. On June 16, Crook's army moved to Liberty, seven miles away. The entire division "thoroughly destroyed the railroad from Liberty to Big Otter Creek by tearing up the track, burning the ties, and bending the rails." Prior to dawn the next morning, Crook marched to New London, where the Confederates were massed. On June 17, Crook's Division was in front as the Union forces advanced some eight miles into Lynchburg and pushed the Confederate pickets back toward the town.

Colonel Jacob M. Campbell reported the 3rd Brigade was "...ordered to the front and formed in line of battle on the left of, and at right angle with, the turnpike. After forming we advanced on the enemy, driving them into their entrenchments, distant about one mile and a half from where we first encountered their line. Darkness having overtaken us, we ceased to press the enemy farther and merely maintained the position we had gained." Colonel Daniel Frost described how the 11th West Virginia "marched to within three miles of Lynchburg, where we engaged the enemy, driving him from his position, and at dark held our advanced position near the principal works of the enemy. Companies B and G of my regiment were thrown forward as skirmishers and advanced past a battery of rebel artillery, the enemy retreating. Finding that our main column had halted, our skirmishers retired with a loss of 3 wounded and 2 missing. Our regiment and brigade held the advance line for an hour, when we were relieved by a brigade of the First Infantry Division; fell back a few rods and slept on our arms until morning...We were relieved about 9 p.m. by the First Brigade, of the First Division, and fell back about 400 yards, where we remained for the night."[23]

That night, Crook's troops replenished their cartridge boxes and slept on arms. The next morning the Confederates attacked Union lines, and Crook was sent some three miles to the right, with intentions of turning their left flank. He found this task impossible and returned under a heavy artillery fire to support Sullivan; however, before Colonel Campbell could reform the brigade front, the main Union lines began retiring "somewhat broken...and in confusion, the enemy advancing against it." He hastily organized his line and advanced, hoping to prevent the Confederates from gaining the crest of the hill, while taking heavy "grape and canister" fire. Colonel Daniel Frost described this phase of fighting, "Our brigade charged the enemy and drove him to his rifle-pits. Here the right giving way, and our brigade being exposed to a cross-fire of musketry, grape and canister, we were obliged to retire about thirty paces to a new line of battle, which was held until orders were received to fall back."

*Colonel Jacob M. Campbell*
*courtesy of Col. Jacob M. Campbell*
*Camp #14, Sons of Union Veterans*

The 3rd Brigade commander, Colonel Jacob M. Campbell continued his account, "We succeeded, however, in driving the enemy down the hill and across a deep ravine, and from there to their intrenchments on the elevated ground beyond, at the same time gaining a position for ourselves comparatively sheltered from the enemy. My line having become somewhat broken by passing through the thick underbrush and in crossing a deep ditch at the bottom of the ravine, I halted my command. I reformed it and again advanced upon the enemy, pressing close upon their works, but were met with such a storm of grape and canister that we were compelled to fall back to the spot where I had reformed my command. We remained in this position, keeping the enemy in their intrenchments, with occasional firing between sharpshooters and skirmishers until 8:30 p.m., when we were ordered to withdraw, which was done in good order, and we took up our line of march for Liberty by way of New London, which latter place we pass through at daybreak on the morning of the 19th. Continuing our march, we arrived at Liberty at 6 p.m., where we encamped for the night." Frost further reported losing one lieutenant and "...5 enlisted men killed, 16 wounded, and 10 missing."[24]

Crook's Division slept on arms briefly, and at midnight marched overnight toward Buford's Gap. There they found the Confederate 3rd Corps under Major General Jubal Early and engaged at approximately 3:00 p.m. Early attempted to flank Crook's Division but failed. Colonel Frost noted his regiment "marched all night and day, the men suffering severely from heat, hunger and fatigue, but bearing all without complaint." Crook withdrew near dark and went toward Salem, where he arrived on June 21. There was only minor skirmishing along the way. En route, hundreds of men fell out of the march from sheer exhaustion in the scorching heat, and Crook halted to rest a few hours. In the afternoon, he resumed marching toward the eastern slope of Catawba Mountain and camped for the night. On June 22, Crook marched through the towns of New Castle, Red Sweet Springs and White Sulphur Springs. On their way through the tedious march, Private David Burrows, Company F, 13th West Virginia, wrote in his diary how he had been "torturing" himself, daydreaming about "home cooked rolls, friend chicken and fresh coffee." A few days later, Burrows recalled how the men were so hungry by then that when they came upon the remains of a recently slaughtered beef cow that was full of worms, they simply cut it up and cooked it. He noted that despite the unsanitary sight, it made a "delightful meal." Crook's forces marched through Lewisburg, West Virginia, on June 25 and encamped at nearby Meadow Bluff that night.

## Crook returns to the Kanawha Valley

The next day, June 26, Lieutenant John S. Cunningham of the 13th West Virginia wrote to his wife near Sewell Mountain, "We are now on our way down to the Kanawha Valley. The Division is on the march down. I am well only would like to take tea with you as I am very hungry...save all the newspapers for me I have not seen a paper of later date than May 27. I do not know what is going on in the outer world." Crook's Division left Gauley Bridge that morning and arrived at Camp Piatt June 29. His troops were exhausted, famished, and many men were still without shoes, with trousers "worn to threads." Young wrote in his diary that they marched eighteen miles in heavy thunderstorms to Dogwood Flats, with much of the command still scattered along the road some ten miles to the rear. They finally met the supply trains, and Young was happy to see his "Boys are making good use of the hard bread. Never were men more worn out than ours at this time." He described Crook's army as "much demoralized," noting that even General Sullivan, their division commander, was "two days in our rear entirely destitute."

After resting a few days, Crook's Division returned to Charleston with no further contact with Confederates along the way other than "an occasional bushwhacker," although they were still "strained for provisions, but came in good shape." During the previous two months, Crook estimated his men traveled an estimated distance of 322 miles from Staunton on June 10. The 3rd Brigade lost twenty-nine men killed in action, one hundred thirty-four wounded, and twenty-seven men were missing on the campaign. Colonel Frost estimated the 11th West Virginia marched a total distance of 672 miles between April 30 and June 30. The 11th West Virginia lost one officer, five enlisted killed, twenty enlisted wounded, and six enlisted captured or missing, for thirty-two total casualties at Lynchburg; Frost further summarized the campaign, "...having marched a distance of 412 miles, in the heart of the enemy's country, over roads rendered dusty by three weeks of drought, without rations much of the time, and with an enemy constantly in our front and rear. The endurance of the men is wonderful, and the spirit of devotion to their cause, which enabled them to bear all the hardships they have seen, is worthy of favorable comment."[25]

During the interim between Crook's Dublin expedition in May and July, a number of changes occurred in the Department of West Virginia. Now known as the "Middle Department," Major General Edward O.C. Ord took command, and Major General Lewis Wallace was given command of the 8th Corps. Note that while Crook's command is commonly identified as the 8th Army Corps in 1864, in reality, the U.S. Army 8th Corps served as guards for the Baltimore and Ohio Railroad system at that time. The Army of West Virginia then had little, if any, contact with the 8th Corps while in the Shenandoah Valley. As many of the units in Crook's Divisions had earlier served as railroad guards, they are often confused with the 8th Corps, but they were two different organizations in 1864. Crook's immediate superior was still Major General David Hunter, with his three divisions then organized as follows: Colonel Joseph Thoburn commanded the 1st Division, Colonel Isaac Duval led the 2nd Division and

Colonel James Mulligan had the 3rd Division.

The latter contained two brigades: the 1st was led by Colonel Thomas M. Harris, former commander of the 10th West Virginia Infantry, and the 2nd Brigade, comprising the 11th West Virginia, 15th West Virginia and 54th Pennsylvania. Within a few days of arriving at Camp Piatt, Crook also consolidated the 3rd Brigade into the 1st Division under Colonel Daniel Frost. Lieutenant Colonel Van H. Bukey then took command of the 11th West Virginia. John Young was home on leave from July 1-5, and when he returned and heard that Bukey was in command, he was most displeased; he and Bukey did not see eye to eye on many issues. Prior

*Colonel Van H. Bukey*
*West Virginia State Archives*

to going home, Young noted in his diary on June 29 that the regiment marched off, but he remained behind to bring up his sick men; the task proved arduous, "Had a great deal of trouble with them – had ten together" and covered twenty-two miles. On June 30, Young's son-in-law, Captain Edgar Blundon, was appointed as commander of the Union garrison at Guyandotte. Blundon took his Company F there to establish his headquarters; Young had still not heard from him in weeks.

Following his retreat from Lynchburg, Confederate Major General Jubal Early moved toward Martinsburg and engaged in heavy skirmishing with Union troops there, under General Franz Sigel, on July 3. Crook was ordered to gather his men and return to Camp Piatt immediately; as they arrived, his men began making preparations for another long campaign. Lieutenant John S. Cunningham, 13th West Virginia, wrote on July 8, "I presume that today or tomorrow we will receive marching orders to go probably to Martinsburg. I leave my silk velvet vest, dress coat and pants and sash with some cartridges for my pistol...with the family that lives in the house Mr. Band lived in before he moved down to Coalsmouth. I think you had better let Father have say $600 in money when the sale takes place to pay on that land...I will furnish you with plenty of money when you wish to go North. You need not say to Father that I advance the money yet, because I will inform him in time."

The Army of West Virginia arrived at Martinsburg July 9 and continued toward

Harpers Ferry. The same day, Union forces engaged Confederates under Major General Jubal Early at Monocacy, Maryland, as Early sought to move toward Washington, D.C., in hopes of capturing the United States capital. Early caused quite a scare in the capital city, and Lincoln himself was especially anxious about the Confederates encroaching on their defenses. Early was close enough so that his men could see the church spires and other buildings in town, but never got into city limits and were repulsed. Crook's command did not participate in the battle at Monocacy, as they were still at Harpers Ferry. Crook soon received orders to join Major General Philip Sheridan's command in Maryland to assist in pursuing Early on July 15; Sheridan would soon take command of the Army of the Shenandoah on August 4.[26]

## Battle of Snicker's Ferry (Cool Springs)
## Death of Colonel Daniel Frost

Crook's force was soon on the road from Harpers Ferry into Maryland, when an observer near the Point of Rocks remarked they were "all footsore and used up" from the previous campaign. While at Hillsborough, Crook received orders to begin immediate pursuit of the Confederates who were near Purcellville, and he also received some good news the army commissary sent "45,000 rations of hard bread and 30,000 rations of beef" that was to arrive that day on the north side of the Potomac River, just waiting for his army to retrieve them. Crook noted his intentions were to return to Martinsburg if he did not encounter the enemy. The Army of the Kanawha re-crossed the Potomac River near Berlin and marched to Purcellville on July 17, with word that an attack was imminent near Cool Springs, a location also known more commonly as Snicker's Ferry. Crook began his movement through Snicker's Gap before dawn the next morning. That afternoon, Crook crossed the Shenandoah River at Snicker's Ferry and attacked the Confederates, meeting strong resistance two miles below the ford. In hours of intense fighting, Crook barely managed to push Early's forces back across the Shenandoah River by nightfall, with heavy losses including Colonel Daniel Frost, who was mortally wounded leading his brigade in repeated assaults attempting to breach Early's lines. Frost was an ardent Unionist who served as Speaker of the House of Delegates in the Restored Government of Virginia in 1861 through 1862. After his wounding, Frost was taken to a nearby farmhouse and wrote his last will and testament. Prior to his death, he tried to contact a nearby family member who was a staunch Confederate supporter. They refused, and Frost died near midnight on July 19.

Captain Young noted in his diary on July 21 that Crook's men were going about the gruesome task of burying the dead and discovered many of the wounded had laid on the field two days "without help." The 11th West Virginia did not otherwise suffer any losses. Afterward, a controversy emerged as rumors spread among Colonel Joseph Thoburn's division that General James Ricketts' division had refused to support them, causing an embarrassing defeat on the field. Rumor had it that Major General Horatio Wright of the 6th Corps had ordered General Crook to attack without consulting General Hunter, whom he had supposedly lost contact with for two days. This was deemed part of a self-serving scheme intended to prevent Thoburn from fighting effectively. Although simplified herein, Crook was essentially blamed for taking matters into his own hands, though he in fact sent a dispatch to General Hunter that clearly stated his intention was to aggressively pursue Early, noting he would not "slip away" this time. There were no ambiguous qualifiers in his dispatch to Hunter, such as "if practicable," etc., so it appears that General Crook clearly intended to aggressively pursue a fight with Early consistent with Hunter's orders.[27]

Following Colonel Frost's death, Colonel John P. Linton was given command of the 3rd Brigade, although he was also wounded shortly after Frost. The brigade command then fell upon Colonel William G. Ely

*Colonel Daniel E. Frost*
*Courtesy of Richard A. Wolfe*

of the 18th Connecticut Infantry. Crook next moved toward Winchester on July 18, passing through Berryville where he encamped for the night. On July 21, the Army of West Virginia received 150,000 rounds of ammunition and 100,000 short rations sent from General Hunter's command. Freshly supplied, Crook's Division then continued toward Winchester, arriving about one mile south of Kernstown, where they encamped that evening. Kernstown was roughly four miles from Winchester, where Jubal Early's

Confederates waited behind heavily entrenchments on the outskirts of town.

On July 22, the 11th West Virginia was reassigned to the 3rd Brigade, 1st Division under Colonel Joseph Thoburn. He was an Irish born Ohio resident, who, like Colonel Thomas M. Harris of the 10th West Virginia, was also a physician. Thoburn previously served as surgeon of a ninety-day regiment, the 1st West Virginia Infantry, in early 1861; during that tenure, he once treated General B.F. Kelley's wound received at the battle of Philippi. He was later commissioned as Colonel of the 1st West Virginia Infantry in August 1861. The 3rd Brigade was formerly under Colonel Jacob M. Campbell and in addition to the 11th West Virginina now included the 23rd Illinois (five companies), 54th Pennsylvania, and the 10th and 15th West Virginia Regiments.[28]

## Kernstown / Second Battle of Winchester

Very early on July 23, Crook received news that a large force of Early's men was advancing toward Winchester from Newtown, and by 9:00 a.m. the Army of West Virginia was formed and waiting for them. Captain Young wrote in his diary that the 11th West Virginia was lying behind a stone wall. Crook engaged at noon and drove the Confederates back as far as Middletown, seven miles beyond Newtown, where he discovered that nearly all of Early's army was massed in his front. Young noted they "maneuvered all day" as Crook's command lost 200 men in the action. Crook returned to Kernstown that evening, and Company G was again posted behind a stone wall, sleeping on arms throughout the night. Skirmishing occurred until early the next morning, as the two armies probed each other's lines. Colonel Thoburn received orders at dawn to move his division into the front as quickly as possible, as Union pickets were then pressed in by Confederates, who drove them back. Within twenty minutes Thoburn was

*Col. Joseph Thoburn*
*Courtesy of Suzanne Spezik*

near the front, and his division quickly took position in some woods to the right and rear of Kernstown, where they had occupied the day previous with strongly barricaded flanks and front defenses supported by rail fences and heavy logs. Colonel Ely recalled: "...At this time the left of General Crook's command was skirmishing heavily. Immediately after taking our first position, I was notified that we should be called upon to charge. We prepared to execute the order by taking down the fences in our front. The next order was to move the left of my brigade forward by right angles with the road and move the whole brigade farther to the right. This movement placed the First and Twelfth Virginia Volunteers within easy range of the enemy's skirmish fire."

Young further recalled, "The line of skirmishers...was pushed forward from the Second Brigade to protect its front and was hotly engaged. The forces on our left [Colonel Mulligan's] were then firing from line of battle. The enemy showed no disposition to attack us strongly in front, but rather a desire for us to advance, while we could see them moving forces along the brow of the hills on our right, preparatory to a flank movement. Orders then came from Colonel Thoburn to move the whole brigade quickly by the right flank toward the hills. While executing this order the enemy annoyed us so much by their fire that I was compelled to order the regiments, as they passed over the rising ground, to face by the left flank and fire by rank into an orchard where the rebels were strongly posted. On reaching the hills Colonel Thoburn ordered me to move the brigade by the left of regiments to the rear." General Crook also recalled: "I repulsed their force twice and was driving them when they partially turned my left and threw it into some confusion. At the same time a heavy column was moving around my right, and I gave the order to fall back. My left soon reformed, and the whole line moved back in good order; the enemy pressing both my flanks and center hard all the time...I fell back to Bunker Hill, arriving there between 9 and 10 p.m., part of the enemy's force camping within ten miles of me."

Captain Young also described, "I came out of the battle at Winchester unhurt, with only two bullet holes through my pants, and they're brand new... We were nearly surrounded when I received orders to fall back. The whole command left me on the battlefield, but I made my way out through a shower of bullets and shells. The whole Regiment had a narrow escape." Occasionally, soldiers would recall more details over time and mention them in later letters home following a large battle, as Young later reminisced: "After Colonel Frost was killed and Lieut. Col. Bukey wounded I took command of the Regiment and had command of it at the Winchester fight, and a hard fight it was. The Rebels outflanked us and gave our men such a gauling [galling] fire from right to left they gave way in confusion and scattered the 11th and 15th Regiment that we did not get them together again until we got to Williamsport. Whole command left me on the field. I don't blame the boys for making their escape. Corporal [Wyatt] Brisco was killed. Sam Landers wounded, William Racer was hurt with a shell."[29]

Crook next ordered the Army of West Virginia to form line of battle on the left of Colonel James A. Mulligan's division; the 11th and 15th West Virginia were detached from the 3rd Brigade and posted on the left of the brigade as skirmishers, a task for which they were becoming particularly well-known among Crook's troops. Captain James W. Myers of the 11th West Virginia wrote: "We occupied a position on the left of the road leading to Kernstown, and at the commencement of the engagement I was ordered with the Fifteenth West Virginia Volunteers forward, the two regiments being detached from the brigade. We advanced, skirmishing, to a stone fence, about a quarter of a mile beyond Kernstown, where we remained, constantly exchanging fire with the enemy, until ordered... to retire, when we did so, rallying behind a second line of stone fence, where we remained a short time and were again ordered to retire to near Kernstown, which we did. We remained here but a short time, when the whole line retiring and the enemy appearing on our flank back to the point north of Winchester near the fortifications. The retreat having become general, the command became somewhat scattered and retreated in some confusion to Bunker Hill, where the most of the command was collected and encamped for the night."

Young wrote further, "The next day we marched to Martinsburg. The fact that this command was detached from the brigade in the early part of the engagement, thus leaving us without knowledge of a point on which to rally, I consider a reason for the confusion arising. Some of the officers and men were cut off from the command and did not join it until its arrival at Martinsburg." The Army of West Virginia marched all night and at approximately 4:00 a.m. was caught in a heavy thunderstorm, but the drenched troops pressed on. Upon arrival at Martinsburg July 25, the 3rd Brigade found two large empty warehouses, which were promptly occupied by the soaked soldiers who made coffee and dried their clothes. Crook next moved toward Williamsport, Maryland, and remained there a few days so the army could obtain fresh clothing. The 11th West Virginia was posted as guards to the wagon trains during that brief respite from marching. Also, during that time, several hundred men thought to be missing were accounted for as wounded. On July 25, George Crook was promoted to Major General and given command of the Department of West Virginia, although he did not transfer into that role until nearly a month later. On July 27, Young noted the Army of West Virginia camped on the battlefield where "many of our brave soldiers slept." They crossed Antietam Creek next morning and went over Maryland Heights, covering twenty-two miles that day. Young recorded in his diary that evening he had forty men present in Company G on July 28, with ten out sick, noting both "Men and officers worn out."

## August 1864 – Constant Skirmishing

Thus far, Lincoln and Grant's scheme to drive the Confederates from the Shenandoah Valley's rich wheat grain harvest had failed, and Grant was pressuring Hunter for results. For example, Private Nathaniel "Nat" Turner of the 4th North Carolina Infantry, Rodes' Division, stated: "Some dwellings were burnt, and many barns with large quantities of grain, forage & c., were consumed. They pressed all the bacon and beef killed all the hogs, sheep, cattle, poultry... whether needed or not...Our corps is faring sumptuously. We get fine new flour and beef of the best quality in abundance, to say nothing of the 'roast-neers' and apples, no small item. I never saw men more gay and cheerful, they evidence have the utmost confidence in Early, who is renowned for his caution and unexpected flank movements, and more for his incessant marching. This Corps has marched hardly less than 1500 miles since the opening of the campaign, yet the men are hearty, generally well clothed and shod, and so much soiled that the assessor would be perfectly justifiable in putting them down as real estate..." General Hunter ordered General Phil Sheridan to take command of the Department of West Virginia on August 6; however, a day later, President Lincoln removed Hunter, and placed Sheridan in command of the Middle Military Division, which included not only West Virginia, but also the Middle Department, the Department of the Susquehanna, and the Middle Military Division. This also meant Sheridan now had command of the Army of the Shenandoah.[30]

Colonel Thoburn's 1st Division relocated from Harpers Ferry to nearby Charles Town in the first few days of August. The 11th West Virginia remained in Crook's 1st Division, 3rd Brigade. From his camp near Wolfsville, Maryland, Young resumed correspondence August 1, writing of his experiences in the recent campaign, which included a brief tenure commanding the regiment when the two senior officers were injured. Knowing his family was worried not having heard from him in several weeks, he began: "Dear Wife and Children: I expect you are anxious to hear from me and to know my whereabouts. We arrived at Martinsburg... proceeded at once to Harpers Ferry. From there to Point of Rocks, waded the Potomac, passed through Loudoun Co., Virginia, to Snickers Gap. Here we found the Rebels in force. After resting two days, Crook crossed the Shenandoah river and attacked them; and after several hours hard fighting we were compelled to recross the river with considerable loss. Here Colonel [Daniel] Frost fell mortally wounded. Lieut. Colonel [Van] Bukey much injured by the fall of his horse, which was shot through. After this, command of the Regiment devolved on me. The next day the Rebs fell back to Winchester. We followed them, passing over the battle ground of Bull's Run. In our fight at Snickers Gap, Company G fought well."

Young chronicled further: "We were out as skirmishers, and never did men fight better without loss. In Company G not one man hurt. But on the 23rd the Rebels attacked us at Winchester and after hard skirmishing we drove them back with some loss. But on the morning of the 24th they again attacked us with great fury and after fighting all day we had again to fall back...Sam Landers was shot through the knee and hand. Wm. Emicks [William Enoch] wounded by the concussion of a shell but now is well and with the company. Sam Landers is in a hospital at Baltimore. We fought the Rebs at Bunkershill [Bunker Hill] and at Martinsburg, but it was no use, they outnumbered us four to one. We fell back to Williamsport and from there to Harpers Ferry and we thought we would have some rest there, but no, the Rebs are out in Maryland and Pennsylvania stealing and robbing the country, and 'old George' as the boys call General Crook, can't rest while the Rebs are so near. The whole command is worn out. Company C and Company D in our Regiment report from eight to ten men present. Company G this morning reports forty-one and two officers. I have had my health well since I left home, but worn out and tired down. Capt. [James T.] Myers the ranking Captain is now in command of the Regiment, which is a great relief to me." Captain James Myers commanded Company B, and had worked his way up through the ranks, enlisting as a private in 1861.

Continuing his account, Young wrote, "We generally have quite a number of good officers when there is no danger...I have never heard from home since I left. I sent four hundred dollars home by our Chaplain and considerable money for the soldiers' families, which I hope you will forward as soon as you get it. We are now in Maryland where we have plenty of everything we want. The roads are lined with ladies cheering the boys as they tug along, bestowing on the poor soldiers, pies, milk, cold water – in fact nearly everything they want. The boys from Winfield are generally well. J.M. Jones has not joined the company yet. I saw him in Martinsburg but he slipped me and where he is now I can't tell. I suppose he is somewhere playing the fiddle. There were a great many on our march yesterday and the day before who fell with sunstroke and died. Alex Henson fell but we carried him to a house and saved him. He was much better this morning. I left William Pauley to nurse him. He will get well. I am satisfied that Wyatt Brisco had a presentiment of his death. He gave J.M. Smith his money and papers, and also his wife's address, saying that he would be killed. But he died like a hero, fighting for his country, and liberty."

Young was also aware of continued threat from guerillas and Confederate raids on his family at home in Winfield, "We are now camped in Wolfsville. The women have baked all their flour for the boys, and wish they had more. Where we will go from here I can't tell but as the Rebels move so will George. The citizens say that the Rebs stole about four hundred head of horses yesterday ten miles from this place. We hear that old Morgan is in Kanawha Valley playing wild with the people. This is what I expected but I don't believe it. I don't think they have force to be everywhere at once...I must close for the want of time...P.S. –I saw...Uncle John D. Young at Snickers Gap. Uncle Charles' John was shot in the back of the head and the ball came out at his mouth. I mean Blue

*2nd Lt. John D. Young*
*Co. L, 7th West Virginia Cavalry*
*West Virginia State Archives*

Creek John Young. He will get well. I suppose that we lost at Winchester, some twelve hundred men, mostly cavalry. The Rebels made some most furious charges on our retreat. Captured a great many of our men and some artillery. But we fought them from Winchester to Martinsburg and fought them there until the trains got away."[31]

Young's paternal uncle, John D. Young, entered the service on May 24, 1864, at age sixty-four years. He received a commission as 2nd Lieutenant in Company L, 7th West Virginia Cavalry and was later placed on disabled service at Charleston, West Virginia, from December 30, 1865. He also refers to another John Young, who was the son of Charles Young from Blue Creek, West Virginia, in Kanawha County; however, that individual does not appear on muster rolls or in the 11th or 13th West Virginia Infantry or the 7th West Virginia Cavalry regiment's service records. Young also mentioned a cousin, Charles Wesley "Wes" Young, who was aged nineteen years and from Blue Creek in Kanawha County. He served in Company E, 13th West Virginia Infantry. Charles was not John D. Young's son but rather a nephew. Young often refers to "Wes" in his letters. Wesley Young enlisted October 9, 1862 at Point Pleasant; he was later hospitalized March – April 1863 at Point Pleasant and promoted to corporal on November 1, 1864.

On August 3, Crook's army marched to Frederick, Maryland, where Young wrote the next morning: "Dear Wife: After a hard day's march yesterday we halted at this place after marching 24 miles by 3 clock PM. I am well at present only I want rest, and I understand that we are to rest here one month. We can't rest too soon for the whole command is worn out, and many brave men have given out and died on the march. Company G is scattered from Parkersburg to this place, only forty five men present this morning, but this is double what other Companies report. I think it is time that General George [Crook] would give us rest. We are as anxious as our General to get the Rebels, but we can't stand everything. The whole command of the Department of West Va. is here and must have rest. The 13th Va. is here. She lost heavily at Winchester. Look out – I understand that General [Jubal] Early says that West Virginia is an enemy to the Southern Confederacy and that he will burn everything in it. Col. McCausland has been burning in Maryland and would not permit the women to take out their clothes. He turned hundreds of women and children out of house and home, without anything to eat or to wear."

Young continued: "I wonder if those honorable Rebels in Winfield will approve this? [John] McCausland burned Secessionists houses as well as Union. General Early says these men who stay at home and take the Union oath are the most detestable and hateful of all mankind, and can't be trusted, and he would kill them as quick as he would a Vermont Yankee. I would like to hear from home very much indeed. Not one word have I had since I left. I would like to know what the Rebels are doing in the Kanawha Valley, and what the 7th Cavalry is doing in the way of keeping out the Rebels. But I know the home Rebels are the worst enemies you have. It is the case in Maryland and in Virginia, east of the Blue Ridge. Those men and women protected by our arms are our worst enemies. In Loudon county, Virginia, we found a village called Lovettsville, that had not a Rebel in it, and they say that they suffer more by the home Rebels than the soldiers; and men and women who profess to be Union. We are now camped on the east side of the Meonty [Monty] River, two miles from Frederick City, Maryland."[32]

Lieutenant General Ulysses S. Grant, the overall Union commander, ordered Major General David Hunter to concentrate all his available forces at Harpers Ferry on August 5, leaving only those troops serving as railroad guards or those protecting public property at their post. Grant met Hunter there on August 7 and according to Captain Young, he also "visited the troops in camp." Crook conducted a division inspection on August 8, and fifteen men were found to have damaged rifles and drew new ones. Young noted Company G had nine men missing or Absent without Leave (AWOL). Grant had received reliable intelligence indicating the Confederates were moving north of the Potomac River in great force, and he was anticipating a large engagement. Grant also knew President Lincoln was concerned about a Confederate push toward Washington, D.C., and directed General Hunter to attack them "wherever found" and follow them south of the Potomac River, pushing them toward the Shenandoah Valley, and to keep the enemy "always in sight..." The 3rd Brigade continued to operate in the vicinity of Harpers Ferry, with Crook's force posted at Charles Town participating in numerous light skirmishes and various reconnaissance patrols.

## Strasburg

On August 6 at nearby Cumberland, Maryland, Companies A, E, F and H of the 11th West Virginia were experiencing heavy skirmishing. A few days later, they again engaged while patrolling at New Creek, West Virginia, receiving "...much credit for their gallantry in defense of those places." The Department of West Virginia was renamed as the Army of West Virginia August 7; from August 9-13, Crook marched toward Cedar Creek, arriving there late in the afternoon on the latter date. Upon arrival, Company G was "fortified in a vineyard overlooking Strasburg," where Young noted Private Joel Nickels was wounded by skirmishers. Young also indicated the "Rebels charged our lines, our men falling back," while Crook described the fight as a "slight skirmish with the Confederates, with the Federals driving those still remaining on the north bank of the creek to the other side." Skirmishing continued again early the next morning, as they marched toward Strasburg. Arriving there that night, they slept on arms. The next morning, Crook found the Confederates had advanced a brigade along a hill overlooking the town and were attempting to drive in his skirmish line. He ordered Colonel Isaac H. Duval's 2nd Division to confront the Confederates, who repulsed them after a brisk fight resulting in six killed and thirty wounded. Afterward in mid-August, Colonel Jacob M. Campbell, who commanded the 3rd Brigade, was replaced by Colonel Thomas M. Harris, the former physician turned warrior who raised and formerly commanded the 10th West Virginia. The 3rd Brigade continued in the 1st Division under Colonel Joseph Thoburn.[33]

## Charles Town and Hall Town

Crook's army encountered numerous small skirmishes and patrols in that area over the next few days, including a small action at Charles Town on August 21. Crook moved to counter Confederate Major General Robert Rode's Division as they marched from Stephenson's Depot to Bruce Town. The Army of West Virginia continued a series of patrols and counter-movements against General Jubal Early's army until August 24, when General Crook was ordered to reconnoiter the Hall Town area. He discovered a large part of the Confederate army lodged there. With the 11th West Virginia in the advance of the army as skirmishers, and Captain Young in charge of the skirmish line, Crook sent orders to make a "feint of attack movement in that direction." The 3rd Brigade attacked Rode's force first and quickly pushed the Confederate skirmish lines backward. Crook recalled that his "...two brigades in position behind a line of works made of rails, logs, and earth, were completely routed...our loss was 17 killed 124 wounded, and 1 missing." General Phil Sheridan later recalled that Crook drove "...the enemy's advance line, punishing him severely and capturing twenty men." The weak Confederate resistance there also caused Sheridan to question their confidence, suggesting that "...the enemy appears in doubt as to what he can do." Crook's forces remained at Hall Town afterward.

From there, Captain Young wrote to his daughter Emily on August 23 and described events at Hall Town: "My heart was made glad last night by receiving a letter from your Ma and one from yourself. I am truly thankful to the Lord for his kindness to us. I have been well ever since I left home but am nearly worn out. My Company is also much worn and tired. We have had hard times since we left the Valley but we are in a good cause and the boys don't complain about hardships. But I think it is hard that they have to leave home to fight traitors, and the home traitors protected. Well, Emma, I have just come off the Battle field. Our Brigade was ordered out to attack the Rebel works at 2 p.m. The 10th, 11th, and 15th Va. took the center. I don't know who was on our left but they had a hard fight. How many killed and wounded I can't tell. The 15th Va. had 2 killed. We none. We have been fighting here three days. We have thrown up breast works that reach from the Shenandoah River to Hall town some 6 miles. We have a great many men here, enough I think to whip the Rebels here. Our fight today lasted two hours, and was very severe while it lasted."

He continued, "A great many must have been killed on our left. The guns are still firing in our front. We expect a big fight here soon, and how we will come out God only knows; but one thing I will do, that is I will trust in the Lord who has blessed me from youth until now. How thankful I feel to God for his goodness to me. In Him will I trust. My dear Emma, He was my hope in youth, so will He be in my old age. We are ordered to have early supper. We will be sent out on the skirmish line tonight, which is a constant shooting day and night. Joel Knuckols [Knuckles] was wounded at Strawsburg [Strasburg] in the arm and sent to the hospital. I have only 48 men with me this morning. Serg. [John] Overshiner, Joseph Griffith, and J.W. Campbell were sent to the hospital yesterday (fever). A great many of my men have been discharged from the Hospital but can't get to me. Milt Jones is reported a deserter. I saw him at Martinsburg but he dodged me and took the cars and went to New Creek. I am glad that the 7th Va. will remain in the Valley. As supper is about ready, I must stop writing...Tell Capt. [John] Bowyers not to sell Mr. [George] Summers property if he thinks there will be any difficulty about it." In common camp parlance during the Civil War, soldiers referred to their friends whom they usually prepared meals with as their "mess" or "mess mates," as Young noted in the latter communication with his daughter. He had earlier purchased ten acres of land from George Summers at Winfield, where Paulina and his family had relocated in 1863. Young contacted Summers about selling part of his land plot sometime in winter 1864 in order to provide his family with financial support.[34]

Also, that day, Young penned a quick note to Paulina: "I suppose you are anxious to hear from me and I assure you that I am fully as anxious to hear from home. I have not received one letter from home since I left Kanawha. I am well and have been well since I left home, but am much word and tired out. We have fought two battles since we came here, and got whipped both times...I have very little time to write. The mail goes out at 5 PM. We are here in sight of the Rebel lines. We have been fighting them for a week and while I am writing the guns are playing freely within a few hundred yards of us. We are fortified near Charlestown and the musketry and artillery have been busy all day. Our boys charged them yesterday and drove them more than a mile. But this morning they are back again, firing away. What will become of us God only knows, but the God in whom I trust will do right. I sent you four hundred dollars by Brothers Lions. Did you get it. Also one hundred for William Tackett, for you to keep for him. Did you get it? I paid Mr. Wilson today for Ben's board...We expect to fight hard battle here in a few days. Nothing more at present – Excuse bad writing I can't write while the Rebs are shooting at our men..."

During a brief hiatus near Hall Town, Lieutenant John S. Cunningham of the 13th West Virginia Infantry corresponded with his wife also: "Day before yesterday evening just as this Regt was ordered out on the skirmish line I received a letter from you dated July 24th...contained the first news I have had from home since I left the valley...you labored under the uncertainty of my whereabouts, which was and always is an uncomfortable uncertainty to anyone...I have suffered from a kind of dysentery for some time but am now better...Father also tells me he is apprehensive of a raid into the [Kanawha] valley during the present month perhaps at this time. I do hope his fears are groundless. At the present time it would be impossible for any force from this command to leave in time to render any assistance, as the troops would have to go via

Pa Central, besides we have a very heavy force before us now and I do not think Genl Crook would spare a force from this point now. Tell Father I read the paragraph in his letter to Col. Brown relating to the invasion and I will ask him whether he has communicated the matter to Brig. Hd. Qtrs. I shall do so myself this evening...Tell ___to trade my pistol off for a Colts navy if he can or sell the pistol for cash. I would rather have a navy Colt, if he can trade for one...Tell Mrs. Overshiner that I saw her husband, [John Overshiner] the Capt [John V.] Young and all the Company that were present last Sunday before the battle. They were then well – that Regt was not engaged consequently they are all right. My dear little wife I have written you a very incoherent letter. I have just read it over and hardly know what I have written to you. I send you ten thousand sweet little kisses. I know you are an excellent little wife to me."[35]

Young was appointed to serve as Division Officer of the Day on August 24 at Charles Town, meaning he was responsible for maintaining order on the picket lines surrounding the Union army. He noted in his diary that the "enemy just before us. Pickets talking to each other and Shooting at each other at the same time. The Virginians won't stop shooting. I was Division officer with orders to stop our men from firing on the Rebel pickets, but the 10th 9th and 12th [West] Virginians would not stop. No engagement today." By the next day, Young recalled that the Confederates withdrew and maintained a "respectful distance" from the Union picket lines. Although Young had somewhat more time to write home in late August, mail service was painfully slow, as usual. He wrote from camp near Charles Town on August 26, accounting for the several days' delay occurring after the Union defeat at Winchester. After he was left on the field, Young apparently took several days to catch up to his regiment. Young recalled, "Dear Wife, I know you are anxious to hear from me frequently and I am as anxious to hear from home. I am still well and able to do my duty in the Regiment and Company."

Young wrote further, "I was very glad to receive your letter of the 14th. It was the first that I have gotten since I left the Valley, and I am truly glad that you are doing so well. We have had hard work to do since we left the Valley. We have been in two hard battles in which we got whipped both times. At Snickers Gap, Co. G fought like tigers until their ammunition gave out, when they were ordered to fall back and cross the river, which we did without the loss of a man. We were on the skirmish line and the Rebs made three charges on us, but were driven back with loss each time. But our great defeat was at Winchester. I had the command of the 11th Va. The 11th and 15th Va. were ordered to advance in the center, on the right of the Berryville Road. We advanced in time and charged the Rebs and took possession of a stone wall on our front, and remained there, fighting like heroes, until we were ordered to fall back; and when we started back we found that we were surrounded and flanked on every side; and every man had to make his way out the best way he could...How I got out is a mystery to me yet."

He further related, "I don't think I could have gotten out had it not been for a cavalry man who was just passing with a lead horse. He gave him to me to ride. The rider had just been shot off of him, and the saddle was a gore of blood, but I was glad to get him. I overtook my company, or part of it, at Martinsburg, but never overtook the 11th and 15th until I arrived at Williamsport, Md. We are now encamped near Charlestown, intrenched. The Rebs [are] all around us. We are fighting more or less every day. There was a hard fight on our right yesterday. It is said that General Averell lost five hundred men, and how true I can't tell. I was officer of the Division yesterday and was out on the picket lines all day, and at night our men and the Rebel pickets are only about four hundred yards apart. I was out this morning at daylight and heard our pickets and the Rebels making a bargain not to shoot at each other, and become very friendly, talking to each other, and finally exchanged papers; and the Rebs offered to exchange tobacco and coffee. They have a large force here, and are very impudent. But I am certain they can't whip us here. There has been come cannonading on our right this morning, and some musketry, and some little shooting in our front, but not worth notice. We have a large army here, some say 1003 men. One thing I know, it takes about eight miles for them to camp on. Where are Captain [Edgar] Blundon and Sallie? Is the 7th scouting any, and do they catch any Rebs? Well Cy Cary he must not let the Gray backs have my black Lynchburg horse. We are now making up our pay rolls again, and if I live to get my money I will send it home at once."

Young reported also, "Everything is very high here. Ham is 28 cents per pound, beef 15 cents. It costs an officer something to live here, but I live as saving as possible for I want to save money to pay the last dollar I owe. If I live to get out of the service, I don't want to owe one dollar, and if I think we are saving we can save enough to pay all. You had better see Captain [John] Bowyers and if there is any difficulty about that property of Mr. [George] Summers, he better not sell it. You know, and so does he, that a Union man can't get justice in Winfield...This, the valley of Virginia, is a good country, and very rich, but poor farmers. Just think, it is said General Early has five thousand men and we have ten thousand, and all living on the roasting ears. Our army will strip a corn field of twenty acres and it won't be hardly one ear a piece, and the Rebels do the same thing and you may guess what will be left for the citizens. And besides this, General Sheridan burned all the wheat, oats and hay on our retreat from Strawsburg to this place, and I don't think the Rebs have much to eat only roasting ears, and they won't last much longer. The 10th, 11th, 15th, 13th Va. and 91st Ohio sallied out day before yesterday and charged on the Rebels and captured 30 head of beef cattle and one Reb, but the 15th Va. had three men killed and 4 wounded. The 10th and 11th were kept back for reserve. Write often..."[36]

## Berryville

About one hour before sunset on September 3, Crook's Army of West Virginia again clashed with Early's Confederates near Berryville, Virginia. Crook wrote: "...the enemy was reported to be advancing, and driving in the pickets...I at once placed Thoburn's division [Sic - First Infantry] in position on this pike with the greater portion of his command to the right of it. Colonel Duval's division was coming up to go into position on the left of Colonel Thoburn's, when the enemy made a furious charge on the latter, driving his two or three left regiments in great disorder, and compelling me to use Colonel Duval's division to check and drive him back and retake the position lost by these regiments. Could I have placed the Second Division - Colonel Duval's - on the left, as originally intended, so as to have come on the enemy's right flank, the movement would unquestionably resulted in the capture of the rebel attacking force - Kershaw's division...our men were posted behind stone walls, and the enemy had to advance to attack over an open country."

General Phil Sheridan reported a somewhat variant account of Berryville, however, noting that when Confederate Major General Joseph B. Kershaw's division of South Carolinians attacked Crook along the Berryville pike in force, they charged well but only to be "...handsomely repulsed with a loss of fifty prisoners and over 200 killed and wounded." General Sheridan was then anticipating a full engagement on September 4, but it did not occur, as the Confederates retired overnight to the west side of the Opequan River. After dark, the Army of West Virginia retreated to their former position and slept on arms. By September 13, General Crook reported that the Army of West Virginia had seven thousand, one hundred forty men available for duty. The effects of constant skirmishing and heavy combat in the Valley Campaign were taking a significant toll on John Young; on September 7, he told his wife for the third time in recent letters that Private Wyatt Briscoe, a young man they knew from Coalsmouth, had been killed at Winchester. He also discussed how the late battle at Berryville was among the worst he had witnessed to date.

From camp near Berryville, Young wrote: "I suppose you are very anxious about me in this land of war and death; and hear many rumors as to our whereabouts. Although I am not prepared to write out here, I will try and let you know that I am well and hearty, but very anxious to hear from home. I received one letter from you, dated Aug. 14th, the first that I have gotten since I left home, and two from Emma. I have written a number since I left. I write one from every place we stop long enough to write. I had written one to Emma on 3rd of Sept. but before I could get it in the mail we were ordered to be ready to march in a few minutes, so I failed to get it off. We marched to Berryville, was attacked at 4 PM by the Rebel forces, and we fought until 9 PM in which time the Rebels made three desperate charges on our whole line, from right to left, but our men repulsed them with great loss. The battle after dark exceeded anything for grandeur that I have ever witnessed. The line of battle was nearly one mile long, and the two armies in close range."

Young went on: "The blaze of fire that issued from the artillery and small arms was awful and terrific. None was engaged but the army of West Va. Our Division repulsed three charges, and lay on the battlefield all night, Col. Thoburn commanding. We lost 300 of our brave men. But the enemy suffered double that number. Co. G lost none in killed or wounded but some acted very shabby in this fight. When day broke I found only 5 men...with me. But the boys did not have a fair chance in the fight. One-half the Company was out foraging when the Rebels attacked us, and did not get with us until next morning. My orderly, Van B. Morris, was absent the first time. I don't think he has been absent in a fight since we left home. Only one of the 11th was killed, although we were in the heat of the battle from 4 until 9 p.m. and out all night. The Rebs kept the battlefield and stripped all of our dead and left them unburied. Our forces fell back 2 miles and fortified where we now lay near Snickers Gap. Co. G are all well, that is all that are with me. But I have only 42 men; 15 at New Creek, the balance in hospitals. I only have lost one man since we left the Valley. Wiatt [Wyatt] Briscoe was killed at Winchester and left on the field. Sam Landers and Wm. [William] Enicks wounded but not dangerous. Joel [Knuckles] Muckels wounded at Strawsburg [Strausburg] in the arm. These is all, and thank God for it. My dear little wife, I can't write much. I am out on picket with my Company and have been for two days, and have to write on my knee. When I have time I will give you a history of our whole march in this valley. Pray for me that we may be permitted to return home in peace after the restoration of our Union. The Putnam boys are well."[37]

## 3rd Battle of Winchester

The 11th West Virginia remained in General Phil Sheridan's army, which had approximately 40,000 men, under General Crook in the 1st Division, 3rd Brigade.

Crook made numerous advances and marches in the Cedar Creek-Opequan area during the next two weeks. Their operations culminated at the third battle of Winchester on September 19. Sheridan described it as "a most stubborn and sanguinary engagement," as he attacked Confederate General Jubal Early's main force of 12,000 men located along the Berryville Pike near Opequan Creek at about 5:00 a.m. A fierce battle raged until after 5:00 p.m. that evening, when the Confederates tried to form a final defensive line on the outskirts of town, as Union troops charged and carried Early's lines, and his men began rapidly falling back into Winchester, running through town. Early had to retreat up the Valley Turnpike, completely routed by the Federals. Sheridan later noted that the mostly hardened veteran Confederates, although defeated, were most "obstinate in their fighting."

Confederate General Robert E. Rodes was struck by a shell fragment on the back of his head, and died shortly afterward; also former Charleston, West Virginia, resident Colonel George S. Patton was mortally wounded in this engagement while commanding a brigade of infantry regiments from the Kanawha Valley. Sheridan also intimated "our losses are severe" despite the men's "superb conduct." Colonel Isaac Duval, former commander of the 9th West Virginia Infantry, was wounded in this battle as well. General Crook executed a daring flanking maneuver with the Army of West Virginia, capturing 2,500 Confederates. Casualty reports varied, but Federal losses are estimated at 697 killed, 2,983 wounded and 338 missing or captured, totaling 4,018, while Confederate losses are thought to have been 276 killed, 1,827 wounded and 1,818 missing or captured for a total of 3,921. Sheridan was so pleased he cited Crook and his men for valor in the official report. On September 20, General Sheridan encountered Early again as he retreated near Front Royal and not at Martinsburg, as he had anticipated. Sheridan attempted to cut off access to Winchester and nearly succeeded until the 6th Corps fell back in confusion. The crisis was remedied by Crook's army, whom Sheridan stated "...was up to that time held in reserve, went in and turned their left, our whole line advanced beautifully, routing the enemy at every point."[38]

Crook next marched thence to Harrisonburg, where Companies A, E, F and H of the 11th West Virginia finally rejoined the regiment after months of railroad duty at Parkersburg. At the third battle of Winchester, the 11th West Virginia lost one officer and two enlisted men killed in action, with eighteen enlisted men wounded. General George Crook afterward continued his pursuit of General Early and moved rapidly toward Fisher's Hill. As he promised her, Young found time to write to Paulina on September 21, "My dear little Wife: As I have just come out of a great battle safely and without the loss of a man of my company, I have reason to be thankful to God. On the

19th inst. we attacked the Rebels at daylight and the battle lasted all day. About 3 p.m. Crook's command was ordered in. After they had repulsed the 6th and 19th Corps we formed in line and charged through the open field, through a storm of shot and shell, but many of our brave officers and men fell in the charge."

Young wrote further, "After hard fighting we succeeded in driving the whole Rebel force from their strong works, and captured between three and five thousand prisoners, several pieces of artillery. Company G and Company J of the 11th Va. were the first that leaped into the Rebel works...Co. G left men in the rear some fifty yards. There were quite a number of rebel soldiers met us in the charge with their hands up, begging for God's sake not to kill them. We captured all the 22nd [22nd Virginia Infantry from Kanawha County] Rebel Regt. except 18 men, according to their own account, but I did not see any of them being ordered forward and the prisoners to the rear – but some of the boys saw them and talked with the Colonel...This morning we received thanks from the president and from General Grant for our great victory. They say they have ordered the firing of one hundred guns in token of our great victory, and in honor of the brave officers and men who gained it. Capt. G. [Greenbury] Slack was killed...Our Division suffered most because we were in the center. But Col. Thoburn who commands one Division is one brave Virginian. I passed through the whole battle at the head of my company untouched. I have some as brave men as ever honored any nation...but I am sorry to say that I have some in my camp that I have never got into any engagement yet. I will have to close as the mail won't wait. Will give you a full account shortly if I live. The Rebs have made a stand at Strawsburg [Strasburg] and our men are fighting while I am writing, so goodbye."[39]

## Fisher's Hill

As Crook moved his army through Hagerstown on September 20, Sergeant John McKee, of the 44th Ohio Volunteer Infantry, observed the 11th West Virginia marching past and noted: "The 11th Virginia Infantry passed through Hagerstown last evening en route for Sheridan's army. They were very loud in their demonstration for Lincoln. If the army meets with no important reverse until the election, the soldiers' vote will be a great deal more unanimous than I expected...." On September 22, Crook's command again encountered General Jubal Early's army at Fisher's Hill. Crook was posted at the extreme right, with the Confederate right located on the north fork of the Shenandoah River. After a great deal of maneuvering throughout the day, Crook was relocated to the extreme right on North Mountain, where about 4:00 p.m. he "furiously attacked the left of the enemy's line, carrying everything before him." Captain Young recorded in his diary, "In line of battle 8 AM, commenced fighting – Crook's command ordered to charge the works, Which they did to the great credit of West Virginia carrying everything before them, routing the Whole Rebel army."

Company G captured ten Confederates as Crook's forces drove them in "the greatest confusion and sweeping down behind their breast works," while the 6th and 9th Corps attacked Early in his front. The Confederates were broken up, and hundreds fled in utmost confusion. General Phil Sheridan was again most pleased with Crook's men, describing the conflict at Fisher's Hill as "a most signal victory." Crook's command pursued Early's retreating army that night. The 11th West Virginia lost one officer and eight enlisted men wounded and one enlisted man captured at Fisher's Hill. Also, during the fight at Fisher's Hill, Private George G. Moore, Company D, 11th West Virginia, captured a Confederate battle flag and later received the Medal of Honor for gallantry.[40]

Young wrote on September 26, "My dear wife and children: I have the great pleasure of announcing to you again that I am well, but have pass through another great battle in which we again have proved victorious and has almost annihilated the Rebel army in the Shenandoah valley. We overtook the Rebs at Fishers Hill, near Strawsburg, and attacked them in their strong earthworks, and although they had a strong force and well-fortified, the boys said they must get out of there. Well, the Army of West Virginia was ordered on the extreme right, and at 3 PM they were ordered to charge the whole Rebel force. The boys raised the yell and started for the Rebels and I tell you that I can't blame the Rebs for running, for the world never saw such a charge before. The yells of the Virginians, and the roar of cannon and muskets was terrific, and awful, indeed, enough to frighten the bravest heart. We captured 23 cannon and a number of prisoners. I don't think there ever was an army so completely routed and demolished as the Rebel army is at this time. There was a Rebel officer captured who told me that as soon as he heard the yell of Crook's men on their right, he knew that they were gone."

Young further recalled, "The 6th and 9th Corps lay still until the army of West Va. routed the Rebels out of their works. It is said here this morning that we captured 1700 Rebs at Fishers Hill, and about 4000 at Winchester; and I am certain that we have passed 2000 in Hospitals, wounded and sick, since we left Woodstock and came to this place. There are four hospitals full of sick and wounded here. The remnant of the Rebels army has dodged us here. I supposed they have slipped through some of those gaps in the Blue Ridge, but our cavalry is after them; also the 6th Corps. They have nothing to hinder them from running, for they burned wagons, threw away arms and everything else they possessed. I would like to know what the Rebs in Winfield think of General Early and his chivalry now. My dear Paulina, the Rebellion is over, and the Union is saved, in spite of armed traitors in the field, and Rebel sympathizers at home."

Young goes on, "I think the intention of our General is to follow the Rebs until they destroy the whole army. I say, and so do the boys, 'Go ahead!' Company G acted bravely in both engagements but I am sorry to say that William Crago was wounded in the last engagement, but not dangerous. He was shot in the breast, but it is a flesh wound. This was the only one wounded in Co. G. Jack Mynes had his cartridge box and canteen shot off while trying to capture a Rebel flag; but, brave boy, he missed it...I will have to stop writing...In fact, the boys are all in fine spirits, and all Lincoln men up to the hub. We have no ink here to write with. We have to do it all with a pencil. I received Emma's letter dated September 8th, the only letter I have received from home for a long time. I found Cousin James Stephenson, Captain Company K 91st Ohio, wounded on the battlefield at Fishers Hill, struck with a shell in the side, but I hope not dangerous. I left him and have not heard from him since. Tell Captain [Edgar] Blundon to announce my name as a candidate for the Legislature if he thinks it proper. You may have your house painted now."[41]

Crook again attacked Early's exhausted troops in a hard fight at Timberville on September 27, and Early again retreated, this time toward Harrisonburg. General Sheridan continued to pursue Early all the way to Port Republic, where the Union army captured several supply stores, and for time being, the Army of West Virginia took a brief respite from heavy combat; the period of October 1-7 was mainly spent combing the valley and destroying potential supply sources for Early's army. Crook's command burnt some two thousand barns and farms in the area of Woodstock, Virginia. Crook moved through Port Republic, Mount Crawford, Bridgewater and Harrisonburg, picking up tons of wheat, hay, flour and some four thousand head of livestock, including another three thousand sheep for food along the way. They also burnt several homes located within five miles of Harrisonburg after a Union lieutenant was murdered by a Southern sympathizer. Crook planned to destroy their entire line of livestock and burn more homes and barns when he received orders to return to Fisher's Hill on October 8.

In West Virginia, Edgar Blundon, who was commanding the Union garrison at Guyandotte, found that several Southern females slandered a close friend of his wife Sarah, attempting to make him suspicious. Sarah had earlier disclosed her anxiety with Edgar being surrounded by so many Southern agitators there, whom she opined would "as soon hang the Federals as look at them." Blundon did not let it trouble him, however. He was instead relieved to learn that Captain Young was enduring the arduous Valley Campaign: "I am happy to hear of Pa's safety. Hope the old Veteran will escape uninjured, though many battles may yet be fought by him."[42]

## Cedar Creek

During the period of October 13-17, the 11th West Virginia was located near Cedar Creek and involved in frequent skirmishing, without a significant engagement. John Young wrote in his diary on October 18 that Union patrols had returned from as far as Middletown and Winchester and found no sign of the Confederates. However, rumors were coming in from cavalry scouts that Early was moving toward them, and Crook's men began to anticipate another large battle brewing, but somehow the command failed to recognize they were in imminent danger. The 11th West Virginia was deployed at the forward edge of the Union line on the eastern side of the pike, overlooking a deep gorge where Cedar Creek flowed into the north fork of the Shenandoah. Their position was protected by breastworks and artillery batteries. The Army of West Virginia then had approximately 4,000 troops and sixteen cannons on hand, which was still less than half strength in contrast to Sheridan's other corps. Aware that Sheridan thought he was gone, General Jubal Early refused to concede. He and Major General John Gordon devised a bold plan to attack the unsuspecting Federal camps at dawn on October 19.

The Confederates quietly moved along a little-known trail at the base of Massanutten Mountain, which brought them to where the Army of West Virginia was encamped behind their earthworks. Word had reached the Federals that Early was moving toward them, as John Young wrote in his diary that his brigade was awake at 3:00 a.m. watching for imminent attack. They had no idea just how close Early was, however, as two of Early's divisions, led by Major General Stephen D. Ramseur of North Carolina and Brigadier General John Pegram, forded the narrow, waist-deep north fork of the Shenandoah River under a full moon and slipped into line of battle without being noticed. A heavy fog blanketed Cedar Creek as dawn approached, which the Confederates exploited to take the Federal army by complete surprise. Flinty General John Gordon, who had been wounded five times in the war thus far, also got his division into position, and at 5:00 a.m., a full engagement began as waves of screaming Confederates attacked Crook, whose hapless divisions were separated. The 1st Division under Colonel Joseph Thoburn was located on the hilltop above Cedar Creek, and they were almost immediately routed by Major General Joseph B. Kershaw's division, killing Colonel Thoburn in the attack and scattering his command.

*The Surprise at Cedar Creek*
*From a war-time sketch by A.R. Waud*
*Library of Congress*

The Confederates also shattered Crook's 2nd Division under future U.S. President General Rutherford B. Hayes. Sheridan had been away from his command at Washington discussing his next deployment when the fight began, and he had recently returned to Winchester some twelve miles away as his entire army was nearly routed. Captain Young was in a habit of nervously writing in his diary to cope with stress just as a battle began; Company G received the full force and fury of the Confederate attack, with Young observing the "Rebels made a most furious assault on our breastworks in front and rear, and in the darkness of the hour carried everything before them our men falling back in great confusion. Co. G lost 6 men missing." At about noon, the fragmented Union army managed to reorganize and repulsed Early's second attack, which lasted until nearly 3:00 p.m. John Young wrote, "Our men turned on the Rebels and drove them back with great loss..." The Union gain did not last long, however, as Early mounted a fierce counterattack, led by Major General Robert Rode's Division, who rolled the confused Union lines back toward Middle Road.

At approximately 3:00 p.m., General Sheridan returned from Winchester, rode onto the field and rallied his troops, riding along the lines yelling and swearing at them to hold their lines in what has become an iconic scenario. Confederate brigade commander Major General Stephen Dodson Ramseur of North Carolina was mortally wounded and captured when Sheridan counterattacked by executing a "left half wheel of the whole line," with a division of cavalry turning each flank of every whole line of advance. The Confederates gave a "stubborn resistance" but ultimately "broke and fled." Lieutenant Colonel Van H. Bukey, commanding the 11th West Virginia, described what happened in the initial assault that morning, reporting his regiment was drawn up in line of battle located "immediately to the left of the battery, on the

*Sheridan's Ride*
*Painting by Thure de Thulstrup*
*Library of Congress*

extreme left of the Army of West Virginia." Bukey reported: "When I arrived at the works I found some of my men firing to the front, and fearing injury to some of our own command in front, and seeing no enemy there at that time, I ordered them to cease firing. I had not passed from the left to right of my regiment, however, before the Fifteenth West Virginia, immediately on my left, fell back from the works, and my flank received a pretty severe, but, owing to fog and darkness, not accurate fire."[43]

Shortly afterward, on Captain Young's left, the 15th West Virginia gave way under a heavy enfilade fire, causing the 11th West Virginia line to break. Lieutenant Colonel Van H. Bukey quickly ordered them to fall back "by companies from the left, oblique to the right and rear down the hill," perceiving he was about to be surrounded if he did not move. The regiment was reformed across the nearby turnpike but had become separated from their brigade. For fear of being cut off and captured, Bukey hastily filed his command in rear of the left of the 19th Corps earthworks, but as they moved the Confederates again attacked on the left and "all in front of us broke." The 11th West Virginia was carried away in the mass confusion that ensued in what became a total rout of Union forces. They retreated to a stone house where Sheridan had his headquarters, and Bukey tried to reorganize the regiment, ordering the eloping officers and men to "rally on General Crook's flag" as they ran by. The situation inside the Union lines had become so disorganized that Lieutenant Colonel Bukey testified "I must confess I did not know where my whole command was."

As Lieutenant Colonel Bukey moved the 11th West Virginia through the woods on their retreat, he found "...those officers whose names I first mentioned [includes Young] on several parts of the field, each with a detachment of command." Young afterward made his way to the rear and told Bukey he was "run over and crippled" in the rout. The regimental surgeon issued Young a pass near Middletown, Virginia, to remain behind to recover; although Young was instead on the battlefield helping bury the dead. He stated in his diary that night he had spent "All day burying the dead, officers searching for their lost men, and soldiers looking up their friends. This is a day that will Long be remembered by many. I was over the battlefield looking for my lost men but I can hear of none but Sergt. Griffith who is wounded. Horses and men laying dead all over the battle field, Union and Rebs." Another officer in Company G, 2nd Lieutenant William G. McDaniel, was missing from the company when the attack began, and Bukey later reported Captain John Young was also missing, noting he had asked for a report from him but last heard from him "... two days ago, I have as yet no explanation."

Not having a complete set of facts to explain the breakdown in command of Company G, Bukey deferred to the officer's statements about the disorganization in the company, later affirming that several officers, including Young and McDaniel, had "acted well in previous engagements...I noticed in particular the good conduct of Lt. [William G.] McDaniel of Company G at Fisher's Hill..." Bukey conceded that during the rout when he ordered officers locating elements of their command to keep them together, all, including Lieutenant McDaniel, "...efficiently obeyed, and when our corps advanced in the evening I had thus succeeded in having the most of my regiment together."

The 11th West Virginia lost five enlisted men killed in action, one officer and twenty-five enlisted men wounded, and forty-nine enlisted men captured or missing at Cedar Creek. Afterward, Sheridan pursued Early to Mount Jackson October 20-21, where they encountered more than two thousand Confederates who quickly broke and again fled after a short engagement. As they ran, Sheridan noted the "flying rebels" left a great deal of debris, including arms and other accoutrements, in order to quicken their pace as they made their way down through the mountainous region. Other than this, after the battle of Cedar Creek, only one other action occurred when Early reappeared near Cedar Creek on November 11 and made only a slight demonstration, which was quickly resolved without an open engagement. Sheridan's army did little that fall and into the winter, as he stated "...nothing of importance occurred in the Valley up to February 27 1865, the day in which my cavalry moved from Winchester to Petersburg."[44]

## After Cedar Creek

Captain Young found means to write home again on October 21 and shared detailed observations of the late battle. Young explained, "My dear Wife and Children: Through the manifold goodness of God I am yet alive and tolerably well. But as I have written you before about the many hard battles that we have been engaged in, I can now record the master one, and I think the final one. I wrote to you in my last letter that there was a large Rebel force in our front, and that we expected an attack. On the 19th inst., at four o'clock a.m., we were aroused by the firing of our pickets, and in a few minutes we were under arms in our breast works, waiting the assault. But to our great surprise the enemy attacked us in our rear. They, during the night, had marched around the Luray Mountain and had entirely surrounded the camp...and just before the break of day made the attack on our rear." He continued: "But before they did this, they captured our pickets, the 11th, 15th, 10th, Va., and the 54th Pa. was on the extreme left and had two batteries of twelve guns, and had the strongest breastworks and was at our post in good time, but the Rebels had taken our right entirely on surprise and the first thing they knew the Rebs were in their camp, and between them and their fortifications, and the consequence was they flanked us out of our fortifications. Such skedaddling has not occurred in this valley often. The whole army of West Virginia left everything in camp and the Rebels got it. We ran nearly one mile through a storm of bullets and shells. Many of our men fell and many were captured, and if it had been broad daylight we all would have been captured or killed. Through the confusion and darkness I lost the command, and made my way out alone. The command was awfully scattered, and was hard to rally. Indeed, many could not be rallied at all."

Young wrote on, "The whole army fell back for two miles, rallied and formed in line, and here the fighting commenced in earnest. The 6th and 19th Corps., with the remnant of West Va. fought them until late in the evening, when the Rebels began to give way, and just as soon as they began to give way our whole cavalry drew their sabers and made a most successful charge, which threw consternation in their ranks and they fled in every direction. Although it is a glorious and a final victory for the Union it has cost us a great deal. O, the brave men and officers who lost their lives in this dreadful engagement, which lasted all day. As I said before, in our confusion and hasty retreat, I lost my command, and in running I sprained my ankle and got my other leg hurt so badly that it was as much as I could do to make my way out. But afterwards, I found that I had made pretty good headway, for when a final halt was made I was at least eight miles from the scene of action; Lieut. Elkins and a few of Co. G were left behind; Lewis L. Griffith is badly wounded, if not killed I have not yet found him, but he is somewhere in the 6th Corps Hospital shot in the back; Sergeant [James R. Holtzein.] Holstine struck in the back with a piece of shell which cut through his blanket and blouse, but not injured badly. He is now doing duty. Lewis J. Persinger is a prisoner; C.F. Gray, James Taylor, John Higginbotham and Joseph A. Griffith missing in action, but I have learned that Lewis Griffith is at Winchester. As bad as our condition is at this time it is not as bad as the Rebels, for we have destroyed their whole army."

Again, he elaborated, "I understand that we have captured 4100 prisoners, 43 pieces of their artillery, all their wagons, and with Headquarters ammunition, ambulance and almost everything that went on wheels; and the whole infantry driven to the mountains in utter confusion and disorder. The whole battlefield was strewed with dead Rebels, and a great number of them conscripts and citizens. But our loss is great. The 13th Va. suffered very much. Colonel Thoburn was killed, and quite a number were killed or taken prisoners. We are all here without blankets, tents or haversacks or even tin cups or coffee pots. We have not anything, only what is on our backs, and it is very cold here. The ground is white with frost every morning. Our Cavalry has just come in with quite a number of the Reb's artillery, and the Johnnies driving their own teams. They look as though they didn't like it much, but they started to the North with their artillery and it is right to make them drive it there. There are a great number of the dead on the field of battle who are dressed in citizens clothes. They were forced out for the purpose of driving us out of the valley. Poor fellows! Many of them, no doubt, were good Union men. O, the horror and wickedness of this Rebellion! I do think if the Rebel sympathizers could see a battle field and have the privilege of walking over it, they would surely say that they were murderers of all these noble men."

Young summarized: "Oh my dear wife, I have just returned from the field of strife, and O, how sickening – not done burying the dead yet, men wounded and killed in every possible shape. There are not only hundreds but thousands lying dead, with heads, arms and legs off, bowels out, brains scattered over the ground. I have been for two or three hours, since I commenced this letter, looking over the battle ground or Sergt. [Lewis] Griffith, James Taylor and Caleb Gray, but I can't find any trail of them. Colonel Bukey told me today that a doctor in the 6th Corps told him the orderly of Co. G was seriously but not dangerously wounded, and was sent to the hospital, but where I cant find. I learned this evening that we have captured and counted 14,353 Rebels, with 53 pieces of artillery, besides what they captured from us on the 19th. I think General Early will have to make another draw on Jeff for more big guns. We have captured nearly 100 big guns since we came into this valley and some 10,000 prisoners."[45]

## Death of 1st Sergeant Lewis Griffith

Young mentioned the Company G Orderly, 1st Sergeant Lewis Griffith, was wounded and taken to a field hospital in Winchester; while there, Griffith met Mollie Hansford-Walls, the elder sister of Victoria Teays Hansford of Coalsmouth, who was helping care for the wounded. Mollie had married a prominent physician from Winchester, Virginia, Dr. John Walls, in 1861 and relocated there. Mollie kept a diary as her sister did and wrote of her interaction with the young soldier whom she knew from Coalsmouth belonging to Company G: "I tried to forget when they brought the wounded into town. The worse time was after the Battle of Cedar Creek in the fall of '64. I went into a storehouse full of wounded and the poor fellows wrapped in their blankets were lying so close together on the floor that they looked like rolls in a pan. I had a basket filled with baked apples and some other delicacies to give out. One got my attention and I have him a baked apple. As I looked down at him, I saw a man with large black eyes and a good face, he reminded me of my brother Carroll. I knelt down and asked him where he was from and he answered Kanawha County. That excited me and I asked him if he was ever in Coalsmouth, my old home."

Mollie went on: "Oh yes, he said that is where I was mustered into the army and where I first joined my regiment. Then I knew he was in the Northern Army so I asked him if he knew any Rebs there. Oh yes he said most of the best people were Rebs. He then asked me if I knew old Major Hansford who had daughters who were two of the most fierce Rebs he ever knew. He said, 'We would always try to get to the boat first when we had to set them across the river. They would always run down the Yankees and snub us like we weren't even there. It was fun.' I then told him that Major Hansford was my father and the girls were my sisters. He was really surprised and wanted to know what I was doing ministering to a Yankee. I told him that he was wounded and needed help and that I always did what I could for the wounded of either army. He said he would like to get someone to wash his clothes...he insisted on me taking his pocket book as he was afraid it would be stolen even though he only had $5.00 in it. He also wanted me to write a letter to his mother. He told me his name was Sergeant Griffith and that his mother lived at Barboursville in Cabell County. I told him I had no pencil or paper but that I would come back the next day to write for him."

Mollie returned the next day: "The next morning was bright and cool and I went down to the storehouse early and found out they had moved most of the wounded to the Lutheran Church. As I got to the church door I saw four dead men wrapped in their blankets lying nearby on the ground. A guard and a regular soldier were standing near them and the soldier was sobbing. I heard him say, 'My poor brother, I knew if he was sent to this valley he would never get out alive.' I asked him why they had come here to fight us anyway. 'Oh, I don't know,' he replied. 'I wish Lincoln and Jeff Davis were both hung.' Just then a Yankee sergeant came out and I told him I wanted to see Sergeant Griffith. 'Why would you want to see a Rebel?' he answered. I told him we were from the same part of the country and I had promised to write a letter to his mother for him. He went inside and when he came back he said I could go in. After looking for some time I found the poor fellow but he was dying. He could not speak, but oh, his eyes. I can still see them now. Anyone who could have seen his eyes could never doubt that man has a soul. I told him what I was writing and if it was all right to raise his hand, and he did so. I sat by him until his last breath and then went home crying. I could not speak of him for a long time without crying. Dr. Walls said that I made such a fuss over that Yank that anyone would think he was a relation. I sent the letter to his mother with the $5.00 but I never heard if she got it. I have often thought of that poor soldier's eyes as he looked at me that bright Sunday morning."[46]

Young next penned the following letter from Cedar Creek, only one day after the battle; he had to certify the death of the young man mentioned in Mollie Hansford-Walls' account as Sergeant Lewis L. Griffith of Company G, 13th West Virginia: "I certify, on honor, that Lewis L. Griffith, a 1st Sergeant of Captain John V. Young's Company G of the 13th Regiment of Infantry Volunteers of the State of West Virginia, born in Kanawha County, State of Virginia, aged 22 years, 6 feet 3 ¾ inches high, light complexion, black eyes, black hair and by occupation a farmer, having joined the company on its original organization at Coalsmouth, and enrolled in it at the muster into the service at Coalsmouth, on the 23rd day of May 1862 by Captain John V. Young, to serve the regiment for the term of Three Years and having served honestly and faithfully with his company in The U.S. Service to the date of his death, October 20, 1864."

Griffith was unmarried; his mother, Sara Griffith, aged sixty-four years, filed a pension claim on June 13, 1865, with the Clerk of Court in Kanawha County, as a resident of Cabell County. She testified she was the mother of "Lewis L. Griffith, deceased, who was a Sergeant in Company G, 13th West Virginia, Volunteer Infantry...who died at Newtown in the Shenandoah Valley on the 20th day of October 1864 of wounds received in the Battle of Cedar Creek on the 19th day of the same month." Young later wrote that a few weeks later, one of the men from the 4th West Virginia Infantry brought him "...two rings off of Sergeant [Lewis] Griffith's fingers. He died at New Town the next day after the fight; shot through the abdomen. This is the first straight account that I could get of him. I will send the rings to his mother as requested by him on his death bed...Serg. [Lewis] Griffith is buried in the Lutheran church yard in Newton, Va. Eight miles from Winchester."[47]

The remainder of 1864 was much less intense for Company G, but the respite was short lived; 1865 would bring an even more dramatic and deadly series of events. Young wrote to Paulina on October 22: "Well, after a miserable night, I will resume my writing. We had rain and cold wind last night, were without tents and blankets. Sat up all night. Had nothing to make coffee in this morning, but a few tin cups. I have not heard anything reliable of my lost men. Poor fellows! It causes me much trouble; I hope they are alive yet and will live to see the end of this infernal Rebellion. The Rebel army has gone, the third time since the 14th day of September, up this valley, minus everything they had, and I hope they will not return this Fall, for I am tired fighting and marching, and I think we ought to have some rest. I assure you that I can't go much longer without rest. There are but few officers in Crooks command that have gone through the campaign Lieut. [George] Mc Daniels and myself have gone through, and have been in almost every battle and skirmish since we started. The Medical director calls me a most remarkable man of my age. I have not taken one dose of medicine since I left the Kanawha Valley...I would write more if I had a larger sheet, but this is all I had and I borrowed this." Young also mentioned he had lost the local senate election and attributed the loss to Southern sympathizers in the area.[48]

Also, on October 22, Young finished an earlier note to Paulina: "...Tell Sarah, Emma, Ben and Jacob that their Pa wants to see them very badly indeed. But they must be good children and obey their dear Ma and cause her no more trouble than they can help. My dear children be good to your Ma for my sake. You know she is a good mother to you. Be kind to one another. The Lord loves good, obedient children. Remember your Ma has worked hard night and day to raise and educate you, and it is your duty to love and obey her. My prayer is, and shall be, that you all may be preserved and kept from evil, and that you may soon be delivered from them who have stripped you and insulted you on account of your loyalty to the best Government in the world and our holy religion. May the Lord bless you all and cause you to remember that this is a world of trouble and disappointment. But may the Lord grant that we may meet again and have peace at home once more. Oh, how I love to think of home...I do not think that General Early will try it again. They say that he begged Jeff Davis to let him come back and try General Sheridan once more after the Winchester fight...as I have told you before that we have destroyed everything in the valley that man or beast could eat; and now the women and children are drawing rations from our commissaries; and their husbands or sons are in the Rebel army, or lying under the sod dead – traitors."

As usual, the mail was slow; Young complained: "It seems very strange that I don't get more letters from home...I think I have written home every week. When I [don't] have ink I write with pencil. As I said before the Johnnies got all my paper and ink, with everything else but the old man, and they tried hard for him. They may get me yet but it will be after I am wounded and can't get out of their way. But I may be disappointed...I have been engaged in twelve regular battles since last Spring, besides sundry skirmishes, in which many brave men were killed, and I have escaped thus far unhurt. It is nothing but the goodness and mercy of God that has warded off the missiles of death from me. I hope that I will be spared yet to return home to the arms of my dear family, and enjoy in my old age the blessing of a restored Government, and the privilege of worshiping God in the old Methodist Church...We have [given] them the best whipping they ever got..." Young relocated his family home to Winfield in 1863, thinking it would be safer due to the large contingent of Union troops and supporters there. The garrison was intended to protect the Court House as well as Union citizens and ensure steamboat traffic on the Kanawha River continued unimpaired. However, the Confederates raided Winfield on October 26, and Paulina and the children were at home during the attack. In this small but vicious affair, four hundred men from Captain Phillip Thurmond's Partisan Rangers and Lieutenant Colonel Vinson A. Witcher's 34th Battalion Virginia Cavalry attacked eighty-three troopers from Company D, 7th West Virginia Cavalry. The hour-long skirmish resulted in Thurmond's death as the Confederates were repulsed.[49]

Young sent a letter to his daughter Emily on October 30: "You can't imagine how anxious to receive letters from my dear family I am, and to learn that they are well...I am well...but have suffered in mind with anxiety since the battle, about my brave men who are lost. There is no doubt but Sergeant [Lewis] Griffith is dead and L.J. Pursinger, John Higginbotham, James Taylor, Caleb F. Gray are prisoners; I understand that Joseph A. Griffith got his knee sprained and was sent to Winchester and is now in the hospital. L.L. Griffith was shot through both thighs and through the loins. When I heard where he was I walked eight miles to see him but he was taken off just a few minutes before I got there, and I did not see him. Poor fellow! I did want to see him so bad but he is gone. We are yet laying on the hills of Cedar Creek watching for old Early. But I don't think he will make another night assault on us. I hardly think the Rebel army will try the valley again this Fall. They met such a magic defeat on the 19th that I think they will be careful how they pitch in next time...But we have no fears while we have our little General Sheridan at the helm. The aggregate of my company is now sixty. There are yet a good many in hospitals sick...left the ranks while going into battle at Winchester on the 19th of Sept. and I have not seen them since but I have learned that they have been detailed as nurses in the hospitals in care of our wounded; but I think a coward would make a poor nurse for a brave soldier.

You said something about my being a candidate and my proverbial defeat. My dear child, this concerns me the least of anything else at present. I am sorry that my name was used as a candidate, but my greatest trouble now is the safety and comfort of my brave men. Even if I had been elected I don't know how I could leave them in the hands of another man. It is just as much as I can do to keep them from being imposed upon, and I with them; and I know if I were away from them I could not enjoy myself under any circumstances whatever. My time will soon be out, and how I can leave my men in the field is more than I can conjecture. But we will see. Some will go out with me, others will have to remain until next August; and besides this trouble, we have the most contemptible Colonel in the U.S. service, who is now engaged in trying to have all the officers of his Regiment that he doesn't like dismissed. And I know he doesn't like me, for I pitch on him whenever he acts mean with me or my men. Well, Emma, I have just eaten dinner. Salt Pork, Coffee and Crackers is our regular living but Silas E. [Elkins] is a good cook and John and I enjoy it very well...We have a very comfortable shanty built out of Cedar logs, and covered with our shelter tents...Yes, Emma, we are like you – we think we have done enough fighting for one campaign, and I assure you that we are tired enough to haul down this year and go into winter quarters. But if the Rebels still insist we will give them another trial and another good flogging if they desire it."

There were several Southern sympathizers suspected of being guerilas in Putnam County that fall, and Young was in favor of their execution, "You spoke of Harvey Bowyers' sentence to be shot. I do wish there were more of the same kind of sentences in Putnam. John Crawford ought to have been shot three years ago. There are many who will be shot without Court Martial when the soldiers get home, in retaliation for their lost comrades, and the insults given to their families and friends while they have been doing their duty in service of their country. I have not received any letter from your Ma since the one sent by Serg. Griffiths...I am glad that Jacob is in the printing office. I hope that he will learn something and be kept out of mischief. Is your Ma going to have your house painted? We are twenty miles from Winchester...Tell the soldiers' friends that the boys are all well, except Will [William] Racer...I wish you would send word to Leander Higginbotham that he is reported absent without leave, and will be punished if he doesn't report at once. He is already reduced to the ranks for his absence. Send him word that if he doesn't come soon he will be arrested and sent under guard, and it will cost him thirty dollars besides transportation. I must close by saying that I commenced on the wrong side of this sheet, but I think it will hold fully as much. You can turn it about and find the beginning and end."[50]

With the 1864 Shenandoah Valley campaigns ended, the 11th West Virginia remained in the Army of West Virginia's 1st Division, 3rd Brigade under Colonel Milton Wells and stayed at Camp Russell. The Army of West Virginia lost thirty men killed in action, 1,947 wounded and 637 missing, totaling 2,855 in minor skirmishes, as well as at the battles of Cedar Creek and Fisher's Hill in 1864. Daily duties quickly became monotonous, and with more time to reflect, Young's thoughts were on his family, the war and its causes. He elaborated on November 4, "Dear Paulina: Through the mercy and goodness of God, I am well yet although I have passed through many dangers since I left home. But I feel thankful that my life and that of my dear family has been spared until the present time, while so many thousands of poor souls have found an untimely grave, caused by this wicked rebellion. Who is to blame or who will have to bear the responsibility of life and property caused by the act of secession and rebellion is a question not yet decided. But awful to relate, our good and great government has for many years pronounced slavery a great evil, political, domestic and social."

Young further explained, "But while acknowledging this to be the case, and that the institution of slavery would finally in the end overthrow the government they of the North acceded to the wishes of the South and still made laws to bind the hateful and sinful institution more tightly and even went so far as to make white men slave catchers in the North; and ministers were not wanting in the North to preach and inculcate from the pulpit that slavery ought to be protected and let alone. Now, I hold that our government is just as guilty as the South. But if I believe anything I believe that the Lord has made use of the South as an instrument to punish and correct the Government for the great sin of slavery. I believe that a nation is punished for crime as well as an individual and if this is the case it will take the blood of the nation to atone for the great national evil. But I ask myself the question many times on the battlefield, when I see the brave soldiers and officers falling on my right and left, torn to pieces, heads, arms, legs off, bowels out, brains scattered over the ground; men wounded in every possible way and crying for help, I ask myself, "Has not enough blood been given to atone for the sin of the Nation, or will not the Lord be satisfied with the sacrifices already made?"

He continued, "But the South is greatly to blame for their conduct since the commencement of the War, and long before. But the Scriptures says that 'the wicked is the sword of the Lord,' and I have no doubt that He is making use of the South as a willing instrument to punish the Nation for the loved and cherished evil of slavery. But this awful crime and sin that is, or ought to be, charged to the South for the abuse of slavery is already being inflicted on the entire inhabitants. Just think of Virginia, 'the mother of states,' sold by her Governor for a battlefield in 1860! And since that time it has become a grave yard, especially in this valley. You can't go anywhere or look in any direction but you can see the marks of the contending armies – the graves of the noble fellows who have been contending for the right (or wrong)."

Young pointed out, "Here in this Valley alone lies more than one hundred thousand brave men. All these have been sacrificed on account of slavery. Virginia has become one graveyard from North Mountain to Richmond and from North Carolina to the Potomac River. This great Valley, which a few years ago, was the great boast of Virginia, is now nothing more than a perfect waste. Negroes gone, property of all sorts swept away, houses, barns and fields left desolate, while some of the owners have gone North, others have fled to the Sunny South, and left everything behind them. But enough of this..." Young also indicated he heard about the recent skirmish at Winfield and was pleased with the outcome. The Union troops were short on rations in Young's division, however, and he indicated many were tired and hungry, after recent unsuccessful attempts at foraging, "There is not to be found within thirty miles of this place, sheep, hogs, pigs, turkeys or fowls of any kind. The fruit and everything eatable has been swiped away by soldiers and the Rebel citizens are reaping their rights with a vim to it..."[51]

On November 10, Young wrote to Paulina, "You can't imagine how anxious I was to hear from home...we were ordered to pack up and be ready to march at ten oclock yesterday...the whole Army has gone in camp. The signs are pretty good for winter quarters but we can't tell...I think it time to let us rest some if not all winter. We have had no fighting to do since the 19th of October but we were up at Woodstock after our wounded. I was so anxious to go for I thought perhaps I might find some of my men but they were not there. We marched that day thirty miles. You may think this strange that after such a campaign I could march thirty miles in one day; but I don't suppose I am so near gone as you think."

Young goes on, "But I would have walked sixty miles to recapture my men. I was notified today that J.A. [Joseph A.] Griffith is in the hospital in Baltimore...I think he sprained his knee...I was glad to hear it for I thought he was a prisoner...but I hope that he is not dead. I don't know what you will do if the Rebs take the Kanawha Valley again but as the Lord has provided for us up to the present time, be assured he never will leave or forsake you in the day of trouble..." Young was also not getting along with the regimental commander, "We have a great deal of trouble with our Colonel. He is the most contemptible detestable ignoramus I ever knew. He is not fit for a Corporal in any company...I am not the Ranking line officer in this Regiment, but have little hopes of raising any higher while Bukey is Colonel. He has his pets and he will have them in the best offices; but we intend to try to have him out...If I had listened to their orders, I today would be in Richmond (in prison) too..."

He continued, "When I leaped over the bank...the bullets threw the dust all over me as I made the last jump. But they might have halted until yet before I would have surrendered...I would rather be with my brave men and hear them tell of their exploits after a battle than to be at...any other place besides home. If you could hear Co. G tell how many they killed and wounded you would think there was not another man left in the Southern Confederacy. Some will swear that they killed a half dozen Rebs when I knew that they had not fired a gun. Let the Rebels rule until we come home and then we will see who will rule. The Rebel sympathizers and the Union soldiers can't live together; those who have given aid or comfort to our common enemy will have to leave the county or go up the spout..." On November 10, Lieutenant Colonel Van H. Bukey wrote to former governor Francis H. Pierpont soliciting his "candid assistance" to obtain a commission as colonel of the 11th West Virginia. He complained that another field officer was "agitating the subject" in their own favor. Young was intimately familiar with this scenario, having dealt with former 2nd Lieutenant Robert Brooks for nearly three years. Bukey soon received his commission as colonel, with date of rank cited October 28, 1864.[52]

Regardless of regimental politics, Young remained focused on his family, writing to Emily on November 20, "My company is in good condition, considering the hard campaign through which we have passed this year. However, some of them are sick and some are not fit for duty...I had forty six on dress parade last night. O, Emma, you can form no idea of how thankful I am to God for his loving kindness to me and my company in this campaign. You may imagine the suffering caused by this war; you may picture in your imagination the horror and suffering on a battle field; and you may hear in your imagination the prayers of the wounded and the cries for help, and the shrieks and groans of the dying; but, oh my dear child, the realities – the realities of a battlefield – I would to God I could forget it. I have seen the poor brave soldiers lying on the battle field with both legs shot off, and sometimes with both arms gone; others with their bowels torn out and they yet living; others torn in every possible shape and yet living, and without even one friend to alleviate their suffering or put to their lips a single drop of cool water. But this picture is too gloomy to dwell upon at this time."

Young asserted, "I firmly believe that peace will soon be made, and that God will be satisfied with the sacrifice already made for the great sin of this nation. I understand that the South is now willing to let their negroes go free; and I firmly believe that whenever they become willing to give up their idols God will accept their sacrifice and restore peace and prosperity to a once happy but now distracted country. How I long for peace...to spend my old days in their presence, and to be interred by my children in a peaceful grave to await the happy morning of the resurrection of the dead. Your Ma, I see with regret, is inclined to think hard of the Methodist Church because there are some Judases in it. O, my dear Emma, let my arm be palsied and my tone [tongue] cleave to the roof of my mouth, but God forbid that I ever should deny the Methodist church. For the liberty of this church I am today in the field, enduring all kinds of suffering. Do you suppose that I would deny the church that has brought me up and made me what I am? Next to my family I love my church. In her I expect to live and die and in her I want my children to remain until death. There are bad men in every church."

Changing the subject, Young indicated the Confederates under General Jubal Early had withdrawn from the Shenandoah Valley; however, the Union camps still received occasional potshots and raids from Confederate cavalry guerillas lurking in the vicinity. As a result, many of the Union men were afraid to leave their camp areas alone. Young's division had finally settled into what was looking like their winter encampment, and he informed Emily: "I wish I could describe our camp to you. Well, we have those little shelter tents just big enough for two to sleep in. Each company has its row of tents with the officers' row of tents on the left. Company G's tents make a pretty long row, and I wish you could see the contrivances of the soldiers for comfort. Some will dig down in the ground, others will build walls out of turf cut and taken out of the commons, and build chimneys out of the same materials, which adds greatly to the comfort of sleeping. I know it would make you laugh to see the shape of some of their chimneys – all sizes and shapes. Some as ugly as ugly can be. John Elkins, Silas [Elkins] and myself have very comfortable quarters. I wish you could see us scrounged in our little house, Silas cooking and John sitting humped up in the corner talking about his time being nearly out. When one of us wants to move, someone has to get up and let him pass. One end of our tent is built up with sod, and a broad plank on each side dug in the ground one foot. The chimney cut in the side built of cut turf in the shape of brick, except a great deal larger...”[53]

Young's daughter Sarah and Captain Edgar Blundon of the 7th West Virginia Cavalry were still newlyweds and were adjusting to their new in-law relationships. Edgar wrote to Sarah on November 23: “I am thankful that Ma Young and Ma Blundon have thus far formed a pleasant acquaintance, and hope it may culminate in binding her new son to the family with the lasting ties of affection...I laughed right out when you told me of the incessant conflabs between our mothers, each of which have their own full complement of talking abilities...Ma Blundon deems this a most unholy war because she has two sons in the Army...while Ma Young thinks Phil Sheridan small beside that embodiment of patriotism who we love to call Pa. God bless him this cold night, where he may be.”

Young wrote to Paulina also on November 23, “This is Thanksgiving Day you know, and the loyal peoples in the States have sent large presents to the soldiers... Company G got three turkeys and three geese. They are now cooking them... it is a gift from the loyal citizens and that is enough to show they appreciate our worth and the high esteem that the country places upon past services through this year's campaign. History has never recorded any campaign like this one. The number of miles marched, the number of battles fought, the hardships endured, is beyond precedence; and the historian will have to record it one of the greatest campaigns of the world. And those detestable characters who stay at home and aid and abet in this rebellion and sympathize with those traitors in arms against our Government will be sought out and hunted down. Covering themselves with Unionism, taking the test oath, voting for Lincoln and hurrahing for the Union will not cover their guilt or remove the stigma of traitor from them or their families. They have shown by their past conduct that they would have destroyed the government if it had been in their power. But when they see their favorite sachem [scheme] of treason fail, they, like Judas, would like to creep back and received as loyal citizens, and have shared to them the benefits of the officers of the country. I will venture to predict that not one Rebel sympathizer or Butternut in the free or slave states, give anything to the way worn soldier of General Sheridan's army for Thanksgiving Day. As I said before I can't tell how long we will stay here. The 2nd Brigade moved today down on the Winchester Railroad and it is thought here today that we will move in a few days somewhere on the road where we can be more easily supplied...”[54]

## Captain Young's Brother Captured by Guerillas

Young was deeply concerned about guerilla activity near his new home at Winfield in Putnam County; however, his family experienced much less contact with Confederates as they did near Coalsmouth. His youngest brother Samuel Early Young (b. 1828) was drafted in September 1864 and assigned to Company G at Young's request. Soon, their cousin John D. Stephenson visited and informed that their next-youngest brother Alexander Samuel Young (b. 1816) was recently captured by guerillas in November. Young wrote to Paulina after working on his winter cabin all day on December 3, "John and Silas [Elkins] and myself have just finished our hut and the worst of all is that it smokes. But we will try to make out with it. We may leave it tomorrow. Samuel and Cousin John D. Stephenson are now with me...I heard that the Rebels have taken brother Alex off. Is it so? If it is the case, you may tell the Rebels in Putnam that if he does not come back safe and sound in a short time that I will avenge his absence on the most influential Secessionist as soon as I return; and if I live it won't be long. O, my dear Paulina, you can't tell how indignant I feel at the information of my brother being in the hands of those roaming devils who have annoyed the country for three long years, and have been fed and protected by those home hypocrites who have been protected by our arms, at the instance of home office seekers."

Furious, Young went on: "Well, I tell you and you may tell them, so help me God, I will avenge his wrongs. The old excuse of 'I can't help it' won't do this time if he is not at home when I come, for I shall come prepared and shall not be very choice in my victims. I know them and have them marked. I know the men who tried to have him and myself arrested in the beginning of the war; and of course they are no better yet, although they have been trying since that time to creep into the Union for the sake of office. You may tell those leading Rebels in your neighborhood that you know they had better go to work and get him back and pay him damages for his absence and confinement. The Rebels may laugh at that and surely will, but the day is coming when they won't laugh. And you may show Captain [John] Bowyer this letter and ask him to warn those men who have been so forward in the commencement of this Rebellion for they will have to atone for my brother's wrongs."

Young continued, "O, my dear wife, I have seen my brave men fall and bleed; I have had my heart rung with sorrow, but to learn that my poor brother was dragged off from his family and has to suffer incarceration at the hands of the enemies of mankind, and enemies of all free institutions, is almost more than I can bear. Sam is nearly crazy about Alex. It is now 9 o'clock and the boys have gone to bed and I have just received orders to be ready with my company at 8 in the morning for picket duty…" Young also asked Paulina to have a new uniform tailored for him, noting he was "ordered" to obtain one with his current garb being in such poor condition after the recent campaign. He continued, "I must close for the want of space. Not any light. My candle is gone…I hope the lord will bless and defend you and our dear children through this wicked Rebellion, and finally save us in heaven where there is no more war, murder or bloodshed, no more of man's taking the life of his fellowman, no more guerrillas dragging husbands away from their wives and little ones." The next morning, he added, "Seven oclock a.m. – All ready for picket. All well, but I am very anxious about Alex…Well, as sure as I live, if Alex is hurt, Crawford, [Peter] P. Bowyer and some others will pay the penalty." Peter Bowyer, Jr., was the brother of John Bowyer of Winfield, a friend of Young's, and Crawford was Peter's brother; he was also a strong southern supporter, however, and served in a guerrilla company.[55]

During the previous year, Edgar and Sarah Blundon had a daughter named Maud, whom Blundon only recently learned had passed away. Sadly, he wrote: "I resume my pen today to express my sorrow occasioned by the severe affliction which God has pleased to send upon us. I would not murmur or complain beneath the chastening rod, but would earnestly pray for grace to say, earnestly and truly: Nevertheless, not my will but Thine be done. Let us not be sorrowful and conclude that ours is a hard lot, but seek that love which applies this mysterious and seemingly severe providence to our especial good…little Maud has been translated in the Paradise of God, where she can sing to all Eternity the praise of Him who gave her but a short existence in this world of sorrow… but to know she is now free from sin and affliction, and that she now resides near the throne of the blessed Redeemer who died to save her, is a consolation rich enough for our comfort… though I regret the necessity of such a providence, yet I am resigned. We may not now see why God sent the affliction – may never see it in this life – but when the great future is unfolded, then we shall know why these strange chastisements. May heaven console our hearts while suffering this bereavement; and prepare us to seek and obtain, with little Maud, the same incorruptible inheritance."[56]

Young never mentions the loss of his grandchild, although he was likely unaware of it. He wrote to Paulina on December 12, "Since I wrote last we have moved our camp two miles on the right and just landed in time to catch the storm…it is very cold and the wind blows hard enough to lift a Yankee out of his boots. Snow fell on the 10th six inches deep, and the wind has been drifting it about ever since. We are now camped four miles above Winchester…I wish you could send me some socks. I am entirely out and can't get any here at any price…I would like to see Mother Blundon very much indeed, but have no hopes of getting home until my time is out, and I don't intend to leave my braves in the hands of any other man as long as I can stay with them. I can get out any time I choose, but my men can't. If I leave them it will be when I am dishonorably discharged like Captain James Meyers because he would not bow to Colonel Bukey. The best Captain we have had in the Regiment. But we will restore him again."

Young continued to tell Paulina about conditions in the winter camp, noting they had built earthworks "across the valley from Fort [Front] Royal Road to the North Mountains" and quipped, "No Rebels in striking distance. Too cold for their bare feet." Captain James W. Meyers enlisted as a private in Company B, 11th West Virginia Infantry on October 28, 1861, and was elected captain on December 24, 1861. At age forty-one-years, he was dismissed from service on November 18, 1864, by a Court of Inquiry initiated by Lieutenant Colonel Van H. Bukey; the matter related to Meyers challenging a questionable order during the battle of Cedar Creek.[57]

Young was correct; their next move would in fact be to the railroad, but not to guard it. Colonel Thomas M. Harris was brevetted as a Brigadier General on December 15. He received orders on December 19 to move the 3rd Brigade (10th, 11th and 15th West Virginia Infantry) by railroad, along with the 1st Division, which also included the 12th West Virginia Infantry, to Washington, D.C., to join Lieutenant General Ulysses S. Grant's army at Petersburg. They arrived on December 22 and established a new winter camp at Deep Bottom. The West Virginians were assigned to the Army of the James on Christmas Eve, in the newly formed 24th Corps under Major General John Gibbon, formerly of the famous "Iron Brigade." The 11th West Virginia remained in the 1st Division, and the 3rd Brigade was reassigned as the 1st Brigade. During the final months of the Civil War, John Young and Company G would see more of "the elephant" than they ever imagined in the trenches at Petersburg.[58]

## Chapter Four References

1. OR, Series 1, Vol. 33, Part 1, 374; 481; 579; Series 1, Vol. 43, Part 1,59; Series 1, Vol. 51, Part 1, 1140.; Roush, 12; Cobb Family Collection, R. Cobb Civil War Letters, MS-2002-117, WV Archives;13th WV Field History, (Part 2), 1.

2. *Weekly Register*, February 11, 1864; Cook, R.B. "Capture of the Government Steamer B.C. Levi." *West Virginia History*, Vol. 23(2), (January 1962), 153-167.

3. Freeman, D. "West Virginia Stakes Oil Claim." *American Association of Petroleum Geologist's News.* (March 1998), 3-5; OR, Series 1, Vol. 5, 604; 647; 706; 733; Series 1, Vol. 19, Part 2, 338; Series 1, Vol. 25, Part 2, 111; 590; Series 1, Vol. 27, Part 3, 449-450; 816; Series 1, Vol. 29, Part 2, 141; 331; 614-616; Series 1, Vol. 33, Part 1, 3; 479-480; 750-756; 1007; Series 1, Vol. 51, Part 1, 1146.

4. OR, Series 1, Vol. 33, Part 1, 479-480; Series 1, Vol. 51, Part 1, 762-735; J.V. Young Diary, March 20-26, and April 4, 1864.

5. CSR, RG 94, M508, Roll 69, National Archives; WV AG Papers, 11th WV, AR 382, Box 1, Folder 42; Roy Bird Cook Collection, Box 1, Folder 2, Call No. A&M 0895, Series 1, Correspondence, WV Archives; Young Letters, April 14 & 23, 1864; Young Diary, April 14-23, 1864.

6. Griffith, 81-83; Michael Ayers. "Journal of the Spring Campaign 1864 in West Virginia." WVU Regional History Collection, A&M 325, WVU Library, Morgantown, WV; OR, Series 1, Vol. 37, Part 1, 23-35.

7. OR, Series 1, Vol. 37, Part 1, 10; 24-34; Ayers Journal May 7, 1864; J.V. Young Diary, May 5, 1864.

8. Ibid., 18; 24; 34; Ayers Journal May 8-9, 1864.

9. OR, Series 1, Vol. 37, Part 1, 10; 25; 54; Ayers Journal May 9-10, 1864; J.V. Young Letters, May 20 & 21, 1864, WVU Library.

10. Ayers Journal May 9, 1864; OR, Series 1, Vol. 37, Part 1, 24-25; J.V. Young Letters May 24 & 30, 1864, WVU Library; CSR, RG 94, M508, Roll 187, National Archives. Private James Davis continued to serve only briefly after the battle of Cloyd's Mountain; he was deemed Missing in Action at Lynchburg, Virginia, on June 18, 1865, and never returned to Company G. Service records note he had become sick and was hospitalized at some point afterward, where he remained until the war's end.

11. OR, Series 1, Vol. 37, Part 1, 10; 33-34; 54-55; See also OR Series 1, Vol. 33, Part 1,721; 723-724; 747.

12. Ayers Journal May 10, 1864; OR, Series 1, Vol. 37, Part 1, 26-27; 34-36; 507. The mountain near Newport, Virginia, where General Crook ordered his wagon

trains to dump hundreds of cases of minié balls is known to locals as "minié ball hill."

13. *Philadelphia North American* newspaper, May 11, 1864. https://chroniclingamerica.loc.gov/lccn/sn86081912/1864-05-11/ed-1/seq-1/ (Hereafter *North American*); OR, Series 1, Vol. 37, Part 1, 27; 35-37.

14. OR, Series 1, Vol. 37, Part 1, 27-28; 35-37; Ayers Journal, May 14-16, 1864; J.V. Young Diary, May 19, 1864.

15. OR, Series 1, Vol. 37, Part 1, 120; 507; Griffith, 103.

16. J.V. Young Letters, May 20 & 21, 1864.

17. Ibid., May 24, 1864.

18. Ibid., May 27, 1864.

19. Ibid., May 30, 1864; CSR, RG 94, M324, Roll 723, National Archives.

20. *North American & United States Gazette.* Philadelphia, PA. May 11, 1864. Vol. 79(155), SN10328, Newspaper reading room, Library of Congress; Roush, 19.

21. J.V. Young Letters, June 9, 1864, WVU Library.

22. OR, Series 1, Vol. 37, Part 1, 120-121; 130-134; J.V. Young Diary, June 12, 1864; Locke, 9-10; 17.

23. Ibid., OR. Vol 37.

24. Ibid.

25. Ibid., WV AG Report December 31, 1864; Roush, 21; Locke, 15; J.V. Young Diary, June 27, 1864.

26. Ibid., 94-103; 169-172; 288-289; 295; CSR, RG 94, M508, Roll 69, National Archives; Locke, Cunningham Letters. July 8, 1864, 17-18.

27. Ibid., OR, Part 2, 290-292; 287-288; 332-355; "Daniel Frost Helped Chart West Va.'s Statehood." *Wheeling Intelligencer,* May 7, 2020; J.R. James, (Ed.). *The Civil War Letters of John McKee, 44th Ohio Volunteer Infantry, 1861-1865.* (Leawood, KS: Leathers Publishing, 1998), 128-129; Scott C. Patchan. *The 1864 Valley Campaign.* (London, NB: Univ. of Nebraska Press, 2007), 60-82; Young Diary, July 27, 1864.

28. OR, Series 1, Vol. 27, Part 1, 428; Part 2, 286-287; CSR, RG 94, M508, Roll 107, National Archives; J.H. Newton., G.C. Nichols, and G. Sprankle. "History of the Pan-Handle, West Virginia." (Wheeling, WV: J.A. Caldwell, Publisher, 1879), 128-236.

29. OR, Series 1, Vol. 37, Part 1, 292; 301-308; Vol. 37, Part 2, 286-287; J.V. Young Letters, August 1 & 24, 1864; J.V. Young diary, June 29, 1864.

30. Ibid, OR, 169-172; 295; 301-308; Part 2, 286-295; John H. Eicher and David H. Eicher. *Civil War High Commands.* (Stanford, CA: Stanford Univ. Press, 2002),

641; *Carolina Watchman,* September 5, 1864. Newspaper Microfilm held in the Edith M. Clark History Room; Brawley Collection, No. NCAAA 39, Rowan County Library, Salisbury, NC; J.V. Young Diary, July 27 & 28, 1864; Philip H. Sheridan. Personal Memoirs. (New York: De Capo Press, Reprinted 1992, Original 1888), 254; OR, Series 1, Vol. 43, Part 1, 709, 719, 721.

31. J.V. Young Letters, August 1, 1864; CSR, RG 94, M508, Rolls 84 &211, National Archives.

32. Young Letters, August 4, 1864.

33. OR, Series 1, Vol. 43, Part 1, 57; 360; 981-982; F.A. Dyer. "A Compendium of the War of the Rebellion." Vol. 2. (Dayton OH: Morningside Books, 1979), 1664-1665; CSR, RG 94, M508, Roll 191, National Archives; J.V. Young Diary, August 7 , 8 & 14, 1864.

34. OR, Series 1, Vol. 43, Part 1, 57; 360; 981-982; F.A. Dyer. "A Compendium of the War of the Rebellion." Vol. 2. (Dayton OH: Morningside Books, 1979), 1664-1665; CSR, RG 94, M508, Roll 191, National Archives; J.V. Young Diary, August 7, 8 & 14, 1864.

35. Ibid. J.V. Young, August 23, 1864; Locke, 18-20.

36. J.V. Young Letters, August 24 & 26, 1864.

37. OR, Series 1, Vol. 43, Part 1, 23; 61; 360-361; J.V. Young Letters, September 7, 1864.

38. Ibid., OR, 24-26; 110-115.

39. J.V. Young Letters, September 7, 1864.

40. McKee, 128; OR, Series 1, Vol. 43, Part 1, 26; 123; Young Diary, September 22, 1864; Record of Rebel Flags Captured by Union Troops after April 19, 1861. Record Group 94, National Archives. The flag is held at the National Civil War Museum in Richmond, VA.

41. J.V. Young Letters, September 26, 1864.

42. OR, Series 1, Vol. 43, Part 1, 28-30; Blundon Letters, October 13, 1864.

43. Ibid., 28-30; WV AG Papers, 11th West Virginia, AR 382, Co. G Muster Roll October 31, 1864, Record of Events. WV Archives; J.V. Young Diary, October 19, 1864; Eicher, 641-642; OR, Series 1, Vol. 43, 32; 135; 394-396.

44. OR, Series 1, Vol. 43, Part 1, 35-37; 135; 394-396; J.V. Young Diary October 20, 1864; J.V. Young Letters, October 24, 1864.

45. Ibid., J.V. Young October 24, 1864.

46. Mollie Hansford-Walls Diary, 51-53.

47. U.S. Army Military History Institute, Carlisle, PA. 11th West Virginia Files; November 20, 1864. Note Sgt. Lewis Griffith's mother wrote in the pension claim that he served under Lieutenant Colonel Van H. Bukey in the 13th West Virginia in 1861; however, Bukey was never a member of that regiment and it was not organized until 1862.

48. J.V. Young Letters, October 22, 1864.

49. Ibid.; Scott C. Cole. *34th Battalion Virginia Cavalry.* (Lynchburg, Virginia: H.E. Howard, 1993), 95.

50. J.V. Young Letters, October 30, 1864.

51. OR, Series 1, Vol. 43, Part 1, 35, 137, 394-396.

52. J.V. Young Letters, November 4 and 10, 1864; WV AG Files, 11th West Virginia Infantry, AR 383, Boxes 1 & 2, Folder 2, WV Archives.

53. Ibid., November 20, 1864.

54. Blundon Letters, November 20, 1864; CSR, RG 94, M507, Roll 69, National Archives; J..V. Young Letters, November 24, 1864.

55. Ibid., December 3 & 4, 1864; Wintz, 54-59; *Wheeling Intelligencer* July 21, 1863.

56. Blundon Letters, December 11, 1864.

57. J.V. Young Letters, December 11, 1864; CSR, RG 94, M508, Roll 192, National Archives.

58. WV AG Files, AR 383, 11th West Virginia Infantry, Boxes 1 & 2, Folders 7, 42, 43 and 44: Morning Reports, Muster-In Rolls, Muster-Out Rolls, and Descriptive Rolls for Company G.

# 5

# Everyone Knew the End Was Near
# 1865

On January 1, 1865, the 3rd Brigade was moved to Chaffin's Farm, Virginia, south of Richmond along the James River, where it established encampment and remained there through early March. The Union and Confederate armies had been locked in desperate trench warfare at Petersburg since June 1864. There were roughly thirty-seven miles of entrenchments running south from Richmond to Hatcher's Run, a stream located just southeast of Sutherland's Station on the Southside Railroad. Company G participated in numerous patrols and skirmishes during this period, and the regiment also engaged in grueling combat during the final assaults in April 1865. At Chaffin's Farm, supplies, uniforms and rations were often limited, and men complained of slow mail deliveries. Hundreds were often completely isolated from their families and friends for weeks at a time. In March 1865, the Army of West Virginia was assigned to Brevet Major General John W. Turner's Independent Division in the 24th Corps under Major General John Gibbon, who formerly commanded the famous "Iron Brigade" and was popular among the West Virginians.

*Major General John Gibbon*
*Library of Congress*

The 11th West Virginia, along with the 10th and 15th West Virginia infantry regiments, remained in Brigadier General Thomas M. Harris's 3rd Brigade; however,

205

shortly after their arrival, the brigade was re-designated as the 1st Brigade of Turner's Division. Harris was a former physician who originally recruited and commanded the 10th West Virginia Infantry. Harris' West Virginians were encamped at Chaffin's Farm until March 1. Generally, combat operations during the months of January and February involved only slight action on picket lines and frequent mortar and cannon fire. Otherwise, the lines were quiet except for "...deserters coming into our lines" daily. The near constant artillery firing in late January along the lines made large troop movements impossible, if not innervating, to say the least.[1]

John Young left a vivid picture of his experiences during the Petersburg and Appomattox campaigns; the war was nearing its apex by the time Company G arrived at Chaffin's Farm. New Year's Day fell on a cold, snowy Sunday in 1865, when Young wrote in his diary, "Some cannonading. Laying between Richmond and Petersburg, in comfortable quarters, but will leave them." He also mentioned Colonel Van H. Bukey's term of service was soon ending and that he announced his imminent departure. Young indicated he was one of the "most contentious men" he had encountered in service, and was relieved to see him go. Bukey was supposed to be replaced by Lieutenant Colonel James L. Simpson, who had only recently returned from being on sick leave since November. Young was excited for Simpson to take over; however, that officer's term of service ended January 23, and he also departed, leaving former Sergeant Major Michael Ayers, who was now an officer with the rank of Major, in command of the 11th West Virginia. Also, in January, Sergeant John Hall Wood, along with a lieutenant and another sergeant, took a wagon train to Washington, D.C., intending to pick up much needed supplies and deliver some wounded men to a hospital. Wood noted, "It was certainly the coldest time I ever saw." Wood was aged twenty-two years when he enlisted in Company G on August 23, 1862, at Coalsmouth and mustered into Federal service there also on October 6, 1862. He was five feet, eight inches tall, with hazel eyes and dark hair, and he resided in Kanawha County prior to the war, where he worked as a farmer.[2]

Company G spent much of January constructing winter quarters; the bitter snowy weather lent a sense of urgency to their labors. Young made numerous, similar diary entries in this period describing how their hastily constructed dwellings often leaked and held water on the ground. He found no less than "4 inches underground" of standing water one night, due to the roofing made only of a "half face of fly tents." This was a large piece of heavy cotton duck canvas material issued to officers, intended as a shade source outside of their larger tents on campaign. Unfortunately, it was not usually adequate protection against heavy rains or snow. At Washington on January 3, Sergeant John Wood and his comrades sought out entertainment at Ford's Theatre, the same venue that would later host the assassination of President Abraham Lincoln. Wood wrote, "It was very interesting and I enjoyed it very much," in contrast to his comrades at Petersburg, who were performing manual labor and sleeping in water. A week later, Young's roof was still incomplete: "Our house not covered - been laying three days by log heap. Cold and snowing. Raining...moved in our cabin. Lay on the wet floor. Slept well..."[3]

As heavy rains continued, he described "the earth is a sea of water." Young also mentioned he was supposed to have received a furlough to visit his wife and family soon, but it was revoked, for which he was most disappointed. Young wrote to his daughter Emily on January 11, again reflecting, "Well, we are here in this swamp yet, in hearing of fighting every day; but, as it happens, we are not engaged in it. But, Emma, this part of Virginia shows what Rebellion does for those who engage in it. East Virginia is one waste from the Allegheny Mountains to the Atlantic Ocean. The eye cannot rest on anything but shows the mark of Rebellion and Secession. We are camped here where our forefathers first landed on the shores of Virginia, where they labored and toiled to build up a great nation for their children, where their fathers, none daring to molest or make them afraid. And the Lord did raise up a great and powerful nation, the happiest people in the world, who had the best institutions in the world, and the freest (slavery excepted)."

He continued, "Three years ago our people were rich, contented and happy, having everything that heart could wish. But those restless spirits in the South could not be satisfied with the full blessings of God on the whole Government but wickedly sought to destroy our Union and build up one whose foundation would be slavery and oppression. Notwithstanding all the light that wise men could give them, and all the entreaties of good men, they persisted in their wicked desire in destroying the Government. But, God will avenge the wrongs done to the oppressed, whether white or black. When I look over this part of Virginia, and my mind runs back...I fancy I see the first poor Negroes landed on the shores of Virginia, and their labor and suffering to the commencement of this unholy Rebellion. Think of the lash – think of the handcuffs – think of the separation of fathers and mothers, sisters and brothers – think of the exposure and suffering in cold and heat – and think of the perpetual ignorance in which they were raised, without one gleam of hope of ever being delivered from that vile bondage."

Young further expounded, "Add to this the effort of the Southern people to bind the fetters still tighter on the suffering race, and then the concessions made by the General Government, to perpetuate the hateful institution – I think of all this and then of the goodness and mercy of God to all mankind. And when I remember His promises to all that trust in him I am forced to believe that the Lord is working out a great salvation for a down trodden people; that cries of these suffering human beings have been heard in Heaven, and the Lord is about to deliver them. We, too, as a nation, have sinned, and the Lord will have a sacrifice. But, Oh, have there not been enough to satisfy Justice? This question doubtless has been asked by thousands. I answer, 'Surely there has.' But unless the Southern people become willing to let the oppressed go free, and lay down their arms and submit to the Government, the whole Southern country will be destroyed and the people annihilated rather than lose the dignity of our Government. May the Lord bless and save our Government and her free institutions forever! Disappointments will come! Just as the boys get ready to start home, with glad hearts, there comes an order revoking all furloughs except in special cases...And then you must send me some socks...I have good comfortable quarters here now. Goodbye for the present." On Friday, January 13, Young scribbled in his diary that some bad luck befell the regiment, "Pontoon bridge broke and left us without rations." Quartermaster Sergeant John H. Wood returned to the camps at City Point and made his way over to the division by crossing the James River, quipping he had traveled over the "worst roads I ever saw in my life."[4]

Young received a letter from Emily on December 13, 1864, and teasing her on January 13, wrote, "Poor little thing. It looked ashamed of itself. It was a dirty and ragged letter, had been on the way just one month. But I was glad to get it. I have no news to write. All quiet on our side of the James. Some heavy cannonading on the south side of the river today...Oh, you cannot imagine how badly all the officers want to get away from here. The sound of those hundred pounders makes them feel unsafe. At least I think they would feel safer in the mountains of West Virginia. The commander sent a circular around this evening to see how many officers of the 11th Va. wanted to be mustered out of the service, and I believe that everyone signed it but myself. I told them if they would muster out my men I would go out too, and not until then. I told them that I loved my family as well as they did, and wanted to go home as much as anyone, but I did not think it honest to get men into service and then run and leave them in danger. I hope that the whole Regiment will go out in February...But I intend to stay with my men just as long as I can, and if they have to fight the enemy more I will be with them...We have a good comfortable house now, and the boys are quite saucy, and Sam keeps singing. He is now singing 'Heaven My Home.' It makes me think of my own happy home and the dear ones there."

Young continued, "This whole country is laid waste and looks desolate indeed. The very negroes that bore the lash here a few years ago now stand between us and their masters with guns in their hands, ready and anxious to avenge their wrongs and teach

Nabobs of the South that a Black man is not a beast of the stall. There are about fifty thousand negroes on the line between Petersburg and Richmond, and I tell you the Johnnies don't like the idea of fighting their own property. The negroes and the Rebs won't make friends. They light in on each other whenever they can. The Rebs will hollow at the negroes on the line – 'There, you smoked Yankees, take your shot,' and then blaze away at the darky; and the Negros will hollow, 'Get in your holes, Rebs, we are going to shoot,' and into their holes they go. If they are careless they soon get a Minnie ball. I think the Government has nearly enough Negroes in the field to whip the Rebs now. I have not seen a citizen, man or woman, since I have been here, although there are large farms, and a few years ago the country was rich and the people had everything that heart could wish.  But Secession:  O, Secession, what hast thou done? Thou hast destroyed the country and murdered thousands of innocent beings who had no interest in Secession... Enough of this at present. I must close...All the Winfield boys are well."[5]

Soldiers in the Civil War often dealt with price gouging by a group of merchants who followed the armies, known as sutlers. They were assigned to specific regiments, selling various dry goods, clothing and often food, but usually at ridiculous prices. The officers in the 11th West Virginia, including John Young, had enough, and they collectively wrote to the War Department on January 13 requesting a new sutler. Company G was placed on heavy "fatigue duty" January 14-17, constructing a new corduroy road from the James River to inside Union lines. When news that Fort Fisher in Wilmington, North Carolina, had fallen to the Union, Young witnessed a heavy artillery barrage in honor of its capture; Wilmington was the last major seaport still under Confederate control that provided vital supply lines. Rumors of peace talks were also rampant in Union camps, but Young remained skeptical. During a heavy sleet storm on January 21, Young had a brief visit with the regimental quartermaster, Sergeant John Wood, seeking a new supply of paper, but it was to no avail as there was a shortage of paper in the army at that time.[6]

On January 22, Brigadier General Thomas M. Harris inspected his brigade, and Young penned, "The 11th Va. pronounced worst Regt. in the Brigade on the account of our camp." Company G next spent three days on picket duty, and early in the morning of January 25, Confederates attacked the 24th Corps in their earthworks where Company G was located. The 25th Corps, comprised primarily of African American troops, were ordered to assist and helped repulse the assault. Young recalled, "Our negroes whipped the Rebs and drove them back." Two days later, the 24th Corps received orders to move south; Young wrote, "Received orders to be ready to strike tents at 8 a.m. this morning, to the great reluctance of the soldiers who have worked hard to make themselves comfortable after building five times this winter." Such was army life, however, and on the next day, the regiment moved to the front lines. Young noted in his diary: "tents down, knapsacks packed. 8 a.m. 'Fall in' the cry. Marched to the front 4 miles. The coldest day this winter. Bad quarters, no fire places. I slept on the cold ground. Suffered with cold..."[7]

On January 28, following guard mount, Company G was ordered back on picket duty, within "speaking distance of the Rebs." Young wrote they had been up all night due to hearing Confederate and Union pickets taunting and harassing each other. Often this was done to not only relieve boredom, but in hopes of drawing the opposing side out into the open to obtain a better shot at them. Young became ill on the picket lines and returned to camp January 29, lying "in bed with a bad cold" the next two days. He wrote to Paulina on January 31, "I am glad to tell you that I am tolerably well this morning, notwithstanding the loss of my officers for they are all leaving as fast as they can get out and wont hardly wait to say 'Good-Bye.' The first thing we know they are out and gone. If they keep on going out Uncle Abe will have to commission the

*Federal pickets at Petersburg, 1865*
*Library of Congress*

darkeys for it does look like the officers are afraid to stay here. I suppose they are afraid General Grant will charge the Rebel works and they don't want to risk their bacon any longer. But, I assure you, some of them never have been in any danger since I have been with them. They were very brave until they had to go to the front, and since that time they have been very sickly all at once. There is no excuse for officers resigning and leaving their men here. I think it would be more honorable to stay until their time is out and then go home. My time is out now and I know that I want to go home just as much as any man in the service, but honor is at stake, and I cannot see that it would be honorable after getting a company of men into the service away from their families into danger, and then run off and leave them just because they happened not to be officers."

He wrote further, "I saw a Lieut. in Company A this morning, running around trying to get out, with a Captain's commission in his pocket. I asked him what he wanted out for – 'Oh,' he said, 'I've been in the service long enough.' The scamp has never been in one engagement since the war commenced. So it is, the great majority of those who are leaving have never done anything for the Government, nor never will. If they could lay around Parkersburg, or some other town, and receive large pay from the Government they would remain in service until dooms day. My dear little wife, can't you, while those fellows about Winfield are so 'greasy,' slide about two thousand dollars into your pocket for our farm? Don't lease, sell if you can. Well, I must close by asking you all to write often. Your letters have come very regularly lately. It only takes them 10 days to come..."[8]

The harsh winter weather continued, and Young found himself in command of the 11th West Virginia. On February 3, President Lincoln sent Secretary of State William H. Seward to meet with Confederate Vice President Alexander H. Stephens, Senator Robert M.T. Hunter, and Assistant Secretary of War John A. Campbell at Hampton Roads to discuss terns for peace. The conference failed to reach any compromises other than prisoner exchanges, but rumors of peace flooded the ranks in the lines at Petersburg. The 42nd Mississippi regimental commander, Colonel L.J.C. Lawson, was also present at the meeting. He recalled that Edwin Stanton, U.S. Secretary of War, told the Confederate delegation they had "no friends" and "nothing to hope for" and to "Lay down your arms, and we will then offer terms," which was bluntly declined by the Confederates. When Colonel Lawson returned to the lines near Petersburg and informed his regiment of the outcome, Wilson stated they shouted through the ranks, "That's enough Colonel, we'll fight till hell freezes over and meet them on the ice!"[9]

Prior to the failed peace talks, Young wrote to Paulina on February 2, "As I am now commanding the Regiment and have taken charge of Headquarters and now have some leisure, I concluded that I would write to you, not that I want to grumble at you for not writing for I have gotten letters very regularly here lately...I don't think my duties will be as hard on me here as they were in the company. But how long I will remain here I can't tell but suppose until we get a Lieutenant Colonel and a Major. But it is hard work to get anyone to accept it. The recommendation of an officer has to go up through all the Headquarters in this Corps and then to the Governor of [West] Virginia, then back and up again before a Board of Examiners, and if he is not sound in every particular he 'can't come it,' therefore I refuse to try it; besides I am tired of the service and I think peace will be made soon. And then I don't want to be forced to go to Mexico or any other place to fight any more. But if I live until company is out, I then want to come home and spend the remnant of my days in peace with you. I will then know how to appreciate home and the loved ones there."

He further related, "We are now laying just below Richmond in talking distance of the Rebels, and they tell our boys that peace will be made before long, but they think the Southern Confederacy will be acknowledged and that we will be glad to make peace on any terms. But how sadly disappointed will be the Chivalry when the thing turns up…I only took command yesterday and the Regiment was in an awful fix – many companies without one commissioned officer, the most of them resigned and gone home, and the rest on somebody's staff. But I have had them coming in all day and sending them to their companies, which they don't like much. But so it is. I now have one commissioned officer to each company, and now I think we will get along much better. You ask what took that contemptible Bukey away from the Regiment. I will just say because he was afraid if he got in another fight company G would mark him out and his fears were well grounded. I have been acquainted with many men in my time but Bukey is the most contemptible man I ever knew. But, as mean as he was, I have outwitted him so far; and I think if ever I see him in private life I shall boot him. Many officers and men have suffered by him…Well, my dear wife, I must close this short letter as night is closing in…"[10]

Young wrote to Paulina on February 7, griping: "You must excuse me for not writing more for I am interrupted at every line – orders, orderlies, Headquarters, and everything else that you can imagine. It is 'Captain' here and 'Captain' there, and 'Captain' every place, night and day… You can't imagine how anxious I am to hear from home. I watch every mail with deep interest…" He also described recent brigade inspections in which the 11th West Virginia had significantly improved under his command; many of the officers also told him they had never had battalion drill until he ordered it the day prior. One incentive for a regiment to improve was that the one deemed "worst" could not obtain furloughs; they had weekly brigade inspections, and names were published intending to shame those responsible. Having received praise from General Harris for the improved state of his regiment, Young bragged: "…all the officers think if I would remain in command the 11th would 'take the horns,' in a few weeks. But I suppose we will soon have a Lieut. Colonel and Major but who I don't know. They will have to pass through a critical examination before they get it. It isn't every man who can get the office here. This army uses a great deal of 'Red-tapeism' and many who are in high position lack brains…"

He continued, "I have bought a new suit of clothes, a short coat pants and waistcoat, sword and belt, which cost me sixty-eight dollars…The officers here think it very strange that I don't resign and go home when every officer is trying to get out except me, but I tell them it is cowardly to bring their men into danger and then run off and leave. I tell them also that I have as good a little wife as any man and that I want to see her just as bad, but I say 'My wife is a brave woman and detests a coward.' But whether it is cowardice or not, I am sure they are afraid of those Big Guns and the coming Spring campaign. I will send Ben 'The Life of General Sheridan.' Tell him to read it. I was with him in every engagement in the Shenandoah. I must close..." In a brief postscript on February 8, Young added: "P.S. Snowed all day yesterday, Sunshine today, but rather cold. Lieut. [Clark] Elkins made application to be mustered out today, but his application was respectfully returned on the ground that he has two days to serve yet (short time)." On February 11, 1865, Quartermaster Sergeant John H. Wood wrote in his diary that the 11th West Virginia "drew some clothing and issued today a very small lot." On February 16, Wood noted, "Lieut. Elkins [Clark] was mustered out this P.M. I wrote a letter home by him."[11]

On February 22, during a heavy snowstorm, Young rejoiced at a recent letter he received from Paulina, who told him she would not try to persuade him to leave his company; he wrote back: "We are here yet, a part of this great army, not fighting but going through an endless routine of inspection, and review, which is nearly as laborious as marching and fighting, but not quite as dangerous...Oh, how thankful I feel to God for his goodness to me since the wicked Rebellion broke out. I can see his goodness in almost every turn I make or have made, since the war. The preservation of my life in so many dangers and the preservation of the health of my dear family are sources of joy and gladness in my poor heart every day; and add to this a companion who heartily co-operates with me in what I think is my duty renders me great pleasure indeed. It holds me up and bears me forward through many trials that perhaps if it were otherwise I would fail. But to think I have a patient wife and children at home, who love their country and hate treason as much as they do, and be willing to make every sacrifice for the restoration of our government. Your expression in your last letter made every nerve in me rejoice, and I could not help shedding tears to think of that letter, and my little patriotic wife at home."[12]

He continued, "Oh, when I read your letter if I could have embraced you in my arms I think I would have had ample pay for all my hardships...So unlike the whining of some officers' wives here, and they have succeeded in tormenting their husbands out of the service, leaving their men here at the mercy of anyone who may be appointed over them. But the signs of the times go to show, my dear wife, that your suffering and surety will come to a close, and we be united again in peace at home. There has been considerable fighting today over the river, but the result I can't give. Some say that Grant has taken Petersburg. Some say it was the negroes and Johnnies fighting. However, it was pretty hard fighting. I had a Johnnie in here tonight who has just deserted. He is from Georgia. He says the Rebels cheered when they heard that Charleston, S.C., had fallen. I asked him what made them charge their commissary the other night. He said the soldiers were only allowed one pint of meal a day and the Quartermaster had a cow that he fed the meal to and they charged and took all the meal and killed the cow and ate her. He said that they charged this commissary three other times this week. He says that Rebels won't fight any longer. There are about one hundred a week coming in our lines. They tell about the same story of their desertion. Well, I must close..."[13]

Young also wrote to his eighteen-year-old son Ben on February 22, whom he discouraged from joining the Army, telling him instead to remain in school, "This leaves us all well and in good spirits, and you need not be surprised at hearing of General Lee's surrendering up the Rebel Army or evacuating Richmond at any day...General Sherman has cut off his supplies and 'General Starvation' is surely marching on Richmond, and will conquer that infernal nest of treason. We had a jolly time yesterday. A dispatch confirmed the fall of Charleston, South Carolina, and Augusta, and also Columbia...This cuts all the grub from Richmond, and Lee will have to get with chivalry. But where will he go? There were a hundred big guns fired in honor of General Sherman and his brave heroes yesterday, but the Johnnies didn't like it much. They hollowed over to our boys to know what was the matter. The boys told them that Sherman was making peace, and the Rebellion would soon go to hell where it belongs. The Rebel soldiers say if their leaders don't make peace by Spring they will make peace for them. They tell us on the picket line that they can eat up seven days rations for breakfast. You may guess what they suffer when I tell you that night before last the Rebels made a charge on their own Commissary with yells that told that they were hungry. When they raised the yell and started for the Commissary, the picket hollowed over to us 'Don't be afraid, Yankees. We are not going to hurt you. We only want something to eat.' One of them deserted that night and came to us, and, poor fellow, he was very hungry and said they did not get anything to eat after they did charge the Commissary. I think quite a number were shot in the charge, for there was a good deal of shooting going on over there."

Young continued to describe the situation at Petersburg to his son, "There has been very heavy fighting over the river today. I suppose the Johnnies have charged the 25th Corps, which is all negroes, and they whip the Rebs every time they fight them, and the Rebs are fighting every day more or less. They won't make friends with 'Nigs,' nor the 'Nigs' won't make friends with them, and the consequence is they shoot every opportunity. Your Uncle Sam [Samuel Young] has built me a nice little office with a little brick chimney, and I have just got in it, but how long I will have the pleasure of staying in it I don't know. We have built so many this winter that I have gotten almost out of heart...Whenever I can get my men mustered out I will come home myself (if I live) but I want to see Richmond first...I tell you that the Rebs will have to leave Richmond or surrender within the next four weeks, or I am mistaken."

Young proceeded, "When I look at the efforts that have been made to put an end to the present national trouble, and then see how little has been done, I come to the conclusion that there is something wrong somewhere. If it is, as Emma thinks, a Divine intention for the purpose of putting down that hateful institution of slavery, peace will not be restored until that is accomplished; for the will of the Lord must be done. And I have long thought that slavery would be done away with through the providence of God. But I know the Lord is with his people on the battlefield as well as at home. When I look back upon the campaign and see what I have passed, and not a hair of my head hurt, what can I say but the Lord has shielded me from the missiles of death that flew around and over me and cut down hundreds of my fellow soldiers. I feel that I am only saved through the mercy of God. But I don't remember of going into a battle without offering up a prayer to God for myself and the protection of my poor men who were exposed as well as myself to the flying missiles of death..."

Sergeant John Wood diarized on February 22, "We drew some stationary..." of which some was delivered to Captain Young, who noted, "The Q.M. [Quartermaster] has just sent me my allowance of paper and I will write more..." Young was having regular discussions with Confederate deserters, informing Paulina: "The Rebels are truly out of heart, and the last deserter says he was conscripted and always knew that they could not whip the Yankees. This is the same whine that we have in the Kanawha with those Rebel sympathizers. They were great friends of the Rebels while there was any prospect of success but as soon as they discovered that the Yankees were determined to restore the Government to them they come whining back with a lie in their mouths, saying: 'We have always been Union.'"[14]

Young noted that everyone realized the end of the war coming soon and prognosticated when he next wrote to Emily on February 15, "...I am satisfied that the Rebellion is in its last throes of agony and despair, and my opinion is that the next four weeks will be the most thrilling and interesting part of the war. All the Rebels this side of the Mississippi will be driven into Virginia and the Union force is large – at least they are large enough to protect the interest of our Cause. I suppose when [Joseph E.] Johnston and [Braxton] Bragg get into Virginia it will be two of the largest armies in the world in front of each other, and the Rebels will have to do something at once or give up all for lost, for the fact that they will have no base of supplies and their great army must be fed and clothed...They must cut their way to some place where they can get supplies for their army. Their boasted plenty has played out. They are conscripting negroes (deep humanity). It would make you laugh to hear our 'smoked Yankees' here talking about fighting the 'smoked Johnnies.' They say that just as soon as Jeff puts arms in the hands of the 'Johnnie Negroes' they will turn on their masters. I wouldn't be surprised."

Young further penned, "There has been a great stir on the Rebel lines for two or three days...The Johnnies are just like a hungry bear in an iron cage, running from one end to the other. They are running from one end of their lines to the other – don't know where they will be attacked first. I can hear their railroad cars running through Richmond day and night taking troops first to the right then back to the left, and in our front. Every time the Reels shift their quarters we have to move to meet them, and thus, you see, all the time watching each other...The South Side road is the only road that they have left, and if they don't avail themselves of that soon they wont have that long. And if they lost that they are gone up, no possible escape for them. Lee is looking for something to turn up in his favor – something disastrous to the Yankees, but this they have so long hoped for that I think it would make them heart sick. But I suppose they hope on and will hope until they are swept away by the Union forces. Well, as it is getting late and we have to be ready for marching at daylight, I must try to sleep a little...".[15]

The mail ran a few days later, and Young received several letters from home. He returned the favor to Paulina on February 28, "Since Lieut. [Clark] Elkins left, I have all the writing to do, and it keeps me busy. He nor Lieut. [William] McDowell have done me any good for nearly one year, but they drew their pay and I did the work. I do not think we are in any danger of having any fighting to do here...you need not be surprised to hear of Lee's retreat at any day between now and the middle of March, in the direction of Lynchburg...I know that their men are deserting faster than they can recruit, if they do take the negroes. But the good of it is the Southern soldiers say they will not fight with the negro. They say that they have been fighting for the rich man's negro but wont fight with him. They say if this is not equality they don't know what is...I will send you some of my photographs that you may see how the old fellow looks yet on duty. You must divide with Sallie and Emma...All the boys are well and in good spirits, waiting until the 23rd of May." This was the date that Company G mustered into Federal service in 1862, and thus would end term of service for the majority of his men.

However, Young had other intentions, "I told the boys the other day that I did not think I could stand another campaign, but their answer was that they did not think we would have much marching to do before our time was out... You spoke of selling our farm. Let her go if you can get enough for it, but don't ask too much for it for fear you don't get anything...I wish I could share your good bed tonight. But never mind, the good time is coming, I hope, when the wicked war will come to an end; when we can spend our last days in peace at home with our loved children and friends...Write often, it doesn't cost much. I am glad to say that I get letters regularly now, at least one a week. So goodnight, my dear wife."

*Captain John Valley Young, circa 1865*
*This is likely the image Young mentioned in his letter to*
*Pauline Young on February 28, 1865.*
*West Virginia State Archives*

As the winter faded into March, hundreds more Confederates deserted into Union lines, many knowing that General Grant had recently offered amnesty to avoid prison camps hoping to induce them to desert. Captain William W. Chamberlaine, of General R.E. Lee's Third Corps Artillery Staff recalled, "It was about the first of March. The number of desertions had increased. Our line was so long that it looked more like a skirmish line than a line of battle..." Young wrote in his diary on March 1: "Some cannonading today...Ordered to take command of the 11th Regt. which I did reluctantly. Received orders to keep 4 days rations in our haversack, and a full supply of ammunition on hand."[16]

Rumors were again circulating that the Confederate government was soon going to begin enlisting slaves as soldiers. Young was convinced the Confederate soldiers would never accept this; many of the deserters he spoke to were angry about the prospect, "They are deserting and coming to our lines by hundreds. One company of the 5th South Carolina came to us this morning and one of the 3rd yesterday morning. They say they are whipped and if Jeff Davis will not make peace they will. There seems to be a great discontent among the Rebel soldiers about arming the negroes. They say that they have been fighting for four years for the negro and now if Jeff wants the negro to fight he must fight them alone, for they are not going to equalize themselves with the negro. Tis laughable to hear some of the deserters talk about negro equality. They say that in 1861 all they could hear was that the North wanted the negro set free, and made equal with the whites, but after fighting four years to prevent this great misfortune, General Lee and Jeff Davis want them to stand up in the ranks with the rich man's negroes to save their necks from the halter. There is such a stampede, such discontent, such desertions in the Rebel ranks that have never been in any nation since the world began, and my opinion is that before the middle of May the Rebellion will be over..."

Young opined further, "We are weakening the rebellion more by lying here barking at Jeff [Davis] than if we were fighting...But I suppose if he gets two hundred thousand negroes in the service he can cut his way to Mexico and he and Lee may have them to dig gold or make tobacco. I am confident that if they start to leave the United States every man who has been galled in this wicked rebellion will leave them. You know that I never had any sympathy for a Rebel but I must confess I feel for those who come into our lines. The most of them are objects of pity. Those poor men never have known what freedom was. They have always been kept under the hammer by those Nabobs of the South, and are made to believe anything that wicked men tell them...The Co. will not get out until the 23rd of May but I have lately learned that my whole company will be mustered out then, which will be a joyful day to us. It is all I desire – to get my brave heroes out at once and to get out with them. Other men may have promotions but if I can get my little band of loyal men all out at once that will be promotion enough for me."

Young wrote on, "The War Department has decided that the 11th Regt. shall go out by companies, that is from the organization [date] of the Company...if even one company has served their country faithfully it is Co. G. We have been chosen and selected out of the Brigade for Sharp Shooters and are to be armed with the Spencer Rifle Seven Shooters. The boys consider it promotion to think that Co. G is the best company in the 3rd Brigade...We have no fighting to do here but the 'Johnnies' and the darkeys keep a constant skirmish up on the other side of the river. There was considerable musketry and a cannon shot last night at Fort Harris, on our left, half mile from here, but this is so frequent that it doesn't create any excitement...the boys are enjoying themselves in a game of ball..." There is no evidence in extant Ordnance records that Company G ever received the Spencer Rifles. Young also included a post-script to his wife on March 5, mentioning a recent photograph he had made wearing "a short jacket, new gloves and a new sword belt," which are consistent with items shown in the earlier photograph. On March 6, 1865, Turner's 1st Division held another grand review by Major General Edward O.C. Ord, commanding the Army of the James of which the 24th Corps was a part. Quartermaster Sergeant John H. Wood wrote: "The boys marched pass in splendid style. I was out on Review with the rest of the boys. Gen. Ord's wife was out to see the W.Va. boys. She is a Virginian."[17]

Young soon received more letters from Paulina and some photos. It is probably well he did not see her immediate reaction when he responded: "My dearest little Wife: I was made glad today by the reception of a bundle and in it I found 'Marsh.' But, O, how careworn does my dear little wife look! But I am so thankful for it. I have been looking at it nearly all day long. I value it as a great prize. It makes me think of better days than these...We all think the Rebellion is going to the wall very fast. The world never heard of such a disorganized body as the Southern Confederacy is at this time. Surely the Lord has darkened their counsels, and the very instrumentality that the South attempted to use against the Federal Government (I mean the everlasting negro) will prove their final destruction...I am satisfied that the Rebellion cannot hold out much longer. They may conscript all the negroes in the South and it will not prolong the war any longer...I am glad that the draft has come in Putnam for there were so many in that county that claimed protection from our arms, that did not care a whit whether the Union was restored or not; and I want them to know what it is to be a soldier, and then I hope they can appreciate home and the loved ones there."

He wrote, "We feel so lonely here in this wretched country, nothing to be seen but soldiers and mules; hear nothing but drums, fifes, brass band, and the yells of the soldiers, which becomes very annoying to me. I feel that I want rest and that in some quiet place. Oh, if I could only spend two or three weeks at my once happy little home. How refreshing to my shattered constitution. But my country, my bleeding country, calls for all my services and duty and honesty compels me to remain at my post. While it is true that I love my wife and children, it is equally true that I love my Government and the cause for which I am contending; and you know if we would count our feeling and ease and relinquish the contest, all our labors would be worse than lost, and we and our children be brought into slavery by those politicians of the South. I know that it seems hard that we have to leave home and all we love in the hands of a coldhearted neighborhood, and go to fight treason far away, when nearly all we leave behind are enemies to the cause that we are now battling for – namely, freedom in every sense of the word, but time finally will settle all these things, and the true and loyal soldier will be fully rewarded by our Government and all good and loyal citizens. There is a time in the future when the brave soldier in this unholy war and his family will be honored everywhere and the enemy of our country and their children will be hunted down and hissed out of society. But now we are apt to murmur at their prosperity. We should pity them for they must live and die in disgrace, and they will have to leave [West] Virginia in order to become citizens."

Young closed with, "My dear Paulina, I know you will think strange when I tell you that I have great sympathy for those Rebel soldiers in the South. I know if you could see them when they come over to us you could not help being sorry for them. You know that they have been duped by their leaders and dragged from their homes to fight and die for the rich man's negro, with no pay or anything for their families to live on while they are in the field. The poor fellows feel as proud when they come into our lines and find that the Yankees are so kind to them. They all say that if the Southern army knew how kind the Yankees are to them they would all throw down their arms and quit fighting. But the Rebel leaders make them believe that Yankees will kill them, or make slaves of them, and put the negroes over them. But the Secessionist in West Virginia is inexcusable. What they did was of their own choice. O, the devastation carnage, bloodshed and misery caused by those wicked leaders who will have to hear their own judgment...It is cold and raining this morning. We are mud bound in this low flat country...Richmond is nearly surrounded and will be soon, then Goodbye Rebs."[18]

On March 12, 1865, Sergeant John Wood met General Ulysses S. Grant during his review of Turner's 1st Division. Wood noted, "The Gen. is a very young man. The first time I have seen him." On March 14, Company G First Sergeant Paul R. Morris was promoted to 1st Lieutenant by virtue of commission from West Virginia Governor Arthur Boreman, dated to rank March 9, and was formally mustered in by Captain Young. The Union army mail delivery was dreadfully slow at Petersburg, and Young reported receipt of only one letter from home to his four sent recently on March 17. He wrote to Paulina again that Friday afternoon, "I was growing impatient about home. It seemed to me so long since I had gotten a letter from you...It does appear to me that I never desired or thirsted for the quiet of home as I do now. I am sick and tired of military life and long for the 23rd day of May to come that I may rest a little from my labors. We have a great deal of duty to do here. It's review after review and inspection after inspection until the men and officers are nearly worn out and disgusted with so much Red tapeism. We had a grand review today by General Grant, General Ord and Vice Admiral [David D.] Porter. General Grant was cheered by every regiment in the Corps. He rode by with his hat in his hand, and as General Ord passed the West Virginia Regiment he would cry out 'Three cheers for the Virginia boys!'"

Paulina informed Young that the Kanawha Valley was once again flooded with war refugees, many of whom were robbing families and stealing cattle. He responded, "I am sorry that the Kanawha Valley is filling up with such stuff as refugees and deserters...I would rather they would stop someplace else. But we must be patient and look at the Great Cause before us to be attained yet, namely, the restoration of our Government with all our free institutions when this is gained and the arms wrested from the hands of the traitors...They are a great aggravation, no

*Lieutenant General Ulysses S. Grant*
*Library of Congress*

doubt, but they cannot do us as much harm as if they were in the Rebel ranks, or raiding through the country stealing what the defenceless citizens have left. Therefore, we ought to bear with them as much as possible. The time has not come yet. The guilty shall not go unpunished. They may be doing business now with a great deal of importance in the very neighborhood that they have lately robbed, but be assured that that place will be a hot place for them when those tired and worn soldiers are mustered out of service and come home. They are sure to remember the suffering and toil of the campaign of 1864 and 1865."

Young also complained that he was being assessed for property taxes by Putnam County; however, being in active service he was exempt and informed Paulina to remind the tax collector of this, noting there was no one in that county he had a lower opinion of than he. While writing this letter, Young noted he fell asleep and continued it next morning, "You said that you were getting almost impatient to have me come home. Well, I can't blame you for it is over three years since we have had any pleasure or quietness at home, and I too am growing impatient about home; and you need not be surprised if you see me as soon as I can get my papers fixed up and Lieut. [Van] Morris is mustered in. I think that I can trust my men with him. I know that I am not able for another campaign. I must close – this is four letters since only one from home."

He wrote again on March 22, as rumors of a large military movement were again circulating the Union camps, "We are yet in the same place. We have remained here longer than at any other place since we left Barboursville twelve months ago. But our time is about out. We started yesterday – was out in line, knapsacks on, tents down, all ready. Orders 'return to quarters, wait for further orders.' But orders have not come yet. Today, we got orders to send our camp and garrison equipage to the rear and to send our great coats and dress coats home or to Norfolk, Virginia. But we concluded to send them home...I sent my overcoat, dress coat, three shirts, two pants, one blouse in a barrel. It will start tomorrow. My overcoat is in a box...We can't tell what minute we will have to leave. Grant is keeping old Lee very busy...He doesn't know where Grant is going to strike him...I tell you the condition is everything else but pleasant. They are expecting every day that the Yankees will come, and the deserters say that we can take it easy; and I assure you that if Jeff doesn't get out soon he never will..."

Company G received twenty-three deserters the night previous, and while Young's men were not engaged, a skirmish took place to their right, "The deserters say that they are badly scared...They say that Lee and Jeff are only trying to get the gold and silver out of Richmond and then they will make for the Mississippi...Surely the Lord has darkened the counsel and confused the assembly and nothing but destruction, disappointment and deep humility awaits them. Well, Lieut. [Van] Morris was mustered in today, 1st Lieut...I have notified the officers all to understand that just as soon as Richmond falls...I will tender my resignation at once, and return home...if my boys have to go I will go with them as far as I can; and when I do all that I can do I think the Government ought to be satisfied, with my honest labor and reward my family...two months from today, Company G will honorably go out, and me with them. Yes, only two months, but it will doubtless seem two years to me...my country calls for my services at this critical time when every officer is leaving the army who can possibly get out. They all dread the coming campaign. I am credited at the War Department with seventeen battles – more than any one West Virginia officer in service. Well, I must stop. It is late. I don't know but I may be routed before day. So goodnight my darling wife, look forward two months and pray our Heavenly Father for my safe return..."[19]

As March drew to a close, General Grant was planning an assault on Confederate lines around Petersburg; his intentions were to send the 6th and 9th Corps along with the Army of the James to attack the weakest parts of the lines in their front, while hoping also to mount a large flank attack on the Dinwiddie Line. Company G was still engrossed in daily duties, however, as Private John Overshiner was assigned to

Turner's Division Quartermaster department, and Private Milton Jones was detailed as Major General John Gibbon's bodyguard. Young sent a letter to the *Weekly Register* newspaper in Mason County "to show the Rebel sympathizers that the West Virginia boys are 'Some punkins' in a great army, as well as good 'bushwackers' at home." Company G was again ordered on picket duty near the end of March, just as Richmond newspapers speculated that peace talks were inevitable. When they returned to camp, Young wrote to Emily on March 24, "As I have just come off picket duty and have obtained a Richmond paper just off the press, I concluded that I would forward the pitiful thing to you that you might see how near the Confederacy is gone up. It is a good sample of everything else in Dixie. On picket yesterday, the Johnnies swarmed around our boys to trade. They wanted salt, coffee, or was willing to trade for the boys old hats. But we had strict orders not to permit the boys to trade with them under any considerations. Although I was Brigade officer of the day, I could not prevent the boys from slipping over the lines and trading their old knives for tobacco and exchanging papers."

Men often traded on picket lines, despite it being against orders. Young related that Corporal Emanuel Higginbotham "got hold of my old pocket knife and exchanged it for three plugs of tobacco. It was diverting to see them start to meet with each other. Both sides had orders not to have any communication with each other. They would watch their officers, and as soon as they turned their backs, would beckon to each other and run with all their might, and meet and trade and then run back. But Emma, I assure you that they are a dirty set of fellows, and if the Southern Confederacy don't go up soon, I am sadly mistaken. How it can hold out much longer is a mystery to me. Jefferson Davis has no other country that he can possibly obtain supplies but East Virginia and North Carolina, and I would suppose that they are pretty well gleaned by this time...Unless the Rebels can defeat Sherman, the cause is a hopeless one. Senator [Robert M.T.] Hunter (Rebel) declares that there is now no issue between the Yankees and the Confederate states from the fact that Rebels has passed a law to arm the negroes and bring them on an equality with the Southern confederacy. I wonder how our Southern sympathizers will like that law? This is what they say they are fighting against. Well, they are now fighting for it."[20]

On the evening of March 24, 1865, Turner's Division received orders to "be prepared to move at daylight tomorrow morn" according to Sergeant John Wood. The veterans' earlier prognostications proved correct; soldiers realized a large campaign was about to open. Wood wrote that the 11th West Virginia left at sunrise on March 25, but the quartermasters were left in camp to ensure all of their equipment was secured: "It is cold and unpleasant, and very lonesome. We don't know what point our boys have gone to." Private Nimrod Loyd, Company F, 10th West Virginia, wrote in his diary they had marched to the Chickahominy River and returned to Deep Bottom the next day. Young noted also they passed through the old Seven Days battle grounds, after they had "Struck tents at daylight this morning, marched twelve miles east and camped in an old field in the swamps... Layed the pontoon across the Chickahominy swamp for Sheridan. One man wounded one captured."

The next day was too "cold and unpleasant" for a long, tiresome march, according to Sergeant John Wood. The regiment again waited several hours for General Phil Sheridan's cavalrymen near Charles City, only to learn they had already crossed the river overnight. The 3rd Brigade wound up marching back toward Deep Bottom a distance of fifteen miles, where they "...camped at 2 P.M. for dinner. Don't know where we are going..." However, at 5:00 p.m. that evening the 24th Corps endured yet another grand review; only this time, they were surprised to find President Abraham Lincoln there to observe them. Lincoln had arrived at City Point to conference with General Grant the day previous. The men quickened their step and were proud to be under Lincoln's calm, deliberate gaze. Quartermaster Sergeant John Wood wrote: "It was a grand thing. It was the first time I ever saw the President of the U.S..."[21]

## Attack of Fort Stedman

Before dawn on March 25, the Confederates mounted what would be their last large-scale offensive attack of the war against Fort Stedman, a large earthen redoubt with nine-foot walls and a moat, located one hundred fifty yards from Confederate lines. Major General John B. Gordon's now commanded Lee's 2nd Corps; his former division led the assault. While they managed to capture about one thousand yards of earthworks, fighting mostly in close-quarter, hand-to-hand combat, they were eventually driven back by the Federals. Private William H. Bachman, Company F, 42nd Mississippi Infantry, was on picket duty during that assault and recalled, "...I was on picket duty Gen. John B. Gordon with a part of his command assaulted and captured Fort Stedman, several miles to our left but soon decided that the Yankees could use it to better advantage and turned it back to them..." During the next four days, March 25-28 General Gibbon's command, including Harris' Brigade, broke camp and went on a twenty-mile long circuitous march along the Chickahominy River, through Deep Bottom, to the Point of Rocks to the Appomattox River, and back to Deep Bottom. After the arduous march, the 11th West Virginia stacked arms and camped on open ground in the cold and frosty night. This movement was part of a larger operation in which Grant simultaneously relocated Foster and Turner's Divisions of the 24th Corps, Major General David. B. Birney's Division of the 25th Corps, and a division of cavalry under Brigadier General Ranald S. MacKenzie, from their positions east of Richmond to location on the right of the 2nd Corps, southwest of Petersburg. Grant's plan was to have these units fill in gaps of the Petersburg line, as the 2nd Corps would soon move out in support General Phil Sheridan's cavalry and the 5th Corps in an upcoming attack at Five Forks on April 1. Once the 24th Corps arrived at their new position, the 5th Corps were then on the extreme left of Grant's line. Grant later recalled "There was considerable fighting in taking up these new positions for the 2nd and 5th Corps, in which the Army of the James had also to participate somewhat, and the losses were quite severe. This was what was known as the battle of White Oak Road."[22]

*View facing Fort Stedman from Confederate lines, 1865*
*Library of Congress*

Meanwhile, from his camp, John Young wrote to Paulina, "...we had orders to march on the 25th, unstruck tents and marched out in the direction of the White House as far as the Chickahominy swamps – 15 miles, camped and laid the pontoons across the swamps, scouted in the direction of York river...we are now lying in Deep Bottom ready to march...At all events we are on the move, and I suppose that we will land somewhere in Dixie. I think the next you hear from me will be away down south. We marched yesterday and the day before over [General George B.] McClellan's battleground in '62, through the wilderness and the Chickahominy swamps. We found one man's skull – whole head, with his teeth yet sound in his head; and I suppose hundreds were left unburied. Our whole Division is lying here together waiting orders. The boys are as lively as school children playing ball all over Deep Bottom, just as though they expected to remain here during the war. The Rebel papers say that Johnston has whipped Sherman, but we don't believe it. There has been no fighting in our hearing for several days, but the Rebels are shifting their forces, first right and then left, as though they expected us to attack them somewhere soon. But our march down to the Chickahominy was only a feint to deceive Lee to make him believe that we were going to attack his right. But the first thing he knows he will hear it thunder on his left. Well, as I am writing on my knee in the open field, you must excuse bad writing...We will remain here until tomorrow, and whether we will march or take transports I can't tell. But I will try to advise you of everything that transpires on our route..."[23]

Resting in camp on March 28, Young heard pickets firing all night, in close proximity, and he did not sleep much; he recalled that more than half of Company G "broke down" on their twenty-mile march that day. Sergeant Wood noted also that night, "We're all tired and sore feet, but we had to make a long march...my feet are very badly blistered and much sore. A great many of our boys gave out and could go no further. I enjoyed my supper very much. There is a good prospect of a big fight soon." On March 29, Brigadier General Thomas M. Harris received orders to move toward the City Point railroad; the West Virginians boarded the trains and traveled to Humphrey's Station, disembarking early on the morning of March 30. The 11th West Virginia did not get to sleep, as they were ordered out on picket upon arrival until 4:00 a.m., when the 3rd Brigade marched thirty miles to Hatcher's Run, arriving there at noon, and with the division's left connected to the 2nd Army Corps' right. Sergeant John Wood observed: "It was a very hard march, very bad roads and teams very much worn out. I marched all night and was desperately tired."[24]

On the afternoon of March 30, Brigadier General Thomas M. Harris was ordered to advance toward the deeply entrenched Confederate lines near Hatcher's Run and quickly pushed the pickets into the earthen defenses, temporarily gaining control of a small section. The Confederates made a fierce countercharge, and the battle raged until afternoon, when General Harris amassed his lines and rushed toward the Confederates, pushing them back toward their lines. The weather was not conducive, with a pouring rain continuing throughout the day. The resultant mud and boggy ground made maneuvering a large force difficult and slow. Due to this, Harris ordered his brigade to entrench themselves at dusk, where they remained all night. The Confederates again renewed their attack in the early hours of March 31, with a "brisk musketry fire." Harris faced a fierce Confederate charge toward his lines at about 9:00 a.m., which was quickly repulsed. The Confederates fell back and again entrenched themselves. Later in the morning, Harris led his brigade toward the Confederate picket lines, and "carried the position handsomely," capturing about one hundred prisoners. His 3rd Brigade lost three men killed, fifty-one wounded, and three missing in the attack. Afterward, there was heavy skirmishing throughout the afternoon and into the night, which continued until the next day from across their entrenchments. The 11th West Virginia Quartermaster John Wood noted that a heavy rain had set in, as he witnessed approximately two hundred "badly mangled" casualties being transported past, which he found disturbing. After the fighting ceased, he and some comrades put up a small tent, which did little to keep out the rain; "It was rather bad time for fighting as it was raining pretty hard."[25]

Private Nimrod W. Loyd, Company F, 10th West Virginia (Harris' Brigade), wrote in his diary, "Move forward from our works and capture a whole picket line some fighting all day in our front." In miserable, rainy weather, Company G was again placed on the picket line that evening. Young could hear the bullets "whistling over our heads" while the army was improving their fortifications. It had rained all day, and the men were drenched. Young noted the action was "furious," but he was proud the regiment had "acted nobly." Two Company G men were wounded: Privates Jeremiah Webb and Hezekiah Henson. Henson enlisted at Coalsmouth on August 6, 1862, at age fifteen years; he was a farmer prior to the war and had been a resident of Hurricane Bridge in Putnam County. He sustained a minor neck wound from a shell fragment but returned to duty the next day. Jeremiah Webb, on the other hand, was aged forty-nine years and had been a close friend of Young's prior to the war. He was one of Young's original company members in 1861 and mustered into Federal service on March 10, 1862, at Coalsmouth. He sustained a serious wound to either the knee or hip; Young indicates it was the knee, but Webb's service files reflect he was wounded in the hip. Either way, it proved mortal, as he died on April 10 at the army hospital located in Point of Rocks, Maryland.26

Clearly, there were signs of a major battle impending, and the veteran soldiers recognized it. On the night of March 31, General Grant had his staff officers out observing Confederate lines, seeking evidence of a weakness or gap in the Confederate lines that the Union army could exploit. The Confederate defenses were massive, spanning nearly fourteen miles in the section facing the 24th, 25th and 2nd Corps, but Grant was determined to find a way to breach Lee's lines. Grant's reconnoitering soon paid off; Brigadier General Lewis A. Grant of the Vermont Brigade was studying Confederate lines through his field glasses that evening, and caught a glimpse of an opening that appeared unguarded from the dam in front of Battery 45 to Burgess' Mill. Captain William Chamberlaine, a Confederate Staff Officer, also described the gap, "It did not appear to me any stronger than a horsehair. We did not have the troops to make it any stronger." When Grant heard of the gap, he began planning his next major attack on Lee's lines and soon began massing the 6th Corps across from the gap that Captain Chamberlaine found.[27]

## Battle of Five Forks

Not only did Grant finally discover a way to breach the Confederate lines, he also found another opportunity he had coveted for months. He would attempt to force Lee out of his massive entrenchments by cutting off his primary supply artery, the South Side Railroad, which ran through Petersburg. He devised a plan for General Phil Sheridan's Cavalry to capture the railroad by way of a strategically important junction, known as Five Forks, on March 31. Lee suspected Grant was building up for an attack in that area and moved Major General George Pickett's division, along with three brigades of cavalry, toward Five Forks in a torrential rain on March 30. The next morning in a surprise attack, Pickett appeared to achieve a tactical victory when he managed to push Major General Gouverneur K. Warren's 5th Corps back to the court house. However, Brigadier General Romeyn Ayre's 2nd Division of the 5th Corps counter attacked and regained their position at White Oak Road, cutting off Pickett's line of communication with his lead elements, forcing him to fall back. Also on March 31, Sheridan's cavalry force moved on Five Forks from north of the Dinwiddie Court House, but Pickett and Major General Fitz Hugh Lee attacked first, throwing Sheridan on the defensive.

After several hours of hard fighting with heavy Confederate casualties, Sheridan was reinforced by two brigades of Major General George C. Custer's cavalry division. Overnight, Brevet Major General Charles Griffin's 1st Division of the 5th Corps counterattacked, and later the entire 5th Corps joined the assault, effectively pushing Picket back. By 7:00 AM on April 1, Sheridan had the 5th Corps and his cavalry in position to take control of Five Forks. Soon, the 5th Corps slammed into Pickett's left and rear, turning his flanks and capturing hundreds of prisoners. General Pickett, who was already the object of derision among many Confederate officers, was busy attending a shad bake (a fish fry) with some chums that morning; he was unaware that his division was under attack, until it was too late to return to his command.

This essentially finished his military career, as General Lee immediately sent orders to remove him from command, but Pickett did not learn of this until days later, as he simply disappeared into the wilderness and avoided a direct confrontation with Lee. The stoic General Sheridan, on the other hand, personally led the Union attack and was often exposed to enemy fire during the battle. Lee lost another important officer in this fight; the young and beloved Colonel William "Willie" Pegram was mortally wounded. He was carried to safety by one of his friends and cared for by his former roommate from West Point. Even though the 5th Corps fought quite well, Sheridan was nevertheless displeased with 5th corps commander General Warren's performance during the battle and relieved him of command. The decisive Union victory set the stage for the breakthrough that would occur on the next day.[28]

*Col. William Pegram, CSA*
*Public Domain*

General Turner reported that General Thomas Harris' and General Andrew Potter's Brigades were directed to drive in the enemy picket line in front of their positions, in order to better develop the division position late in the day on April 1. As a result of the assault, the Confederate artillery was silenced in front of the 24th Corps, enabling Turner to strengthen his entrenchments and better position his corps for the massive assault General Grant was planning. Some four miles north of Five Forks, also on April 1, the 123rd Ohio Volunteer Infantry under Lieutenant Colonel Horace Kellogg were deployed forward of Harris' West Virginia Brigade as skirmishers. Confederates again charged their lines just after dawn, as a diversion to the intended attacks at Five Forks. According to Private J.B. Willoughby, Company F, they "had it hand to hand for a time, but we overpowered them and captured 30 of them." Private N.W. Loyd wrote in his diary that evening, "...at dark we are deployed across our division front heavy cannonading to our right all night and before daylight heavy musketry commenced at daylight." Despite exhaustion, John Young hastily recorded in his diary that night: "Hard fighting all day. Tremendous firing all night, under arms all night. The enemy charged our lines three times. No sleep."[29]

At nightfall on April 1, General Harris' 3rd Brigade was held in reserve near Hatcher's Run, a small stream running southwestwardly just behind the Confederates' forward defenses. Recent heavy rains had swollen its banks; the currents were not only moving rapidly, but the water was also bitter cold. Private William H. Bachman, Company F, 42nd Mississippi Infantry, was not far from where Harris' Brigade was located on April 1, across Hatcher's Run to the Burgess Mill area, near their former winter quarters. Bachman's regiment was part of Brigadier General Joseph Davis' Mississippi Brigade; Davis was the nephew of Confederate President Jefferson Davis.

Bachman recalled details of that fateful night, "After Dark on Saturday evening the first day of April we left Fort McRea where we had been the winter months and moved about one mile to the right and took a position in the fortifications with the right of the brigade resting near the big dam in Hatcher's Run. All along the line to our left firing was kept up all night with both cannon and small arms. We had no pickets in our immediate front that night a fact that was unknown to the writer else he would not have slept so well."[30]

On April 1, General Harris' 1st Brigade was comprised of the 10th West Virginia Infantry under Captain Marshall W. Coburn; the 11th West Virginia Infantry under Major Michael Ayers; and the 15th West Virginia under Lieutenant Colonel John W. Holliday. General John Gibbon, commanding the 24th Corps, placed the mountaineers in front of Brigadier General William B. Curtis' 2nd Brigade and to the left of Brigadier General Thomas O. Osborn and Brigadier General Andrew Potter's Brigades. Somehow, Young again found time to write to his wife late in the evening of April 1. Many soldiers wrote home during or just before battles during the Civil War; people experiencing protracted periods of duress often seek out readily means of accessible escape from their immediate hardship.

*Brigadier General Thomas M. Harris*
*Library of Congress*

Young penned the following from Hatcher's Run, "In the field...I just have a little time to drop you a few lines. We have been fighting here for three days. Yesterday we advanced four hundred yards and fortified, where we lay now. Co. G has just returned from the front where we have been fighting. None hurt...We are now in hearing of the South Side Railroad and the Rebs are making a powerful and determined stand, but I have no fears as to the result. I received your kind and welcome letter yesterday and read it under fire of the enemy; and now the guns are roaring close by...We have a great many men here and one Corps of negroes just behind us. They are chafing to get in the fight. They say the white folks are suffering and they want to charge the fort in our front. We are so close to it that the gunners cannot work their guns. Every time he shows himself he is sure to hear a bullet. I think we will take it today. Some of Co. G was within one hundred and fifty yards yesterday and captured some Johnnies. The boys are all well....The boys have thrown away the most of the clothing. Well, my wife,

I must close. I can't tell what moment they may call for Captain Young and Company G. We have been out once this morning but were driven back faster than they came. I don't know whether you can read this or not, but you can make out enough of it to know that I am yet alive and well. I cannot describe anything to you now under fire, so goodbye for the present – May the Lord in whom I trust defend us all is my prayer."[31]

## Grant Attacks

During the night on April 1, 1865, General Grant ordered a massive artillery bombardment all along the Confederate lines. The firing began at about 11:00 p.m. and continued for at least three to four hours into the morning of April 2, 1865. After months of scheming and planning, constantly probing Confederate lines, Grant's efforts were coming to fruition. Veteran troops on both sides were fully aware of what was transpiring and what was at stake. John Wood, the 11th West Virginia quartermaster, reminisced that late Saturday evening, April 1, "All seemed quiet until 11 o'clock when there was commenced the most terrific cannonading I ever heard in the direction of Petersburg and continued until daylight, and the news is that our boys captured several thousand prisoners and the first line of works." Another Union soldier opined: "No other Union Army bombardment equaled this one...a constant stream of living fire. It was indescribably wild and grand." Major Michael Ayers, commanding the 11th West Virginia, wrote: "This night I shall never forget. The earth trembled under our artillery." On the other side of the lines, a young Mississippi private took cover in the massive earthworks and observed, "...The [cannonade] was so intense that the bright fusillade lit up the night sky as day." Colonel Samuel Walkup commanded the 48th North Carolina Infantry. He nervously wrote home to his wife the night prior during the awful bombardment, having prophetically discerned what was about to transpire in the coming hours: "You need not send clothes, nor flour, nor anything else to me my dearest...We will either be killed or captured or the road will be destroyed before this letter reaches you...Be prepared for bad news from Lee's Army. There is no reasonable prospect of good news."[32]

## Federal Breakthrough: Hatcher's Run, April 2, 1865

On the morning of April 2, 1865, Confederate commander Robert E. Lee knew the situation for his Army of Northern Virginia was growing desperate and time was short; his quickly thinning ranks of effective troops were now spread out across lines spanning some thirteen miles before Petersburg. Further illustrating the dire straits Lee found himself in, there were an average of six- to ten-yard intervals between each man in the lines due to depleted manpower, caused by illnesses, casualties and desertions during the winter. Major General Ambrose Powell Hill commanded Lee's 3rd Corps which was posted on the Confederate right, southwardly from Fort Alexander. The division holding the extreme right was commanded of Major General Henry Heth, whose lines stretched from the center, near Fort Gregg, southwestwardly toward a small stream known as Hatcher's Run, over a distance of roughly five miles. One historian recently estimated that Lee's left, comprising the section of Confederate lines commanded by Heth, only had a density of approximately fourteen hundred troops per mile. This translates to roughly barely one rifleman per yard.[33]

At 4:30 a.m. on April 2, 1865, General Grant ordered the 6th Corps, commanded by Major General Horatio Wright, to attack en masse at a point near Fort Alexander, on Lee's already thinned and weakened right and near the center of his lines. The 6th Corps' juggernaut plowed into the Confederate earthen forts where the two armies clashed in the chaos of bitter hand-to-hand fighting, with clubbed muskets, bayonets and fists, for almost an hour. The first man thought to breach the Confederate works was Captain Charles Gould, 5th Vermont Infantry, whose attack was "direct and rapid." Gould was awarded a Medal of Honor, but it was not until 1895, as there were many other soldiers claiming to have been the first to top the Confederate works, most of which were disputed for several years.[34]

Private William Bachman, 42nd Mississippi Infantry of Davis' Brigade, testified, "...we discovered by the noise of firearms and the yelling and hurahing of humanity that our lines had been broken in front of Petersburg and that the enemy was fast approaching our rear from that quarter but unfortunately for us at that time we had no officers either regimental or brigadier that were willing to assume responsibility and take us out of danger of being captured as others did that were similarly situated." Major Michael Egan of the 15th West Virginia observed, "About two or three o'clock in the morning of April 2, 1865, there burst upon the ears of the armed mass of expectant listeners such a thunderous sound of Bellona's pent-up resources as never before or since reached the eager hearing of her chivalrous votaries. A simultaneous advance on the enemy's works throughout the length of the whole line extending several miles was now inaugurated. All of the many appliances of modern warfare, from the great siege-gun and other monster cannon down to the death-dealing Gatling gun, the sixteen-shooting breach-loading rifle, carbines, muskets, and even the six-shooting navy revolvers, were brought into the combined and terrible requisition by the determined and frenzied forces of the two great contending armies engaged in the last supreme struggle of a long and bitter war."[35]

As Union officers desperately tried to reform their regiments into brigades, orders were given to charge further down inside of Confederate lines, swinging like a giant door to their left. Troops on the right wing of this onslaught soon came across General Heth's headquarters, and Private George Loyd, Company A, 122nd Ohio Volunteer Infantry, discovered Heth's headquarters flag and captured it. A Maryland officer recalled the fierce, albeit futile, Confederate resistance: "It seemed to those devoted troops that second day of April morning that the whole Federal Army had been let loose. Everywhere was heard the roar of artillery and the rattle of musketry. That handful of men composing the Army of Northern Virginia was not but a pigmy battling with a giant and still that pigmy had not been of much greater

*Major General Henry Heth, CSA*
*Library of Congress*

proportions for many months and yet the giant had not before ventured an attack along the line. But the end was fast approaching and the end was as glorious as the beginning."[36]

## Lee Notifies President Jefferson Davis to Evacuate Richmond

Shortly after dawn, General Lee learned of the breakthrough and sent word to President Jefferson Davis in Richmond that Petersburg and Richmond would have to be evacuated, as he could no longer provide protection. Meanwhile, as Federal troops poured through Confederate lines, Major General A.P. Hill's infantry suffered heavy losses, and his artillery lost several guns and men killed, captured, or wounded. One of the artillery units near the 6th Corps breakthrough was a section of rifled guns belonging to Captain Charles R. Grandy's Battery of the Norfolk Light Artillery Blues; a few hundred yards to their left was a section of smoothbore Napoleon guns under Lieutenant James W. Gilmore. Occupying another redoubt on Grandy's right was Captain George M. Cayce's Battery of Virginia Light Artillery (Crenshaw's Battery); both were in close proximity to the 11th and 52nd North Carolina Infantry, commanded by Lieutenant Colonel Eric Erson, of Brigadier General William MacRae's Brigade, and the far right of General James Lane's North Carolina Brigade. On Erson's right was Brigadier William McComb's Tennessee Brigade. Note that many historians consider accounts of Heth's artillery positions generally tentative due to conflicting sources and the general chaos on the morning of April 2.

As a result, these and other batteries along with infantry were positioned "nearest the enemy" when the Federals turned their front southward after the breakthrough, and they highly vulnerable to capture. At some point in the fighting that morning, Purcell's Battery lost their battery colors to Private Isaac James, Company H, 110th Ohio Volunteer Infantry, for which he later received a Medal of Honor. According to one soldier who witnessed the initial assault, "...the storm culminated in the pouring over of a vast column of Federals on [Lieutenant Colonel Eric] Erson crushing it, and utterly destroying it." Erson reported he lost more than two-thirds of his command in that attack. Sergeant Frances McMillen, Company C, 110th Ohio Volunteer Infantry, also captured the 11th North Carolina Infantry battle flag, and Corporal Milton Blickensderfer, Company E, 126th Ohio Volunteer Infantry, took the 52nd North Carolina Infantry battle flag in the chaos of battle that morning. Each later received a Medal of Honor for gallantry capturing the colors.[37]

Once inside the Confederate lines, soldiers from the 2nd, 6th and 11th Vermont Infantry regiments captured a piece of artillery that had belonged to Purcell's Battery and turned it on the retreating Confederates. They could not find the friction primers (a device used to create a spark and ignite the powder charge inside of the gun), however, so a soldier cleverly devised a plan to ignite the cannon by firing blank musket rounds into the cannon vent, causing the charge to explode and send the projectiles "howling through the woods after the very men who had prepared the compliment for us." The distance from the area where the 6th Corps broke through Confederate lines to Hatcher's Run was about five miles, and there were numerous small ravines, creeks and obstacles placed inside of Confederate works, making it difficult to again maintain order in ranks as the Federals pressed southward. A Federal officer from Vermont recalled they were so close to Petersburg at this point, he could see churches: "the spires of which were plainly visible in the distance. The ground between this formation and the city consisted of a series of hills and marshy ravines..." Men scurried in and out of embrasures, looking for Confederates in squads of three or four, or often singly, and charged "whatever obstruction came in their paths."

At approximately 6:30 a.m. that morning also, General A.P. Hill was returning from a meeting with General Lee and was informed that the lines were broken by a massive Federal assault. Hill rode forward, intending to meet with General Heth. Hill rode along with only Sergeant George W. Tucker as his guard, they countered two Union soldiers, Corporal John Mauk and Private Daniel Wolford of the 138th Pennsylvania

Infantry. General Hill and the sergeant pointed their weapons at the two Union soldiers, who managed to take cover behind tree; Mauk fired at Hill, killing him instantly. The general was knocked off of his horse and landed face down. Command of Hill's 3rd Corps then fell upon General Heth.[38]

Advancing southward, the 6th Corps also encountered Brigadier General William McComb's Tennessee Brigade (formerly Archer's Brigade), who, similar to their counterparts in Lane's and Erson's regiments, were spread thin. McComb had enlisted as a private in the 14th Tennessee regiment in 1861, but by September 1862 was commissioned as colonel. Captain William Harder recalled having only one hundred thirty men on line, and, "Everything seemed to be covered with darkness and gloom. It was raining, the snow was gone, and mud took its place...Thirty four stands of colors could be counted

*Major General A.P. Hill, CSA*
*Library of Congress*

in the Federal line and column. Our four gun battery was well served, and the flashes of the Federal rifles were terrible. Presently they moved forward with terrible loss of men, under our fire across the break on the little bridge in a fast run...The fire never slackened along our little line The yell of our men never ceased. The column of Federals to our right plunged forward without firing and came through our fire and through the fire of the two pieces that was run out of the fort, up to our right, passing us and covering the cannon and the fort, capturing them in 40 yards of our right wing." Realizing his lines were in chaos, General William McComb gave the order for his brigade to retreat toward Hatcher's Run.

Also that morning, Private Milton Matthews, Company C, 61st Pennsylvania Infantry, attacked the color bearer of the 7th Tennessee Infantry and captured their colors. He was later given a Medal of Honor for his actions. Corporal Charles Marquette, Company F, 93rd Pennsylvania Infantry, also captured General McComb's Brigade headquarters flag in the attack, and he also later received a Medal of Honor. During the chaos of the attack, Sergeant Lester Hack, Company F, 5th Vermont Infantry, came upon the 23rd Tennessee Infantry and saw the color sergeant attempting to rally his comrades about one hundred yards distant. He recognized the flag bearer was surrounded by the color guard who were armed with bayonets, but loudly called out, "I am going after that flag!" Hack's cohorts tried to dissuade him from going, knowing that capturing a battle flag usually meant certain death.

Regimental colors during the Civil War had great significance to the men who fought under them; they associated the flag with not only former battles they had survived, but also with the honor of their friends who died in battle. Hack refused to listen and rushed toward the color bearer, whom he confronted and demanded he surrender the flag. The ensign refused, and Hack knocked him down with his bare fist and took the flag. Another soldier in the 5th Vermont who witnessed the incident later recalled that Hack next presented "...his empty musket, and ordered the squad to surrender. They did so very quickly..." Hack also later received a Medal of Honor for heroism.[39]

## McComb's Counterattack

Once his brigade had reached a large wooded area some four hundred yards to their rear, General McComb quickly reorganized them and mounted a brief but furious counterattack on the Federals who drove them from their works. McComb reported: "...the Second Maryland and the Tennessee troops comprising the brigade held every foot of line entrusted to them until they received orders to evacuate it. A part of said line was broken on the left, but was retaken in less than thirty minutes by the Second Maryland, First, Seventh and Fourteenth Tennessee regiments..." On McComb's right was Davis' Mississippi Brigade; the 1st Confederate Battalion under Colonel Andrew N. Nelson held Davis' left, who assisted the Marylanders and Tennesseans in their countercharge. Some historians have erroneously thought Davis' Brigade was located further to the north, between McComb's Tennessee Brigade and General Lane's left. As a result, many have thought it was MacRae's North Carolinians, along with elements from Cooke's Brigade, occupying the earthworks in front of General Harris' West Virginians.

However, documents related to both Davis' Brigade and the Tar Heel Brigades shows neither were posted in the locations formerly supposed at the time of the 6th Corps breakthrough. Although they were in the vicinity earlier, General MacRae stated that at 4:30 AM that morning, two of his regiments, the 11th and 52nd North Carolina Infantry, were detached to the left of McComb's Brigade, and his remaining three regiments were located west of Hatcher's Run. General Cooke further indicated his brigade was scattered "in parts," on April 2, across the creek inside of Fort Euliss at the time of the Federal breakthrough. A soldier from the 27th North Carolina in Cooke's Brigade noted they were relieved of their former post by Davis' Mississippi Brigade at approximately midnight on April 1, and they crossed the creek to Fort

Euliss, where they remained until they retreated later that morning.[40]

While McComb was in retreat, a few of his men reached Hatcher's Run, and several were shot or drowned trying to swim across the creek, which was much swollen due to the recent heavy rains. Major Andrew O'Neal, commanding the 1st Confederate Battalion, recognized an opportunity to mount a countercharge when he saw that several men from the 2nd Maryland Battalion (whom had earlier occupied McComb's left) were cut off from their own brigade and had halted, becoming intermingled among his own men along the creek bank. O'Neal's battalion was trained as sharpshooters, and they were widely esteemed as such. These crack troops were handpicked from each of the brigade regiments, and many carried the coveted Henry Repeating Rifles. Following A.P. Hill's death earlier that morning, General Heth took command of his Corps; command of Heth's division then devolved upon General Cooke, who ordered a general retreat shortly after their lines collapsed. However, O'Neal apparently failed to receive, or ignored, Cooke's order, as he quickly rallied his men, along with the Marylanders present on his part of the line, and attacked the Federals concordantly with McComb's counterattack. They pushed the Federals out of the works, who fell back toward the former Confederate skirmish line rifle pits.

O'Neal's ad hoc force managed to hold off the Federals for about three hours, although they were eventually pushed out by overwhelming numbers under heavy musketry and artillery fire and had to again retreat. O'Neal was severely wounded in the Federal counterattack and surrendered the entire battalion at once. A private in the 2nd Maryland Battalion found himself in dire straits and was forced to have a very unhappy birthday: "In a few minutes after we got into the pits we found we had Yanks on all sides but the right flank. Tried to get out that way and found ourselves completely surrounded and the Capt commanding said it was useless to show a fight. Hence about 7 a.m. I found myself again a prisoner...It is a sad way of having my birthday celebrated." During the intense hand-to-hand combat occurring with the 6th Corps, as McComb's and O'Neal's troops desperately tried to hold their works, Corporal Charles Dollaff, Company K, 11th Vermont Infantry, and his comrades suddenly found themselves face to face with the color guard of the 42nd Mississippi, who were in line of battle to the immediate right of the 1st Confederate Battalion.

Dollaff promptly attacked the color bearer "...in a hand to hand fight." He received a Medal of Honor for his actions; the citation states, "Seeing the furious charge of the Union troops, the Rebel color bearer tore the flag from its staff, and tried to destroy it. It was prevented by the quick action of Cpl. Dollaff, who captured the flag and the color bearer." Color Sergeant John McCarrell was also captured, along with the battalion battle flag. The Confederates on this section of Heth's lines were being caught in a giant vise-grip; the 6th Corps was on their immediate left, and elements of the 24th Corps were now amassed on their front, forcing them to evacuate toward the swollen banks of Hatcher's Run. While there was a small bridge crossing the run to the southwest, the Federal 2nd Corps had taken nearby Fort Euliss across the bridge, just as General MacRae's and General Cooke's brigades retreated toward Sutherland's Station. Many of McComb's men drowned trying to cross Hatcher's Run, but a few managed to float across on logs, under heavy musket fire from the Federals.[41]

## Attack of the 24th Corps

Following the breakthrough on April 2, General Grant ordered the Army of the James, commanded by General Edward O. C. Ord, to assist the 6th Corps protecting the breakthrough gap. At that time, the Army of the James was divided in two locations; southwest of Petersburg was the 24th Corps under General John Gibbon, who had Brigadier General Robert S. Foster's 1st Division; Division; Brevet Major General John W. Turner's Independent Division (2nd Division), and one division of United States Colored Troops from the 25th Corps in reserve. Captain John Young's regiment, the 11th West Virginia Infantry was then part of General Harris' 3rd Brigade of Turner's Division, along with the 10th and 15th West Virginia Infantry regiments. Note that the 123rd Ohio Volunteer Infantry was also later attached to Harris' Brigade on April 2. East of Richmond, were Major General Godfrey Weitzel's two divisions of the 25th Corps, and Brigadier General Charles Devens' 3rd Division of the 24th Corps.

General Foster's division was positioned to participate in the initial assault at about 4:30 a.m. on April 2, but the order was remanded. By 8:00 a.m., they had moved farther north to the breakthrough area, entering the captured lines, and then moved toward Petersburg, near Forts Greg and Whitworth, where they stopped and awaited further orders. Shortly after daybreak, as Foster's Division moved off, General Turner ordered Brigadier General Thomas M. Harris' brigade to advance a strong skirmish line up to the Confederate works, probing to ascertain whether they were retreating, of which he had "strong suspicions." General Harris deployed the 123rd Ohio Infantry, under Lieutenant Colonel Horace Kellogg, forward as the 3rd Brigade skirmish line, spread out some three hundred yards across their brigade front. Across from them were Confederate skirmishers from the 42nd Mississippi, who belonged to Davis' Mississippi Brigade. Davis' men were heavily entrenched some three hundred yards directly in front of Harris' West Virginians and supported by Letcher's artillery battery, in the redoubts where the line refused into a "fishhook" shape against Hatcher's Run.[42]

General Joseph Davis often wrote to his uncle, Confederate President Jefferson Davis, requesting his personal intervention with General Robert E. Lee in military situations that he did not agree with. Earlier, Davis had temporary command of General Heth's Division in February 1865 while Heth was home on a furlough. Heth returned in mid-March, and Davis resumed command of his brigade. However, on the morning of April 2, Davis was not present with his brigade. Many historians have supposed he was off visiting other officers in Heth's division just prior to the 6th Corps attack. However, Davis wrote a letter to President Jefferson Davis on April 4 stating he had went "on foot" to Richmond, presumably during the night of April 1, (a distance of over twenty-one miles) hoping to see his uncle, but found it was "too late" because he had already evacuated. General Davis noted that he was aware his brigade was captured, although it is unclear as to whether he knew that before leaving for Richmond or learned of it ex post facto.

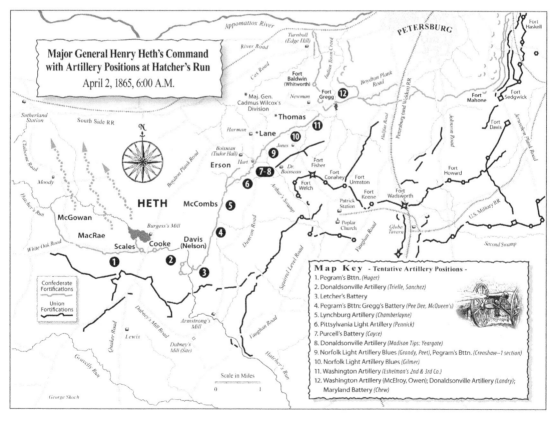

His absence ironically left senior Colonel Andrew M. Nelson, who was not one of Davis' favorite officers, in command of the brigade. Nelson had tendered his resignation to Davis only a few weeks prior to April 2; Davis accepted it, but by April 2 it had still not been processed through the upper echelons of command to the

Confederate War Department and Confederate Congress. Davis' Brigade was then comprised of the following units, deployed from left to right on the morning of April 2: the 1st Confederate Battalion (Confederate Regulars composed of three companies of the 2nd Alabama Infantry Regiment and one company each from Georgia, Tennessee and Florida); 42nd Mississippi Infantry; 11th Mississippi Infantry; 26th Mississippi Infantry, and 2nd Mississippi Infantry. The latter regiment held the earthworks located on the extreme left at the point where they "refused" the "fishhook" against Hatcher's Run.[43]

General Henry Heth reported that Cooke's North Carolinians had already vacated their position and were "making good" their retreat from the southwest side of Hatcher's Run prior to McComb's Brigade being overrun by the time Harris' West Virginians were called into line of battle shortly after the massive Federal bombardment ended that morning. In silence, they watched while the 6th Corps attacked some four miles to their right, kneeling in the mud for about three hours behind their own hastily constructed breast works. Their anxiety piqued as they peered across the marshy, wet field at the heavily fortified works with dread, knowing all too well what lay ahead. Most had tossed away excess articles of clothing, bed rolls, etc., knowing they needed to travel light and fast to cross the three-hundred-yard gauntlet in their front. The 123rd Ohio Regiment under Lieutenant Colonel Horace Kellogg was posted in front of Harris' Brigade as skirmishers. Prior to stepping off as skirmishers, Lieutenant Colonel Kellogg was intensely anxious anticipating orders to lead his men out. One Buckeye soldier recalled "Twice he sent for permission before it came."[44]

Major Michael Egan, 15th West Virginia recalled: "For some time after the thunderous opening of hostilities by the cannon from the batteries on our right and left we were compelled to stand inactive, awaiting the break of day before moving on the forts in our front, one of which lay on the opposite side of Hatcher's Run...These were times that truly tried men's souls." While awaiting their orders to advance, the 11th West Virginia color guard were ordered to advance forward into the earthworks with their colors visible, just before orders came to charge the enemy works. The Confederate artillerymen of Letcher's battery across from them quickly spotted their flags and fired at them; a shell exploded on the parapet and threw large logs about the inner works, killing one man and injuring four others. Captain Young later described the incident, "I lost one man. David Stephens [Private John David Stephenson] was killed early in the morning, and eight wounded but slightly. The most of them are with me. Jerry Webb [Private Jeremiah Webb] is the only one who is badly hurt, and he was shot in the knee." Webb was aged forty-nine years when he was wounded earlier on

March 31; he died in an army hospital on April 10 at Point of Rocks, Maryland. Webb was one of Young's original company members, having enlisted at Coalsmouth in 1861. Webb had no children, but his wife, Clarissa Webb, later filed for a Widow's Pension, and those documents indicated Webb was wounded in the hip, not the knee.

A large piece of wood struck Private David Stephenson on the base of his skull, instantly killing him. Private Stephenson enlisted in Company G on February 10, 1862 at Coalsmouth. His widow and five children continued to live there after the war. Hezekiah Henson was slightly wounded earlier on March 31 when the 11th West Virginia attacked the Confederate picket lines, but he had managed to stay on duty. Private Andrew J. Mynes was also in the color guard, and described Private Hezekiah Henson's second wounding: "Early on the morning of that day...the Color Guard of which he was a member was ordered to advance into the breastworks which order we obeyed and as soon as we were in the works, the rebels opened fire upon us and knocked a slab from off the breastworks which struck him...in the chest knocking him down and inflicting injuries in his chest and back..." Henson also had several previous medical problems throughout the war. Andrew Mynes later provided an affidavit for Henson's post-war pension claim, stating he was with him in July 1863 when he was treated for pleurisy at Point Pleasant, and was also with him later on the Lynchburg Road when Hensley fell out of the column ill, "as he couldn't stand to march." Despite receiving two wounds in nearly as many days, Private Hezekiah Henson was up and walking the next day. Henson survived the war and died in 1927 aged eighty-one years from rheumatism and heart disease. Ironically, Henson was married in 1872 at Coalsmouth by Captain Young's former nemesis, Robert Brooks, who became an ordained minister after the war.

Corporal Fretwell Hensley, also in the color guard, sustained a severe back and chest injury from the flying logs, but he survived the war. He died on September 26, 1899, from chronic nephritis complicated by pleurisy, rheumatism, heart disease, hearing loss, neuralgia of the stomach, vision loss and senility. Four other unidentified men from Company G received minor shrapnel wounds and lacerations from flying debris. Afterward, anxiety was at a terrible level among the mountaineers, who wanted to move forward and fight instead of passively awaiting the next incoming shell hoping not to be struck. General Harris finally received orders to move his brigade forward; he reported, "I assaulted the works of the enemy, at about 7 o'clock in the morning, at the point where his lines begin to refuse on the north bank of Hatcher's Run, striking them at the fort which defends the angle and from that to the run, a distance of about 300 yards.."[45]

## Harris' West Virginians attack

Amidst the heavy rattle of musketry in their front, left and right, and the pounding artillery tossing canister at them, Harris' mountaineers finally stepped off at double-quick time. Racing through the sloppy ground, they were almost to the fort when they encountered several dozen felled trees placed in their way, intended to delay their advance; they served their purpose most effectively. Harris' men were stuck in that position for more than an hour and a half, trying to bypass the obstacles and return fire under a rain of musketry, canister, shot and shell from Letcher's Battery of artillery. Oddly, there were only minimal casualties during their entanglement in such an exposed position. Major Michael Egan, 15th West Virginia, described their attack: "When the faint dawning of day gave us light to see our way, 'Forward March' was given. It was a general move all along the line, and it was grimly understood by everyone that earnest business...We were not to be denied admittance to their inner circle much longer, and so, when we came to the water, which was intended to check our aggressive advance, we tarried not on the brink of that Rubicon to think, but plunged right in, and the trees and debris which the enemy had cut down and thrown into the water, and which were now floating in there, designed as another obstruction to our advance, proved rather a benefit instead, affording us a chance to get to one fallen tree to another, and by holding the limbs a number of the foremost men scrambled across without getting wet. While making this difficult crossing our comrades on dry ground in our rear diverted the fire of the enemy within the fort from us considerably."

Once Harris' Brigade managed to move forward after being stalled under heavy musketry and artillery fire, oddly there were only minimal casualties. The 123rd Ohio Infantry was earlier assigned to be posted as Harris' Brigade skirmishers. Their skirmish line was nearly three hundred yards wide, spanning the earthworks from the far right of McComb's Tennessee Brigade, to just south of the earthworks occupied by Davis' Mississippi Brigade near Hatcher's Run. They quickly encountered the Confederate skirmish line, composed of elements from McComb's Tennessee Brigade, along with Davis' Mississippi Brigade, the latter mostly from the 42nd Mississippi. Skirmishers rapidly poured musket fire back and forth from roughly one hundred fifty yards away, and Harris' men soon pushed the Confederates back toward their own works and managed to silence the artillery battery with a heavy, rapid masking fire until the remainder of Harris' Brigade caught up with them.

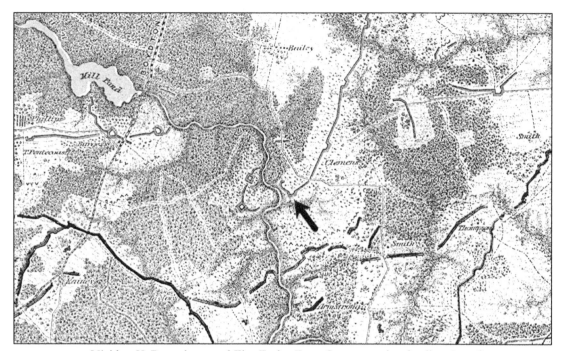

*Michler, N. Petersburg and Five Forks, From Surveys under the direction of*
*Bvt. Brig. Gen. N. Michler, Major of Engineers, By Command of Bvt. Maj. Gen. A.A. Humphreys. 1867.*
*US Library of Congress, Geography and Map Division. Arrow shows vicinity of Harris' West Virginia*
*Brigade attack on April 2, 1865. The "fishhook" is left center against Hatcher's Run.*

The Buckeyes and West Virginians were battle-tested, hardened veterans; each unit had established a valiant and bloody record of themselves in prior campaigns and were determined to oust the Confederates of this position. The Mississippi Brigade were also veteran troops, however, and promptly unleashed another sheet of heavy musketry and artillery into Harris' Brigade as they finally advanced. Lieutenant Colonel Kellogg's skirmishers continued to exchange heavy musket fire back and forth with the Confederates from roughly one hundred fifty yards away, eventually pushed the Confederates back into their own works, and silenced Letcher's artillery battery with a heavy, rapid masking fire, buying a few precious minutes of time until the remainder of Harris' Brigade caught up with them. Despite a disintegrated command and hundreds captured along with their colors, a stubborn remnant of Confederates yet remained behind the earthworks when Harris' West Virginians, who were determined to put up a fight, charged at about 7:30 a.m.[46]

After driving the Confederate skirmishers inside the works, around 8:30 AM, Lieutenant Colonel Kellogg ordered the 123rd Ohio Infantry to close ranks and form line of battle; General Harris called out to continue the advance upon the works, and as they drew closer, Kellogg saw many of the Confederates were "leaving their works in great haste and at the same time a white flag was seen close to their works." He immediately ordered the regiment forward at the double quick and "...had the satisfaction of seeing my regimental colors planted on the enemy's works in advance of all others. The result of the movement was the capture of 200 prisoners, 2 brass 12-pounders, 3 cassions, about 500 stand of small-arms, and 2 of the enemy's battle-flags...After resting my command a short time and collecting the captured property I proceeded to rejoin the brigade." Private Nimrod W. Loyd, Company. F, 10th West Virginia, said that as Harris' Brigade entered the Confederate earthworks, they moved "...rapidly forward and take the whole line of works in our front we cheer lustily..."

However, Private J.B. Willoughby of Company F, 123rd Ohio Volunteer Infantry, offered a somewhat different account of the captured artillery pieces on April 2, "Today the ball commenced early, our forces to our right charged about 4 a.m., and drove the Rebs...Our Regt took 2 brass 20 pounders, 2 battle flags, and over 300 stand of arms, and a lot of prisoners." One of the prisoners taken that morning was Private William M. Graham, 26th Mississippi Infantry of Davis' Brigade, who stated, "Davis' Brigade was captured on the 2d of April 1865, while holding the right of the works, and we were sent to Fort Delaware. We had to live on six crackers and about three or four ounces of meat a day." The 26th Mississippi Infantry lost their colors to Private Richard Mangum, Company H, 148th New York Infantry (4th Brigade, 1st Division), at the time the massive 24th Corps skirmish line advanced on April 2. Colonel John B. Murray, commander of the 148th New York Infantry incorrectly reported the colors taken were from the 8th Mississippi Infantry, who were never in the Army of Northern Virginia. During the fighting that morning, the 2nd Mississippi color sergeant William Byrn refused to surrender the regiment's battle flag. According to Private George H. Bynum, Company A, that banner was carried since July 1863 and had "courageously borne through shot and shell...through all the bloody battles of Virginia until the surrender of the regiment on April 2, 1865." George Bynum also recalled that his brother Nathan Bynum had torn "...it from the flag staff, concealed it beneath his little gray jacket and carried it through prison at Ft. Delaware." The color bearer, William H. Byrn, carried it home from prison after the war. It was taken to the Mississippi State Archives and donated by the Bynum brothers and William H. Byrn in August 1916.[47]

The 123rd Ohio Regimental historian later recalled his regiment captured two battle flags. One of the battle flags belonged to the 2nd Maryland Battalion, whose remnant earlier helped the 1st Confederate Battalion retake their earthworks as McComb's shattered Tennessee Brigade retreated toward Hatcher's Run. That flag was found furled and hidden behind a log near Hatcher's Run. The other flag captured by the 123rd Ohio belonged to the 11th Mississippi Infantry of Davis' Brigade. Lieutenant Colonel Kellogg personally kept that flag, and he later handed it down to his descendants. Despite their sterling performance that morning, the 123rd Ohio Regiment was prone to misfortune; nearly the entire regiment was later captured at Burkesville on April 6 and held until paroled at Appomattox on April 9. The regiment had been on an expedition to burn High Bridge along the South Side Railroad that day, when they became entirely surrounded with only a handful of men managing to escape.[48]

Major Michael Egan, 15th West Virginia, was grateful for the 123rd Ohio pouring such heavy musketry into the works while the brigade stalled, entangled on the obstacles: "While making this difficult crossing our comrades on dry ground in our rear diverted the fire of the enemy within the fort from us considerably. The first over did not even wait to be reinforced by those immediately following them but went at once into the fort. This little band was very much scattered and entirely exposed to the fire of the enemy, who had us under such close range that a plucky resistance on his part musty have inevitably caused great havoc amongst us. As it was, however, they became panic-stricken, and threw away every impediment to their very expeditious flight. While thus engaged I had not much chance to take notice of what was going on in the fort to the right of us; but it was carried at the same time and in much the same manner as was ours. In both of these forts there were large numbers of men and material captured." General Harris indicated his brigade had rapidly charged into the works and "...carried them successfully without loss on my part, capturing 2 guns, 3 battle-flags, 1 captain, 1 lieutenant, and 28 men, the greater portion of the defending force making good their retreat whilst my men were struggling through a very dense difficult slashing in front of these works, and those who remained surrendering as soon as my men entered the works."[49]

## Company G's Corporal Adam White earns the Medal of Honor

Captain Young wrote in his diary later that evening: "Daylight fighting commences in earnest. A shell strikes our works, kills David Stephenson, wounds four more of Co. G. 8 a.m. – Charged the Rebel works, route the Rebels, captures the whole thing. Co. G captured a Brigade flag." Captain Young indicated Company G captured a brigade flag; this was the third captured flag referenced by General Thomas Harris in his official report. Although yet speculative, there is a great deal of evidence that this flag was the headquarters flag of General Joseph Davis, who commanded the Mississippi

Brigade. As noted earlier, Davis was not present with his command on April 2. Forty-one-year-old Corporal Adam White is credited with capturing the flag thought to be Davis' Brigade Headquarters flag, which is identified as War Department Capture No. 491. White migrated to the United States from Switzerland in 1826 with his parents, and lived in Wood County, West Virginia, when the war began. When Company G charged into the earthworks that morning with their bayonets flashing, they found that most of the Mississippians had already abandoned the works or surrendered to Federals from the 6th Corps on the brigade's left wing. However, there were still pockets of Confederates offering a stubborn resistance to the Federal attack.[50]

*Davis' Brigade Headquarters flag*
*War Department Capture No. 491*
*Captured by Corporal Adam White*
*National Civil War Museum*

As White rushed into the works, he encountered a group of enlisted men and officers, along with two of Davis' brigade staff officers, huddled near the eastern bank of Hatcher's Run. In their midst was a color bearer holding Davis' Brigade headquarters flag. White and some comrades quickly charged and captured the entire works; in a brief, but violent hand-to-hand fight, White took the flag as Company G routed the Confederates. Corporal White was later cited for displaying "exceptional heroism" in capturing the flag from its bearer "with his own hands."

Davis Brigade's color ensign was 1st Lieutenant Moses D. McNeely, who was in charge of the brigade color guard; it is unknown whether he held the flag on April 2, but he survived and surrendered at Appomattox on April 9. Also captured in that attack was Captain Thomas A. Brander and 1st Lt. James E. Tyler of Letcher's Battery, with three bronze Napoleon guns in the earth works adjacent to Hatcher's Run. However, the Letcher Battery flag evaded capture and is now held in the Virginia Military Institute Museum at Lexington, Virginia.

Corporal Adam White received the Medal of Honor on June 13, 1865, in Richmond, Virginia, for gallantry in "capturing a Rebel flag at Hatcher's Run before Petersburg, on April 2, 1865." White was born on December 21, 1823, in Trub, Bern, Switzerland as Adam Weiss. His family migrated to the United States during the 1840s and settled in Wood County, Virginia, and he changed his surname to the English transliteration, White. Deeply devoted to his new homeland, White enlisted in Company G, 11th West

Virginia Volunteer Infantry, at Parkersburg, West Virginia, on March 27, 1864, for three years or the duration of the war. He formally mustered into service on March 30, 1864, at Wheeling. White stood five feet, nine inches tall, with black hair and blue eyes. He married Magdalena Frankhauser on February 5, 1847, at St. John's German Evangelistic Church of Switzerland, Powhatan Point, Monroe County, Ohio, and they had thirteen children together.[51]

White died from heart failure caused by Bright's disease of the kidneys on May 19, 1895. His wife, Magdalena Fankhauser White, died from severe burns in a house fire on February 27, 1915. Both are buried in Wadeville Cemetery, Wood County, West Virginia. Two days after White received his Medal of Honor citation in Richmond, he and thirty-some other Medal of Honor recipients traveled to Washington, D.C., with the flags they captured to meet the Secretary of War and tell their stories of how they had taken the flags. 24th Corps commander Major General John Gibbon accompanied the men. Adjutant General Edwin Townsend was present when White told his story to Secretary of War Edwin Stanton. White left to go home on twenty days' leave, and Townsend requested on April 11, 1865, that White be given an extension of ten extra days "as a mark of appreciation for his gallantry." White was also promoted to Sergeant on May 17, 1865, while on furlough.[52]

*Corporal Adam White*
*Original in Private Collection*
*Used with Permission*

## 24th Corps Assaults on Fort Gregg and Fort Whitworth

With General Henry Heth's line collapsed, the Confederates retreated northwest toward Sutherland Station. Late in the afternoon on April 2, Major General Nelson Miles' division of the 2nd Corps caught up with the retreating Confederates at Sutherland Station and engaged in a sharp battle. Four brigades of Heth's division, including the North Carolinians of Cooke and MacRae's brigades, stubbornly repulsed two attacks before Miles received reinforcements. In the third assault, Miles overpowered Heth's troops, and they began retreating further south, losing over 1,000 men captured at Sutherland Station. As the remainder of A.P. Hill's 3rd Corps fell back toward their last line of earthworks near Petersburg, troops from Mississippi, North Carolina, Georgia and Louisiana were ordered to take position in the area along the Boydton Plank Road, near Fort Gregg and Fort Whitworth, in what would become one of the most vicious and controversial assaults of the Civil War by the 24th Corps. Fort Gregg (a.k.a. Battery Gregg) and Fort Whitworth were two large but unfinished earthen enclosures located some six hundred yards apart. Fort Whitworth was also known as Fort Anderson, Fort Baldwin and Fort Alexander at various times.

The latter name had to do with a young North Carolinian private, who became derelict in his duties and was punished by being forced to carry a large log on his shoulders, while standing on top of the parapet during the preceding winter months. The two forts were part of a series of similar earthworks located around the interior lines of Petersburg, intended to allow defenders to effectively resist any breach in the main lines. Fort Gregg was the larger of the two, but it was weakened by Confederates encamped in dozens of nearby log cabins during the previous winter, who frequently cut large logs out of the works for firewood. Nonetheless, it was still a formidable position.

One of the soldiers who defended Fort Whitworth on April 2 was Private Frank Foote, of the 48th Mississippi. He described, "Fort Gregg was one of a series of strong enclosed works, about thirty feet high, built inside the main lines, and was intended for just what happened. A deep moat or ditch surrounded the fort, but it contained very little, if any, water at that time... Whitworth or Alexander was patterned after Gregg, but was never completed. These two forts were intended to be connected, but other work requiring more attention it was abandoned. No moat surrounded Whitworth, and the winter rains had nearly washed the structure level." The Confederates had two three-inch rifled cannons posted inside of Fort Gregg that fateful day, manned by the Washington Artillery and some soldiers from Maryland. Nearby Fort Whitworth had three similar guns within its placements, although it was still less imposing according to one of the defenders. Foote further described Battery Whitworth as "Unfinished...an indefensible work, being a washed-out redoubt only, and not over knee high." Forts Gregg and Whitworth was roughly one mile from Lee's interior lines close to Petersburg, so close that soldiers from both sides mentioned they could see the church spires rising from the downtown area.[53]

A controversy emerged after the war as to exactly which Confederate units had defended Fort Gregg, where the most intense fighting of the assault occurred. Known as Lee's last stand of the war, it seemed everyone who had anything to do with it wanted to claim the last bit of honor for their regiment. Several years after the war, Brigadier General James H. Lane published a letter in the *National Review*, claiming it was his brigade alone which posited the defense of Battery Gregg; Lane dismissed the notion that Brigadier General Nathaniel Harris' Mississippi Brigade (12th, 16th, 19th and 48th Mississippi Infantry) had anything to do with it, asserting that the Mississippians had abandoned Fort Whitworth before the attack on Fort Gregg began. This resulted in a flurry of rebuttles in post-war veteran publications, as well as debates as to who was entitled to such, which continued for several years afterward. A Mississippi soldier who was inside of Fort Gregg that fateful day became so frustrated with the post-war conflict over which units had defended the bastion that he later questioned, "Will we ever get a correct history of Fort Gregg?"[54]

Although an in-depth study of this issue is well beyond the present work, the bulk of evidence, including both Union and Confederate accounts, suggests the primary defense of Battery Gregg was wrought by some two hundred fifty to three hundred men from the 12th Mississippi, under Captain A.K. Jones, and the 16th Mississippi, under Lt. Col. James H. Duncan, who was identified as the garrison commander, but all were under charge of their brigade commander, General Nathaniel Harris. In addition, there were elements of the 33rd and 37th North Carolina Infantry regiments, some Georgians as well as artillerymen from the famed Louisiana battery, the Washington Artillery, and a few gunners from Chew's Maryland Battery present. The latter were identified as "Supernumeraries" because they had dual training as both infantry and gunners; many of them served as riflemen in the defense of Fort Gregg. Multiple sources also agree that Fort Whitworth was defended by roughly another two hundred to two hundred fifty men from the 48th Mississippi Infantry under Colonel Joseph M. Jayne and the 19th Mississippi Infantry under Colonel Richard Phipps. During the assault, General Nathaniel Harris was inside of Fort Whitworth with the latter regiments also, along with three rifled, three-inch cannons manned by members of the Louisianan Washington Artillery.[55]

The Federal infantrymen in the 24th Corps were well aware their work was not yet finished that day following the breakthrough in Confederate lines. Brigadier General John W. Turner, commanding the 2nd Division, 24th Corps, received orders to move toward the Union signal tower near Fort Gregg, shortly after the West Virginians attacked Davis' Mississippians earlier that morning. The 1st Division under General Robert Foster followed suit later that morning as the 6th and 24th Corps pushed the retreating Confederates back through an intricate series of "double lines" of earthen works around Petersburg, until they arrived in front of Fort Gregg early that afternoon. General Turner wrote, "Before General Harris had reached the enemy's line I received an order to send two brigades to our signal tower near Fort Gregg in support of the Sixth Corps, which I was then informed had broken the enemy's lines. I accompanied these two brigades (the First and Second), and subsequently in the afternoon formed them in support of Foster's division, which immediately after my arrival moved to the assault of Fort Gregg..."

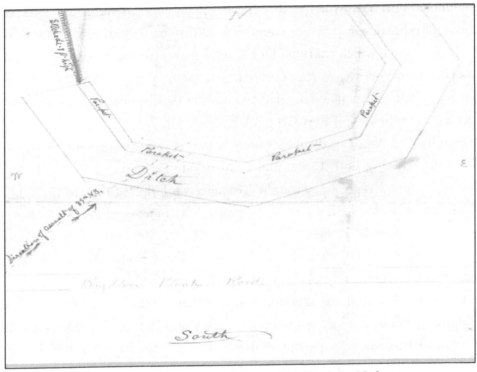

*Sketch of Fort Gregg by Frank Foote, 48th Mississippi Infantry*
*Courtesy of Jim Myers*

Harris' West Virginia Brigade was placed in front of Fort Whitworth and directed to await orders to attack. Major Michael Egan, who commanded the 15th West Virginia Infantry, recalled a stirring and unusual event, as General Grant appeared in view of his troops prior to the assaults on Fort Gregg and Fort Whitworth: "Before making the assault on the two nearest forts we were halted for the purpose of making a reconnaissance. While thus halted we were within easy range of the enemy's sharpshooters, who commenced making it decidedly unpleasant for us. Soon we noticed, on a gently elevated plateau to our right, a splendid troop of handsomely equipped and richly caparisoned horsemen cantering briskly forward in a diagonal direction to the front. It was a thrilling, and in a soldier's eye, an admirable sight to see such 'shining lights' thus expose themselves to the discretionary action of the enemy, who, had he been so disposed, could have annihilated the larger portion of that distinguished party. This was Grant and his staff making a personal observation of the field before us." Soon after Grant and his staff fell back, Turner's division was ordered to advance on Forts Gregg and Whitworth.

Major Egan further described: "In advancing, the 1st and 3rd Brigades had a fort to each encounter; the 1st on the left confronting Fort Whitworth, the 3d Brigade on the right in front of Fort Gregg. In moving on a right line of the 3d Brigade became engaged first, as Fort Gregg was, as I have before stated, the most advanced in position. As we neared these works the enemy's fire therefrom became very fierce and destructive, and the two brigades halted at nearly the same time to lay down. At the time of lying down I found myself, with two of the men of Company K of our regiment, a few yards in advance of the remainder of the troops of our brigade; these boys kept steadily on at their work of loading and firing at the heads of the enemy whenever he exposed himself to fire at us. I assisted by biting cartridges for them ready to ram home, and while thus employed, a bullet passed through my left sleeve at my wrist, and came out at the elbow; on glancing involuntarily behind me after this narrow escape I saw two men lying dead, one across the other, the uppermost just receiving a bullet in the centre of his forehead. Whether or not this bullet was the one that first passed through my sleeve I can only surmise."[56]

General Foster ordered the attack at approximately 1:00 p.m., and following a light bombardment of artillery, the massive blue waves of infantry hurled themselves forward into a murderous and galling fire from the Mississippians inside of Fort Gregg. A private in the 12th West Virginia Volunteer Infantry, of the 2nd Brigade, Turner's Division, indicated, "Our brigade was halted in line on high ground facing toward Fort Gregg to the north. All was quiet as yet, there being no firing. When we reached this ground we could see some of our troops, a part of the First Division of our corps, a little to the right of a direct line from us to the fort, and pretty close up to it. They were in a wavering condition, having failed to enter the fort. A little later an aid rode up to Col. [William] Curtis, evidently giving an order. The colonel looked a little pale, but unflinching, and almost before we had time to think, and without any announcement of what we had to do, the order of 'Attention, Second Brigade, shoulder arms; right shoulder shift, arms; forward double quick march,' was given. The boys seemed to know by a common understanding what was wanted, and, giving a yell, a sort of 'Rebel yell,' they started on the charge, running like mad their very best, seeming to realize that the sooner they got to the fort, the fewer of them would get killed."

Lieutenant Colonel Andrew Potter, commanding Turner's 1st Brigade, advanced in support of Foster's division and encountered Confederate skirmishers entrenched in rifle pits dug in front of Fort Gregg, whom he said "annoyed my flank at first." The pickets were from Brigadier General Nathaniel Harris' Mississippi Brigade and were also some of Lane's North Carolinians. Private Frank Foote, 48th Mississippi Infantry, knew they were in for it, and their ranks filled with dread and anxiety in anticipation of what lay ahead. He recalled, "As far as we could see long lines of infantry, artillery and cavalry in parallel columns, in all the 'pomp and circumstance of war,' were crossing our broken works heading in the direction of Petersburg. It was Gibbon's [24th] corps, and they presented a magnificent spectacle...the sight was enough to quail the heart of the stoutest soldier there. We turned to each other, and wondered if only four hundred (400) of us had to stem that torrent. It was enough to dampen the ardor of the stoutest..."

Another Mississippi soldier commented that the 12th Mississippi battle flag was inside of the fort, with "Every big battle of the Army of Northern Virginia" printed on it. Meanwhile, Lieutenant Colonel Potter and his 1st Brigade continued their advance as the skirmish lines moved inside of Fort Gregg, taking direct fire in front and enfilade fire from the west coming from Fort Whitworth. They rapidly advanced without firing a shot until some fifty yards from the fort, when they "lay down and poured in a rapid and accurate fire." Potter's Brigade suffered heavy losses to that point and now had to make the best of it. After lying here some twenty-five minutes, they succeeded in temporarily silencing the Confederates, Potter's men arose and again charged the works, and were able to plant their regimental colors on the parapet, but the bearer was quickly shot down. Soon the Federals had to fall back and reform their lines.[57]

During the heavy, rapid firing in the Union assault, the air around Private R.B. Thetford of the 12th Mississippi seemed like a sheet of lead. A passing Minié ball struck and bent his ramrod, just as he was ramming a cartridge down the barrel. As the battle for Fort Gregg pitched, the battlements became wreathed in a heavy, gray smoke. The Confederates in nearby Fort Whitworth, the 19th and 48th Mississippi, poured a heavy enfilade fire into the advancing Federal troops, and as one private recalled "...we judged by the stream of the wounded, very effectively... We sprang upon the parapets and 'Yelled our joy' at the defeat of the first attack. The smoke cleared away, and we could trace many black spots on the ground that counted for human beings. For four hundred yards back we could trace these blue dots, and showed how the deadly bullet had found a lodgment."[58]

Foster's Division desperately tried to capture the earthen Goliath, through three failed assaults. Hundreds of dead and wounded soldiers in blue littered the blood-soaked fields around Fort Gregg, and casualties inside the bastion were also beginning to mount. Frank Foote wrote, "The fourth assault that reduced the fort was planned in the ditch around the fort, for it was full of Federals. They were to push each other up the slope, and simultaneously up the unfinished rifle pits that were intended to connect Gregg and Whitworth, and with a rush from those not in the moat. The signal was a flag to be thrown on or in the fort, which was done, (I saw it in the air as it was pitched by the color bearer,) and the rush was successful. As the Federals gained the parapet they poured into the defenders a volley that did great execution, and the place surrendered before another fire could be put in...A friend of mine claims that he shot over twenty Federals that day, as he had a loop hole and all he had to do was load and fire, and see them kick..." The Confederate defenders inside both forts had two to three rifles each on hand, and they were rapidly firing as their comrades stood behind them quickly reloading the rifles and passing them back to the shooter. Foote also recalled that the fire was so intense that many Federals thought the Mississippians had repeating rifles. Afterward, Foote estimated there were approximately seven hundred casualties lying in and around Fort Gregg.[59]

*Assault on Fort Gregg, sketch by A. Waud*
*Library of Congress*

Major Michael Egan, 15th West Virginia Infantry, was stunned by the violence he witnessed at Fort Gregg: "I have never witnessed anything to compare with the bloody struggle for its possession on the one side and retention on the other. While gazing at this desperate hand-to-hand encounter going on upon its ramparts I lost all thoughts of personal danger under the excitement of the moment, and lay spell-bound, waiting the final issue of the struggle. A few men of the 3rd Brigade nearest Fort Gregg were seen to make a sudden break and climb the breastworks of the rebel stronghold, only to be immediately bayoneted by its reckless defenders. Another heroic band, bearing the Stars and Stripes, instantly followed, and a moment later proudly planted the beautiful banner high on the rebel ramparts. I cheered immediately, and the shout was taken up and repeated by comrades all around me; but, alas!

Our joy was but momentary; a second later the Union flag, together with its noble defenders, fell, and in its place stood the Stars and Bars. And now, unbidden, another handful of men scaled the fort, and once more the rebel insignia is hauled down and our colors again float triumphantly in the blood-charged breeze. And so the flags alternated, carrying with them in their rise and fall the hopes and fears of the thousands of overwrought onlookers; but at last the officer in charge of this gallant brigade gave the word to charge, and in they went, with an irresistible rush, maddened at the slaughter of their late comrades, and determined to avenge their deaths. That onslaught could not be checked, and though the reckless rebels fought to the bitter end the struggle was soon over." Corporal Andrew O. Apple of the 12th West Virginia Infantry received a Medal of Honor for his bravery trying to plant the regimental colors on the parapet at Fort Gregg. Apple was desperately trying to lodge the colors when he realized many of his comrades were out of ammunition: "We came from the left of the line and took the fort after a terrific struggle, during which there was no time to reload our muskets after first discharging them, and the greater number of us were forced to use our bayonets during the entire assault."[60]

Frank Foote of the 48th Mississippi witnessed the 12th West Virginia, of Turner's division, lose six color bearers, who were all killed in succession during the fourth and final assault on Fort Gregg. Private William Hewitt, 12th West Virginia Volunteer Infantry, received a Medal of Honor for finally planting the regimental colors on the parapet that day. Hewitt recalled: "After our men had got into the ditch surrounding the fort, they remained there perhaps twenty minutes before they made an entrance...the Rebels were throwing dirt, stones and various kinds of missiles upon them... the gallant [Private Joseph R.] Logsden undertook to plant the flag of the Twelfth upon the parapet, and was killed, falling back into the ditch. The colors were then seized by 2nd Lieutenant Joseph Caldwell of Company A, who leaped upon the parapet, and in attempting to plant the colors there was killed, falling also into the ditch. The flag fell inside of the fort. Then the brave boys of the Twelfth rushed to the parapet to recover their flag. They were joined by comrades of the rest of the brigade. Pouring a volley into the Rebels, the boys of the Twelfth leaped into the fort and planted their flag on the parapet - the first colors on the Rebel works. The fort and its brave defenders were soon ours, all the troops present joining in their capture. But the reduction of the fort was at fearful cost to the Union troops, the loss being in killed and wounded 715..." Private R.B. Thetford of the 12th Mississippi wrote of the Federal onslaught during the final attack, "Yanks helped each other over the parapet, and came on over us, with such overwhelming numbers that they killed and wounded nearly all of us." Thetford also noted that after the Mississippians ran out of ammunition, they began lighting fuses on artillery shells and tossing them over the parapet as hand-grenades, which enraged the oncoming Federals.

Colonel William Curtis, former commander of the 12th West Virginia Infantry, was in command of Turner's 2nd Brigade, which was composed of the 12th West Virginia, 54th Pennsylvania, and 23rd Illinois Volunteers. Curtis' Brigade was the first to enter the fort; he witnessed: "The resistance of the enemy was desperate. Those who were foremost in entering the fort were shot down or bayoneted, and several were killed on the top of the parapet in the act of leaping inside..." Curtis indicated the first man entering the fort was "instantly killed with a bayonet." Captain William A. Smiley of Company D received the surrender of Fort Gregg by Lieutenant Colonel James Duncan, who commanded the fort and gave his sword to Captain Smiley. The colors of the 12th and 16th Mississippi were both captured, "one each by Privates J.W. Johnston, Company B, and Charles A. Reeder, Company G, Twelfth West Virginia Volunteers." The 16th Mississippi color bearer, Sergeant B.F. Chisholm, was killed defending his flag. Both Reeder and Johnston each received the Medal of Honor for their gallantry.[61]

## Harris' West Virginia Brigade Assaults Fort Whitworth

At the same time the general advance was ordered on Fort Gregg, General Thomas Harris, commanding the 1st Brigade, gave the word to charge on Fort Whitworth. The 19th and 48th Mississippi regiments produced a heavy, galling masking fire towards Harris' West Virginians during the initial three assaults on nearby Fort Gregg. During the last attack, the Mississippians continued rapid firing and reloading by ranks, like the defenders at Fort Gregg had done. The sharpshooters were placed in the front ranks, and their comrades behind them would quickly grab the empty musket and reload it, while handing the shooter a freshly loaded weapon. This process was deadly, and it continued until Harris' Federals were finally about forty yards away, when they charged into the fort. An intense but brief close quarter fight erupted, as Federals quickly secured the fort.

Frank Foote recalled: "In Whitworth we kept up a heavy fire, and prepared for the assault on us, and it came in heavy columns. The flag of the 48th [Mississippi] floated defiantly over our heads and was twice shot off the staff; the third time it was attached to a rifle, and flaunted in their faces. Near and nearer came the Federals, and the quicker did our rifles crack, that counted every instant. In reckless abandon, Gen.

Harris sprang upon the low parapet, and with our flag in his hands yelled out 'Give them hell!' For a moment, the enemy slacked their steady tramp; then seeing no chance for us to repulse them Gen. Harris gave the word 'Every man for himself...'" As Fort Whitworth fell into the hands of Harris' West Virginia Brigade, the Federal soldiers were enraged because they had lost so many of their comrades while taking the fort.

They rushed in screaming and cursing so loudly, bayoneting and shooting Confederates with such intensity and vengeance, that many of the veteran Rebel soldiers were quite visibly shaken. Among the few survivors were two privates from the 48th Mississippi who, when they observed the Union General Officer entering the fort, ran to him and surrendered, begging him to protect them because "they feared being given no quarter." The survivors now began their retreat toward the inner works, near the town of Petersburg, which was roughly one mile away. The Federals had Fort Whitworth surrounded; the Mississippians had to withdraw under a heavy crossfire from not only the troops in their immediate vicinity at Fort Gregg, but also friendly fire from those located at Battery 45, a Confederate fort located near the Appomattox River.[62]

Major Michael Egan, 15th West Virginia, was again profoundly affected by the sanguinary horrors of what awaited them: "This latter fort was the larger one and had more than twice the number defending it...We found upon our entrance the remaining half, with one exception, submissive captives; this latter was the youngest member of the crowd, and he was the last to quit shooting at us. Even after he had been disarmed, he kept shaking his little fist defiantly in our faces, and offering to fight all the Yankees in the field, single-handed and alone...after the severe fighting of the previous two days a cessation of hostilities, apparently by mutual consent, succeeded, and we had time to look about us, and take a view of the havoc done in the recent struggle. I can compare the appearance of Fort Gregg to nothing but a slaughter-pen. The blue and gray were there promiscuously heaped together. Their kindred blood commingling presented a sight that could not fail to impress one indelibly with the horrors of a civil war."[63]

Captain A.K. Jones of the 12th Mississippi recalled, "...the slaughter was appalling. I saw the field at Fredericksburg, Chancellorsville, the Wilderness, and on the 12th of May 1864, at Spotsylvania Court House, and at neither place were the dead half-so thickly strewn as at Gregg. The dead were lying two hundred and three hundred yards in front of the fort, and increased in numbers as the fort was neared, until immediately at the fort it was simply fearful. Men shot off the parapet fell back into the ditch, and were pitched out behind, and actually lay in heaps..." As the beleaguered Mississippians tried to escape or surrender en masse, color bearer Thomas J. Newman of Company D, 48th Mississippi, eloped with the colors, only to have them torn to shreds a week later at Appomattox.

Frank Foote described the incident: "Our guns were broken. The colors were torn to pieces, and the bits preserved as souvenirs and mementos." Foote saved a piece of the torn battle flag and inscribed the following on a piece of paper that is with the fragment: "Before me lies a piece of the battle flag of the 48th regiment. It has a bullet hole through it, received at Fort Gregg. What associations this bit recalls - what events the mind flashes back to, since its baptism at Chancellorsville. Once a proud banner that waved over a hundred fields, now a mere remnant fraught with interest, and treasured most carefully...These colors were presented to the regiment at Fredericksburg Va January 1863 on the occasion of our formation from a Battalion into a regiment. In every action from Chancellorsville to the day of surrender these colors waved, and in the glorious action of Fort Gregg April 2, 1865. Forty-two bullet holes were made in it. Three staffs were necessary others being shot in two in action."[64]

After the war, Thomas Harris maintained correspondence with several other veterans, including Frank Foote, whom he fought against on April 2. Harris received a letter from Foote on March 5, 1884, requesting details of the assault on Fort Whitworth, and he responded to Foote as follows on March 13, 1884: "Dear Sir, I have the pleasure of acknowledging the receipt of yours of the 5th inst. and am happy to have an opportunity of collecting your acquaintance under more favorable

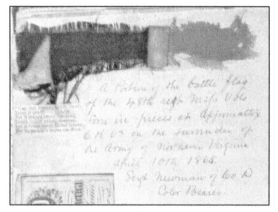

*Fragment of the 48th Mississippi Infantry Battle Flag. Courtesy of Jim Myers.*

auspices than when we met on a former occasion April 2nd 1865 at Fort Whitworth the fact owing to your defense we did not meet except at long range...for I was in command of a Brigade that got all the benefit it could from the cover of your cabins out in front of that battery of that had been used as winter quarters by your men. Hence, any advance did not have that wish and impetuosity in or that indicated a burning desire to make your acquaintance – In fact, we felt that we could afford to be somewhat contrary about it and it was not until the time of the capture of Fort Greg that we made the final rush for the fort. The reason for this was no doubt happy for us both for which the losses in the capture of Fort Greg were very large on both sides and particularly on the side of the Union forces my losses were comparatively light. Hence, my inaction was the saving of human life in which I rejoice...It would give me great pleasure to see you and talk the matter over but as I am now in my 71st year it is not likely that I shall have the opportunity. It was an accidental circumstance that enabled me to find Col [Joseph] Jayne and thus enabled me to return him his sword. I will close by wishing you a life of peace pleasure and prosperity."[65]

Oddly, Captain Young said very little about the brutal series of assaults in which his brigade participated on April 2. He wrote in his diary that day, noting only that they had "Stormed two strong forts and took them [Fort Gregg and Fort Whitworth]. Losses, a great many men and officers." It has been said that people making history usually have no time to write it; this is certainly the case for John Young during the eventful days following the Federal breakthrough on April 2. There was no correspondence to his wife for several days afterward, likely attributable to the intensity of Grant's pursuit of Lee to Appomattox. Young was clearly proud of himself and Company G, however, and wrote to Paulina again on April 17: "Since my last writing we have had hard fighting and harder marching. We have taken Richmond and Petersburg, followed old Lee to Appomattox Court House and whipped and captured his whole forces. Then we went to Lynchburg and captured that Rebel hole. Remained there three days and destroyed all the Rebel property and are this far back on our way to Richmond where, it is said, we will remain until our time is out. We have had a hard time of it but we have cleared Virginia of the Rebel army. Never did men fight harder than the West Virginia boys did in storming the Rebel forts before them on the 2nd of April. I lost one man. David Stephens [Pvt. John David Stephenson] was killed early in the morning, and eight wounded but slightly. The most of them are with me. Jerry Webb [Pvt. Jeremiah Webb] is the only one who is badly hurt, and he was shot in the knee. Company G was the first in the Fort at Hatcher's Run and captured one stand of colors and several cannon and horses. Our Division charged on Forts Whiting [Battery Whitworth] and Gregory, [Fort Gregg] and the hardest fighting in the war was done there. There was at least three hundred men lying dead on the ground when we took the fort. [Fort Whitworth] Out of two hundred Rebels who were in the fort, only about eighteen came out alive; and our officers could hardly save them. After we had taken the place, General Grant said that the men who took that Fort took Petersburg and Richmond. But we are done fighting in Virginia."[66]

## Appomattox Campaign

After the fall of Petersburg and Richmond, the Army of Northern Virginia retreated southwest toward the small village of Appomattox. General Robert E. Lee wanted to get to North Carolina, in hopes of uniting with Major General Joseph E. Johnston's army. General Grant's pursuit was rapid and aggressive; Lee would only make it as far as Appomattox. Turner's Division chased Lee toward Appomattox, and the 11th West Virginia moved along a course parallel with the South Side Railroad from April 3 to 6. Early the next morning, Foster's Division of the 24th Corps moved toward Farmville on a rapid forced march of thirty-five miles, intending to block Lee's retreat by burning a bridge in advance of the Confederate movement. Union morale was high, although most of the soldiers had had enough of the war by this time. Private William Hewitt, 12th West Virginia Infantry, wrote of an incident occurring near Farmville, "On this forced march the boys struck up a discussion as to the probability of overtaking Lee's army, the likelihood of a battle, and the probable result of it. Finally some of the boys said that they had seen enough of the Johnnys and that they wished that they, the Johnnys, would go on until they should run into the Gulf of Mexico. Fighting the Johnnys was no longer a picnic. The time had passed when the boys were 'spoiling for a fight,' and as the average man is generally willing to postpone a possibly fatal ordeal, so the most of the boys were doubtless willing to delay an engagement with the enemy..."[67]

Turner's Division chased Lee toward Appomattox, and the 11th West Virginia moved along a course parallel with the South Side Railroad from April 3 to 6. Rapidly marching those three days, they passed quickly through many small towns and villages, including Poplar Grove Station, Wellsville, Amelia Court House and Burkeville Junction, covering a distance of more than two hundred miles. 11th West Virginia Quartermaster Sergeant John H. Wood recalled the roads were muddy and difficult to march on. Exhausted from the rapid marching over many miles, he briefly wrote in his diary prior to falling asleep on the night of April 3, "We have the glorious news this morning that Petersburg and Richmond is in possession of (our) boys. I have not heard the particulars of the loss on our side. We moved at 7 o'clock this a.m. out to the South side R.R...moved 12 miles and camped...Pitched our tent and got supper and rested very well."[68]

On April 4, Sergeant Wood indicated his brigade left at 10:00 a.m. and marched steadily for fifteen miles, stopping at Wilson's Station, roughly twenty-nine miles from Petersburg. He wrote, "I was very tired and went to bed early. No fighting today. I captured a large amount of tobacco and forage, - no fighting." Captain Young also made a note in his diary while resting on the evening of April 3: "Started early this morning on the heels of the retreating Rebs. Their camps all left with the camp and garrison equipage...12 a.m. – The cannon thundering some ten miles ahead of us. News of Richmond's fall – grate [great] cheering and music." Young also made note that Generals Grant, Ord, & Gibbon were with them that day but they saw "No Rebels.

They are running for their life. Say they won't fight any more." On April 5, Turner's Division marched all day and all night, stopping at Burkeville Junction for breakfast, covering more than thirty miles in two days.

Harris' West Virginia Brigade moved toward Farmville early on April 6, after learning Confederates abandoned their positions at Burkeville overnight. Afterward, Turner's Division moved parallel with the Lynchburg and Danville Railroad, encountering numerous skirmishes with Lee's rear guard at Rice's Station. Heavy fighting occurred there, according to General Thomas Harris: "My command was engaged in a skirmish with a force thrown out by General Lee for the protection of the flank of his retreating army on the evening of the 6th instant, in the vicinity of High Bridge, on the South Side Railroad." These skirmishes only delayed the inevitable retreat a short time, however, as the Confederates found Union cavalry under General Phil Sheridan at Sailor's Creek. Sheridan's troopers defeated the hardened veterans who were desperately trying to make a stand; a remnant of the 44th Tennessee Infantry, formerly of McComb's Brigade, had managed to keep their regimental colors during the massive assault at Hatcher's Run on April 2. During the fighting at Sailor's Creek, 1st Lieutenant E.M. Norton, adjutant of the 6th Michigan Cavalry, captured the colors and the color bearer. Lee was hoping to delay the Federal pursuit at Sailor's Creek, but he failed to do so as Sheridan pushed the Confederate rear guard further westward, finally entrapping them at Appomattox Station.

Sergeant John Wood recalled that while at Burkeville on April 7, the 11th West Virginia halted their march late in the evening, but no sooner than they had gotten their tents up, "we have them took down and got ready to march." The command moved out again, but their supply train stayed all night. Harris' Brigade marched at 2:00 a.m., rapidly moving west until April 8, when at 5:00 a.m. the 24th Corps arrived at the Lynchburg Road and fell in behind Sheridan's cavalry. Gibbon's Corps marched all day and encamped near Appomattox Station just after sunset. Wood diarized: "I feel very sleepy and bad getting up early....got some supper and went to bed at 12 a.m. The roads from Farmville to Walker's church were very good. I got very tired and weary before we stopped for the night."[69]

Harris' West Virginia Brigade arrived at Appomattox Court House at about 3:00 a.m. on April 9, moving at the double quick along the Lynchburg Road, stopping one mile east of the Court House. They went into line of battle and quickly engaged the Confederates, fighting for two hours and "gaining a decided advantage..." Private William Hewitt, 12th West Virginia Infantry recalled, "Before daylight on the morning of the ever memorable 9th of April, a day that will stand out as conspicuously in our history as that of the surrender at Yorktown, if not more so, we started to cut off and surround the Rebels in their retreat, to engage and vanquish them in their Last Ditch, and give a finishing stroke to the Lost Cause and thus to give to the loyal people of the Nation the fruition of their indomitable struggles, through hope through darkness and doubt, for four long and bloody years; to illuminate the land with joy, and to fill it with a great gladness such as it had not known for generations."

Hewitt continued, "We marched not very far when we were started on the double-quick along the road, just as day was breaking. We had marched thus rapidly only for a few minutes, when some cavalry were observed coming out of woods on our right at a rather rapid rate, though in good order. It appeared that the Rebels had been driving them, and that they were withdrawing to uncover the infantry. Just as a squadron emerged from the woods opposite our regiment, one of the cavalrymen exclaimed: 'Here come the Doe boys!' and then he gave us the further encouragement of assuring us that the Johnnys had up the black flag. Every soldier who served any considerable time in the late war will bear out the assertion that in no kind of civil life during the same length of time could a man bear a tithe of the rumors, startling in purport that he could hear during the war. So the boys had heard too many rumors to be frightened by this story of the black flag."

Continuing, Hewitt wrote, "In a few minutes our regiment was halted, the ranks closed up and formed into line upon the road...We moved in line toward the enemy and at nearly right angle to the road, through some woods in such a manner as to place our regiment in the west line of the closing in lines. Our two divisions from the Army of the James and Sheridan's cavalry were now barring the Rebel retreat. We advanced rather cautiously, moving up a little, then halting, waiting on the disposition of other troops. It was not long till shells began to crash through the tree tops above us, from the enemy's batteries. They did no harm to us, however. We now halted and remained in line for perhaps two hours, expecting to have a battle that day. The boys of the Twelfth seemed confident. There was no disposition shown by any to flinch. They no doubt were cheered by the thought that for once, since joining Grant's army, they were about to get a whack at the Rebs without having to fight them behind breast works; when about 9 o'clock a.m., the order came very unexpectedly and to our great gratification and relief, to cease firing until further orders. We did not then know that a flag of truce had been sent by Gen. Lee; but the boys generally seemed, in the phrase of the present time, to 'catch on' to the fact that this probably meant the surrender of Lee's army, the mainstay of the Rebellion; and their countenances accordingly lighted up with the thought of the pleasing prospect of this glorious consummation, which all felt was devoutly to he wished for, and which had been hoped, prayed and fought for through four long years of blood and tears, and tears and blood."

When the word reached the 24th Corps that General Lee had surrendered his Army of Northern Virginia to General Grant, hostilities ceased at once, with the two armies literally facing each other just a short distance apart while terms were negotiated. The 11th West Virginia lost one wounded in the last battle of the war, Private John Smith, Company F, who was shot in the shoulder. As the Confederates were paroled, they were given supplies and rations, and Harris' Brigade encamped near where they had stood in line of battle, remaining there until April 12. Captain Young described events on April 9, "At 2 P.M. we got the glorious news from the front that Lee and his whole army had surrendered. The boys were almost carried away with joy at the news. We arrived up at the command at or near Appomattox. I went up and saw the rebel camp of all whom had surrendered. Great joy among everybody. Our wagons were not up to the Regt. today as it was against orders but parked ½ mile in rear." On April 10, Turner's Division was supposed to participate in the formal surrender ceremony at Appomattox Court House, but the weather was "foggy and damp, cannot see any distance" and it was postponed. Young wrote that the 11th West Virginia stayed in their camp until noon, had a formation, and ate dinner. Young surmised, "The boys are all very much pleased with the condition of things."[70]

## Lee's Surrender

On April 12, the Surrender Ceremony occurred, and the Army of Northern Virginia stacked arms for the last time. General Lee gave his stirring "General Orders Number Nine" to his troops prior to dismissing them, stating he saw no reason to continue on in the face of overwhelming resources and numbers, assuring them that his decision was in no way due to "no distrust of them." He continued that it was rather the "feeling that valour and devotion could accomplish nothing that could compensate for the loss that must have attended the continuance of the contest, I have determined to avoid the useless sacrifice of those whose past services have endeared them to their countrymen..." Harris' West Virginia Brigade was present during the ceremonies that day. Afterward, they received orders to march toward Lynchburg, a distance of twenty miles.

Arriving there late that evening, Harris discovered that huge stores of supplies had been nearly destroyed by the Confederates. The remaining stores were given to local citizens, including food and clothing. Young was sent out on forage detail, scavenging the countryside some eight miles from camp. He returned with "...some grain and hay, but nothing to eat for many" of his men. Harris' men rested until April 17, and over the next few days several men in the 11th West Virginia began to receive discharges from the army. On April 15 it rained hard in the morning but cleared by afternoon. Young observed the grass was "a lovely green" as the brigade marched through Concord and back to Appomattox. They continued to Farmville and camped there until April 19. By all accounts, the war was over for Captain John Young and Company G. From this point he spent several weeks processing paperwork for his soldiers' discharges and settling pay and clothing accounts with the army paymasters.[71]

Young again wrote to Paulina on the evening of April 17, "...I received your letter dated April 2nd one hundred miles from Richmond yesterday, and you can't imagine how glad I was to hear from home once more. I know you have troubles, my dear wife, but be patient. The Lord is on our side and He will make all things right. I will be home now shortly after discharging my whole duty to my God and my Country, and have not disgraced my loved family. Be of good cheer, my love. As the Lord has spared me thus far, He will permit me to return home to the embrace of my wife...I must close."[72]

## On to Richmond –Final Muster

On April 20, Harris' Brigade moved to Burkeville Junction after marching all night. There they saw hundreds of Confederates taking the Oath of Allegiance to receive their paroles. The brigade stayed there for four days and was then ordered to Richmond. Arriving there on April 25, they remained in Richmond until mustered out of service. General Harris estimated the distance marched by his brigade from April 3-25 was two hundred fifty-nine miles, with total losses being five killed, fifty-four wounded and three missing in the Petersburg-Appomattox Campaigns. On April 25, the 24th Corps participated in their last formation together, in a parade of Union troops passing through the city of Richmond at 9:00 a.m., according to Young. He recalled a "grand reception" as the division marched through "the upper part of the city," and afterward, they went into camp one mile north of the city. The day was "warm and the boys were very much fatigued by the march at shoulder arms," he later observed.[73]

On April 14, President Abraham Lincoln was assassinated by John Wilkes Booth at Ford's Theatre in Washington, D.C. The country was stunned and in mourning, as John Young learned of it in Richmond. He lingered there for several weeks, completing company business and mustering his men out of the army. He sent Paulina several letters, indicating a significant relief that the war was ended. He mentions nothing of his health condition, although men who were with him later indicated that he was rapidly deteriorating. He wrote on April 27, "I know you are anxious about me and would be glad to know my whereabouts. Well, the fighting is over and I am at Richmond sound and well. Thank the Lord in whom I have trusted. I have seen the fall of Richmond and the surrender of Lee's whole Army. Company G was on the skirmish line when Lee hoisted his white flag...There are several of the boys sending their money in your care to be sent to their wives...You must not be uneasy about me for the fighting is over, and just as soon as I get my business settled up I will be at home, if the Lord permits, to spend the remnant of my days. O, how impatient I am to get home! Since the fall of Richmond each day is like a week to me. But I hope it will not be long before I can embrace you in my arms conscious that I have discharged my duty to God and my country, and satisfied that traitors will get their just reward. The death of our President is the death blow to traitors."

Young continued, "It would be useless for me to try to describe the suffering of the citizens of Old Virginia. The Rebel Army and our army had swept everything off and left the people destitute. Hundreds of women come to the Provost Marshall crying for bread for themselves and children, and women who twelve months ago would turn their noses up at the name of a Yankee, the very women who contributed to the suffering of our prisoners in Libby, are now crying for bread. The most humiliating thing is the freedom of the negro, and his privilege among Southern chivalry. We had a hard march from Petersburg to Appomattox Court House, and from there to Lynchburg, and then back to Richmond, but I made it about as well as the youngest of them. The First Division and our Division which is now called the Second in the 24th Corps, were all that went to Lynchburg. We have the honor of capturing Lee's Army...Nothing more, but I want to see you very bad. I often look at your photograph but it is not 'Marsh.' I am still your devoted husband."[74]

Young was at Jerusalem Park in Richmond on May 4, writing to his daughter Emily, "I am getting so anxious to hear from home – I have not had a letter since the fall of Richmond, and what it is I can't tell. I think if you all knew how anxious I am to hear from my loved ones at home you would write oftener. The last I have heard from you was a letter you wrote April 20th. I received an order yesterday to make up the boys' Muster-Out Rolls, and they would be mustered at once. But this morning the mustering office refuses to muster them out without an order from the Secretary of War; and before we could get that order our time would be out. Only eighteen days more. There will be only thirty of Company G left, and I think they will get out by the first of June. Lieutenant [Van] Morris will come home with me. He can't stay without forty men and there will be only thirty left. I wish he could stay with the boys. The boys are all anxious to get home. They think they have done enough for the Government for one time. But they are proud that they helped to take Richmond and General Lee. The

Rebels here are the humblest things you ever saw. They are entirely dependent on the Yankees for everything they eat and wear. They curse Jeff Davis and the Southern Confederacy, and say the Southern leaders only wanted to steal their silver and gold, and get all the property they could in their hands and then cut out."

He further penned, "I was in Richmond yesterday and was at the Capitol and saw the statue of General Washington. But a great part of the business part of the city was burned down by the Rebels. But the Yankees are building it up and in a few weeks it will be as good as ever. The Rebel ladies are riding day and night with the hated Yankee officers. The Yankees are all the go here with Rebel women. General [O.C.] Ord sees their love for the Yankee soldiers and has issued an order prohibiting any from marrying without taking the oath. This they don't like but rather than miss a good chance they will take it. I will start home just as soon as I can get my business settled up. I think we will be at home by the first of June, if we have no bad luck. I think we will get another order to be mustered as soon as General Harris returns from Washington. If so, we will be at home sooner. O, what a happy time for a way-worn and tired soldier who has served his country for more than three year, and has been in many hard-won battles, and at last has come out gloriously triumphant and tired, to see this wicked unholy and uncalled for Rebellion under his feet and the perpetrators punished. I will not write any more before I go home unless I get a letter from home..."[75]

## Final Business, Mustering Out

Young spent the month of May in Richmond buried in "red-tapeism," which he loathed, trying to settle company clothing and ordnance accounts so that he could receive his final pay before his term of service ended on May 23. He was grateful to be alive and was becoming intensely anxious to return home. He was reminiscing and reflecting on the war, disclosing more of his thoughts to his wife, "...I can return home knowing that I have done my duty to God and my country. It can never be said to my children that their Pa acted dishonorable in this Rebellion; nor can the enemies of our Government say that I have ever acted cowardly in any engagement that my command has been in. But I assure you that the campaign of '64 and '65 has taxed my strength to the very utmost. But I was determined to stick to my brave boys, until Richmond was ours; and then after Richmond and Petersburg fell I wanted to help capture that old traitor Lee, which we did at Appomattox Court House, which ended the war. So I can say that through the Providence of God, I have lived to see the end of this Rebellion; and hope through the goodness of God to be permitted once more to join my family

*Ruins of Tredegar Iron Works, Richmond, Virginia, 1865*
*Library of Congress*

under the time honored stars and stripes to spend my remaining days in our accustomed peace and love with ourselves and God and our neighbors. Since the fall of Jeff Davis' assumed throne and the surrender of the thousands of poor dupes under his iron sway, and hearing them tell of the tyranny used over them, all malice and hatred have given way to sympathy for the poor, down trodden of East Virginia. There was no such tyranny used in West Virginia; neither did the leaders usurp such power over them as they did here. You have no idea of the ignorance of the poorer classes of whites here, or how they have been oppressed by the slave holders. They were forced to leave their wives and little ones to die for the rich man's negro; and the poor, desolate wife dare not speak one word in favor of the Government of her Fathers."

Young was also anticipating trouble when he arrived home; there were accounts to settle with those who did his family harm, as well as the horse thieves: "I know there is no excuse for those horse thieves and Rebel sympathizers in West Virginia. But they will have to answer for their doings, and doubtless many will yet feel the soft end of the halter or perhaps hear the report of more than one musket. This whole country is one waste, and there are at least ten women to one man. Whether the men are all killed or are yet hidden out I can't tell, but there are but few, and most of the women are wearing black. O, who will have to answer to God for the loss of life and the sorrow of the widow and orphans, made so by this unholy and wicked and uncalled for Rebellion? I saw a fine young Rebel officer lying on the battlefield at Appomattox Court House, mortally wounded, away from home, without friends to give him one encouraging word. He told me that he must die. He said that he was suffering much and begged me to pierce him through with my sword and put him out of his misery. But I told him that I was no murderer and he had little enough time to prepare for death. But he said that he was ready to die, so I left the fellow and saw him no more. A great many Rebels were killed at Farmville and Appomattox Court House. You spoke of Tom Markham coming back. I tell you Putnam will soon be too hot for Rebels."

Young was ordered to Washington, D.C., on May 24, ostensibly to settle with the government. He took a steamer from City Point near Richmond, and he was frustrated because he paid $12.00 fare and $1.00 per meal, which he noted was "not good." Young arrived in the capital city that evening and "proceeded to get my business completed. Took my papers to the agent and had them examined." On May 28, Young was still awaiting clearance from the War Department on company business matters and was "Sitting on an iron bench, waiting on the War Department to deliver my papers. Hundreds of citizens as well as soldiers is visiting the capital square while I am writing, both men and women, and children." The next morning, he still waited: "Beautiful morning, waiting at the Quartermaster's Dept., sitting in the adjoining park. The city crowded with soldiers and citizens from every state in the Union." Young made several fruitless attempts to settle with the quartermaster in the coming days but could not complete business until June 3. That evening, he left for Richmond and began making preparations to return home as soon as he arrived the next morning, but he was still unable to leave. After he arrived in Richmond, Young received a letter from the Officers of the 11th West Virginia Infantry thanking him for his faithful, devoted service and recognizing his bravery throughout their time together.

Also, when he returned to Richmond, Young found that twenty-three of his men had been mustered out of service and were on their way to Putnam County, West Virginia. Greatly annoyed, Young had to wait until the last man in Company G was mustered out of service on July 5, even after he was already mustered out on June 17. Young was agitated and desperately anxious to get home, but even at war's end, he kept the welfare of his soldiers above his own – even above his own families. At age fifty-two years, Young ended his military service at 10:00 a.m. on a warm, sunny day in Richmond, Virginia, and began the long trek back to his home at Winfield, in Putnam County, West Virginia, at 9:00 p.m. that evening. He wrote in his diary, "This day ends my soldiering."

Young boarded a train for Grafton, West Virginia. En route, he discovered that not only was his baggage missing, but also a young former slave named Pete he had hired as a camp servant while at Petersburg, who was supposed to be going home with him. Oddly, Young had not mentioned Pete prior to this time, but it was common practice for Union officers to hire former slaves to manage their camp duties such as cooking and laundry during the war. Young arrived at Grafton the next afternoon and found several men from the 13th West Virginia Infantry there whom he knew. Socializing and catching up on "old times" all night, he still heard nothing of his baggage or Pete when he left for Parkersburg the next day, July 7. Concluding that his servant had "ran off," Young boarded the steamer Mattie Roberts on the Ohio River, traveled to Gallipolis, Ohio, and arrived at Winfield late that evening. Young did not document the doubtlessly joyful reunion he experienced with his family, but we can surmise it was a wonderful moment, although Young was suffering from a severe respiratory condition that he had not spoken much to his wife about. Now, the war was finally over for Young and his family, who, beyond shadow of doubt, had paid dearly to "Sacrifice all for the Union."[76]

Chapter Five References

1. OR, Series 1, Vol. 46, Part 1, 135; 579.

2. CSR, RG 94, M508, Rolls 194-195, National Archives; John H. Wood. Wartime Diary, January 1, 1865 to August 22, 1865. Civil War Collection, Series 1, MS 79-18, WV Archives; WV AG Report December 31, 1864; Note the typescript of Wood's diary states he was a 1st Lieutenant; His service file indicates he held the rank of Sergeant.

3. J.V. Young Diary, January 3, 4 & 7, 1865; OR, Series 1, Vol. 51, Part 1, 1197-1198; Wood Diary, January 4 and 13, 1865, 1-2.

4. Ibid., January 9-13, 1865; Young Letters, January 11, 1865.

5. J.V. Young Letters, January 13, 1865.

6. J.V. Young Diary, January 14-21, 1865; Wood Diary, January 21, 1865; CSR, RG 94, M508, Rolls 185 & 195, National Archives; WV AG Report December 31, 1864.

7. J.V. Young Diary January 22, 25, & 27, 1865.

8. Ibid., January 25-31, 1865; Young Letters, January 31, 1865; Putnam County, West Virginia, Clerk of Court's Office, Winfield Plot Map 1855.

9. James W. Silver (Ed.). *The Confederate Soldier: Reminisces of Dr. Legrand J. Wilson, Confederate Surgeon, 42d Mississippi Infantry during the Civil War.* (Memphis TN: Memphis State Univ. Press, 1973), 186-187.

10. J.V. Young Letters, February 2, 1865.

11. Ibid., February 7-8, 1865; Wood Diary, February 10 & 16, 1865.

12. J.V. Young Letters, February 22, 1865.

13. Ibid.

14. Ibid., February 22-23, 1865; Wood Diary, February 22, 1865.

15. J.V. Young Letters, February 1865, to Emily Young.

16. J.V. Young Letters, February 28, 1865; William W. Chamberlaine. *Memoirs of the Civil War Between the Northern and Southern Sections of the United States of America, 1861-1865.* Vol. 1. (Washington DC: Byron S. Adams Press, 1912), 113-116 J.V. Young Diary, March 1, 1865.

17. J.V. Young Letters, March 5, 1865; Wood Diary, March 5 & 6, 1865.

18. Ibid., March 9, 1865; Wood Diary March 18, 1865.

19. Wood Diary, March 12, 16, 17, 1865, 6; WV AG Papers, AR 383, 11th WV Infantry, Boxes 1 & 2, Folder 7, Muster In Roll March 14, 1865. WV Archives.

20. J.V. Young Letters, March 23, 1865.

21. Wood Diary, March 24-26, 1865; Nimrod Wesley Loyd, Co. F, 10th West

Virginia Volunteer Infantry. Record of a Diary kept of the Campaign of 1865. No. MS 98-14, WV Archives; J.V. Young Letters, March 25 and 26, 1865.

22. William H. Bachman. Recollections of the Civil War, March 31, 1865. Manuscript: Call No. Z/2266.000/S Box 1, Mississippi Archives, Jackson MS. Transcribed from originals by the author. Ulysses S. Grant. *Personal Memoirs.* (Old Saybrook, CT: Konecky & Konecky, 1885), Vol. 2, 597-603; OR, Series I, Vol. 46, Part 1, 134-135; Part 2, 1214-1216.

23. OR, Series 1, Vol. 46, Part 1, 135; 1214-1215; Wood Diary, March 27, 1865; J.V. Young Diary, March 27, 1865; J.V. Young Letters, March 27, 1865.

24. Wood Diary, March 28-30, 1865; J.V. Young Diary, March 28-29, 1865.

25. OR, Series 1, Vol. 46, (1894), 1219-1221; Wood Diary, March 30, 1865.

26. J.V. Young Diary, March 30-31, 1865; Loyd Diary, March 28 & 29, 1865; Wood Diary, March 28, 1865, 7; CSR, RG 94, M508, Roll 189, National Archives; WV AG Papers, AR 382, Box 2, 11th WV Infantry, Co. G, Muster Cards. WV Archives; Hezekiah Henson Pension & Widow Pension File, No. MT288, Roll 212, Pension File No. 157815, Widow Pension Application No. 827241, National Archives.

27. J.V. Young Letters, April 1, 1865 Loyd Diary, March 28, 1865; Bachman, March 28, 1865; C.M. Keyes, (Ed.). *The Military History of the 123rd Regiment, Ohio Volunteer Infantry.* (Sandusky, OH: Register Steam Press, 1874), 107; George S. Maharay. *Vermont Hero: Major General Lewis A. Grant.* (Rizzoli, NY: Universe Publishing, 2006), 210-212; Chamberlaine Memoirs, 113-116.

28. Wilson A. Greene. *The Final Battles of the Petersburg Campaign: Breaking the Backbone of the Rebellion.* (2nd Ed.). (Knoxville, TN: Univ. of Tennessee Press, 2008), 179-188; John Horn. *The Petersburg Campaign June 1864-April 1865.* (Cambridge, MA: Decapo Press, 1999), 219-240; Chris Calkins and Edward Bearss. *The Battle of Five Forks.* (Lynchburg, VA: H.E. Howard Publishing, 1985), 73-113.

29. James B. Willoughby Civil War Diary 1862-1865. Entry from April 1, 1865. Civil War Manuscripts, Special Collections, and Archival Holdings, Ms94-46, WV Archives. CSR contains only a general index of soldiers from Ohio in Record Group 94, National Archives, but Willoughby's name appears as a musician in Co. F, 123rd Ohio Volunteer Infantry; J.V. Young Diary, April 1, 1865; OR, Series 1, Vol. 46, Part 1, 1214-1215.

30. Bachman, April 1, 1865.

31. OR, Series I, Vol. 46, Part 1, 579; Part 2, 1173-1179; 1221; OR, Series 3, Vol. 5, 179; J.V. Young Letters, April 1, 1865.

32. Wood Diary, April 1, 1865; Joseph Wheeler. *Their Last Full Measure: The Final Days of the Civil War.* (Boston, MA, Decapo Press, 2015), 80-181; Frank H. Foote. Private, 48th Mississippi Infantry. "Harris' Mississippi Brigade at the Siege of Petersburg and Appomattox." Letter to *New Orleans Times-Picayune* Newspaper, September 15, 1902. Online: http://www.beyondthecrater.com, September 15, 1902); Walter Clark, (Ed). *Histories of the several Regiments and Battalions from North Carolina in the Great War 1861-1865.* Vol. 2, (Goldsboro, NC: Nash Brothers Printing, 1901), 576.

33. Greene, 189.

34. OR, Series 1, Vol. 46, Part 1, 953-955; A.F. Walker. *The Old Vermont Brigade: Military Essays and Recollections; Papers Read Before the Commander of the State of Illinois, Military Order of the Loyal Legion of the United States.* Vol. 2. (Chicago: A.C. McClurg and Company, 1894), 189-209; H. Stevens. *The Storming of the Lines of Petersburg by the Sixth Corps, April 2, 1865: Personal Narratives of Events in the War of the Rebellion.* (Providence, RI: Soldiers and Sailors Historical Society, 1904), 5-40.

35. Bachman Diary, April 1, 1865; Egan, 384-385.

36. OR, Series 1, Vol. 46, Part 2, 981; 983; William W. Goldsborough. *The Maryland Line in the Confederate States Army.* (Bloomfield, Michigan: Easton-Franklin Classics, (Reprint October 2018), 149.

37. Walters & Riley, Norfolk Blues, 216-218; Marshall, 327-330; CSR, Grandy's Battery, RG 94, M325, Roll. 305, National Archives; OR Series 1, Vol. 46, Part 1, 1273-1274; Part 2, 903, 994, 1000; 1257, 1260; *Vermont Watchman and State Journal,* April 14, 1865; Crew and Trask, 49-51, John S. Fox. *The Confederate Alamo: Bloodbath at Petersburg's Fort Gregg on April 2, 1865.* (Eldorado, CA: Savas Beatie Publishing, 2014), 312-313; Carmichael. The Purcell, Crenshaw, and Letcher Artillery, 43; 111; 219, 223-228; "The Vermont Light Battery." *Vermont Watchman and State Journal,* (Montpelier, VT: April 14, 1865), 2; Captain Thomas Elliott. (Compiled by Charles P. Young). History of the Crenshaw Battery, with its engagements and Roster: Pegram's Battalion, 3rd Corps, Army of Northern Virginia. SHSP, Vol. 31. (1903), 275-290; John Goolsby. "The Crenshaw Battery." SHSP Vol. 31, (1903), 275-278; Samuel Z. Ammen. *Maryland Troops in the Confederate Army from Original Sources,* Vol. 1 and material relating to the life of S. Z. Ammen. Copy of Scrapbook: MSA SC 2356, Maryland State Archives, Annapolis MD. Samuel Ammen later founded the Kappa Alpha Fraternity, and served as the literary editor

of the *Baltimore Sun*. He died Jan. 5, 1929, in Daytona Beach, Florida, and is buried in Stonewall Jackson Cemetery in Lexington, Virginia; William Henry Harder Memoirs, 1861-1865: 23rd Tennessee Infantry Regiment. Manuscripts on Microfilm, Mf-574, Typescript, 106. Tennessee State Library and Archives, Nashville, TN; OR Serial 7, Vol. 7 Supplement, Part 1, 1997, 813-814; Record of flags captured by Union forces after April 19, 1861, RG 94, WD No. 460, National Archives.

38. OR, Series 1, Vol. 46, Part 2, 969-973; 993-995; 1259; 1274; George Benedict. *A History of the part taken by Vermont Soldiers and Sailors in the War for the Union 1861-1865.* (Burlington, VT: Free Press Association, 1886-1888), 204-205; S.Z. Ammen, Maryland Troops.

39. CSR, 18th Tennessee Infantry, RG 94, M268, Roll 177, National Archives; Harder Memoirs, 125; 139; 141; 143; 153; OR, Series 1, Vol. 46, Part 2, 790-792; 969-975; 1259; OR Serial 7, Vol. 7 Supplement, part 1, 1997, 816-817; Benedict, 203-204; Record of Rebel Flags Captured, RG 94, WD No. 362; Lew Wallace, (Ed.). *The story of American Heroism: Thrilling Narratives of Personal Adventures during the great Civil War as told by The Medal of Honor Winners and Roll of Honor Men.* (Springfield, MO: J.W. Jones Publishing, 1897), 467-468; S.F. Beyer and O.F. Keydel. *Deeds of Valor: How America's Civil War Hero's Won the Congressional Medal of Honor.* (New York: Smithmark Publishing, 2000), 507-508.

40. OR, Series 7 Supplement, Vol. 7, 810-812; 813-814;814-815; 816-817; Virginia Historical Society, Lee Headquarters Papers, Call No. MSS-3L515A508. Report of Brigadier General William MacRae, April 11, 1865; John A. Sloan. *Reminiscences of the Guilford Greys, Company B, 27th North Carolina Regiment.* Washington, DC: Polkhorn Printers, 1883), 112; Clark, Vol. 3, 33-34, 31 and Vol. 4, 509; Major Robert Bingham. "44th North Carolina." *Southern Historical Society Papers*, Vol. 20, 1877; 267-268 (Hereafter *SHSP*); *SHSP* Vol. 25, 1897, 345; *SHSP* Vol. 40, 34; Peter S. Carmichael. *The Purcell, Crenshaw and Letcher Artillery.* (Lynchburg, VA: H.E. Howard, 1999), 218-227; Recollections of Brigadier General William M. McComb, in Confederate Memorial Literary Society Collection; No. E483.75.A22, Virginia Historical Society Manuscripts, Virginia Museum of Culture and History, Virginia Richmond, VA; Randy Bishop. *The Tennessee Brigade.* (1st Ed.). (Baton Rouge, LA: Pelican Publishing, 2010), 1-12, 301-302. Letter from Captain Robert T. Mockbee to General William McComb, February 16, 1911 and Letter by William McComb to Lamar Hollyday, from December 16, 1876 (Hereafter Hollyday Letter); Harder, 153-157, 161, 167: Robert T. Mockbee Post war recollections, cited in Harder. Major

Alfred M. O'Neal to His Wife. Letter published in *Confederate Veteran*, Vol. 18, (February 1910), 86- 88.

41. Cambridge Dictionary of American Biography. (Cambridge, MA: Cambridge Univ. Press, 1995), 41; R.J. Driver, Jr. *First and Second Maryland Infantry, CSA.* (Bowie MD: Heritage Books, 2003), 333: Cites Diary of J. William Thomas 1861-1865 entry from April 2, 1865. Original is held in private collection at Severna Park, MD; Mockbee, 301-302; T.P Williams. *The Mississippi Brigade of Brigadier General Joseph Davis, An Historical Account of its Campaigns and a Biographical Account of Its Personalities, 1861-1865.* (Dayton, OH: Morningside Books, 1999), 194-196; CSR, 1st Confederate Battalion, RG 94, M258, Roll 61; National Archives. The 1st Confederate Battalion carried a Mobile Depot 12-star battle flag; there was no evidence found indicating receipt of an ANV Pattern flag at Petersburg; Hollyday Letter, 8-9; OR, Series 1, Vol. 46, Part 2, 790-792; 970-973; 1173-1174; 1221; 1257-1260; 1272; Benedict, 203-204; Record of Rebel Flags Captured, RG 94, WD 289 & 270; Richard Rollins, (Ed.). *The Returned Battle Flags: Returned to those who bore them.* (Redondo Beach, CA: Rank & File Productions, 1995), 27. This work contains a reprint of the rare Charles Ware's 1905 "Flags of the Confederate States Army: Returned to those who bore them": Presented to the Confederate Veterans Reunion, Louisville, KY. Unfortunately, the original and reprint both relied on War Department records citing Charles A. Reeder, Co. G, 12th West Virginia Infantry as the person who captured the 42d Mississippi Infantry battle flag; however, that flag was taken by Corporal Charles Dollaff of the Vermont Brigade. Reeder's regiment was in the 2nd Brigade, Turner's Division, 24th Army Corps, and they were not present when the 24th Corps attacked McComb's and Davis' Brigades at Hatcher's Run. The 12th West Virginia Infantry were engaged during the assault on Fort Gregg later that day, and Charles Reeder there captured the 16th Mississippi Infantry flag during that attack (cf. Reference No. 61 in this chapter: S.F. Beyer and O.F. Keydel. Deeds of Valor).

42. OR, Series I, Vol. 46, Part 1, 4; 576-580; Part 2, 491-492, Part 3, 1179-1182, 1214-1215.

43. Ibid. OR, Part 3, 1219; 1221; 1272; Williams, 192; 194-196; Carmichael, 218-219; 227; L.L. Crist, (Ed.) *The Papers of Jefferson Davis.* Vol. 2, September 1864-May 1865. (Baton Rouge: Louisiana State University Press, 2003), 502; William M. Graham. "Twenty-Sixth Mississippi Regiment." *Confederate Veteran,* Vol. 15(4), (1907), 169. Graham recalled the 26th Mississippi were posted on the "right of the

works" at the fishhook; CSR, RG 94, MR269, Roll 61, National Archives.

44. Supplement to the OR, Serial 7, Vol. 7, Part 1, 1997, 810-815 (Reports of Major General Henry Heth; Brigadier General John R. Cooke; and Lieutenant Colonel Eric Erson); Roland R. Dunbar. *Military History of Mississippi, 1803-1989.* (Spartanburg, SC: Reprint Co., Reprinted 1978), 124-125; *J.A. Sloan. Reminiscences of the Guilford Grays, Company B, 27th North Carolina Regiment.* (North Charleston, SC: Createspace.com, 2012 Reprint), 112; Greene, 212-214; 265-273; Christopher M. Calkins. *The Appomattox Campaign, March 29-April 9, 1865.* (Philadelphia, PA: Combined Books, 1997), 43-47; OR, Series, 1, Vol. 46, Part 2, 1216-1221; Keyes, 108-109; Egan, 384.

45. J.V. Young Letters, April 2 & 17, 1865; CSR, RG 94, M508, Roll 189, National Archives; Corporal Fretwell G. Hensley, Pension Application, May 1, 1877. Claim No. 235534, also Widow's Claim No. 706864; Widow's Pension Application, Clarissa Daily Webb, RG 15, Claim No. 266676, December 27, 1880; Widow's Pension and Minor Children Pension Applications, Rhonda Stephenson, RG 15, WC No. 667-563, July 11, 1884; Hezekiah Henson Pension File No. 157815, National Archives; OR, Series I, Vol. 46, Part 2, 1221-1223.

46. OR, Series I, Vol. 46, Part 2, 1219; 1221; Egan, 384-385; J.V. Young Diary. April 2, 1865.

47. Loyd Diary, April 2, 1865; Willoughby Diary, April 2, 1865; Letter from G.W. Bynum, Co. A, 2nd Mississippi Infantry, August 1, 1916, to Rowland Dunbar, Chief Archivist, Mississippi Department of Archives and History, Accession No. 68.42., Manuscripts, Mississippi State Archives. All five Bynum brothers served in Company A, 2nd Mississippi Infantry; "Confederate Flags at Washington." Confederate Veteran, Vol. 1(9),( January – December 1893), 247; OR, Series 1, Vol. 46, Part 2, 970; cf. OR, Series 1, Vol. 46, Pt. 2, 1203; 1207-1208; 1258-1260; Record of Rebel Flags Captured, RG 94, WD No. 289; Frank Foote, Co. F, 48th Mississippi Infantry. "Last Days of Harris' Brigade." Letter to *The Clarion,* Jackson, MS, October 8, 1884. Original copy in personal collection one of Jim Myers. Used with permission. (Hereafter Foote, October 8, 1884); WD No. 289 Howard Madaus Sketch and Fact Sheet, Museum of the Confederacy; Note that Capture of WD 289 is incorrectly attributed to Corporal Charles H. Dollaff of the 11th Vermont Infantry in the War Department Capture File; he received a Medal of Honor for capturing the 42d Mississippi battle flag on April 2, 1865. Colonel J.B. Murray's report in the Official Records states the flag was taken by Private Richard Mangum belonged to the

8th Mississippi; however, they were never part of the Army of Virginia. Other researchers have posited that Murray refers to the 48th Mississippi Infantry, who were at Petersburg on April 2, 1865; however, they were at Fort Whitworth that afternoon and Private Frank Foote, Co. F, stated their flag was not captured. Also, the 148th New York marched two miles to the right from their earlier position to the point where the 6th Corps broke through well before dawn that morning (cf. OR, Series 1, Vol. 46, Part 2, 1203.); Civil War Vexilliologist, Howard Madaus, examined WD 289 and opined the flag likely belonged to the 26th Mississippi.

48. OR, Series, 1, Vol. 46, Part 2, 456; 458; 1216-1221; Keyes, 108-111; Arlington Dunn Collection, Transcript of Civil War diary, 1862-1865. Call No. 285; Loc: LH242; Accession No. 5082-5112; Rutherford B. Hayes Presidential Library, Freemont, OH; "State will Restore Banner: Ohio to Return Confederate Flag to Maryland." *Worthington Advance*, May 15, 1908, Worthington, Ohio and *The Cecil Whig* January 16, 1909; Original copies held at Ohio History Center, Columbus OH; Robert J. Driver, Jr. *The First and Second Maryland Infantry, CSA.* (Bowie, MD: Heritage Books, 2004), 330-333; Milton A. Reckord. Maryland Adjutant General. *Guide Book and Descriptive Manual of Battle Flags in the Flag Room of the State House.* (Annapolis, MD, 1965), 24. Image No. 34D, 2nd Maryland Infantry Battalion Battle Flag. David C. Love. *The Prairie Guards: A History of their Organization, their Heroism, their Battles and their Triumphs.* (Topeka, KS: Bonnie Blue Press, 1999 Reprint, Original 1890), 18; Howard Madaus. Flag Sketch and History, 11th Mississippi Volunteer Infantry, CSA. Email communication from Greg Gibbs, Civil War Flag Message Board. http://www.history-sites.com; Rowland Dunbar. *Fourth Annual Report of the Director of the Department of Archives and History of the State of Mississippi from October 1, 1904, to October 1, 1905.* (2nd Ed.), (Nashville, Tennessee: Brandon Printing Co. 1911). Original copy on file at Mississippi Department of Archives and History, Jackson MS, Call No. 843, MDAH Collection; Record of Rebel Flags Captured, RG 94, WD No. 460. There is conflicting evidence regarding the fate of the 11th Mississippi flag. Sgt. David C. Love indicated "Frank Hope, the color-bearer, tore the flag of the regiment into shreds, tied them to the flag staff and threw them into Hatcher's Run. About this time the regiment was entirely surrounded, and all the members surrendered." Also, Lieutenant Colonel Horace Kellogg, 123rd Ohio Infantry kept the 11th Mississippi Infantry flag his regiment captured on April 2, 1865, and left it to his descendants. Civil War Flag Vexilliologist Howard Madaus inspected WD No. 460 and verified it

as the 11th Mississippi Infantry colors carried on April 2, 1865, which contradicts Sgt. Love's account, i.e. it apparently wasn't torn to shreds. Note also the 1904 Mississippi Archives Annual Report contained the following in reference to a bunting battle flag once thought to be that of the 11th Mississippi: "This flag with its bearer was captured at Selma AL., April 2, 1865, by Private Charles A. Swan, Company K, Fourth Iowa Cavalry, First Brigade, Fourth Division Cavalry Corps, M.D.M. The bearer stated that it belonged to the 11th Mississippi. It is probable that accrediting the flag to this regiment is a mistake, as the 11th Mississippi Regiment served in Virginia, and it is hardly probable that the flag was captured at Selma, Alabama. The mistake seems to have arisen in the difficulty in deciphering the figures, which are very much faded."

49 .Egan, 385; OR, Series, 1, Vol. 46, Part 2, 1216-1221.

50. J.V. Young, Diary, April 2, 1865; J.V. Young Letters, April 17, 1865.

51. OR, Series 1, Vol. 46, Pt. 2, (1894), 1261; Medal of Honor Case File, Sergeant Adam White, Co. G, 11th West Virginia Infantry, Adjutant General Records 1762-1984, Files 519694.2092 and 28878.477, RG 94, 8W3/16/32/1, Box 781, R&P 519, 694, National Archives; J.V. Young Diary, April 2, 1865; Record of Rebel Flags Captured, RG 94, WD No. 491 and 362; Love, 265; CSR, RG 94, M269, Roll No. 395, National Archives; *SHSP* Vol. 40, 34; *SHSP* Vol. 14, January 1886, 6-21; Carmichael, 227; United Daughters of the Confederacy Magazine, Vol. 78(3), (March 2015), 8-20; *Daily State Journal* newspaper, Parkersburg, West Virginia, May 20, 1895, Adam White Obituary. Newspapers on Microfilm, Misc. Reels M-20, WV Archives; Email communication of August 29, 2018, with John Coski, Historian, and Cathy Wright, Flag Curator, National Civil War Museum regarding WD 491, (formerly Museum of the Confederacy). The capture of WD 491 is attributed to Corporal Adam White, Co. G, 11thWest Virginia Infantry on April 2, 1865. The flag is 36"x35" and unmarked; Civil War Flag Vexilliologist Howard Madaus indicated it was possibly an artillery flag; however, Captain John Young stated Company G captured a brigade flag that day; Turner's 1st Brigade (Harris' West Virginians) captured three flags, two being that of the 11th Mississippi, and the 2nd Maryland Battalion. McComb's Brigade Headquarters flag (WD 362) was taken by Corporal Charles Marquette, Co. F, 93rd Pennsylvania Infantry. Remnants of McComb's Brigade were either captured by the 6th Corps or had evacuated by the time Adam White's regiment attacked Davis' Mississippians, and all of Davis' regimental colors are otherwise accounted for. Letcher's Battery did not lose their colors on April 2,

1865.

52. 1840, 1850, & 1870 US Census; Adam White Biography, Unpublished Manuscript, 2019, by Mike and Sylvia Nicholas. Mr. Nicholas is Adam White's descendant. Used with permission; Adam White Pension application, RG 94 US National Archives; WV AG Papers, AR 382, 11th West Virginia, Muster Roll December 1, 1864; Adam White MOH file; CSR, RG 94, M508, Roll 195. Adam White's family settled in Monroe County, Ohio, in 1826. He married Magdalena Funkhouser there in 1846 and relocated to Wood County, West Virginia. They had thirteen children together. White died in 1895 from a chronic illness.

53. Frank H. Foote. "Harris' Mississippi Brigade at the Siege of Petersburg and Appomattox, Part 2"; Letter to *New Orleans Times-Picayune*, September 15, 1890. Also, "Death Grapple at Petersburg: Last Days of Harris' Mississippi Brigade. Part 3." Letter to *The Clarion*, Jackson, MS, September 24, 1884. Transcribed from originals in private collection of Jim Myers. Used with permission; OR, Series I, Vol. 46, Part 2, 1173; 1216-1217; Frank H. Foote, Letter to *National Tribune*, May 1, 1890. Online: http://www.beyondthecrater.com.

54. Ibid., Frank H. Foote Letter, May 1, 1890; OR, Series 1, Vol. 46, Part 2, 1894-1895, 770, 1179-1182; 1214-1220; 1272-1285; *SHSP* Vol. 3(1), (January 1877), 19-28; 82-86; 301; *SHSP* Vol. 4(1), (July 1877), 18-33; Vol. 7(10, 11 & 12) (October-December 1880), 475-488; Vol. 19, (January 1891), 65-71; Nathan H. Harris. "Nineteenth Mississippi Regiment." *Confederate Veteran,* Vol. 6(1), 1898, 70-71; Buxton R. Connelly. "How Fort Gregg was Defended." *Confederate Veteran,* Vol. 15(11), (November, 1907), 505-507; E.C. Cotrell. "The Fight at Fort Gregg." *Confederate Veteran,* Vol. 7(5), (May, 1899), 200, 308; Unidentified. "Defenders of Fort Gregg." *Confederate Veteran,* Vol. 25(1), (January, 1917), 23. The article mentions Dr. George W. Richards, who was a surgeon inside of Fort Gregg on April 2, 1865; some believe it was he who wrote the article; R.B. Thetford. "Commands Holding Fort Gregg." *Confederate Veteran* Vol. 29(9), (September, 1921), 335-336; A.E. Strother, Irwin Artillery, Cutt's Georgia Battalion. "Battle and Capture of Fort Gregg." *Confederate Veteran* Vol. 29(9), (September, 1921), 425-426, 505-507.

55. Ibid.

56. OR, Series I, Vol. 46, Part 2, 1179-1189; Egan, 384-392.

57. Ibid., OR Part 2, 1203; William Hewitt. *History of the 12th West Virginia Volunteer Infantry.* (Charleston, West Virginia: 35th Star Publishing, Reprint, 2012, Original 1892), 572-585.

58. OR, Series I, Vol. 46, Part 2, 1179-1189; 1214-1217; E.C. Cotrell. "The Fight at Fort Gregg." *Confederate Veteran,* Vol. 7(5), (May, 1899), 200; *Confederate Veteran* Vol. 29(9), (September, 1921), 335-336; *Confederate Veteran* Vol. 29(9), (September, 1921), 425-426, 505-507; Foote, Letters of September 15 1902 & September 24, 1884.

59. Ibid., September 15, 1902.

60. Ibid., September 24, 1884.

61. Egan, 384-392; J.W. Jones, (Ed.) *The story of American Heroism: Thrilling Narratives of Personal Adventures During the Great Civil War as told by the Medal of Honor Winners and Roll of Honor Men.* (Springfield, Ohio: Werner Company, 1897), 619-622.

62. Foote, September 24, 1884; Hewitt, 575-578; OR, Series 1, Vol. 46, Part 2, 1173-1174; 1179-1182; 1219-1221; 1256-1260; Robert U. Johnson and Clarence C. Buel (Eds.). "Five Forks and The Pursuit of Lee." *Battles and Leaders of the Civil War.* (New York: Century Books, 1956), Vol. 4, 717; Rollins, 27; *SHSP,* Vol. 7, (October – December 1880), 475-488; "Appomattox Paroles." *SHSP,* Vol. 15, (1887), 328-329; Record of Rebel Flags Captured, RG 94, WD 270 and WD 285; National Civil War Museum, Museum of the Confederacy flag collection, No. 174. Note that the capture file contains an error; Private Charles Reeder did not capture the colors of the 42d Mississippi, rather it was the 16th Mississippi colors that he captured. S.F. Beyer and O.F. Keydel. *Deeds of Valor: How America's Civil War Hero's won the Congressional Medal of Honor.* "A Hero from the South: Private Charles Reeder, 12th WV." (New York: Smithmark Publishing, 2000), 514-515; CSR, RG 94, M508, Roll 202, National Archives. Charles Reeder was born in Virginia in 1844. He enlisted as a private in Company G, 12th West Virginia Volunteer Infantry at Shinnston, WV, on August 18, 1862. Reeder was reported Missing in Action near Winchester from June 15, 1863, and returned August – September 1863 and was present during the 1864 Shenandoah Valley Campaign and at Petersburg in 1865. Following the assault on Fort Gregg, Reeder was detailed as Brigade Orderly and promoted to Corporal.

63. Egan, The Flying Gray-Haired Yank, 392-393.

64. *SHSP,* Vol. 7, (October-December, 1880, 10, 11 &12), 475-478; OR, Series 1, Vol. 46, Part 1, 1894-1895, 1220; Foote, September 15, 1902; October 1, 1884; Foote, May 1, 1890.

65. Letter of March 13, 1884by Brigadier General Thomas M. Harris, Commanding

Turner's 3rd "West Virginia" Brigade, to Frank Foote, former member Co. D, 16th Mississippi Infantry. Transcribed by the author from the original, held in Jim Meyers' private collection. Used with permission.

66. J.V. Young Diary, April 2, 1865.

67. Ibid., April 17, 1865; Hewitt, 580-581.

68. Ibid., Hewitt.

69. J.V. Young Diary, April 4-5, 1865; Thomas M. Harris Letter March 13, 1884; Hall Diary, April 3-4, 1865.

70. OR, Series 1, Vol. 46, Part 1, 135-136; 1214-1215; Hall Diary, April 6-8, 1865.

71. Ibid., OR, 1223; Hewitt, 582-585.

72. J.V. Young Diary, April 12-17, 1865.

73. Ibid., April 17, 1865.

74. Ibid., April 20-25, 1865; OR, Ser. 1, Vol. 46(1), 136-137.

75. Ibid., J.V. Young, April 27, 1865, WVU Library.

76. Ibid., May 4, 7 & 16, 1865; J.V. Young Diary, May 16-June 5, 1865; Letter from 11th West Virginia Volunteer Infantry to Captain John V. Young. Letter to Captain J.V. from 11th West Virginia Officers, May, 1865. Roy Bird Cook Collection, Call No. A&M 0895, Series 1, Correspondence, Box 1, Folders 2, WVU Library.

# 6

# Return to Civilian Life

July 19 was a cloudy, rainy day. Former 11th West Virginia Infantry Quartermaster Sergeant John Wood, a resident of Coalsmouth, was traveling home and stopped by John Young's house to pay a social call. Wood "put on clean shirts and got ready to go to Winfield," after boarding a steamer and traveling from Parkersburg. He ate dinner with Young and his family that evening, and they somberly reminisced on their wartime experiences. Having his fill of melancholy, Wood also paid former Lieutenant Van Morris a visit that night. Once they teamed up, Wood learned that all of the Company G men who left Richmond together made it home safely. Often, friendships among soldiers during wartime are "forged in fire" but Wood and Morris had known each other for years before the war, and decided to celebrate the Union victory by going on a "drinking spree." Wood recalled later that "Van was very tight." The next day both were hung-over, and spent the day mowing grass "very dryly." Wood soberly reflected, "I felt very bad today from the effects of our spree yesterday." They were soon joined by several other men from Company G at Winfield, and spent a few days reminiscing and celebrating together.

Wood stayed with the Young family until July 22; after dinner that evening, he left for Coalsmouth. He found his family well, and after catching up with them, he went out and discovered, "It is a very drunken place-some considerable fighting at Coal today." Some of the veterans not only had a hard time letting their friends go, but were apparently unwilling to end the celebration anytime soon. Wood and many other veterans continued their celebration through August 11 when he wrote, "There are several of the boys from Company G here today and most of them are on a spree." On August 15, Wood again imbibed, "Drank some whiskey today though not much." Wood was a schoolteacher prior to the war, and he soon desired to return to his former profession. He also continued to make the rounds visiting his old friends on August 17-19: "Went down to see Jim Mynes in regard to getting a school. Also went down to the Hurricane Bridge. Got dinner there...At the bridge I hired a horse from Geo. [George] Duke and rode to Coalsmouth by sundown...Got on a big spree this evening." Wood again visited John Young on August 21. While there, he consulted Judge James Hoge, former colonel of the 181st Militia Regiment, who gave him a "certificate to teach" school again, and spent the evening with Ben Morris' family.[1]

After visiting with former Company G men for a few days, Young settled into domestic life again, and spent his last years quietly working on his small farm. He also served as a minister in the Methodist-Episcopal Church. Typically stoic, Young never told Paulina about his severe respiratory condition while he was in the army. His correspondence with her rarely mentioned having any health issues other than rheumatism and an occasional fever, although several men from Company G later testified that he had been quite ill for the last two years of the war. Lieutenant Colonel Van H. Bukey, who commanded the 11th West Virginia Infantry, recalled that Young was quite ill during 1864-1865 but did not allow his health condition to affect performance of his military duties. On October 21, 1866, Young received word from the U.S. Treasury Department his account with the War Department was yet unsettled regarding "clothing, supplies and equipage used by Co. G, 13th WV for part of the 4th quarter 1862." Doubtlessly annoyed with the "red-tapeism" as Young called it, they requested yet another task of him: to have former Company G members "who have not signed a muster roll...those names be verified by affidavit." Young's reaction is undocumented, but we can easily infer that he was less than pleased to receive the latter; many of those men were killed in the 1864-1865 campaigns in the Shenandoah Valley, and at Petersburg, and like himself, were trying to put the war behind him. The treasury official also requested he provide an itemized list of "each piece of equipment on hand" when he mustered out of service, which he had already turned into the War Department in June 1865.

John Young died at home on November 13, 1867 from consumption, a condition known to modern physicians as tuberculosis. He was aged fifty-four years and five months; Young is buried at Cary Cemetery near Poca, West Virginia. Paulina Young filed for a Widow's Pension on January 4, 1869, in Putnam County, West Virginia. Oddly, she said of Young's relationship with his former regiment that he was a "Stranger to the Officers of Said regiment" with only "few acquaintances save those of his own company." Van Morris of Company G enlisted as a sergeant on August 22, 1862 and stated he was well acquainted with Young before and during the war, having lived near their home. Morris described Young as healthy before the war and remained so until July 1, 1864. After that point, he recalled that as the regiment returned from General David Hunter's expedition to Lynchburg, Virginia, Young began to complain of "...being feeble, and during the campaign in the Shenandoah Valley in the summer, Fall and winter of said year, his health gradually grew worse, which was affliction of the lungs, but he continued to do duty down to the date of his discharge, at which time his health was bad, and continued to grow worse until he died of consumption."[2]

Another officer from Company G, 1st Lieutenant Clark Elkins of Putnam County, also testified that Young became ill on the retreat from the battle of Lynchburg occurring June 18, 1864 and remained sick until the end of the war. Elkins mentioned he frequently warned Young of the dangers of continued service with a severe illness and encouraged him to accept a discharge on account of disability, describing Young as "a broken down man" until the day he left the service. Not surprisingly, Young refused, telling Elkins that he "...would try and remain with his company until they were discharged." Dr. Andrew Barbee, a Putnam County physician who enlisted in the 22nd Virginia Infantry (Confederate) in 1861, was Young's doctor for two years before the war. He testified that before military service, Young was well capable of doing physical labor for a livelihood, and was a "sound man," known as "Temperate, and Sober and a Minister of the Gospel." Dr. Barbee visited Young only ten days after his discharge in 1865, and then found Young "broken down in health," diagnosing him with consumption. In the interim before Young's death, Dr. Barbee continued as Young's physician. During this time, Young's health intermittently improved, and he would "go around the neighborhood and do some light work when the weather was favorable thereby taking some exercise and he would when the weather would become unfavorable he would again become worse." Paulina was awarded a Widow's Pension of $20.00 monthly effective May 27, 1871, with retroactive pay to November 13, 1867.[3]

John Young's last will and testament was written by a friend, David Dix, on September 11, 1867 at his request, due to being too ill to write it himself. The will states: "I John V. Young of sound mind and disposition do hereby for the love and affection I have for Pauline M. Young my wife, give and bequeath to her during her life time or until marriage (1) tract of land lying in Teays Valley containing (125) one hundred and twenty five acres, Bounded as follows, on the East by Major Sims and Capt. John Bowyers lands, on the south by said Bowers lands, and on the west by Mahlon Chapman's & Miller's heirs, on the north by various Surveys. I do also bequeath to her all the personal property in my possession, namely, horses, mules, cattle, sheep and hogs, also all the corn, oats & tobacco, also (1) one wagon and all farming utensils, also the household and kitchen furniture, also all claims and money now in the hands of Charles Mollohon [Mollohan], my lawful attorney for collection or that may be collected. It is my request that Pauline M. Young my wife to settle up all my just debts, I do give and bequeath to Benjamin L. Young my son my Silver watch and service sword, I do also give and bequeath to Jacob R. Young my son my carbine and revolver, I also request that Pauline M. Young my wife give Sarah F. Blundon and Emily A. Cassady [Cassidy] each a cow, when they shall need them."

Putnam County court documents indicate John Young and Paulina purchased a land plot of one hundred twenty-five acres located at Teays Valley (Winfield) from George Dix in 1855. Young relocated his family there in 1863, due to the incessant dangers at their former residence near Coalsmouth, along the eastern face of Coal Mountain. Paulina lived in Winfield for the remainder of her life. One week prior to his death, John Young sold one-half acre of his parcel of land, located at Block Two along Ferry Street on the southern bank of the Kanawha River in Winfield, to John Bowyers. Incidentally, the home of Colonel James W. Hoge, the attorney and former state representative from Winfield, was also located just a few blocks from Young's house. On May 8, 1875, Paulina Young sold eighty-three and one-half acres of her land to John H. Payne.[4]

Summarily, when Young wrote in his diary at Richmond that his time soldiering had ended, it was not entirely true. He was now home safe with his family, but his former problems with pay and rank had yet to be resolved, in what amounts to a sad, but ironic, twist of events. When Young was at the War Department in Washington during May 1865, he filed a claim for back pay due from the time he entered service in 1861 through the time he began to receive pay as a captain in 1864. This matter was not fully resolved until November 22, 1888, eleven years post-mortem. The original claim was filed on April 23, 1862, in a sad testament to government bureaucracy, or "Red-tapeism" according to Young. Adding insult to injury was the fact that his final account for clothing and camp equipment from Company G was not settled, either, until October 20, 1866. This means he did not receive his final pay until some point afterward.

Paulina Young died on December 19, 1883, aged sixty-five years. She is buried in Franklin Cemetery near Poca, in Putnam County, West Virginia. Captain Edgar Blundon, Young's son-in-law, was ordained as a "Circuit Rider" in 1865, and served in the ministry for one year in Putnam County, and was admitted to the Methodist Conference as a minister in March 1866. Stationed at Malden, West Virginia, and other locations, he continued to serve for the next six years. Blundon also had a post office named after him on August 17, 1888, located along Leatherwood Creek, near Elkview, West Virginia. The Blundon Post of the Grand Army of the Republic, No. 73, at Charleston was named in his honor, but he was never a member. Edgar Blundon died of tuberculosis at the parsonage in Burning Springs, Wirt County, West Virginia, on March 6, 1873. He is buried close to the grave of John Young at Cary Cemetery near Poca. His tombstone epitaph states, "Saved by the omnipotence of Grace." His wife Sarah later served as a member of the Ladies Auxiliary of the Blundon Post of the Grand Army of the Republic in Charleston following his death. Sarah Francis "Sallie" Blundon, died in Charleston, West Virginia on December 14, 1920, aged seventy-eight years. She is buried in Spring Hill Cemetery. The Blundons had three children: Maud, who passed away during infancy, Nina (b. 1866) and Lizzie (b. 1868).

Young's daughter Emily married Captain James Cassidy, who served in the 7th West Virginia Cavalry with Edgar Blundon, on February 19, 1867, at Charleston, West Virginia. John Young was the minister officiating the ceremony. Emily died young, at age twenty-seven years in Fayetteville, West Virginia, of an unspecified pulmonary disease. Young's son Benjamin Lewis Young relocated to Huntington, West Virginia, sometime before 1920. Little is known of his activities there, although family records show Benjamin married Melissa Thornton at Charleston on January 12, 1881, and he died at age seventy-five years on October 28,1922 of "chronic Pericarditis." His younger brother,

*James and Emily Young Cassidy*
*Courtesy of Steve Cunningham*

Jacob, died at age thirty-one years in Kanawha County on January 31, 1876.

In the end, Captain John Valley Young is best remembered as a devout Christian, who fiercely loved his family and friends. He was fiercely patriotic, and became an excellent officer, leading his men into the fiery trials of combat from the front, always putting their welfare above his own. John Young's family paid a dear price for his service in the Civil War, and it ultimately cost him his life. Truly, the captain and his family lived his own epithet, "Sacrifice all for the Union."[5]

Chapter Six References

1. J.V. Young Letters, May 16, 1865; J.V. Young Diary, July 5-7, 1865; CSR, 11th West Virginia Infantry, RG 94, M508, Roll 195; Wood Diary, July 19-August 21, 1865.

2. J.V. Young Pension File, February 1, 1871: Paulina F. Young Widow's Pension Application, April 27, 1871: Letter from Van B. Morris, Buffalo, West Virginia.

3. Ibid., J.V. Young Pension File: February 24, 1871, Clark Elkins testimony for Captain J.V. Young, May 26, 1869; also letter by Dr. Andrew Barber, Putnam Co., West Virginia of May 27, 1871.

4. Last Will & Testament of John Valley Young, Will Book No. 1, 36, Putnam County Clerk of Court Records Room, Putnam County Court House, West Virginia. Also: Deed Book No. 4, 423; 485.

5. Dr. George C. Wilding. *Promoted Pioneer Preachers, West Virginia Conference of the United Methodist – Episcopal Church: A Sketch of her Early Ministers.* (Parkersburg WV: Charles L. Scholl, Publisher, 1927), 25-26; Edgar Blundon Obituary. *Pittsburgh Christian Advocate*, (No. 24, June 1873), 1; Young Family Marriages, Birth and Death Record from Family Bible, 2-6. West Virginia Vital Records, Death Certificate of Jacob Lewis Young, WV Archives.

# Appendix A

Company G Members on State Militia Rolls Prior to Enlistment

| NAME | UNIT | RANK | COMMENTS |
|---|---|---|---|
| Brooks, Robert | 153rd Reg't | Lt. Col. | Commissioned July 1863, also formed Scout company |
| Brown, Robert | 153rd Reg't | Pvt. | Co. K. per 08/11/1862 roll |
| Burdett, H.F. | 153rd Reg't | Pvt. | Co. D. per April 1862 roll |
| Campbell, James M. | 153rd Reg't | Pvt. | Co. B. Blake's Co. July 1862 |
| Johnson, Chastian, T. | 153rd Reg't | Pvt. | Co. A. per 04/10/1862 roll |
| Cristman, Charles | 153rd Reg't | Pvt. | 1861 |
| Holley, George W. | Putnam Co. Scouts | Pvt. | Enlisted 07/01/1864; present on 12/31/1864 militia roll |
| Higginbotham, Seander | 153rd Reg't | Pvt. | Co. B. undated roll |
| Higginbotham, Jno. | 181st Reg't | Pvt. | 1st Co. Capt. E.H. Ferguson, present 09/04/1861, Unsworn |
| Higginbotham, Samuel L. | 181st Reg't | Pvt. | 1st Co. Capt. E.H. Ferguson, mustered in 09/05/1861 |
| Holztein, James R. | 153rd Reg't | Pvt. | Brooke's Scouts |
| James A. Johnson | 80th Reg't | Pvt. | Co. A. per 04/10/1862 Roll |
| George A. Leadmon | 181st Reg't | 1st Lt. | Co. 1. Capt. Bailey's Co. 07/13/1863 roll. Paid as 1st Serg't. Enlisted 08/11/1862. Also served in Hurricane Creek Home Guard 1861. Commissioned 2d Lt 08/16/1862, DOR 08/11/1862. Died 02/01/1863. |
| Pauley, William J. | 153rd Reg't | Pvt. | Co. G. 1861 |
| Racer, John S. | 80th Reg't | Pvt. | Undated roll, presumed 1861 |
| Racer, George A. | 80th Reg't | Pvt. | Undated roll, presumed 1861 |
| Smith, John M. | 80th Reg't | 1st Sgt | Co. E. per 04/10/1862 Roll |
| Stephenson, Jno. D. | 153rd Reg't | Pvt. | Co. I |
| Benjamin A. Tackett | 80th Reg't | Pvt. | Undated roll, presumed 1861 |
| Young, William Samuel | 153rd Reg't | Pvt. | Co. B 1861 |

Source: WV Adjutant General Records, AR 354, Union Militia, Box 10. WV Archives.

# Appendix B
Company G Muster Roll 1861

| NAME | RANK | AGE | DATE |
|------|------|-----|------|
| Young, Jonathan V. | Capt. | 48 | April 61 |
| Brooks, Robert | 1st Lt | 49 | 05/23/62 |
| Elkins, Poindexter | Serg't | 39 | 05/23/62** |
| Holstein, James R. | Serg't | 18 | 05/23/62 |
| Nicholas, Andrew J. | Serg't | 39 | 05/23/62 |
| Higginbotham, E. | Corp'l | 20 | 05/23/62 |
| Pauley, William J. | Corp'l | 21 | 05/23/62 |
| Stevenson, David | Corp'l | 34 | 05/23/62 |
| Elkins, John S. | Corp'l | 18 | 05/23/62 |
| May, Jacob C. | Corp'l | 20 | 05/23/62 |
| Mynes, Andrew J. | Corp'l | 18 | 05/23/62 |
| Allen, Henry | Pvt. | 20 | 05/23/62 |
| Allen, Charles | Pvt. | 29 | 05/23/62 |
| Bays, Lewis | Pvt. | 41 | 05/23/62 |
| Burnes, Harvey | Pvt. | 21 | 05/23/62 |
| Bryant, Gabriel | Pvt. | 22 | 05/24/62* |
| Campbell, John W. | Pvt. | 20 | 05/23/62 |
| Crosan, David H. | Pvt. | 25 | 05/23/62 |
| Davis, Silas James | Pvt. | 24 | 05/23/62 |
| Elkins, Silas | Pvt. | 26 | 05/23/62 |
| Ellis, Lewis H. | Pvt. | 44 | 05/23/62 |
| Griffith, Joseph H. | Pvt. | 18 | 05/23/62 |
| Griffith, Lewis | Pvt. | 22 | 05/23/62** |
| Gray, Caleb | Pvt. | 36 | 05/23/62* |
| Holley, John L. | Pvt. | 27 | 05/23/62 |
| Holley, Joseph S. | Pvt. | 31 | 05/23/62 |
| Horton, William | Pvt. | 37 | 05/23/62 |
| King, James P. | Pvt. | 18 | 05/23/62 |
| Larter, James G. | Pvt. | 20 | 05/23/62 |
| Overshiner, John W. | Pvt. | 44 | 05/23/62 |
| Paul, James | Pvt. | 27 | 05/23/62* |
| Pauley, Buren | Pvt. | 33 | 05/23/62 |
| Racer, Wm. B. | Pvt. | 37 | 05/31/62* |

| NAME | RANK | AGE | DATE |
|------|------|-----|------|
| Rains, William | Pvt. | 21 | 05/23/62 |
| Tackett, James | Pvt. | 43 | 05/23/62 |
| Taylor, Isaac | Pvt. | 40 | 05/23/62 |
| Webb, Jeremiah | Pvt. | 42 | 03/10/62 |
| Wells, John | Pvt. | 31 | 05/23/62* |
| Young, Wm. Samuel | Pvt. | 18 | 05/15/62* |

NOTES: Ages are those reported at enlistment. Men with * are not on muster rolls but are found in other records. Those with ** are shown as dead or transferred on the 1864 muster roll. Cpl. James D. Johnson appears on the October 1, 1862 muster roll as Pvt. James A. Johnson with muster date of 08/21/1862: each has same age (18 years); however, James D. mustered in on October 6, 1862 as Corporal. Isaac Taylor (age 40) enlisted for 3 years on Mar 27, 1862 at Coalsmouth, Kanawha Co., [West] Virginia in Co. G as a Sergeant. Record of Isaac's discharge in May 1865 is found in Will Book 2, page 612 at the Cabell County, West Virginia Courthouse. It was recorded on November 22, 1866. Sources: WV Adjutant General Records, AR 373, Box 10, Union Militia, Kanawha County. See Also AG Order Book Number 1, Commissions; and WV Adjutant General Annual Report, December 1, 1864, 11th West Virginia Infantry, Company G; also WV AG, AR 382, Boxes 1 and 2, Muster In and Muster Out Rolls, and Morning Reports. WV Archives.

# Appendix C

Company G Muster Roll, October 1, 1862

Captain J.V. Young's Co. "Few recruits"

| NAME | RANK | AGE | DATE | LOCATION | MISC |
|---|---|---|---|---|---|
| Brown, Robert | Pvt. | 42 | 08/24/62 | Coalsmouth | |
| Bryant, Gabriel H. | " | 22 | 05/24/62 | " | |
| Brisco, Wyatt | " | 19 | 08/20/62 | " | |
| Bess, John A. | " | 26 | 08/25/62 | " | |
| Burdett, Henderson | " | 18 | 09/18/62 | Pt Pleasant | |
| Cyrus, John H. | " | 20 | 07/27/62 | Coalsmouth | |
| Carter, Lewis V. | " | 25 | 09/18/62 | Pt Pleasant | |
| Campbell, Henry T. | " | 44 | 08/06/62 | Coalsmouth | |
| Campbell, James M. | " | 19 | 08/30/62 | " | |
| Cash, Ferdinand S. | " | 18 | 08/23/62 | " | |
| Crago, Harrison | " | 22 | 09/18/62 | Pt Pleasant | |
| Crago, Wm. | " | 30 | 09/18/62 | " | |
| Enicks, Wm. H. | " | 21 | 08/25/62 | Coalsmouth | Wounded 3rd Winchester 7/24/64 |
| Epling, Miles Philip | " | 19 | 08/30/62 | " | Wagoner |
| Felder, Sanford | " | 36 | 09/19/62 | Pt Pleasant | |
| Griffith, Joseph A. | " | 18 | 03/10/62 | Coalsmouth | |
| Henson, Hezekiah | " | 18 | 08/06/62 | Coalsmouth | |
| Holley, George W. | " | 18 | 08/24/62 | " | |
| Hamick, Burton VJ | " | 18 | 07/20/62 | " | |
| Higginbotham, Seander | " | 20 | 09/18/62 | Pt Pleasant | |
| Hamrick, Noah J. | " | 19 | 07/26/62 | Coalsmouth | |
| Johnson, James A. | " | 18 | 08/21/62 | " | |
| Johnson, Asa S. | " | 22 | 08/21/62 | Pt Pleasant | |

| NAME | RANK | AGE | DATE | LOCATION | MISC |
|---|---|---|---|---|---|
| Jones, James M. | " | --- | 08/20/62 | " | |
| King, Martin E. | " | 29 | 09/18/62 | Pt Pleasant | |
| Leadmon, George A. | " | 19 | 07/14/62 | Coalsmouth | |
| McDowell, Eli | " | 23 | 07/27/62 | " | |
| McGlaughlin, Lewis E. | " | 25 | 09/22/62 | Pt Pleasant | |
| Morris, Van B. | " | 22 | 08/23/62 | " | Mustered 10/06/62; elected Sgt |
| Moses, James R. | " | 25 | 08/15/62 | Coalsmouth | |
| Mynes, John W. | " | 20 | 07/27/62 | " | |
| Nickels, Joel | " | 19 | 08/09/62 | " | |
| Nickels, Francis M. | " | 24 | 08/18/62 | " | |
| Paul, James F. | " | 20 | 07/27/62 | " | |
| Paul, Wm. F. | " | 20 | 08/15/62 | " | |
| Price, Peter | " | 21 | 06/21/62 | " | |
| Smith, Albert P. | " | --- | 06/12/62 | " | |
| Smith, John M. | " | --- | 09/18/62 | Pt Pleasant | |
| Racer, Wm. B. | " | 37 | 05/31/62 | Coalsmouth | Cut off by Rebels |
| Racer, John S. | " | 31 | 08/15/62 | " | Cut off by Rebels |
| Racer, George A. | " | --- | 08/30/62 | " | Cut off by Rebels |
| Tackett, Benjamin A. | " | 19 | 07/06/62 | " | Captured by Rebels |
| Tyler, James | " | 19 | 08/09/62 | Coalsmouth | |
| Wells, John | " | 31 | 02/16/62 | " | |
| Wood, John H. | " | 22 | 08/25/62 | " | |
| Walls, Augustus | " | 44 | 08/06/62 | " | |
| Young, Wm. F. | " | 18 | 05/23/62 | " | |

Source: WV AG Papers, AR 382, 13th WV, Box 1/1. WV Archives.

# Appendix D

Adjutant General's Report

## Company G – 11th Regiment West Virginia Volunteer Infantry

From the Annual Report of the Adjutant General of the State of West Virginia, for the year ending December 31, 1864.

| NAME | RANK | AGE | DATE OF RANK | COMMENTS |
|---|---|---|---|---|
| Young, John V. | Capt. | 49 | 08/29/62 | |
| Elkins, Clark | 1st Lt. | 32 | 12/14/63 | Pro. fr. 1st Sgt to 2d Lt 06/06/63; Pro. to 1st Lt. 12/01/63 |
| McDaniel, Wm. G. | 2d Lt | 22 | 12/14/63 | Pro. From 1st Sgt, Dec. 1, 1863 |
| Morris, Van B | 1st Sgt | 22 | 10/06/62 | Pro. Fr. Sgt 11/01/64 |
| Nicholas, Andrew J. | Serg't | 39 | 05/23/62 | |
| Holtzein, James R. | Serg't | 18 | 05/23/62 | |
| Taylor, Issac | Serg't | 40 | 05/23/62 | Pro. fr. Pvt. 11/01/64 |
| Wood, John H. | Serg't | 24 | 10/06/62 | Pro. fr. Pvt. 11/01/64 |
| Higginbotham, E. | Corp'l | 20 | 05/23/62 | |
| Carter, Lewis V. | Corp'l | 25 | 10/06/62 | |
| Pauley, Wm. J. | Corp'l | 21 | 05/23/62 | |
| Stevenson, David | Corp'l | 34 | 05/23/62 | |
| Elkins, John S. | Corp'l | 18 | 05/23/62 | |
| May, Jacob C. | Corp'l | 20 | 05/23/62 | |
| Mynes, Andrew J. | Corp'l | 18 | 05/23/62 | |
| Johnson, James D. | Corp'l | 18 | 10/06/62 | |
| Epling, Miles P. | Wag'r | 19 | 10/06/62 | |
| Allen, Charles | Priv. | 29 | 05/23/62 | |
| Adkins, Hiram | Priv. | 18 | 02/01/64 | |
| Bays, Lewis | Priv. | 41 | 05/23/62 | |
| Burnes, Harvey | Priv. | 21 | 05/23/62 | Wounded by accident |
| Brown, Robert | Priv. | 42 | 10/06/62 | Hospital Sandy Hook Maryland, to July 1865 and mustered out at Harpers Ferry WVA |
| Bess, John A. | Priv. | 26 | 10/06/62 | Wounded by accident |
| Burdett, John W. | Priv. | 18 | 10/06/63 | |

| NAME | RANK | AGE | DATE OF RANK | COMMENTS |
|---|---|---|---|---|
| Burgey, [Burgess] Benedict | Priv. | 40 | 03/30/64 | In US General Hospital Fort Monroe Virginia; mustered out May 3, 1865 |
| Campbell, Henry T. | Priv. | 44 | 10/06/62 | |
| Campbell, John W. | Priv. | 20 | 05/23/62 | |
| Crago, Harrison | Priv. | 22 | 10/06/62 | |
| Crago, William | Priv. | 30 | 10/06/62 | Wounded in action Sept. 22 1864 |
| Cristman, Charles | Priv. | 18 | 01/28/64 | |
| Crosan, David H. | Priv. | 25 | 05/23/62 | |
| Davis, James S. | Priv. | 24 | 05/23/62 | Capt'd at Lynchburg, June 17, 1864 |
| Elkins, Silas | Priv. | 26 | 05/23/62 | |
| Ellis, Lewis H. | Priv. | 44 | 05/23/62 | |
| Ellis, Lewis J. | Priv. | 19 | 08/05/63 | |
| Enicks, William H. | Priv. | 21 | 10/06/62 | Wounded |
| Fielder, Sanford | Priv. | 36 | 10/06/62 | |
| Flint, Daniel | Priv. | 37 | 12/17/62 | |
| Grass, Richard | Priv. | 41 | 12/17/62 | |
| Griffith, Joseph H. | Priv. | 18 | 05/23/62 | Sick in Stewart Hospital Richmond VA. Mustered out June 1865. |
| Gray, Caleb F. | Priv. | 36 | 05/23/62 | Captured at Cedar Creek, Va. Oct. 19, 1864 |
| Higginbotham, Samuel L. | Priv. | 20 | 10/06/62 | Wounded in RT Leg (flesh wound) at Lynchburg, June 17, 1864 |
| Higginbotham, Jno. | Priv. | 18 | 10/06/62 | Wounded at Lynchburg, June 17, 1864 |
| Hensley, Coleman S. | Priv. | 33 | 10/06/62 | |
| Hensley, Fretwell G. | Priv. | 31 | 10/06/62 | |
| Henson, Alexander | Priv. | 19 | 10/06/62 | |
| Henson, Hezekiah | Priv. | 18 | 10/06/62 | Minor wound at Hatcher's Run, March 31, 1865 |
| Holley, John Leander | Priv. | 27 | 05/23/62 | |
| Holley, George W. | Priv. | 18 | 10/06/62 | |

| NAME | RANK | AGE | DATE OF RANK | COMMENTS |
|---|---|---|---|---|
| Holley, Joseph S. | Priv. | 31 | 05/23/62 | |
| Hamrick, B.V.T. | Priv. | 18 | 10/06/62 | Wounded by accident, July -, 1863 |
| Hart, Calvin | Priv. | 31 | 02/01/64 | |
| Horton, Samuel | Priv. | 44 | 10/06/62 | Captured at Lynchburg, June 18, 1864 |
| Johnson, Chastien T. | Priv. | 20 | 12/17/62 | |
| Jones, James M. | Priv. | 20 | 10/06/62 | Wounded by accident. |
| King, Martin E. | Priv. | 29 | 10/06/62 | |
| King, James P. | Priv. | 18 | 05/23/62 | |
| Landers, Samuel | Priv. | 19 | 06/28/64 | Wounded July 24, '63 |
| McDowell, Eli | Priv. | 23 | 10/06/62 | |
| Mynes, John W. | Priv. | 20 | 10/06/62 | |
| Moses, James R. | Priv. | 25 | 10/06/62 | |
| Moses, William H. | Priv. | 18 | 10/06/62 | Mustered out in Army Hospital Gallipolis Ohio 06/14/1865 |
| McLauglin, L.E. | Priv. | 22 | 10/06/62 | |
| Nuckels, Joel | Priv. | 19 | 10/06/62 | Wounded |
| Nuckels, Francis M. | Priv. | 24 | 10/06/62 | |
| Overshiner, John W. | Priv. | 44 | 05/23/62 | |
| Paul, James T. | Priv. | 20 | 10/06/62 | |
| Paul, William M. | Priv. | 21 | 10/06/62 | |
| Paul, James | Priv. | 27 | 05/23/62 | Wounded Sept. 8, '62 |
| Pursinger, Lewis J. | Priv. | 39 | 10/06/62 | Capt'd Oct. 19, 1864 |
| Racer, William B. | Priv. | 37 | 12/17/62 | Cut off by Rebels 1862 |
| Racer, John S. | Priv. | 31 | 12/17/62 | Cut off by Rebels 1862 |
| Smith, John M. | Priv. | 22 | 10/06/62 | |
| Stephenson, Jno. D. | Priv. | 35- | 09/23/64 | Drafted |
| Seites, Henry | Priv. | 18 | 12/18/62 | Missing in Action, June 18, 1864 |
| Tacket, James | Priv. | 43 | 05/23/62 | |
| Tacket, William P. | Priv. | 18 | 01/28/64 | |
| Tyler, James | Priv. | 19 | 10/06/62 | Missing in action, Oct. 19, 1864 |

| NAME | RANK | AGE | DATE OF RANK | COMMENTS |
|---|---|---|---|---|
| Webb, Jeremiah | Priv. | 42 | 03/10/62 | Died April 10, 1865 from GSW to hip or knee sustained on March 31, 1865 at Hatcher's Run. |
| Wells, John | Priv. | 31 | 05/23/62 | |
| Wall, Augustus | Priv. | 44 | 10/06/62 | |
| Wall, Asbury | Priv. | 18 | 10/06/62 | |
| White, Adam | Priv. | 36 | 10/06/62 | |
| Young, William L. | Priv. | 18 | 10/06/62 | Wounded by accident |
| Young, Samuel E. | Priv. | 35 | 09/23/64 | Drafted – J.V. Young's brother also as Samuel B. |

## DISCHARGED

| NAME | RANK | AGE | DATE | COMMENTS |
|---|---|---|---|---|
| Brooks, Robert | 1st Lt. | 49 | 05/23/62 | Res'd June 2, 1863 |
| Epling, Philip | Priv. | 44 | 10/06/62 | Dis'd Oct. 4, 1863 |
| Pauley, Buren | Priv. | 33 | 05/23/62 | Dis'd Oct. 14, 1863 |
| Chandler, Richard H. | Priv. | 44 | ------ | Dis'd by G.C.M. |

## TRANSFERRED

| NAME | RANK | AGE | DATE | COMMENTS |
|---|---|---|---|---|
| Cunningham, Jno. S. | 2d Lt. | --- | ------ | Pro. Adjutant 13th W.V. Inf. |

DIED

| NAME | RANK | AGE | ENLISTED | DATE OF DEATH |
|------|------|-----|----------|---------------|
| Cyrus, John H. | Priv. | 18 | 10/06/62 | 11/05/1862 |
| Ellis, Charles A. | Priv. | 21 | 12/17/62 | 01/28/1863 |
| Price, Peter | Priv. | 21 | 10/06/62 | 01/14/1863 |
| Mynes, Anderson R. | Priv. | 18 | ------- | 12/31/62 |
| Leadmon, George A. | Priv. | 20 | 10/06/62 | 02/10/63 |
| Hamrick Noah J.J. | Priv. | 19 | 10/06/62 | 02/10/1863 |
| Allen, Henry | Priv. | 20 | 05/23/62 | 07/24/1863 |
| Burdett Henderson F. | Priv. | 19 | 10/06/62 | 07/09/1864; Left leg shot off 06/18/1864 |
| Campbell, James M. | Priv. | 20 | 10/06/62 | 09/10/1864 |
| Horton, James H. | Priv. | 18 | 01/28/64 | 11/21/64 |
| Elkins, Poindexter | Serg't | 39 | 05/23/62 | 03/23/1863 |
| Griffith, Lewis L. | 1st Ser. | 22 | 05/23/62 | 10/20/1864 from wound received 10/19/1964 |
| Bryan, Gabriel H. | Corp'l. | 21 | 10/06/62 | 07/27/1863 |
| Brisco, Wyatt | Corp'l. | 20 | 10/06/62 | Killed July 24, 1864 |

DESERTED

| NAME | RANK | AGE | ENLISTED | DATE |
|------|------|-----|----------|------|
| Tacket, Benjamin | Priv. | 18 | ------- | 09/05/1862 |
| Horton, William | Priv. | 37 | 05/23/62 | 09/12/1863 |
| Smith, Albert P. | Priv. | 33 | 10/06/62 | 06/20/1863 |
| Larter, James G. | Priv. | 20 | 05/23/62 | 11/05/1863 |
| Rains, William | Priv. | 21 | 05/23/62 | 11/20/1863 |
| Nicholas, Ephraim | Priv. | -- | 06/28/64 | 07/06/1864 |
| Tacket, Elijah | Priv. | 44 | 06/28/64 | 07/06/64 |

Aggregate: (total in company) 113 men

SOURCES: WV AG Report, 11h Regiment W.VA. Infantry, From the Annual Report of the Adjutant General of the State of West Virginia, for the year ending December 31, 1864; Company G Muster Roll. WV Archives; See Also: WV AG, AR 382, Box 1/2 Folders 43 and 72; Box 2/2, 11th West Virginia, Company G, Muster Cards. WV Archives.

# Appendix E

## Soldiers found only in 11th WV Co. G in Compiled Service Records (CSR)

| NAME | RANK | AGE | DOE * | LOCATION | COMMENTS |
|---|---|---|---|---|---|
| Davis, Silas | Pvt | 25 | 05/23/62 | Coalsmouth | Died Chas. Hosp. 06/27/64 |
| Hamrick, Barton | Pvt | 18 | 10/08/62 | Pt Pleasant | Accidental wound 07/63 |
| Henson, Orem | Pvt | 19 | 08/01/63 | Ravenswood | WIC Petersburg 03/31/65 |
| Webb, George | Pvt | -- | 08/01/63 | Coalsmouth | WIC Petersburg 03/31/65 |

[*] Date of Enlistment

Source: CSR, Union Regiments, 11th West Virginia, RG 94, Microfilm Roll No. 189, National Archives. George Webb is mentioned in John Young's diary on March 31, 1865 but is not found on muster rolls or CSR.

# Appendix F
### Soldiers found only on December 17, 1862 13th WV Co. G Return

| NAME | RANK | AGE | MUSTER DATE | COMMENTS |
|---|---|---|---|---|
| Cites, Henry | Pvt. | 18 | 02/26/1862 | Coalsmouth |
| Ellis, Chas. | Pvt. | 23 | 11/29/1862 | " |
| Ellis, Lewis J. | Pvt. | 19 | 11/29/1862 | " |
| Flink, Dan'l | Pvt. | 37 | 08/30/1862 | " |
| Grass, Richard | Pvt. | 41 | 02/20/1862 | " |
| Johnson, Christian F. | Pvt. | 22 | 08/21/1862 | " |
| Mines, Anderson Reed | Pvt. | 18 | 12/3/1862 | " |
| Racer, William | Pvt. | 37 | 05/31/1862 | "Cut off by Rebels" |
| Racer, John S. | Pvt. | 31 | 08/13/1862 | " " |
| Racer, George A. | Pvt. | 26 | 08/20/1862 | " " |
| Tacket, Benjamin | Pvt. | - | - | Captured by Rebels August 1862 |

Source: WV AG Files, Union Regiments, AR 382, 13th West Virginia, Folders 55. WV Archives.

# Appendix G

Soldiers found only on August 13, 1863 13th WV Co. G Muster-In Roll

| NAME | RANK | AGE | MUSTER DATE | COMMENTS |
|---|---|---|---|---|
| Bordell, John W. | Pvt. | 17 | August 13, 1863 | Coalsmouth |
| Lewis, Ellis | Pvt. | 19 | August 3, 1863 | Winfield |
| Horton, Samuel | Pvt. | 44 | August 11, 1863 | Coalsmouth |
| Moses, Samuel A. | Pvt. | 23 | August 23, 1863 | " |
| Moses William H. | Pvt. | 17 | August 23, 1863 | " |
| Persinger, Lewis A. (I) | Pvt. | 39 | August 19, 1863 | " |
| Wall, Asbury | Pvt. | 17 | August 15, 1863 | " |

Source: WV AG Files, Union Regiments, AR 382, 13th West Virginia, Folders 52. WV Archives.

# Name Index

# About the Author

Philip Hatfield, Ph.D., is a member of the Company of Military Historians, and holds a doctorate in psychology from Fielding University; a master's degree in psychology from Marshall University; and a bachelor's degree in psychology and history from the University of Charleston. Dr. Hatfield is a veteran of the U.S. Air Force and is the author of five books and numerous scholarly articles related to the Civil War.

35th Star Publishing
www.35thstar.com

Made in the USA
Coppell, TX
22 July 2020